The Bugis

The Peoples of South-East Asia and The Pacific

General Editors
Peter Bellwood and Ian Glover

Each book in this series is devoted to a people (or group of associated peoples) from the vast area of the world extending from Hawaii in the north to Tasmania in the south and from Fiji in the east to Thailand in the west. The books, written by historians, anthropologists and archaeologists from all over the world, are both scholarly and accessible. In many cases the volumes are the only available account of their subject.

Already published

The Peoples of Borneo
Victor T. King

The Khmers
I. W. Mabbett and David Chandler

The Balinese
Angela Hobart, Urs Ramseyer and Albert Leeman

The Bugis
Christian Pelras

In preparation

The Melanesians
Matthew Spriggs

The Lapita People
Patrick Kirch

The Maoris
Altholl Anderson

The Peoples of the Lesser Sundas
James L. Fox

The Malays
A. C. Milner and Jane Drakard

The Fijians
Nicholas Thomas and Victoria Luker

The Bugis

Christian Pelras

BLACKWELL
Publishers

First published 1996

2 4 6 8 10 9 7 5 3 1

Blackwell Publishers Ltd
108 Cowley Road
Oxford OX4 1JF
UK

Blackwell Publishers Inc
238 Main Street
Cambridge, Massachusetts 02142,
USA

British Library Cataloguing in Publication Data
A CIP catalogue record for this book is available from the British Library

Library of Congress-in-Publication Data
Pelras, Christian.
The Bugis/Christian Pelras.
p.   cm. – (The Peoples of South-East Asia and the Pacific)
Includes bibliographical references and index.
ISBN 0–631–17231–9 (alk. paper)
1. Bugis (Malay people) – History.   2. Bugis (Malay people) – Social life and customs.
I. Title.   II. Series.
DS632. B85P45   1996
959.8′4–dc20   95–42827
CIP

Typeset in 11 on 12.5 pt Sabon
by Pure Tech India Ltd, Pondicherry, India

Printed in Great Britain by Hartnolls Limited, Bodmin, Cornwall
This book is printed on acid-free paper

This book is dedicated to all my Bugis friends, colleagues and hosts, too numerous to be named individually; to my dear driver Djafar, who was my trusted daily companion during my stay at the Social Science Training Centre of Ujung Pandang and again in 1984, shortly before his untimely death; to my son who, at the age of three, was already playing with Bugis children and who, at the age of twenty, accompanied me as a photographer; and to my wife, who accepted the hardships of fieldwork without enjoying the excitements of research.

Contents

List of Illustrations

Map 1 Sulawesi in its historical south-east Asian context

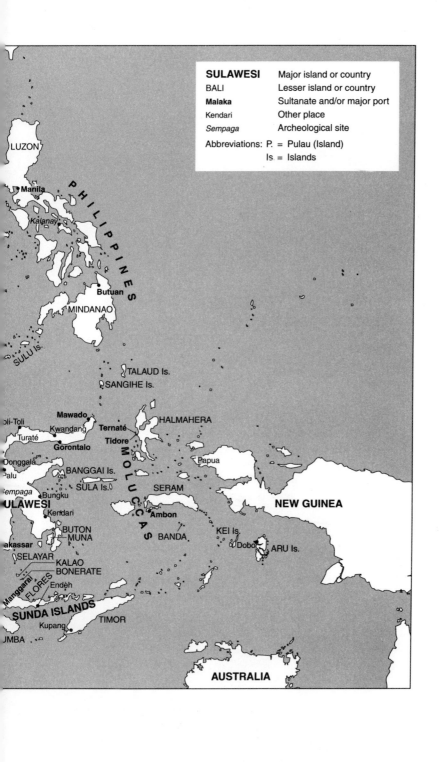

SULAWESI	Major island or country
BALI	Lesser island or country
Malaka	Sultanate and/or major port
Kendari	Other place
Sempaga	Archeological site

Abbreviations: P. = Pulau (Island)

Is. = Islands

LUZON

Manila

Kalanay

PHILIPPINES

Butuan

MINDANAO

SULU Is.

TALAUD Is.

SANGIHE Is.

Mawado

oli-Toli

Kwandang

Ternaté

HALMAHERA

Turaté

Tidore

Gorontalo

MOLUCCAS

Donggala

Papua

Palu

BANGGAI Is.

Sempaga

SULA Is.

SERAM

Bungku

NEW GUINEA

ULAWESI

Kendari

Ambon

BUTON

MUNA

BANDA

KEI Is.

akassar

Dobo

ARU Is.

SELAYAR

KALAO

BONERATE

Manggarai

FLORES

Endèh

SUNDA ISLANDS

TIMOR

Kupang

UMBA

AUSTRALIA

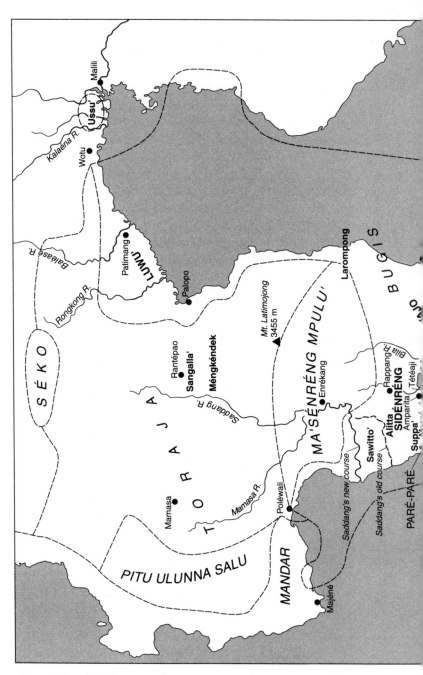

Map 2 South Sulawesi ethnic groups and toponyms of the
historical period

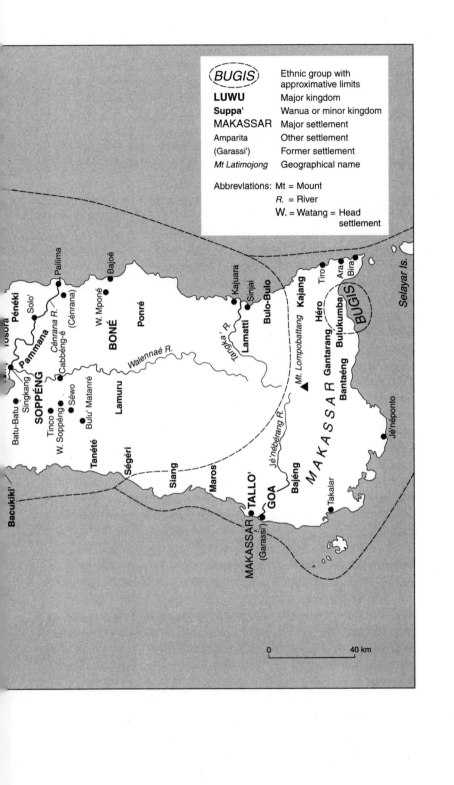

BUGIS	Ethnic group with approximative limits
LUWU	Major kingdom
Suppa'	Wanua or minor kingdom
MAKASSAR	Major settlement
Amparita	Other settlement
(Garassi')	Former settlement
Mt Latimojong	Geographical name

Abbreviations: Mt = Mount
R. = River
W. = Watang = Head
settlement

Selayar Is.

Pallima
Péneki
Solo'
Bajoé
Kajuara
Tiro
Ara
Bira
BUGIS
Cénrana R.
(Cénrana)
W. Mponé
Sinjai
Héro
Bulukumba
Iosora
Cabbéng-é
BONÉ
Ponré
Tangka' R.
Lamatti
Bulo-Bulo
Kajang
Gantarang
Pammana
Cénrana R.
Walennaé R.
Bantaéng
SOPPÉNG
Singkang
Séwo
Bulu' Matanré
Lamuru
Mt. Lompobattang
MAKASSAR
Batu-Batu
Tinco
W. Soppéng
Tanété
Séyéri
Siang
Maros
Bajéng
Takalar
Jénéponto
Ségéri
Jé'néBérang R.
TALLO'
GOA
MAKASSAR
(Garassi')
Bacukiki'

0   40 km

1

Introduction

The Bugis are a south-east Asian people, numbering more than three million, whose homeland is the south-western peninsula of Celebes island – Sulawesi in modern Indonesia. They belong to the great family of the Austronesian peoples.

As a result of both internal evolution and interaction with different civilizations (China, India, the Islamic world and finally European peoples), the Austronesians of maritime south-east Asia, where they have lived since before the Christian era, have developed into many different societies and cultures. Of these, the best known include – besides the Bugis – the Malays, the Javanese and the Balinese. Centuries of separate history have widened the differences between these peoples and their Austronesian cousins in Melanesia, Polynesia and Micronesia. Within maritime South-east Asia, however, their relationships with one another and common traits remain clear and strong. There are so many similarities and continuities in their geographical environments – in type, physical setting and climate – and so many historical, political, commercial and other links that since the earliest times all foreign travellers have been conscious of their basic cultural unity, giving to this part of the globe, successively, the names 'Malay world', 'Indonesia' and 'Malaysia'. However, as all these names now have political or national associations, in this book the older names 'Insulindia' and 'Insulindians' will be used to designate this area and the family of peoples who constitute the most immediate world of the Bugis, those with whom they most frequently come into contact.

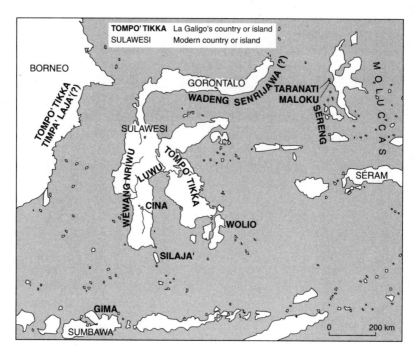

Map 3 The La Galigo *geography of Sulawesi and its surroundings*

Who Are the Bugis?

Although their name may sound familiar to readers of Conrad's novels or to travellers who remember having seen their smart schooners in Indonesian harbours, the Bugis have for centuries been among the most imperfectly known of the Insulindian peoples; and what little was 'known' about them was often in large part wrong. For example, because their boats were until recently seen all over the region, from Singapore to New Guinea and from the southern Philippines to north-western Australia, it was widely thought that they had long been mainly a seafaring people, perhaps the most important one in the whole south-east Asian archipelago – indeed, some even credited them with having crossed the Indian Ocean to Madagascar – whereas in fact they are primarily farmers, and their maritime activities did not gain momentum until the eighteenth century. Their former reputation as

Plate 1   A Bugis woman

pirates is almost entirely without foundation; and their famous *pînisi'* schooners, far from being hundreds of years old, took their final shape between the end of the nineteenth century and the 1930s.

Yet the Bugis display many other fascinating features. They provide an example, rare in this area, of the formation of states outside any Indian influence and without the development of real cities. Their literature, whose many written works in manuscript form are still read and copied, exists alongside a rich oral tradition that continues to thrive, and has produced one of the world's major epics, the *La Galigo* cycle, which is longer than the *Mahabharata*. Having become Muslims since the beginning of the seventeenth century, they are reckoned, together with the Achehnese and Minangkabau of Sumatra, the Malays of Sumatra, Malaya and Borneo, the 'Moro' of Mindanao,[1] the Banjar of Borneo, the Sundanese of West Java, and the Madurese of Madura and East Java, as among those Insulindian peoples whose Islamic identity is the strongest; and Islam is indeed an integral and essential part of the Bugis' culture and way of life. At the same time, however, much of their pre-Islamic heritage remains alive and well. Perhaps the most fascinating of these survivals is the *bissu*, a class of transvestite priests who still practise shamanistic rituals and communicate with the deities of the ancient pantheon.

The Bugis are known by their neighbours for their fierce character and sense of honour, which sometimes result in violence; and yet they are among the most hospitable and amicable peoples and the most faithful in their friendships. The cohesion of their society is based largely on the existence of a system of pervasive and interlocking clienteles; and yet most of them have a strong sense of their individuality. Bugis society is one of the most complex and apparently rigidly hierarchical of any in Insulindia; and yet competition for office or wealth ranks high among their motivations.

The coexistence of these conflicting traits is perhaps what makes the Bugis so mobile, and lies behind another of their

[1] 'Moro', a term of Spanish origin, is the commonly accepted collective designation for all Muslim peoples of the southern Philippines.

characteristic features, namely their propensity to migrate. All over Insulindia, from Malaya to western New Guinea, from the southern Philippines and north Borneo to the Lesser Sunda Islands, they can be found, busy in navigation, trade, agriculture, plantation work or forestry – whatever occupation is most appropriate to time and place. Their most valuable assets are certainly this versatility and adaptability which have enabled them to survive over the centuries, always changing and yet always the same.

The Land of the Bugis

The geographical and ecological conditions of Sulawesi, particularly those of its south-western peninsula, have been determining factors in the history and identity of the Bugis from the very earliest times. Despite the fact that its surface area (189,000 sq km, including its dependent islands) exceeds that of Java and Madura combined (132,000 sq km), making it one of the major Insulindian islands, Sulawesi appears to be one of the least known. In the sixteenth century it took the first European navigators in the area thirty years to discover that the land they had arrived at consisted not of two archipelagoes ('the Celebes islands' in the north and 'the Macassar islands' in the south) but of one big island. These first European visitors to both North and South Sulawesi were Portuguese. In the south, traders began visiting the west coast around 1530, but regular relations with Malaka were not established until after 1559, and it was not until about 1625, when all the major European trading nations (the Netherlands, Denmark, England and France as well as Portugal) had opened trading posts in Makassar, that the mapping of the rest of the island reached an adequate standard. The first European maps ignored Sulawesi altogether; those published between about 1534 and 1580 gave only a fantastic outline of its western and northern coasts, showing nothing of either its large gulfs or the southern and eastern coasts (Pelras, 'Premières données').

It is not entirely surprising that the first Europeans to hear about this land thought of it as several distinct islands, since there was virtually no overland route linking the four peninsulas stretching out from the mountainous nucleus: right up until the construction of roads in the 1920s it was often easier to travel by sea. The coastal plains are in many places very narrow, and in other places often swampy and bordered by inundated mangrove forest; and in contrast to other islands such as Borneo and Sumatra, not many rivers are navigable far into the interior.

One important exception in South Sulawesi is the waterway formed by the Cénrana river, which was passable by large craft as far as Lake Témpé, and, further south, by the Walennaé river; an easy crossing of the peninsula was also possible from Lake Témpé to present-day Paré-Paré on the west coast. A similar crossing of North Sulawesi was possible in Gorontalo by navigating from the Gulf of Tomini up-river to Lake Limboto, from where a short pass led to the bay of Kwandang on the northern coast: this was thus a relatively easy short cut compared to the long route by sea round the northern peninsula. Another crossing existed between the port of Tobungku in the Bay of Tolo (East Sulawesi) and Ussu' Bay at the head of the Gulf of Boné, via Lake Matano. Yet another short cut was provided by the Kalaéna river in Luwu', which led through a steep pass over the mountains to Lake Poso and then down the Poso river to the Gulf of Tomini.

Other rivers were navigable only in their lower reaches, but further progress could be made by following their valleys further inland on foot. On the western coast, for example, the Saddang river could be navigated as far as Enrékang, from where the Toraja country could be reached by continuing up the valley on foot. Further north on the west coast another important route to the interior seems to have been the Karama river, whose valley led far inland into the mountains. The shorter rivers also had their uses, for their outlets provided anchorage for trading boats and, on swampy coasts, permitted travellers to cross the mangrove belt easily.

All these routes, and others by sea and land, were important in gaining access to the island's natural resources and in transporting them to points of connection with the sea routes of the inter-island trade network, to which the people of Sulawesi have belonged for a very long time indeed. These resources, including iron and copper ore, gold dust, sandal-wood, rattan, resins and vegetable poisons, as well as products of the sea and seashore such as tortoiseshell, mother-of-pearl and mangrove dyes, have presumably been exploited here since before the beginning of the Christian era.

Sulawesi's position between Borneo and the Moluccas makes it a natural port of call on the age-old sea routes between the latter and the Malacca straits, through the Buton and Selayar straits. As early as 1511 the Portuguese Tomé Pires advocated the use of this shorter route rather than the southern one usually taken by his compatriots; the reason why it took them about twenty years to follow this advice is probably that the southern route, along the north coasts of Java and Bali and through the Lesser Sunda Islands, was at that time the most frequented and the most profitable. There was also a much longer northern route around North Borneo and North Sulawesi. As for the Makassar strait between Borneo and Sulawesi, it seems on the map to offer one of the most direct routes from the southern Philippines to Lombok, Bali and East Java on one side and to the eastern Lesser Sunda Islands on the other. However, several accounts testify to the fact that sailing along this route could be made difficult by the frequent lack of wind at the equator, which divides the island between Toli-toli and Palu.

South Sulawesi – the Bugis' native home – is the part of the island where human action has put its most marked imprint on the landscape. It has long been the most densely populated of the four peninsulas: in 1990 its inhabitants numbered about seven million on a land area of nearly 83,000 sq km, giving an average of about 84 inhabitants per square kilometre. This is not a high density when compared with overcrowded Java and Bali, but is much higher than that on Sumatra and Borneo. However, there are substantial disparities between districts, with only 20 per cent of the inhabitants living in the five northern ones, which represent about 48 per cent of the province's land area, at about 30 inhabitants per square kilometre, while 80 per cent live in the seventeen southern districts, at about 112 per square kilometre. The most densely settled parts of these southern areas are the agricultural plains of the interior and the two important harbour cities of the

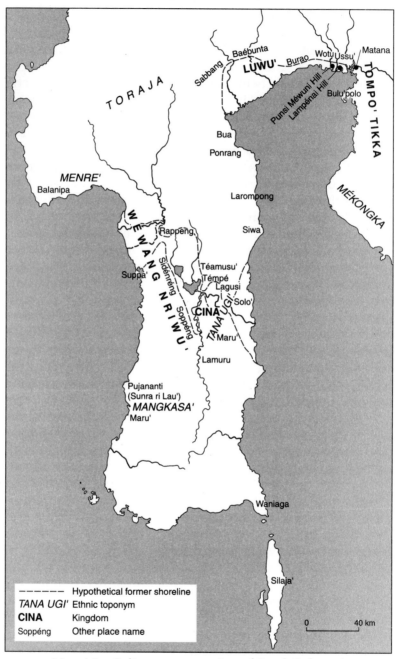

Map 4 La Galigo *representation of South Sulawesi*

west coast, Paré-Paré (110,000 inhabitants) and Ujung Pandang, known in the past as Makassar (915,000 inhabitants).

The north of the province is covered by mountains, geographically an extension of those in Central Sulawesi; the highest peak is Mt Latimojong at 3,455 metres. Of its rivers, the Karama, Mamasa, Saddang and Mata Allo drain into the Makassar strait, the Bila into the central lakes (Témpé and Sidénréng) and the Kalaéna and Malili into the Gulf of Boné. The southern end is dominated by an extinct volcano, formerly known as Bonthain (for Bantaéng) Peak, with two summits, Mt Bawakaraéng and Mt Lompobattang, of which the latter is the higher at 2,871 metres. From south to north, parallel and very close to the western coast, runs a cordillera which forms a kind of backbone to the peninsula; with an average height of 1,000 metres, it becomes progressively lower towards the northern end, providing the Saddang river with a passage to the Makassar strait and giving easy access to the central plains. These extend from north to south around Lakes Sidénréng and Témpé and in the basin of the Walennaé river, and are bounded on the east by a low range of limestone hills. Further coastal plains surround the Gulf of Boné: the Luwu' plain at the head of the gulf, the Wajo' along the basin of the Cénrana river, which connects Lake Témpé with the gulf, and the Boné.

Forest covers just 38 per cent of the province's land area, and 70 per cent of this is in the mountainous northern districts; just 8 per cent remains in the more populous southern areas. Nostalgic memories of an omnipresent virgin forest remain in the collective psyche, as expressed for instance in tales of the oral tradition, but in reality deforestation has been extensive since probably the fourteenth century, with the opening up of more and more wet ricefields in the lowlands and valleys and over-intensive shifting cultivation on the hills and in the highlands. This has resulted not only in an impoverishment in the variety of plant life but also in a dramatic denuding of the slopes, leading to severe gullying and silting up of the lakes and estuaries.

The climate is equatorial, with average temperatures ranging between 23 and 31 degrees Celsius along the coasts, falling as the land rises into the mountains by about one degree Celsius for every 200 metres elevation. In the southern part of

Celsius for every 200 metres elevation. In the southern part of the peninsula the climate is characterized by the alternation of trade winds. From late November to March the winds blow from the west, bringing heavy rain on the west coast – heaviest in December and January – and some rain also on the central plains just behind the mountains; from April to October they blow from the east, bringing relatively moderate rain on the eastern and central plains, with May and June the wettest months. There are, of course, many local variations on this pattern: Palopo in the Luwu' plain has on average 2,200 mm of rain over 167 days, for example, in contrast with just 1,350 mm in 100 days in Bantaéng at the southern tip of the peninsula. Some years, too, bring more rainfall than others; at any particular moment in a relatively wet year, there is always a good chance of rain falling in some parts of South Sulawesi, while other areas will be dry.

The main agricultural product in the south-western peninsula has for centuries been rice. Although wet ricefields cover only 20 per cent of the area, this still amounts to over three times as much land under rice as in all the remainder of Sulawesi (Whitten et al., *Ecology of Sulawesi*: 584). The ease with which rice can be grown here has undoubtedly been a major factor in the growth of the population. Moreover, as the two sides of the peninsula have alternating rainy seasons there is nearly always harvest in progress somewhere, and thus it has always been possible at any time to compensate for any local deficit. Traditionally, the lowland wet fields have been rainfed, with no real irrigation, and despite governmentinitiated irrigation schemes, especially since the early 1970s, most are still cultivated in this way, giving just one harvest a year with an average yield of around 1–1.5 tons per hectare. Until relatively recently this was large enough to meet local needs and even to produce a surplus for export as well. Besides the wet fields, there were also dry ricefields in hilly areas, cultivated through the slash-and-burn technique which unfortunately, having been pursued too intensively, was probably the main cause of the deforestation which has occurred in most of the seasonally dry hilly regions.

Besides rice, the ancient Bugis also cultivated millet and Job's tears;[2] these crops have now virtually disappeared, persisting only on a small scale. Maize has been cultivated quite successfully since its introduction in the sixteenth century, while sago, which from time immemorial had been the staple food in Luwu', retains some of its former importance there although it has been increasingly replaced by rice. Other substitutes for rice are taro, sweet potato and even, in the Mandar area, banana.

South Sulawesi has perhaps less variety in fruit and vegetables than other parts of the archipelago: as well as bananas, aubergines, breadfruit, cucumber and various kinds of gourd and pumpkin are grown, and tomatoes have recently been introduced. The coconut, as everywhere in the Pacific world, has many uses: its outer envelope furnishes fibres for making ropes, its nut can serve as a container, its water is drunk when the fruit is still young, and its flesh is eaten at various stages of maturity and is used to produce coconut milk (a basic ingredient for cooking) and oil, while the sap of its inflorescences yields sugar, palm-beer and vinegar.

The main source of proteins has always been fish, caught variously in the open sea, on the coral reefs near the coasts or in the freshwater rivers, ponds and lakes inland. Fish are raised in ponds in the middle of ricefields, while aquaculture of milk-fish and shrimps in brackish coastal ponds is widespread, and has been much developed recently.

Cattle husbandry has never been very sophisticated in spite of the role of the buffalo as sacrificial animal and symbol of wealth. In former times the agricultural use of the buffalo was limited to treading the ricefields; they do not seem to have drawn ploughs until the fourteenth century. In the twentieth century the buffalo has largely been replaced by Balinese cattle. The meat of both species is eaten only at feast times. More care seems to be given to horses, which are everywhere used as both riding and pack animals; in a few regions they are also used for ploughing. Most meat comes from fowls; domesticated ducks are raised usually for their eggs only, not for their meat, but a related wild species (*Dendrocygna javanica*)

---

[2] 'Job's tears' is a tropical grass which bears edible grains; its scientific name is *Coix lacryma Jobi (L.)*.

from islamized areas and deer hunting has become the privilege of the nobility.

In summary, South Sulawesi provides its inhabitants with an environment which – excessive deforestation apart – compares favourably with that of other rural areas in south-east Asia. It has permitted a reasonable growth of population and possesses many assets conducive to the development of local states on an economically well balanced foundation.

South Sulawesi Languages

The Bugis, along with the Mandar, the Toraja and the Makassar, are one of the four main ethnic groups of South Sulawesi, all of which belong to the same West Austronesian linguistic sub-group. The Mandar (numbering about 400,000) live on the north-western coast of the province, the Toraja (about 600,000) mainly in the northern mountains, though increasing numbers of them are settling in the Luwu' plain. The Bugis (over three million) occupy the mainly lowland and hilly areas to the south of these two groups, with a few living in the Luwu' plain, mostly near the coast around and to the south of Palopo, while the homeland of the Makassar (about 2,000,000) is the southern end of the peninsula, both along the coasts and in the mountains. Each of these groups is further divided into local sub-groups with more or less distinct dialects.

The Bugis still distinguish themselves according to their former major states (Boné, Wajo', Soppéng, Sidénréng) or groups of petty states (those around Paré-Paré and Suppa' on the west coast; those around Sinjai in the south). The languages of these areas, with their relatively minor differences from one another, have been largely recognized by linguists as constituting dialects: recent linguistic research has identified eleven of them, most comprising two or more sub-dialects (Friberg and Friberg, 'Geografi dialek').

There are also a number of small groups in Luwu' whose members speak languages related to those of central or south-east Sulawesi. One of the most fascinating is perhaps the Wotu people, who are to be found only in one particular village in the Luwu' plain which is held to have special links with the origins of the Luwu' kingdom. These people stress their own special relationship with Selayar and Buton, two islands located respectively at the south-west and south-east of the entry to the Gulf of Boné. Recent preliminary linguistic research has indeed found a relatively high percentage of correlations between their language and the Wolio dialect of Buton and the Layolo of Selayar (Sirk, 'Wotu Language').

A very different ethnic group are the Bajo, who call themselves Sama. The most numerous (an estimated 800,000 in 1995) and famous of the 'sea-peoples' of south-east Asia, usually, although wrongly, called 'sea gypsies', they live in scattered groups in the islands of the Sulu Sea, along the coasts of Mindanao (southern Philippines), north-west Borneo (Malaysia) and north-east Borneo (Indonesia) and all around eastern Indonesia, especially in Sulawesi, where they live in various locations in the Gulf of Boné, in Buton and on the neighbouring Muna and Kabaéna islands, in the Bonératé archipelago south of Selayar, and on the islands of Makassar. They speak a dialect closely related to those spoken by other Sama/Baja/Bajau of North Sulawesi, north Borneo and the southern Philippines, with obvious connections with Malay.

The Bugis and their Neighbours

Most of the South Sulawesi peoples are closely interconnected, not only linguistically but also through many cultural and historical links. Settled as they are in the middle of the peninsula and being the only group in contact with all of the others, the Bugis share common elements with all of them; but as they are also the most numerous they sometimes overshadow their neighbours, especially those who are, like themselves, Muslims.

Bugis and Makassar

As Makassar is both the most widely known harbour city in South Sulawesi and, since the eighteenth century, home to many Bugis, there is often confusion between the Bugis and

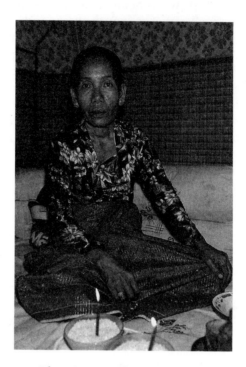

Plate 2 A Makassar woman

Makassar peoples; indeed, the names Bugis and Makassar are usually so closely identified that many think they are synonymous. Even local intellectuals have recently contributed to the loss of the distinction between the two peoples by resorting to the composite term 'Bugis – Makassar' (Mattulada, 'Kebudayaan Bugis – Makassar'; 'Bugis Makassar'; Hamid Abdullah, *Manusia Bugis – Makassar*). This confusion is, of course, not without its grounds, and it certainly reflects the present feeling, among at least part of the South Sulawesi Muslim population, of a common identity which supersedes ethnic and linguistic differences. This can be neither denied or disregarded. However, it must be stressed that from their emergence as separate entities up until the present century, the Bugis and the Makassar were quite distinct, notwithstanding their numerous and intimate interrelations.

The Bugis and Makassar languages, although closely related, are not mutually intelligible; they are even, of the four main languages of their group, the two that have diverged from each other the most (Mills, 'Proto South Sulawesi': 492). However, mutual cultural borrowing in various domains including material life, the arts and literature has resulted in the emergence of a kind of cultural commonality which even in the nineteenth century made it possible for the Dutch scholar Matthes to append to his Makassar and Bugis dictionaries the same ethnographic atlas, with the same houses, boats, agricultural tools, items of clothing and so on represented, differentiated only by the terminology used to describe them. Nowadays, once outside his province of origin, any Muslim from South Sulawesi, whether a Makassar, a Mandar, a Duri, somebody from Wotu or even a Bajo, will readily identify himself to other people as Bugis.

Bugis and Toraja

To many eyes, whereas the Bugis and the Makassar seem to have most in common among the South Sulawesi peoples, the Bugis and Toraja seem to be the most distinct. In fact, the Toraja language is clearly derived from the same ancestral language as the other South Sulawesi tongues, and Bugis shares more cognates (about 45 per cent) with Toraja than it does with Makassar (about 40 per cent) (Mills, 'Proto South Sulawesi': 492). Myths of origin show both similarities and differences: both the Bugis and the Makassar represent their ancestors as native sons of the land to whom divine heroes were sent from the heavens or from the abyss, bringing order and social rules to the earth. Some of the Toraja – in Rantépao, Ma'kalé and Méngkéndék – have a similar myth structure, while others have traditions about arriving from over the sea, and coming to settle in their present area by following the Saddang river from its mouth. The latter tradition might refer to the actual arrival of the common ancestors of the Mandar, Toraja, Bugis and Makassar, while the former, clearly a political myth, might be rooted in the attempt to establish the superiority of an aristocracy of newcomers over the autochthonous population.

A common opinion today is that the Bugis and Toraja have been implacable enemies since ancient times. There have indeed been wars between the two peoples with, in later times, Toraja prisoners of war sometimes enslaved; but generally speaking their relationship was one less of competition than of complementarity, based on the exchange of iron, gold, forest products and later coffee from the highlands for the products of the lowlands such as salt, salted fish or the expensive white or spotted buffalo required for religious rituals, as well as luxury goods from overseas – silks and the glass beads from which ornaments were made. In earlier times the Toraja even appear to have maintained close relations with both Luwu' and the Bugis proper. A number of seignories in north Wajo' and in Sidénréng are even said by the Bugis themselves to have been created some time around the fourteenth or fifteenth century by Toraja aristocrats from Sangalla'.

Culturally, the Bugis and the Toraja have much more in common than might appear to be the case at first glance; however, differences between them have been enhanced in present times by the conspicuous character of particular traits in, for example, house construction and clothing which play a role as indications of identity. There are nevertheless many similarities in their agricultural and manufacturing techniques and in their traditional weaponry, and the Bugis may even have borrowed their techniques for working silver, gold and iron from the Toraja: oral tradition in the main Bugis smithing community in Amparita, Sidénréng, attributes its foundation to an exiled Toraja smith. Furthermore, descriptions of funerary rituals as performed on the west coast of South Sulawesi around 1540 (Jacobs, 'First Christianity': 299–300) are strikingly reminiscent of the great Toraja funerary feasts of today.

Later, from the seventeenth century onwards, differences between the 'pagan' Toraja and their Muslim (Bugis and Ma'sénrémpulu') neighbours became greater, and in recent decades the development of tourism based on the 'originality' and 'unique character' of the Toraja culture has led both local Toraja guides and foreign writers of guidebooks to stress the differences from, and rivalry with, their neighbours.

Bugis and Bajo

From the first occasions on which they were mentioned by European writers as seafarers, and on many other occasions since, there has frequently been confusion between the Bugis and another maritime people, the Bajo. As early as 1511 the Portuguese Tomé Pires mixed up the Bugis traders coming to Malacca from the so-called 'Macaçar' islands with the Bajo, whom he characterized as pirates.

What we do know about the Bajo in historical times is that, far from being just sea nomads depending exclusively on fishing for their subsistence, they were always very active in the quest for such commodities as were in demand on the international markets – both products of the sea, such as mother-of-pearl, sea slugs, tortoiseshell, pearls, seashells, coral and seaweed, and products of the coasts off which they were living or which they visited, such as the dye-yielding roots of coastal forest plants, mangrove bark and wood, eagle-wood, resins, honey, beeswax and birds' nests (Andaya, 'Aquatic Populations': 36). This activity involved them in a close relationship of exchange and complementarity with the Bugis and Makassar kingdoms.

Nowadays, South Sulawesi Bajo have a relatively high rate of intermarriage with Bugis, and some of those I have met in the Gulf of Boné were able to speak four languages: Sama, Bugis, Makassar and Indonesian.

Part One

The Shaping of Identity:
From Origins to the Classical Age

2

Evidence and Source Material

The origins of Bugis history are clad in obscurity and uncertainty. Unlike the western Indonesian regions, South Sulawesi lacks Hinduized monuments and inscriptions on stone or metal which would enable us to construct a reliable framework for its history from the first centuries of the Christian era to the period for which abundant Western sources are available. Local written sources give reliable information only from the fifteenth century. For earlier times, therefore, we have to combine a cautious use of the available texts with the evidence offered by archaeology, external sources, comparative linguistics and ethnography.

Archaeological Data

In South Sulawesi, as in many other parts of Indonesia, archaeological research is not so far advanced as in mainland south-east Asia – to say nothing of western Europe. However, notable progress has been made since the mid-1970s concerning both the earliest period of human occupation and the proto-historical period.

The Earliest Times

In 1972 Van Heekeren took the view, on the basis of surface finds in Cabbéngé (Soppéng) in the Walennaé river valley, where evidence of a flake industry appeared alongside the fossil remains of animals long since extinct – such as the stegodon, a kind of small elephant – that human occupation here might date back to the middle or late Upper Pleistocene period, that is, around 50,000–30,000 BC (Heekeren, *Stone Age*: 66–72). Although later studies (Bartstra, 'Note') have claimed that the fossil material was not associated with the stone artefacts, and that the latter might have been of much later origin, other scholars (Glover, 'Late Stone Age': 275) have inclined to accept a date of perhaps 40,000 years BP for these traces of human activity, thus making them contemporary with Wajak Man in east Java, Niah Cave Man in Sarawak, north Borneo, and the Tabon Cave finds in Palawan, south Philippines (Soejono, 'Prehistoric Indonesia': 55).

Overlapping sequences, mainly excavated in caves in the vicinity of Maros, show that the early (Cabbéngé) flake industry was succeeded, at Léang Burung 2, by an industry characterized by the presence of Levallois points and dated, by means of the carbon-14 dating of shells associated with these artefacts, at between 31,000 and 19,000 years BP. There are so far no identified remains from the final stages of the Pleistocene. The next level, dating from about 10,000–8,000 BP at Ulu Léang 1, has shell middens, thick steep-edged scrapers and high-domed core scrapers. Then, around 6,000 years ago, comes an industry of long-backed blades associated with bone points. Glover ('Léang Burung 2': 372–3) writes that 'the archaeological sequences suggest the slow evolution of a cultural tradition, perhaps with some input about 6000 years ago, but not a series of population movements with each "people" bringing new cultural patterns.'

The last stone age culture in South Sulawesi, usually called 'Toalean culture', is based on a blade, flake and microlith complex which may have been begun some time before 5000 BC and is known from many rock shelters, some of which display paintings such as hand stencils and simple animal (babirusa) figures.[1] These caves, which were probably used as

---

[1] The babirusa (*Babyrousa babyrussa*) or 'deer hog', a kind of wild pig of the *Suidae* family, is endemic to Sulawesi; its upper tusks grow up through the skin and curl around towards the skull, looking like horns.

occasional camp sites near fields or on hunting expeditions rather than as regular habitations, are very rich in denticulated arrow-heads, geometric microliths and hollow-based points called Maros points. These are said to be 'the most refined products of the Indonesian flake industry' (Soejono, 'Prehistoric Indonesia': 57). This culture is not totally isolated, but is 'the local expression of the widespread flake and blade technocomplex of the Philippines, eastern Indonesia and possibly even further afield' (Macknight, 'Rise of Agriculture': 2). The early hunter – gatherers who lived here were probably of Melanesoid or Australoid stock, and thus not unlike the present inhabitants of New Guinea or Australian aborigines.

Vegetable and animal remains of this period include those of *Canarium* almonds, many kinds of wild seeds, freshwater molluscs, tortoises, wild pigs, anoas[2] and babirusas. In some of the caves a few human remains have been found, but the 'Toalean' people did not regularly dispose of their dead in caves. Carbonized rice grains, estimated to date from about 4000 BC – certainly before 2000 BC – have been found which constitute one of the earliest examples of rice found so far in insular south-east Asia (Glover, 'Late Stone Age': 277–8). Of course, at that time rice may have been just one among many edible plants.

Pottery, usually considered to be associated with the beginnings of plant and animal domestication and as an indicator of an Austronesian culture, first appears about 3000 BC (Bellwood, *Prehistory*: 223–8). The neolithic innovations found in South Sulawesi seem to have come through the Philippines from south China via Taiwan, which was probably the point of dispersion of the Austronesian peoples. The first, plain earthenwares are succeeded by a different, decorated kind of pottery, somewhat like that found in Kalanay (central Philippines) and Sa-Huynh (Vietnam). This latter type is usually related to the further expansion of iron use in the late first millennium BC (Ngo Sy Hong, 'Sa-Huynh').

[2] The anoa (*Anoa depressicornis*), of the *Bovidae* family, is a wild pygmy buffalo, endemic to Sulawesi.

The Age of Metal

Artefacts found from around the beginning of the Christian era are still neolithic in appearance and include polished quadrangular and rounded stone axes, adzes, stone beaters for bark cloth, harpoon heads, bone spatulae, shell scrapers and decorated (incised) pottery. This kind of technical complex may have lasted well into the first millennium, for instance in Kalumpang, west–central Celebes, although this site is not definitively dated, and includes no metal finds.

Some locally made bronze and iron tools were used, however, though when exactly Celebes peoples gained knowledge of iron-working techniques is still uncertain. On the mainland they were known by 700–600 BC, but there is no evidence of iron use in the archipelago from earlier than 300–200 BC (Glover, personal communication). The earliest evidence for bronze-working in south-east Asia comes from central Vietnam and Thailand and can be dated at around the late third millennium BC (Glover and Syme, 'Bronze Age'): iron in Vietnam and Thailand can be dated at the earliest at around 700–600 BC (Bellwood, *Prehistory*: 275, 292). Both bronze and iron techniques seem to have spread from contintental to maritime south-east Asia.

The early metal phase of Sulawesi is, like that of the Moluccas, poorly known, although rich in material (Bellwood, *Prehistory*: 304). Selayar is well known for its Heger I bronze drums, which are found in the archipelago from Malaya to New Guinea along what clearly seems to have been a sea trade route in use since well before the beginnings of the Christian era: most of these artefacts were originally made in north Vietnam and south China between 500 and 100 BC. Ceremonial bronze axes, also found in Selayar and in Makassar, may be of a different origin, perhaps cast in Java or Bali. These are the first clues to the existence of trade relations between South Sulawesi and the surrounding world, through which new technological knowledge could be diffused. Other metal objects, such as iron knives, bronze fish-hooks, bracelets, pendants in animal form, statuettes and betel boxes, some of which have ended up in private collections, have also been found at several prehistoric sites, but none of these can be dated with certainty.

The most famous bronze object from Sulawesi, the Buddha image in the style of Amaravati (second to fifth centuries AD) found at Sempaga near the mouth of the Karama river, is probably of Indian manufacture (Bosch, 'Buddha-beeld'); it is similar to other bronze images found in east Java and in Palembang at the site of Bukit Siguntang, the traditional centre of the famous kingdom of Srivijaya, and is one of the earliest pieces of evidence of a religious influence from India in Indonesia. It is interesting to note that the prehistoric site of Kalumpang, excavated first by van Stein Callenfels and later by van Heekeren, lies upriver from Sempaga. It should also be noted that the Karama valley was one of the possible routes to the iron ore-producing area of Séko, one of the few places in the archipelago where iron could be extracted relatively easily in ancient times, which suggests the existence there of early trading. Some copper ore also exists in the mountains of central Sulawesi, and copper ingots may have been exported to Java, which is very poor in metal ores; but many prehistoric Indonesian bronzes include lead, which is not to be found in Indonesia and so had to be imported from overseas. We know for certain from Sanskrit inscriptions on seven Sivaite sacrificial columns in eastern Borneo that around the fourth century an Indianized state existed just across the Makassar straits from Mandar: here Hinduism might well have coexisted with Buddhism, in view of the discovery in that area of another bronze Buddha image of the Gandara style (Fontein, *Sculpture of Indonesia*: 23).

Other evidence of South Sulawesi's far-reaching links in ancient times is provided by three other bronze Buddhist statuettes (two Buddhas and one Avalokitesvara) found near Bantaéng at the peninsula's southern tip; cast by the lost wax process, they are now in the Rijksmuseum, Amsterdam. According to the authors of the catalogue in which their details are published (Scheurleer and Klokke, *Divine Bronzes*: 111–13), stylistic analysis suggests a date around the seventh or eighth century AD and points both to south-east Indian influence and to links with similar artefacts from south Thailand (Songkhla) and Borneo. Excavations near Bantaéng have produced potsherds and many bronze artefacts of the early metal age together with polished stone axes, while many glass beads of Indian origin have been found in nearby Ara, pointing to the existence there of maritime trade as early as 300–100 BC. We may thus surmise that from the beginning of the early metal period South Sulawesi was incorporated into a huge trading network with connections with east Borneo and presumably also with Java, Sumatra, Vietnam and perhaps indirectly Sri Lanka and India.

According to oral information many golden objects have also been found in South Sulawesi, either accidentally or through illegal digging for ancient ceramics, but few of them have found their way into museum collections or indeed ever come to the notice of experts, since they are usually sold for the price of the metal and made into modern jewellery. I was told, for instance, of the discovery in Mandar of a golden image which, from the description given by someone who had seen it, could well have been a reclining Buddha. Golden images were also formerly kept as the regalia of several seignories on the southern coast of the peninsula, among them Bantaéng itself (Goedhart, 'Bonthain': 158, 174). Two gold masks, presumably funerary masks, have been found, one near the former Siang, on the south-western coast of the peninsula, the other again in the vicinity of Bantaéng. The Siang mask is strikingly similar to another said to have originated in east Java, which Miksic (*Javanese Gold*: 54–5) terms a 'preclassic object', since hinduization changed Javanese funerary practices from inhumation to cremation; it might thus date from before AD 500, though neither location nor dating can be confirmed. Another beaten gold mask discovered in Butuan in the North Agusan province of Mindanao in the southern Philippines might date from the ninth to the thirteenth century (Battesti and Schubnel, *Trésors des Philippines*: 9, 13; Villegas, 'Tradition de l'or': 32). Spanish testimonies bear witness to the use of funerary eye- and face-covers in the Philippines up to the sixteenth century (Miksic, *Javanese Gold*: 50–7). There are also reports of frequent finds in Selayar (Heekeren, *Bronze–Iron Age*: 85) and in Luwu' of gold leaves, apparently similar to those discovered in the southern Philippines as well as in Santubong (Sarawak) and Bali, which appear to have been used as funerary eye-or mouth-covers (Miksic, *Javanese Gold*: 56–7).

Megalithic remains

Other, quite conspicuous, ancient remains, in the form of monuments of megalithic type which are to be found in several parts of the province, are difficult to interpret. Some of them are presumably of great antiquity while others may be quite recent: not far from the Bugis country, the Toraja still erect menhirs, sometimes of immense size, at the funerals of prominent individuals. No precise date can be given for the complex of large stone jars and statues found in the Bada district of central Sulawesi, west of Lake Poso, although it appears to be associated with iron and pottery working. In Bugis history, the custom of 'stone planting' to solemnize a treaty was still in use in the sixteenth century, and stones

Plate 3 A so-called dakon *stone at Lawo near Soppéng*

known to have been erected on such occasions are still to be seen in several places. Ashes found under some menhir-like stones in areas inhabited by the Bugis indicate that they were erected on the tombs of prominent individuals from the time before islamization until well after it. Dolmens, by contrast, seem to have been abandoned as burial markers following islamization.

Other large stones, now locally called 'stone mortars', are likewise undatable; in spite of their name and the fact that a few of them may have been used as rice mortars recently, their original purpose is doubtful. Some of them are marked by several holes, the size and shape of which certainly seem to make them unsuitable for pounding rice. Moreover, they are usually associated with what Indonesian archaeologists refer to as 'scraped stones' (carved with parallel or hatched lines) and '*dakon* stones'. *Dakon* is the Javanese name for a board game called *a' galacangeng* in Bugis, which is played with two roles of holes, each with a bigger hole at either end, and small stones or cowries used as pawns. However, only a few of the stones with holes in conform to this model: some have seven series of seven holes arranged as a square; in others the holes are in an irregular pattern. They may have had a ritual use, for until recently the Bugis reserved such games as *a' galacangeng* or knucklebones for the period of mourning. Such stones are often found, sometimes alongside twelfth-century imported ceramics, on or near sites linked in oral tradition with the origins of the first Bugis dynasties; they might predate them, but it is impossible to tell by how long. Similar groups of stones are to be seen in Pasemah, south Sumatra and central Java, suggesting the diffusion of a cultural complex possibly based on a common religious ideology.

Many sacred places in South Sulawesi are marked by the presence of stone monuments, but it is not possible to determine whether the stones were put there because the places were considered sacred or whether the places came to be deemed sacred because of the presence of these stones, of an origin unknown to the present inhabitants – possibly erected there by earlier settlers. One such sacred place is a hilltop in Kajang where a number of boulders, possibly natural features, are the subject of local myths about the appearance of humankind on earth, the first incest, and the origin of agriculture and the stars that govern it; a particular spot is considered as the 'Navel of the Earth'. At this place communal rituals were held, and here too was the stone where the lords of Kajang were consecrated. Elsewhere in the peninsula large stone structures often mark places associated with stories about the appearance of divinely descended founders of local dynasties, and the consecration of most Bugis and Makassar rulers usually took place on special stones; indeed, the princes were described figuratively as 'stone-treaders'.

Imported Ceramics

The first relatively precise dates to be obtained from archaeological finds in South Sulawesi are from high-fired ceramics imported from mainland Asia, mostly from China; it is indeed one of the richest of all Indonesian provinces in these materials (Hadimuljono and Macknight, 'Imported Ceramics'). Although there have been a few finds of earlier ceramics from the Tang period (ninth century), for instance that of a phoenix-headed ewer from Maros (Macknight, 'Emergence of Civilization': 130), most of this trade in ceramics dates from the middle and late Sung period (eleventh to thirteenth centuries) to the present.

Potsherds are found in very large quantities on the sites of former settlements, and complete pieces have been dug out from many ancient burial sites. Prior to islamization, in most parts of the Bugis area the dead were cremated, and the ashes of noble people were interred in jars together with other porcelain wares which were deposited in the tomb either as costly belongings of the deceased or as containers for the offerings. Porcelains were also buried with corpses in the western and southern parts of the peninsula, where cremation was not practised. In spite of large-scale plundering by uncontrolled antique dealers, sites rich in ceramics can still, as a recent thesis by David Bulbeck (*Historical Archaeology*) brilliantly shows, provide precious clues about the historical geography and chronology of former South Sulawesi states.

Epics and Historical Texts

The Bugis themselves see their own past through two kinds of anonymous handwritten texts which can be respectively characterized as mythic/epic and historical. The first kind consists of a huge corpus or cycle of versified stories, collectively referred to by the Bugis as *Sure' Galigo* after one of its protagonists, La Galigo. The other kind, to which we shall turn first, includes a great number of not only Bugis but also Makassar and Mandar local chronicles.

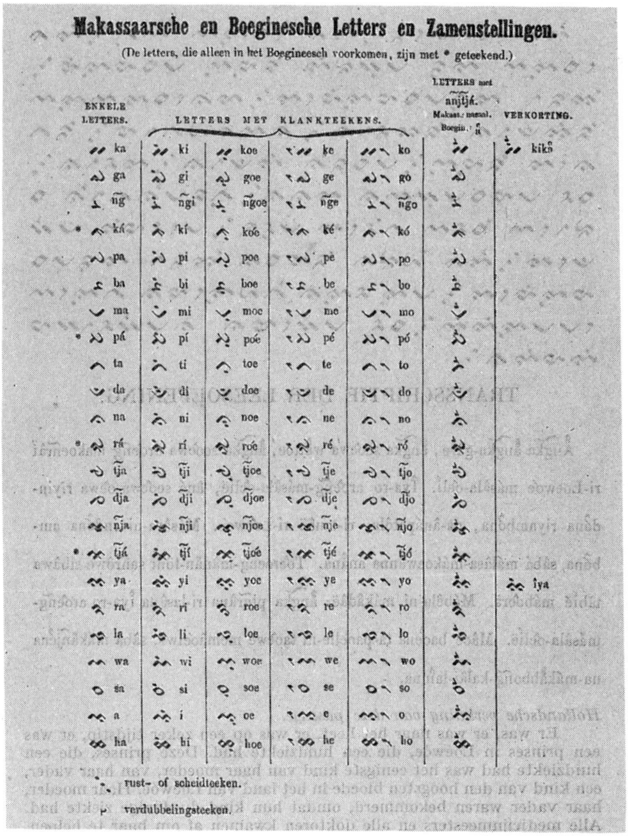

Plate 4   *Reproduction of the table of Bugis and Makassar scripts from Matthes, Boegineesche Spraakkunst*

Bugis Chronicles

While nearly all Bugis kingdoms, seignories, chiefdoms or domains, from the most powerful to the most minor, have their own chronicles, very few of these texts treat of the whole area as an entity. These manuscripts, kept by the Makassar as well as the Bugis and called by the Bugis *lôntara'*, record detailed genealogies of noble families, dynastic tables, ancient diaries – which in South Celebes have been kept in some courts or by some noble households since the seventeenth century – and other sundry items such as vassal lists or texts of treaties and political contracts. The chronicles appear to have drawn much of their data from these kinds of primary sources as well as from local oral tradition. They focus for the most part on specific developments in individual polities – their origins; the progressive organization of their territorial and political institutions; the deeds (wars, conquests, treaties, alliances) of their successive rulers, and also their talents, insufficiences and wrongdoings and the technical innovations made in their time – and they list the marriages and births in princely families (Noorduyn, 'Historical Writing').

While Bugis and Makassar chronicles have been hailed by many Western scholars as notably objective and reliable, at least from the time (*c.*1400) when they appear to have been based on contemporary documents and notes, they nevertheless usually lack a reliable measure of time. This deficiency is only imperfectly remedied by the expression of time-lengths: how long successive rulers held sway, at what age important individuals died, or how many years elapsed between one event and another. Therefore, in order to establish chronologies one has to apply to these texts the technique of 'back-dating', taking as starting point a securely dated event (such as the birth, death or accession of a ruler, or a military operation) known through an external source and then counting years backwards, cross-checking with other chronicles of neighbouring polities: in this way quite good results can be achieved. This technique was first used by Noorduyn (*Kroniek van Wadjo*: 88), who then brilliantly applied it to arrive at a precise dating for the islamization of Makassar (Noorduyn, 'Islamisering van Makassar'). Where time-lengths are not given, one can work towards a chronology by using and cross-checking genealogies, taking an average of twenty-five years per generation. In this way scholars have established quite reliable chronologies from about the beginning of the fifteenth century.

For the earlier parts of the chronicles, which usually deal with the founding of the original settlements, the legendary origins of the ruling dynasties and the establishment of a governmental contract between the first rulers and the local inhabitants, any attempt at dating is almost irrelevant, since these texts have more an ideological than a truly historical significance. Most chronicles state that the first rulers, be they male or female, were either 'people descended from heaven' (*to-manurung*) or 'people sprung up from the abyss' (*to-tompo*'). Of divine origin, they were sent to humankind to put an end to the time of anarchy – how long this was is uncertain, as it is described as lasting seven *pariama*, a period of disputed length – which had followed the departure from earth of the *La Galigo* heroes, who are also described as earlier descendants of the gods.

The La Galigo *Cycle*

The *La Galigo* manuscripts, rhythmically segmented texts written in a highly literary style and archaic language, narrate in detail the destinies over five generations of hundreds of princely characters of divine descent living at an undetermined period in a number of South Sulawesi kingdoms and on adjacent islands. Until well into the twentieth century these texts were widely considered to be sacred, and could not be read without appropriate rites being performed. Most of the Bugis still believe that the events described really occurred in a golden age of the past when things were different from the present and humankind was nearer to the gods. A complete version of the epic cycle is nowhere to be found; most extant manuscripts, many of which begin and end abruptly, cover no more than a few, sometimes disconnected, episodes. However,

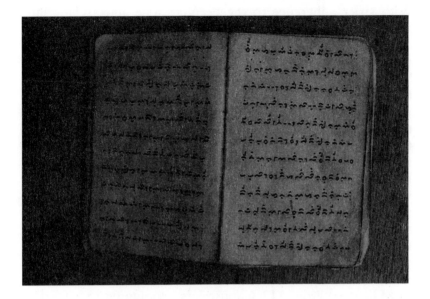

Plate 5 A La Galigo *manuscript*

many Bugis *literati* and in some areas even ordinary villagers
have a good knowledge of a great part of the whole cycle,
acquired through public readings or oral transmission.

The *La Galigo* cycle is obviously not the work of a single
author, for many of the known episodes exist in several versions which appear to be more than simple variants descended
from a single ancestor text. While the overall course of events
and the relationships between hundreds of protagonists display a consistence and coherence that are quite extraordinary
in view of the innumerable episodes, there are variations in
wording, composition and important detail from one version
of any episode to another. One way in which the whole cycle
may have come into being is progressive composition: in the
beginning only the general setting and the main story lines
would have been established, including the genealogical relationships between the main characters, while later poets
would have periodically composed new episodes in the same
language and style and in keeping with the already existent
episodes. The accretions then became integrated into the cor-

pus and even gave rise to yet further versions by other poets. With strict adherence to the peculiar style and archaic language of the *La Galigo* cycle such a process could well have lasted over a relatively long period of time, making even more difficult any attempt to establish a date for the whole cycle. What kind of historicity can be attributed to these texts, when they were composed or even over what length of time they were composed remain uncertain. However, their striking internal coherence indicates that at least the basic framework, the main episodes and the relationships between the principal figures were constructed within a relatively short time-span. Presumably they originally came into being in oral form and were transcribed later.

In approaching this immense corpus of material, the foreign student of Bugis letters is fortunate to be able to rely on the remarkable work done by the Dutch scholar R. A. Kern in publishing detailed catalogues of all *La Galigo* manuscripts present in European libraries and at the former Matthes Library in Makassar. From 113 manuscripts, amounting to a total of 31,500 pages, he has distilled 1,356 pages of detailed summaries, to which are appended extensive lists of the hundreds of characters who appear in the course of the narrative (Kern, *Catalogus* I and II). An abridged Indonesian version has recently been published (Kern, *Cerita Bugis*). On the basis of this quite invaluable work it is possible to reconstitute in detail nearly all the episodes of that remarkable saga, surely one of the world's greatest epics – longer than the *Mahabharata* itself.

External Sources

Recourse to external sources would be most valuable to complement local sources, to establish dates with accuracy, to gain an alternative point of view on known facts and to fill gaps in information. Unfortunately, very few such sources are available before the sixteenth century. One of the earliest is the Javanese poem *Nagarakertagama*, written in about 1365, in which several place-names in and around South Sulawesi are mentioned (Pigeaud, *Nagarakertagama*, 3: 17; 4: 34); for the fifteenth century, a few laconic allusions are to be found in later Malay texts (*Sejarah Melayu*: 151–3; Abdul Rahman al-Ahmadi, *Sejarah hubungan*: 4–5). Chinese sources, so useful (despite the difficulty of interpreting the Chinese rendering of foreign names) in reconstructing the early history of other places in the archipelago, are disappointingly silent on South Sulawesi prior to the fifteenth century. Even the first Portuguese accounts are relatively late and terse as compared with similar sources on Malaka, Java and the Moluccas.

Although some indirect information was recorded by a few Portuguese authors (Pires, *Suma Oriental*: 220), the first Portuguese eye-witness account of South Sulawesi is that given by the Malakan merchant Antonio de Paiva, who stayed there for a year in 1542–3 and returned in 1544 (Jacobs, 'First Christianity': 282–303). The second is that of one Manuel Pinto (not to be confused with the more famous Mendes Pinto), who arrived with an expedition from Malaka and stayed from 1545 to 1548 (Wicki, *Documenta Indica*, II: 420–2). Other Portuguese documents were written at the turn of the seventeenth century by Diogo de Couto (Couto, *Decadas*, V: 86), and by Manuel Godinho de Eredia (Eredia, 'Description of Malacca': 54–7), the son of a Bugis princess. From that time onwards, with the first visit of the Dutch in 1605 quickly followed by the arrival of the English, Western sources become more numerous, more diverse and more precise. After the fall of Makassar to the Dutch in 1666–9, Dutch accounts – both archival and published – dominate, although a few other Western sources are available, for example the reports written in 1688 by the Frenchman Nicolas Gervaise (*Description historique*) and in 1848 by the future 'White Rajah' James Brooke (*Narrative of Events*) about his experiences a few years earlier in the then virtually independent Bugis state of Wajo'. But while external sources can supply interesting material to complement extant local sources from the sixteenth century onwards, they are cruelly lacking in respect of earlier lacunae.

3

The World of Early South Sulawesi

In view of the available sources and their reliability, we can divide the Bugis past into three periods: the historical period, for which we can rely on Bugis chronicles supplemented by external sources; the early Bugis period, for which the only written sources come from the *La Galigo* cycle, information from which must be used with great caution; and the prehistoric period, for which no written sources are available and where we must rely on archaeological evidence alone. The knowledge we amass for each of these periods can be related to what is more generally known of the past of both continental and insular south-east Asia and supplemented by analysis of linguistic and ethnographic evidence. Notwithstanding their limitations, these sources encourage me to attempt a provisional reconstruction of the Bugis prehistorical past; further research will progressively clarify and amend the picture.

A Hypothetical Reconstruction of the Prehistoric Past

The Early Settlement of South Sulawesi

From an early time, probably well before 50,000 years BP, South Sulawesi, like the other islands of south-east Asia (Bellwood, *Prehistory*: 65, 91, 98) was inhabited by people contemporary with Wajak Man of Java (Soejono, 'Prehistoric Indonesia': 55) and probably not very different from those who settled Australia around that time. In south-east Asia they went through a process of some facial and cranial gracilization, but remained phenotypically Australoid. Some descendants of these populations have survived up to the present as isolated groups in Malaya (e.g. the Sakai) and the Philippines (e.g. the Aeta), or mixed to some extent with later arrivals.

At the beginning of the twentieth century, the Swiss explorers and cousins Paul and Fritz Sarasin put forward the hypothesis that the To-Ale' of South Sulawesi ('people of the forest', wrongly written by them Toala), a small group who lived partly in caves in the mountains near Lamoncong (south Boné), were the direct descendants of the prehistoric cave dwellers, and related to the Veddah of Sri Lanka (Sarasin and Sarasin, *Reisen*): hence the term 'Toalean' still used by modern prehistorians to denote the late prehistoric culture of South Sulawesi. However, measurements made in 1933 by van Stein Callenfels proved that there were in fact no differences worth speaking of between the so-called Toala and their ordinary Bugis neighbours (Heekeren, *Stone Age*: 109). From documents in the archives of the Dutch Royal Anthropological Institute in Leiden it further appears that, far from being living fossils maintaining their primitive way of life and pagan practices, as the Sarasins imagined, these people were simply modern Bugis exiles condemned by the Boné rulers for serious breaches of the customary law to banishment in those inhospitable tracts, where they lived in destitution.

Nonetheless, oral tradition in South Sulawesi does refer to original inhabitants whose physical appearance was different from that of present-day Indonesians. In Luwu' and north Wajo' people call them Oro and say that they looked like Papuans; in the south, for instance around Sinjai, they are called to-Marégé, which was also the name given by the South Sulawesi navigators who visited the north-west coast of Australia to the Australian aborigines, and are said to have had the same physical characteristics as the latter. Interestingly, no Toalean remains have been found north of Singkang (Heekeren, *Stone Age*: 114), which invites the hypothesis that, surviving as isolated groups, the to-Marégé may indeed have retained physical traits inherited from the pre-Austronesian population.

However, not only the Sarasins' Toala but all present inhabitants of the southern part of South Sulawesi may number the Toalean palaeolithic cave dwellers among their ancestors. Toalean culture persisted in some areas until around 1000 BC, and Toalean flakes and neolithic adzes have been found in many caves together with earthenware, glass beads, fragments of bronze and iron objects. This continuity until long after the presumed date of arrival of the Mongoloid, Austronesian-speaking agriculturalists indicates sustained interaction and progressive assimilation between the older inhabitants and the Austronesian newcomers.

In spite of the marine regressions which occurred during the Pleistocene, with the sea level at its lowest (*c.*150–130 metres) around 20,000 BP (Dunn and Dunn, 'Marine Adaptations': 248), Sulawesi was not then linked to the mainland of southeast Asia. We may therefore assume that early Australoid populations used some form of elementary water transport of a kind similar to that used by the ancestral Australian aborigines to cross from the nearest Indonesian islands: even when the sea level was at its lowest, Australia was never less than 80 km away. According to Dunn and Dunn ('Marine Adaptations': 265), coastal subsistence was at that time probably still based simply on strand gathering. With the rise in sea level which began in around 15,000 BP the Indonesian archipelago took its present form, and it is fair to assume that the technology of water transport became much more advanced, to allow fishing in the open sea if not yet deep-sea voyages. By about 4000 BC, at a time when Toalean culture was still flourishing and the first Austronesian incomers were arriving in the archipelago, the pre-Austronesian peoples were probably very competent seafarers and open-sea voyaging already common.

If this progress in the methods of water transport was indeed the result of local technological evolution within the culture of the south-east Asian Australoid/Melanesian islanders, it may have enabled the spread from the north of technical innovations such as pottery or some sort of horticulture, and later their diffusion throughout the whole island world of the South Seas, before any substantive Austronesian migration – which, indeed, it may even have facilitated. Prior to this time, the neolithic techniques and artefacts which came to South Sulawesi from south China and Taiwan via the Philippines may likewise have travelled in the absence of large-scale migrations or even direct contact. It is also possible that, besides hunting and gathering, some groups among the early settlers on Sulawesi were already exploiting taro and other aroids,[1] yams and some other plants still used in an area covering the whole of the Pacific – for example *Cordyline fruticosa* or *Erythrina sp.* (Bellwood, 'Horticultural Prehistory': 68); the discovery at Ulu Léang 2 of very early grains of rice even raises the question whether its arrival predated or accompanied that of the Austronesians.

The Coming of the Austronesians

The dispersal of Austronesian-speaking populations with a basically Mongoloid genetic inheritance is now generally estimated to have begun around 4000 BC, when groups of people whose economic activity centred on plant cultivation expanded southwards from Taiwan through the Philippines (Bellwood, *Prehistory*: 88). The first Austronesian settlers in South Sulawesi may have arrived from the southern Philippines via North and Central Sulawesi *c.* 3000–2500 BC.

Linguistic analysis suggests that the first Austronesian settlers in South Sulawesi were related to the present-day inhabitants of its central and south-eastern parts, and spoke languages related to the present-day Kaili-Pamona, Bungku-Mori and Muna-Buton groups. The existence of such a link seems obvious from the analysis of certain words and forms which are to be found particularly in the Makassar and Toraja languages as well as in old Bugis and in the sacred language of the Bugis *bissu* priests (Mills, 'Proto South Sulawesi': 508, 513–21; 'Reconstruction': 218; Sirk, 'Basa Bissu': 235–6; Bulbeck, *Historical Archaeology*: 512–13). Other evidence of this inheritance, and perhaps also of previous non-Austronesian languages, could be found by thorough comparative linguistic

---

[1] Taro (*Colocasia esculenta (Schott)*) is a plant of the Aroidae family whose root is eaten all over south-east Asia and the Pacific area.

analysis of river, mountain and other place-names which have no known meaning in Bugis or other contemporary South Sulawesi languages, even in their archaic forms. Such is the case for mountain names like Latimojong, Aruang and Népo, the last of which is also to be found in Central Sulawesi; Kambuno, the name of a mountain in Central Sulawesi, is also the name of an island in the Gulf of Boné. Likewise, most of the names of the oldest Bugis principalities, including Luwu', Cina, Témpé, Sidénréng and Suppa', have no known meaning in Bugis, in marked contrast to those of polities founded later.

It seems likely that before the Christian era people belonging to the Muna-Buton linguistic group whose heirs are today to be found in Wotu (Luwu'), Layolo (Selayar), Kalao (near Selayar), Muna and Wolio (Buton) were settled on the coasts all around the Gulf of Boné (Bulbeck, 'Historical Archaeology': 509), while the rest of the peninsula was sparsely populated by people belonging to the Panoma group (Mills, 'Reconstruction': 218; Sirk, 'Basa Bissu': 235). The previous Australoid – Melanoid inhabitants of the peninsula had probably been so few and scattered that, through a process of genetic absorption resulting from the incomers' substantial superiority in numbers and, perhaps, technology (Bellwood, 'Horticultural Prehistory': 63), they were easily assimilated, with the exception of a few remnant groups (Bulbeck, 'Historical Archaeology') which may have become a source of slave labour: Oro slaves are frequently mentioned in *La Galigo* texts. Interestingly, Mills ('Proto South Sulawesi': 622) relates the word for 'slave' in Bugis and Makassar (*ata*) to the name Aeta which is given in the Philippines to residual negrito populations.

Later came people speaking the proto-South Sulawesi language – or languages – from which all the present-day South Sulawesi languages are descended. These languages were shown to form a distinct group in 1938 (Esser, *Atlas*); later research by other authors has confirmed and refined this view (Mills, 'Proto South Sulawesi'; Friberg and Friberg, 'Geografi dialek'; Grimes and Grimes, *Languages*; Bulbeck, 'Historical Archaeology'). According to Mills, who used a mainly qualitative approach ('Proto South Sulawesi': 500–8), the Makassar language seems to have remained the most isolated of all the proto-South Sulawesi languages and shows the fewest affinities with its closest neighbour, Bugis; he thinks that the speakers of the proto-language must originally have been settled along the lower course of the Saddang river to its outlet into the Makassar strait, an area situated between present-day Paré-paré, Rappang and Pinrang. The ancestors of the various groups of today were presumably still in close contact, for the languages of the Bugis, Makassar, Mandar, Toraja and Ma'sénrémpulu' peoples seem to have undergone common development for some time; later the groups moved apart, the ancestors of the Makassar southwards, of the Mandar north-wards along the western coast, of the Bugis into the central lowlands, of the Toraja northwards into the mountains and finally those of the Pitu Ulunna Salu upriver along the Mamasa towards the area they inhabit now.

Many features point to a long period during which Makas-sar was relatively isolated from other South Sulawesi lan-guages; an explanation for this, according to Mills, may be that the peninsula's southern part was still separated from the rest, if no longer by the inland sea of around 5000–500 BC then by a continuous belt of swamps, lakes and rivers which made it into a virtual island, cut off from the proto-Bugis and other peoples. Later, in their southwards movement, the Bugis would thus have progressively occupied an area previously settled, perhaps only thinly, by Makassar.

Although Bulbeck criticizes many of Mill's arguments, his own computerized analysis of the Grimes' lexico-statistical data ('Historical Archaeology': 487–515) also points to the 'great distinctiveness of the Makassar language from those surrounding it', which 'implies that "proto-Makassar" was the first language to split off the main line of descent of the South Sulawesi languages'; he accounts for that distinctiveness by the inclusion of a substratum which 'could have been provided by the original, Toalean inhabitants'. However, he thinks that the next group to split off from the common line was the Bugis, followed by the northern South Sulawesi family (including the Mandar and Toraja).

It is not yet possible to tell when the process of ethnic differentiation among the peoples of South Sulawesi began. A clue to the date of their emergence may perhaps be found in comparative onomastics. While the name for Bugis is in Bugis itself Ugi' or Wugi', it is Bugisi' in Makassar, Bugi' in Toraja and Bugis in Mandar and in Malay; the name for Makassar is Mangkasa' in Bugis, Mangkasara' in Makassar itself, Mangkasar in Mandar and Mengkasar in classical Malay; the name for Mandar is Menre' in Bugis, Manra' in Makassar, Mandar in Mandar itself and also in Malay. The Mandar language has clearly retained the original forms, which appear also to have been known to the first Malays or pre-Malays who visited the island, perhaps in association with trading ventures of which the earliest evidence is provided by bronze statues which have been approximately dated to around the first centuries of the Christian era.

Where did the South Sulawesi peoples' common ancestors come from? Mill's guess ('Proto South Sulawesi': 499–501) is that they arrived by sea, as indeed is told in a number of Toraja traditions, from some other island; this probably happened, he suggests, not in a single large migration but in a series of perhaps closely spaced movements. The other island could be anywhere in the south or west, but if Mills is correct in locating the first settlement near the mouth of the Saddang river, the nearest possibility appears to be either east Borneo around Kutei-Samarinda or south-east Borneo around Pegatan-Pulau Laut. (Both of these places were in later times settled by Bugis colonists, who may thus have unwittingly returned to the place of origin of their ancestors.) These areas are easily reached by boat from the western coast of South Sulawesi: Makassar is one or two days' sailing from Pulau Laut, and regular maritime links between Samarinda and Paré-paré have lasted up to the present day. Last but not least, there is new linguistic evidence in favour of a Bornean connection. It has recently been shown, on the basis of an extensive body of phonological, morpho-syntactic and lexical data (Adelaar, 'Borneo as a Cross-roads') that the Tamanic group of languages spoken in the north-eastern part of west Borneo is closely related to the South Sulawesi languages, particularly Bugis and Toraja. This can best be explained by the former cohabitation of the ancestors of both peoples in a common homeland. Adelaar ('Asian Roots') has also recently found evidence of some influence from South

Sulawesi languages on the south-east Barito languages of Borneo and on Madagascan – two languages whose links had
already become established. This influence must have predated the seventh century AD, which Adelaar thinks is the
most probable period of migration to Madagascar of people
of Bornean ancestry. As the Tamanic peoples (the Embaloh,
Taman, Kalis and Palin), as well as the south-east Barito
peoples, are definitely inlanders, while the South Sulawesi
peoples have for centuries been sailors and enthusiastic maritime traders, Adelaar favours the scenario of an early migration of the Bugis from Sulawesi to Borneo; this hypothesis
would be in accordance with Sirk's views about a development of proto-South Sulawesi languages in South Sulawesi
itself. An alternative explanation is that, on the contrary, the
ancestors of both groups, Tamanic and proto-South Sulawesi,
lived in close contact in south-east Borneo before moving
westwards overland (the Tamanic group) or eastwards overseas (the proto-South Sulawesi group).

Mills believes that trade may have been a major factor in
motivating the migration to Sulawesi. Trade may in fact have
led to the early settlement of both sides of the Makassar strait
by proto-South Sulawesi speakers, who would have maintained frequent and long-lasting exchange links. Such a situation might reconcile the two conflicting hypotheses of a
development of proto-South Sulawesi languages in either Borneo or Sulawesi. Both east and south-east Borneo show traces
of indianization from perhaps as early as the second century
AD and from quite ancient times the region had had trading
links with neighbouring areas, including the western coast of
South Sulawesi. These connections may very well have fostered the expansion of the South Sulawesi peoples. The process would have begun with annual visits, traders coming
from Borneo on the west monsoon and returning on the east
monsoon. The mouth of the Saddang river gave access to
forest products, the iron and gold of the mountains and also
presumably to a channel crossing from the Makassar strait to
the Gulf of Boné: thus it was the best possible place to establish a trading settlement. Bulbeck misses this point when, in
his criticism of Mills's hypothesis, he doubts that this area
'could have held such extraordinary benefits for population

growth that it remained the static centre for four successive migratory waves' (Bulbeck, 'Historical Archaeology': 514).

Another strategic settlement point could have been the 'seven river mouths' on the Mandar coast, including the mouth of the Karama river, where the famous Amaravati-style bronze Buddha was found, which leads to the iron ore of the Séko area. Other possibilities are the eastern outlet into the Gulf of Boné of the hypothesized trans-South Sulawesi channel, in what was later to be known as Tana Ugi', and the Luwu' area at the head of the Gulf of Boné, giving access to gold, iron and copper. Moreover, the coast of Makassar and Bantaéng provided possible ports of call for craft navigating between the western and eastern parts of the archipelago. The possible association of the ancestors of the South Sulawesi language family with metal-producing sites is the more significant in that the linguistically related Tamanic groups of Borneo are 'famed as itinerant silver-smiths and workers in brass and copper' (King, *Borneo*: 48).

Early South Sulawesi Lifestyle and Culture

For most of the first millennium AD, the daily life of the South Sulawesi peoples may have been rather similar to that of the Toraja at the beginning of the twentieth century. They probably lived in communities scattered along river banks or sea and lake shores, living in houses raised on piles; they supplemented their subsistence swidden farming of rice and other edible crops by catching fish and shellfish. From comparative lexicography and comparative ethnography one can surmise that they also ate sago, tubers (especially yam and taro), millet, Job's tears and many kinds of vegetable, including cucumbers and aubergines. They also had sugar cane, bananas, breadfruit and, above all, the coconut tree, from which they derived palm beer, palm sugar, coconut milk, oil and vinegar, as well as other forest products such as honey, wild plants and the betel nut, which they chewed. They hunted indigenous game such as wild boar and babirusa and also the imported deer. Also imported were the buffaloes they raised for sacrifices and great occasions. It is not certain whether

Plate 6   Sago processing in Luwu'

they raised domestic pigs and goats; these animals are not mentioned in *La Galigo* texts, but pig bones, perhaps the remains of funerary offerings, have been found in excavated burials (Macknight, 'Emergence of Civilization': 130); however, these may have been from wild boars.

The first Austronesian settlers in South Sulawesi probably did not weave cloth; the technique of weaving, although part of the stock of knowledge of their Austronesian ancestors in Taiwan *c*.4000 BC, seems to have been lost by those who migrated to eastern Indonesia and Sulawesi via the Philippines. According to Glover (personal communication), woven cloth does not appear on mainland south-east Asia until about 700–500 BC. It spread to maritime south-east Asia later, perhaps at the same time as metal technology. Right up to the twentieth century, the peoples of central Sulawesi did not know how to weave and produced textiles by bark-cloth beating, a technique known widely in south-east Asia and the Pacific, including by the speakers of the proto-South Sulawesi languages. Evidence of bark-cloth beating which Bellwood (*Prehistory*: 248) would be inclined to date at around 1000 AD, though no radio-carbon dates are available, has been found at the Kalumpang site: there is an old Bugis word for bark-cloth, *ujang*, and some South Sulawesi Toraja were still practising this technique in the late 1960s. However, their ancestors, the later settlers of South Sulawesi, practised weaving using unspun fibres and perhaps also cotton on back-strap looms with a circular warp. The names for cotton (*ape'* in Bugis, *kâpasa'* in Makassar, *kapas* in Malay, from the Sanskrit *karpasa*) even suggest that weaving was brought to South Sulawesi by people already in direct or indirect contact with Indian trade. It must also be noted that the word for heddle – *are'* in Bugis, *kara'* in Makassar, *kala'* in Toraja and in Luwu', *arra* in Wotu – is akin to the Malay *karap* also found in east and south-east Borneo, indicating that proto-South Sulawesi weaving terminology was received from more or less indianized south Sumatran Malays via south-east Borneo.

For clothing, the men probably wore a loincloth and possibly a headcloth, and the women a skirt. There is archaeological evidence that they used bronze and sometimes gold ornaments. They had pottery, although they made extensive use of bamboo containers, and used iron weapons and tools alongside bamboo knives and spears; ground stone tools may also have coexisted with iron implements for a long time. For fishing, they used pronged and simple harpoons, hooks, various kinds of traps and nets, and also vegetable drugs; for hunting, they may still have used bows, a weapon which later disappeared (a common Austronesian name for bow, *pana*, is still used in Bugis for the carding bow); they also had spears, spear-throwers and blowpipes with poisoned darts, as well as a kind of lasso attached to a long pole. Most of these weapons were also used in war, along with short swords and, for protection, rattan helmets and long shields.

The early Bugis must have practised head-hunting for ritual purposes related to agriculture and fertility. They generally buried their dead, but they also disposed of some corpses by immersion (in the sea or lakes), or by putting them in trees. Their ancient megalithic sites probably bear witness to their practice of double funerals.[2] Their religion was dominated by the worship of ancestors and spirits, to whom offerings were made through specialist intermediaries. It is of course difficult to determine what their theological system was, but it is reasonable to surmise that, as among many other Insulindian peoples, it was based on the idea of a socio-cosmic order, in which the world was viewed as a polarized entity whose opposed pairs in a generalized system of symbolic equivalencies were sky and earth, mountain and sea, rising sun and setting sun, right and left, sun and moon, male and female, life and death. Mythological elements still surviving in Bugis esoteric texts and popular folklore, or alluded to by ancient sources, as well as surviving pre-Islamic rites, still show traces of a former cult of the sun – moon/above – beneath duality, with offerings presented to the 'above' on mountain summits, clifftops or other elevated places and to the 'beneath' on the seashore, river banks and at subterranean pools. The proto-Bugis people, like the Toraja of today, may also have distinguished between the rites 'of the rising sun' for the gods and deified ancestors and those 'of the setting sun' for the dead.

Early South Sulawesi peoples, although scattered in small communities, were not isolated. Trade was already important to them. The finds near Bantaéng and Ara of objects dated from 300 to 100 BC, the bronze drum found in Selayar, the bronze axes also found there and at the peninsula's southern tip, the Buddha image found in Mandar and the Buddhist statues found in Bantaéng all show that South Sulawesi had been incorporated quite early into a network of trade relations extending from the far west to the far east of the archipelago, which must have included not only the eastern and south-eastern coasts of Borneo but also Sumatra and

[2] The 'double funeral' is a practice known all over the Austronesian world, whereby the dead are subject to two different sets of ceremonies, the first immediately after death, the second several months or even years later. Among the Toraja, who are the only people still to follow this practice in South Sulawesi, the corpse is kept between the two sets of ceremonies, wrapped in many layers of cloth making a long cylinder, in the traditional house (*tongkonan*) of their family group.

continental south-east Asia, where similar finds have been made (Fontein, *Sculpture of Indonesia*; Scheurleer and Klokke, *Divine Bronzes*). The very existence of bronze objects, at a time when the tin necessary to make bronze alloys could only be obtained in Malaya, implied the import either of ready-made artefacts later to be recast or of tin or tin/bronze alloys in ingot.

The goods exported from South Sulawesi in the sixteenth century, such as sandalwood, tortoiseshell, resins, gold and other metals, must have been among those picked up there by early traders in the first centuries of the Christian era. Gold was in great demand everywhere, either for local use or for export to India, and gold dust was obtained by panning the rivers in the mountains of west central Sulawesi. The natural outlets for this product were the above-mentioned river mouths on the western coast and at the head of the Gulf of Boné, later the location of the kingdom of Luwu'. Iron was also much in demand: the Javanese kingdoms do not seem to have exploited what little iron was available in Java (Bronson, 'Metal Trade'), and so they had to import it. One source was the central Sulawesi mountains, among the very few locations in the archipelago where abundant ore deposits are found, with a few traces of copper; Sulawesi iron was particularly sought after for the forging of the most highly praised weapons because of its nickel content, which produced some of the best *pamor* (welded steels) in the archipelago for pattern-welded swords and knife blades. The iron-producing areas were accessible through the head of the Gulf of Boné or through the Gulf of Tolo. In both cases the most direct sea route from Malaya, Sumatra or Java passes through the strait between the island of Selayar and the Bira peninsula, which have accordingly long been strategic points. Mt Bawakaraéng, known by sea charts under the name of Bonthain Peak, has been used as a navigational mark by generations of sailors; and the south-western and south-eastern tips of Sulawesi were natural ports of call on the northern route from the west of the archipelago to the Moluccas, which were certainly visited from very early times by spice traders. The earliest evidence of long-distance trade in cloves, which were not available elsewhere in the world, comes from a find dated about 1700 BC at

which to reconstruct that part of South Sulawesi's past which lies beyond the reach of available historical sources; unfortunately the limited space available in this book does not permit the full development of my arguments, which will be resumed at length in a forthcoming publication (Pelras, 'Regards nouveaux').

I am well aware that this use of material of a largely legendary character may sometimes lead to mistaken conclusions. However, in view of the fact that most of my conclusions tally with the opinions of many of my elderly Bugis informants, taking into account not only written data but also their inside knowledge of Bugis society and culture, I am confident that at least some part of these reconstructions will be confirmed by further research.

The Discontinuity between La Galigo *and Historical Texts*

Interestingly, although some of the kingdoms or important domains of the Bugis, for example Luwu', Témpé, Cina, Lamuru, Soppéng, Sidénréng and Suppa', are mentioned in the *La Galigo* cycle, none of the chronicles of these places tries to relate the mythical ancestors and founders of its historical dynasty to the heroes of the *La Galigo* texts. At the end of the *La Galigo* cycle, Luwu' and *La Galigo*'s three other most important kingdoms (Wéwang Nriwu', Tompo'tikka and Cina), are the only kingdoms where descendants of the gods are said to have been left to rule: with the exception of these royal couples and their offspring, all the heroes of godly origin have to leave Earth after Sawérigading's youngest daughter, who reigns in Luwu' with her husband, has produced a child able to succeed, and after all the rites required at the birth of a royal child have been performed. Yet there is no real attempt in later texts to link this couple with the mythical founding couple of later Luwu' or Cina chronicles and genealogies, who have different names and stories. A standard beginning of Bugis chronicles, used in that of Boné for instance, describes a time before the appearance of dynastic founders when 'those who had ruled the land during the age of *La Galigo* had returned to the abode of the gods', or that 'those whose ancestry could be traced to the age of *La Galigo* were no more' and that 'for seven periods [*pariama*] the people had been left without rulers' and submitted to the rule of the stronger, when 'the people were eating each other like [big] fish [eat small fish]'.

Indeed, the assertion of a gap between the two periods seems to have had considerable significance in political mythology. This does not mean, however, that it is not based on some reality, to which I think a number of facts bear witness. One of these is the marked discontinuity between the *La Galigo* universe and that of the chronicles. Another is the disparity of language: although the terminology of the chronicles and associated texts does contain archaisms, it is more or less understood by modern Bugis, while the *La Galigo* texts, by contrast, use so many obsolete words and phrases that at first hearing they are almost unintelligible to untrained Bugis listeners. Irrespective of the actual time of their transcription in manuscript form – and even of the actual time of their oral composition – there is no doubt that they have conserved a much older form of the Bugis language, more different from the language of the earliest chronicles than Chaucer's English is from Defoe's. No extant Bugis historical text in its present form, with the possible exception of a few very short documents such as the Luwu' vassal list published by Caldwell ('Bugis Texts': 75–80) seems to predate the second half of the seventeenth century. Even the earlier elements that they incorporate seem to have been rewritten in more contemporary wording; by contrast, while *lôntara'* can be copied, in whole or in part, and the copyists, who are usually specialists in their subjects, feel free to make additions or modifications based on their knowledge of other texts or oral tradition, *Sure' Galigo* are treated as sacred texts and may not be modified at all (Pelras, 'Oral et écrit'). The extreme textual and linguistic conservatism of the *La Galigo* texts strongly supports the view that when they refer to geographical and political conditions very different from those we know from even the earliest historical texts, or when they describe elements in Bugis society and culture which were not found later, even as early as the fifteenth century, while in other aspects continuity is evident, they are referring to an actual past reality.

In toponymy and topography, both continuity and discontinuity are evident. Many place-names cited in *La Galigo* texts, such as Luwu', Wotu, Baébunta, Larompong, Témpé, Soppéng, Lamuru, Sidénréng, Suppa', Sawitto' and Maru'/Maros, and geographical names such as Mt Latimojong, Cape Marasanging and Silaja'/Selayar, are still in use in present-day Sulawesi. For others, local experts have offered identifications: in a few cases, for example Waniaga, which all agree corresponds to present-day Bira, there is virtual unanimity, whereas in others, for example Cina, Wéwang Riwu', Pujananti, Tompo'tikka, there is more dispute. Strikingly, however, a number of important historical place-names are conspicuously absent from *La Galigo* texts; these include those of kingdoms such as Wajo', Boné, Goa and Tallo', which were already important at the beginning of the sixteenth century and which certainly existed, although still in the early stages of development, in the fifteenth and probably in the second half of the fourteenth too. If these kingdoms already existed at the time the *La Galigo* stories were created, the question arises why they are not mentioned when other places, some important, some not, are. Even if the tales were fictive history one would expect them to attribute glorious forebears to contemporary leading powers. Another curious detail is that, although Témpé and Sidénréng are named in these texts, no mention is made of their being situated, as they nowadays are, on a lake shore: people from far away overseas are portrayed arriving there directly in seagoing boats, as if they were on the sea coast. Consequently, the contention that the *La Galigo* cycle was composed after the fourteenth century has to account for its description of a South Sulawesi different both from that of known historical times and from the political myths of historical text, yet one that is quite consistent and that seems to be confirmed in certain details by external evidence.

Archaeology and the Proto-history of South Sulawesi

Research on South Sulawesi proto-history, which is still at a fairly early stage, is likely in the coming decades to bring to

light many as yet unknown facts. For the time being we have
to content ourselves with the scarce available evidence. One
set of evidence concerns Indic influences: although there are
no indianized architectural remains on the island, the Buddhist bronze images found in Mandar and Bantaéng, and the
few Sanskrit loan-words in Bugis (especially conspicuous in
La Galigo and *bissu* texts), seem to point to the presence from
as early as the fifth century of foreign, Buddhist traders who
may have had some limited influence on native religious representations and practice, and in the development of native
states. In contrast, the undated gold finds in Siang and Luwu'
are obviously related to a funerary tradition of which examples have been found in several places in the archipelago,
including the southern Philippines, west Borneo, Java and
Bali, but had nothing to do with indianization, whether it
preceded it or remained untouched by it. As for the continental Asian – mostly Chinese – ceramics found all over the
peninsula, even when not properly excavated they constitute
precisely datable archaeological evidence. An interesting com-
ment on their geographical distribution is made by local antique dealers, who say that most of the older finds, of which
only a few are Tang pieces, come either from Luwu' or Mandar, or from the southern coast of the peninsula, especially
around present-day Pangkajé'né, Takalar, Bantaéng and the
Selayar island, all places whose strategic importance in inter-
insular trade has been stressed above.

Some very interesting results have emerged from the archaeological survey carried out in 1988 by a joint Indonesian–Australian team on twelve sites in Soppéng mentioned by the
chronicles as early settlements or as cremation and burial sites
(Bulbeck et al., *Survey Soppéng*). Dating of sherds collected on
the sites has provided evidence that three of them were settled
from the middle and late Sung period (twelfth century); two-
thirds of the sherds from that time have been found at Tinco,
which the chronicles identify as the site of a palace inhabited
by the founder of the historical dynasty of Upper or West
Soppéng. Twenty-eight megaliths have also been counted on
this site, which is just one kilometre away from the famous
megalithic site of Lawo, where more than eighty megaliths of
different types, but no sherds, have been recorded. The second

site dated to this period is in Watang Soppéng, the present-day capital city of Soppéng; the third is Séwo, a mountain site with many megalithic remains which are still considered sacred. Another mountain site, Bulu' Matanré ('High Mount') has yielded no sherds from earlier than the Yuan period; Yuan sherds have been found in three more sites, but these were where historical rulers were cremated, and their ashes may have been buried in heirloom ceramics. Finally, sherds from the beginning of the fifteenth century up to the present century have been found in increasing numbers on all twelve sites.

David Bulbeck has attempted to convert tradewares counts into chronological information and has produced 'chronological histograms' for each of the sites surveyed. This work suggests a high density of occupation at Tinco for the oldest period and a relative decrease after the thirteenth century in Watang Soppéng; the general increase in sherds from the beginning of the fifteenth century appears to be caused mainly by the appearance of many new settlements. If we compare these results with statistics produced by the South Sulawesi Archaeological Service about the ceramics finds reported for the whole province (unfortunately with no details about the location of the individual finds), as well as about registered ceramics in private collections and authorizations for export of ceramics from Ujung Pandang, we find that both sets of data indicate relatively fewer finds from the Yuan period followed by a relative increase for the Ming period (Hadimuljono and Macknight, 'Imported Ceramics': 77). Rough calculations of finds in relation to the length of the respective Chinese dynasties produce an average rate of ceramics finds of 4.6 per year for the Sung (1127–1279), 1.1 for the Yuan (1280–1368) and 13.6 for the Ming (1368–1644). For Soppéng, where the variation is less marked, the relative decrease in the proportion of sherds at the most ancient archaeological sites, calculating in periods of fifty years, occurs between 1300 and 1400, with the lowest rate for Tinco between 1300 and 1350 (Bulbeck et al., *Survey Soppéng*: 56–60).

Although no indication of disturbance has been detected on any site, it seems to me significant that at precisely that period a mountain settlement was founded at Bulu' Matanré, obviously a place of refuge in times of insecurity, and also that

the number of settlements multiplied at the end of the fourteenth century. I am inclined to relate the figures and evidence
cited above to what the chronicles say about a period of
anarchy between the age of the semi-divine rulers of *La Galigo*, which might thus be situated between the eleventh and
thirteenth centuries, and that of the historical dynasties, which
would begin in earnest in the late fourteenth and fifteenth
centuries. The increase in imported sherds in the latter period,
corresponding to the founding of new settlements, might point
to economic changes, perhaps linked to new political developments with either the cultural renaissance of older polities
such as Sidénréng, Soppéng or Cina, or the birth of new ones
such as Boné or Wajo'.

A Possible Scenario for the Origins of the La Galigo Texts

As a working hypothesis, I suggest that the *La Galigo* texts
began to take shape, at first orally, around the middle of the
fourteenth century, in an intermediate period after a prestigious, economically successful and (presumably) militarily
powerful dynasty with Luwu' and Cina as its main centres had
either been kept out of power or temporarily lost its previous
ascendancy. This change in its fortunes could have resulted
from changes either in the local economy or in the international or inter-insular trade and political balance. Those earlier times may have been remembered, particularly by poets
associated with the former dynasty, as a kind of golden age,
and described in epic terms, integrated with mythic elements
of even older origin. These texts would have provided the
newly emerging chiefdoms or seignories of the second half of
the fourteenth century, as well as the reviving older polities
and their nobilities, with the archetypal model of appropriate
princely rituals and conduct, always to be emulated, never to
be equalled – as indeed they have done for Bugis nobility up to
the present day. I am further inclined to think that the *bissu*
clergy played a major role in this process, indeed that they
may have been responsible for the origin and development of
the whole cycle. This would be in keeping with the status of
the *La Galigo* manuscripts, until fairly recently, as holy books,

Plate 7 Pulling the honoured guest by means of a lawolo: *a rite carried on since* La Galigo *times for members of the high nobility*

and with that of the *bissu* as among the best experts in that literature.

Other clues supporting this date for the main composition of *La Galigo* include the reference within it to the Javanese kingdom of Majapahit ('Mancapai') as a dominant sea power, and to the use of instruments and weapons such as the compass (*padoma*) and cannons (*ballili*), which appear to have been introduced to Indonesia from China during the fourteenth century. According to Pierre-Yves Manguin (personal communication), cannons were used in Java by the Chinese during the Yuan campaign of 1293, and a mortar bearing a Chinese inscription dated 1421 has been found in Java. Javanese attempts to control the Luwu' trade might have contributed to its economic and political decline. Contrary to Bulbeck, I do not think that fourteenth-century Luwu' was under the influence of Majapahit (Bulbeck, 'Historical Archaeology': 478).

The La Galigo *Cycle and Oral Tradition*

Oral tradition can be helpful in locating places named in *La Galigo* texts and understanding why they were important. One such place is the sacred hill called Punsi Méwuni, situated in Ussu' at the head of the Gulf of Boné between the Cérékang river and an equally sacred stream called Waé Mami, where

Plate 8   The purported site of Tompo'tikka near Malili

Batara Guru, the founder of the Luwu' dynasty, is said to have descended from heaven. This hill is guarded by a very exclusive and impenetrable mystic community of about forty families living in the small settlement of Cérékang. Bugis speakers in an environment of Mori (Kinadu and Padoé) speakers, they form the nucleus of a network of adepts called Tossu' (from *to-Ussu'*, 'Ussu' people') scattered all over Luwu'. Around the hill, and around the bay of Ussu', are several places associated with various *La Galigo* episodes following the descent of Batara Guru or related to the felling of the giant Wélenréng tree and to Sawérigading's sinking into the abyss. According to oral tradition, Batara Guru's palace used to stand on top of the hill, which only adepts of the higher degrees are permitted to climb. The surrounding forest is all sacred and no one is permitted to fell its trees.

Significantly, to the east of Cérékang is the head of the track which, following the left bank of the Ussu' river, led to the iron deposits near Lake Matano. According to my informants, a place marked by heaps of slag can still be seen near the lake, where up to forty iron smelters are said to have practised their trade. The nickel-bearing iron, most of which was traded in Ussu' for textiles, was known in Luwu' as *bessi Tossu'* ('iron of the Ussu' people') and throughout the archipelago as *bessi Luwu'* ('Luwu' iron'); it was much sought after for the making of krisses.[3] The Matano people also exported through Ussu' small amounts of copper, which they obtained further up-country. They were often at war with their eastern neighbours, the to-Bungku, who were also iron miners and smelters, and were known (particularly by the sixteenth-century Portuguese) under the name of Tambuco for the swords which they exported from the east/central coast of Sulawesi to the Moluccas (Andaya, *Maluku*: 87). Further east from Ussu', the Malili river, which also gives access to the Matano region, is said to have been the border between the kingdoms of Luwu' and Tompo'tikka. Malili people point to many sacred places linked with the beginnings of Tompo'tikka, including the site of one of its ancient palaces.

---

[3] The kriss (pl. krisses; also spelt kris, creese and crease) is a type of dagger, often with a wavy blade, used all over the Malay world.

Many oral traditions about ancient Luwu' are also retained to the west of Ussu' in Wotu, whose villagers are mentioned in *La Galigo* as the carpenters who built the king's ships. Overlooking the Péwusoi river is the hill of Lampénai, said by local informants to be the site of the original settlement of Wotu and also said to be the site of another of Batara Guru's palaces. People say that when they dig at its foot they often find gold leaves, thus echoing the finds in ancient burials elsewhere in the archipelago. Gold was panned near here until relatively recently. A few centuries ago, it is said, this hill was by the sea coast (van Vuuren, *Celebes*: 431) and thus controlled access to the river. From its summit one enjoys a beautiful view over the whole Luwu' plain and gulf and the mountains which surround them; it thus also controls the passage from the south-eastern to the south-western peninsula, as well as access to the track leading northwards across the mountains to Lake Poso and further to the Bay of Tomini. This track began at Wotu, which was thus the only way to the short cut across Sulawesi from one gulf to the other. Much later, at the time of the historical kingdom of Luwu', Wotu was the official intermediary between the Luwu' ruler and the peoples of the mountain east of Lake Poso.

Another Bugis holy place, the site of the palace of Sawérigading and his wife Wé Cudai', was situated in Cina. Although there are disputes about its precise position, most local specialists in *La Galigo* texts tend to locate it in Pammana (south Wajo') on top of a hill called Alangkanang-é ri La Tanété ('the place of the palace on the plateau') which is surrounded by various megalithic remains. On the plateau itself several individual sites are distinguished: one is that of a relatively recent cemetery, and the palace site is elsewhere, now overgrown by a wood. Another site is said to be that of the meeting hall (*baruga*), and yet another that of the cockpit. At the foot of the hill people show a place which, although it is now quite remote from the nearest river, the Cénrana, they insist was the landing stage. Oral tradition elsewhere also tells how water formerly covered places which are now inland on the other bank of the Cénrana.

I do not share Caldwell's opinion in rejecting this traditional location of *La Galigo*'s Cina in favour of a hill called Bulu'

Cina ('Cina hill'), also on the right bank but near the mouth of the river: there are in fact several toponyms in the area including the name Cina, which means that they belonged to Cina but not necessarily that any was the centre of Cina. My own view is that the ancient Cina corresponded to the whole right bank, including Caldwell's Cina and the hill La Tanété, from which the *La Galigo* texts say Témpé hill was visible – which is indeed the case.

It is true that any identification of ancient and present places may be made fictitiously by later inhabitants in order to lend legitimacy to a ruling dynasty by giving it prestigious fore-bears; however, such identification has to take into account previous oral traditions and should not be discarded without a thorough examination of the evidence and, we must hope, future archaeological research.

The Early Bugis World of the *La Galigo* Texts

By putting together pieces of information scattered throughout texts from the *La Galigo* cycle and setting them against oral tradition one can obtain a picture of the political situation and state of civilization in South and Central Sulawesi and the surrounding world before the fourteenth century; this may or may not tally with the reality, but its coherence and plausibility are striking. Later research will perhaps permit scholars to distinguish among fact, anachronism and fiction. For the time being we have to be content with a general summary of the ancient Bugis world as it appears from these sources – in many respects quite a different world from that of later pre-Islamic times of which we know from historical sources.

La Galigo's *Physical Geography of Sulawesi*

The most obvious difference, often confirmed by local oral tradition, between what the *La Galigo* texts tell us about the geography of South Sulawesi in those ancient times and the situation today is that they imply the existence of a channel between the Gulf of Boné and the Makassar strait, with some of the present-day lowlands being under water. At the mouth of the Cénrana river, instead of the present delta there seems to have been a wide estuary, narrowing into a first pass at Solo', then widening again into a vast, presumably brackish, lake into which water poured from what is now Lake Témpé through narrow straits, creating dangerous whirlpools. On the hills which stretch out to the south and south-east from present-day Pammana to Cina—Boné lay Cina; on the hills to the north were the domains of Paccing, later known as Singkang, and Témpé. Beyond, where nowadays rich ricefields form a vast plain surrounding the shallow lakes Témpé and Sidénréng, an 'inner sea' covered most of the land as far as Soppéng in the south and the hills to the west which lead into the high cordillera running parallel to the western coast, with an outlet on this coast near Suppa'.

At first sight it seems difficult to accept such radical differences in coastlines for a period so comparatively recent as the eleventh to thirteenth centuries. According to geologists the sea level of the archipelago did indeed rise and fall several times between about 35,000 and about 5000 BP, and at least one oscillation carried the sea level above the present elevation, making an island of the southern part of South Sulawesi; but this happened in the immediate post-Pleistocene period (van Vuuren, *Celebes*: 149; Dunn and Dunn, 'Marine Adaptations': 248) – very much earlier than the period of the *La Galigo* texts. Recent palynological research has also confirmed that the sea once extended from the present mouth of the Cénrana river to the ridge of 'Celebes molasse' immediately east of the Témpé depression, but only between 7100 and 2600 years BP (Gremmen, 'Palynological Investigations', cited by Bulbeck, 'Historical Archaeology': 515). Yet the geographical picture painted by the *La Galigo* texts is unambiguous; and modern Bugis or Ma'sénrémpulu informants also insist that the southern part of the peninsula south of Lake Témpé was formerly an island and that it was possible to sail directly from the Gulf of Boné to the Makassar strait. Moreover, many local traditions in Wajo' or Luwu' consistently mention places now well inland which are said formerly to have been near the sea or even under water, or hills which are said to be former islands (Pelras, 'Regards nouveaux'). These convergent indications cannot easily be dismissed.

There is a body of evidence showing that in the sixteenth century the Témpé depression was still occupied by only one deep and very large lake, which progressively became more and more shallow. In 1548 (Wicki, *Documenta Indica*, II: 420–2) the Portuguese eye witness Manuel Pinto described this lake, which the Bugis then called Tappareng Karaja ('the great lake') as criss-crossed by many sailing ships; he also says that a large *fusta* (a long Portuguese ship with sails and oars) could sail upstream from the sea to Sidénréng. According to Pinto, this lake had a width of 5 Portuguese leagues of the time (about 25 km) and a length of 20 leagues (about 100 km); these measurements do indeed sound extravagant. However, about 180 years later Valentijn was still writing about a single lake which, even if it largely dried up during the dry season, always retained in the middle a deep navigable channel supplied with water by rivers coming from the surrounding mountains (Valentijn, *Beschryvinge*: 140). In 1828 Crawfurd (*Descriptive Dictionary*: 74, 441), basing his view on information from 'respectable members of the [Wajo' people] trading to Singapore', gave it a length of 25 miles (about 38 km). He further wrote that 'villages in [its] banks . . . carry on a considerable foreign trade. The trading praus are tracked up the stream of the Chinrana river . . . The depth of water is abundant during the rainy season for the largest praus, but not so in the dry.'

From another source of the same period (Nahuis van Burgst, *Brieven*: 54) it appears that there was already a Sidénréng (then called Western) Lake distinct from the larger Lake Témpé and communicating with it through a short channel. Lake Témpé was said to be 16 'hours' (48 English miles or 72 km) in circumference, and 6–30 ft deep. An estimate of Lake Sidénréng's surface in 1884 put the area at about 30 square miles, and that of Lake Témpé at about 50 square miles, with a depth of 4–5 metres in the rainy season (Staden ten Brink, *Zuid-Celebes*: 11); but the latter, as observed in 1888, could almost dry up in the dry season, while in flood conditions the two lakes merged into one again (Haan, 'Aanteekeningen': 27). Ever since the lakes have been silting up, and nowadays even at the highest water only canoes can sail on them. A similar process has been taking place in the eastern depression, where the Cénrana river flows to the Gulf of Boné. In 1920, Bugis *palari* could sail upstream to the halfway point; this is no longer possible, and the small lakes bordering the left bank have become mere swamps, although the whole area is regularly flooded in the rainy season.

To the north-west of Lake Sidénréng, where the western cordillera falls gradually to the level of the plain, local tradition has it that there was a link with the Saddang river, which then flowed out into the Makassar strait not through its present outlet but much further to the south at Suppa'. This accords with the conclusion reached in 1918 by the mining engineer, geologist and geographer E.C. Abendanon (*Voyages*) and confirmed by van Vuuren (*Celebes*: 191–6) that the old course of the river was through the former Lake Alitta, which at the beginning of this century still survived as a swamp and has now completely dried up. Another link from the Saddang to the lake may have flowed through Rappang; at the end of the eighteenth century or the beginning of the nineteenth the ruler of Sidénréng had formed a plan, presumably based on this tradition, to dig the channel anew over a length of 4 'hours' (12 miles or 22 km) in order to divert to the west coast the trade then going via the Cénrana (Nahuys, *Brieven*: 53).

Over the centuries an enormous quantity of alluvial silt has been deposited by the Saddang as well as by the Walennaé and Cénrana rivers, changing the single, large lake of the sixteenth century into three smaller, shallower ones. It can easily be imagined that between the time when an inland sea actually divided South Sulawesi in two and the situation described by Western witnesses there was an intermediate period, recalled in the *La Galigo* texts and in oral tradition, when the Témpé basin was occupied by a kind of freshwater inland sea; and this is precisely the name given by the Makassar up to the beginning of the nineteenth century to the 'great lake': Tamparang Labaya, or 'freshwater sea' (the contemporary Malays called it Laut Salah, 'false sea'); while the Makassar *tamparang* retains the meaning of 'sea', its Bugis counterpart *tappareng* has come to mean 'lake'. As I conceive it, this 'freshwater sea' was mainly fed from the south by the Walennaé river and from the north by the Salo Bila river (and perhaps also by a branch of the Saddang river); its outlet to the east flowed into a shallow bay on the southern bank on which Cina was situated, and its outlet to the west was probably through a channel linking up with the low course of the Saddang river, at the mouth of which Suppa' was established. I am not certain, however, whether such a situation still prevailed between the eleventh and thirteenth centuries; as is often the case in epic works, the texts may mix memories from different periods in the past.

La Galigo's *Political Geography*

Against this geographical background the *La Galigo* texts describe a political situation which certainly includes epic embellishments and anachronisms, and perhaps project into the past a scenario which is in part fictitious and is certainly not systematic; the following presentation of this picture rests on my putting together scattered elements.

In this undated past, Central and South Sulawesi are dominated by three leading powers: Wéwang Nriwu', Luwu' and Tompo'tikka, each of which appears to control one of the three areas which remain of strategic importance. Even now, in *bissu* hymns the totality of Earth is symbolized by (western) Wéwang Nriwu', (central) Luwu' and (eastern) Tompo'tikka, while Silaja' (Selayar), guarding the south-western access route to Luwu', and Wolio (Buton), guarding the south-eastern route, are generally named in parallel verses (Hamonic, *Language des dieux*: 78, 93). According to my reconstruction, access to the Saddang valley, the Mandar coast and the mountainous country of west – central Sulawesi was controlled from Suppa' by Wéwang Nriwu' ('Tremor of the Hurricane'), which may also have exercised some kind of suzerainty over the Makassar western coast with Pujananti/Gossabare' under Sunra ri Lau', and further south as far as the bay of Bantaéng. In the centre, Luwu' controlled the rest of the Torajaland and the mountains to the Malili river in the east, the northern and western coast of the Gulf of Boné from Ussu' to Bira ('Waniaga') and the island of Selayar, as well as part of the eastern coast of the gulf and of the south-eastern peninsula (the Mékongka/Mingkoka country), but neither Buton ('Wolio') nor the adjacent islands. Cina or Tana Ugi', while acknowledging the suzerainty of Luwu' to a degree, controlled the eastern end of the east – west channel linking the Gulf of Boné to the Makassar strait. The story of how Sawérigading, in order to marry Wé Cudai', won control, after several victories in sea battles against foreign ships, including some from Java, may reflect the memory of competition for this economically strategic place. The third leading power, Tompo'tikka ('Rising Sun'), controlled areas to the east: the iron-rich mountains around Lakes Matano and Towuti, with their outlets in the Gulf of Boné via the Malili river and in the Gulf of Tolo through the country of the To-Bungku, whose exports of iron and forged weapons to the Moluccas are reported in the earliest Portuguese testimonies; the Luwuk peninsula in east – central Sulawesi; and the island of Banggai, also rich in iron, which is mentioned in a Chinese work of 1304 in connection with its trade with the Moluccas (Ptak, 'Northern Route': 29–31).

The author of the Javanese poem *Nagarakertagama*, dated 1365 (Pigeaud, *Nagarakertagama*, 3:17; 4:34) names as tributaries of the powerful east Javanese kingdom of Majapahit 'the countries of Bantayan [Bantaéng], the principal is Bantayan, on the other hand Luwuk, then Uda, making a trio; these are the most important of those that are one island; then those that are, island by island: Makasar, Buton, Banggai, Kunir, Galiyao and Selayar' (English translation by Pigeaud). I think that a systematic order is discernible here, one that echoes the tripartite division depicted in the *La Galigo* texts, Bantaéng possibly being the heir of Wéwang Nriwu' and Uda that of Tompo'tikka. As Bantaéng lies at the tip of the south-western peninsula and Luwu' at the head of the Gulf of Boné, it seems to me that Uda should be sought somewhere on the other side of the gulf, and not, as has recently been suggested, in the Talaud archipelago or in North Sulawesi (Sollewijn Gelpke, 'Udama Katraya': 240, 244), because the Western concept of a single and indivisible island of 'Celebes' did not appear until well after the first visits of the Portuguese navigators (Pelras, 'Premières données': 229). This makes it unlikely that Uda would be named among 'the countries of Bantayan . . . that are one island'. As the other places named in the *Nagaraker-tagama* – Buton (*La Galigo*'s Wolio), Banggai (in my interpre- tation part of Tompo'tikka) and Selayar (in the Luwu' sphere of influence) are different islands off mainland Sulawesi, this must also have been the case for 'Kunir', 'Galiyao' and even 'Makasar'. We should not be led astray here by the relatively recent use of the name 'Makasar' for the harbour city now known as Ujung Pandang, for it was originally an ethnic name and could apply to any settlement of Makassar people, even away from mainland South Sulawesi; this *Nagarakertagama* 'Makasar' might well be the same as the 'Makassar island' situated between Buton and Muna (Berg, 'Poelau Makasar': 366). As for 'Galiyao', in spite of a recent hypothesis which identifies it as Pantar in the Lesser Sunda Islands (Dietrich, *Galiyao*), I remain inclined, in view of the system which seems to underlie the *Nagarakertagama* list, to accept an earlier identification with Kalao (Fraassen, 'Plaatsnamen').

La Galigo's *Geography of the Archipelago*

Among kingdoms in and around Sulawesi with which Luwu', Wéwang Nriwu' and Tompo'tikka had dealings, some are easy to identify: 'Taranati' is obviously Ternaté in the north- ern Moluccas; 'Maloku' must be one of the latter's neighbour- ing islands, perhaps Tidoré; 'Gima' is the name given by the Bugis, even now, to Bima, the eastern part of Sumbawa; 'Séreng', a name used since the sixteenth century for Seram Island, seems here to apply to the northern Moluccas in general. The precise location of some other places is uncertain, although it is obvious from the sea routes described as leading to or from them that they are located in north-eastern Indone- sia: according to oral tradition, 'Wadeng', a kingdom closely linked to Tompo'tikka, corresponds with present-day Goron- talo, whose former indigenous name was Wada (Nur, 'Sawé- rigading di Gorontalo': 440–4), while 'Senrijawa', on the route between Wadeng and Taranati, must have been some- where on the coast of Sulawesi's north-eastern tip. Other place-names, however, remain obscure.

To all of these kingdoms the *La Galigo* texts ascribe Bugis rulers (or at least rulers with Bugis names), most of them related to one another by matrimonial, political and presumably commercial links. This is, however, not the case for such seemingly transparent place-names such as 'Sunra ri Aja' (West Sunda), 'Sunra ri Lau' (East Sunda), 'Jawa ri Aja' (West Java) and 'Jawa ri Lau' (East Java); descriptions of journeys to and from these places seem to indicate that they were not on Java Island itself but were settlements of outsiders, perhaps situated on the southern end of the peninsula.

Maritime Links and Trade

All of the above-mentioned kingdoms ruled by Bugis dynasties form in the *La Galigo* texts a kind of common socio-cultural space to which Bugis maritime travel was restricted. The ships used appear from their descriptions to have been very similar

Plate 9   Sawérigading's ship, as drawn in a La Galigo *manuscript*

Plate 10   One of the Borobudur ships

to those of ninth-century Java or Srivijaya, as pictured in
Borobudur's famous reliefs (Horridge, *Sailing Craft*: 6): they
are big boats with double outriggers presumably made of
giant bamboo stems; to come aboard one had to step on the
outrigger boom. Their masts, usually dismantled at mooring,
were probably crook-ended, of tripod form, with large,
tilted, rectangular sails; those of the *La Galigo* hero Sawérigading's flagship *Wélenréng* are said to have been made of
precious imported *patola* silks. On the vast platform of bamboo lathing, one or several deck-houses were built. The keel
seems to have been made out of a huge tree-trunk, hollowed
out as for a dugout canoe and supplemented with side planks,
probably 'sewn' to each other.[4] Steering was by means of

---

[4] The technique of 'sewn boats' was a general feature of Austronesian boat
building before the availability of iron tools made dowelling more common,
and it remained in use in some places even long after that. Holes were made
all along the sides of the planks, and stitches of fibre string were passed
through them to make seams. The holes were then packed with absorbent

lateral rudders. Wind propulsion could be supplemented by one or several ranks of rowers, usually people from 'Waniaga' (Bira) and Selayar.

These epic texts, of course, attribute gigantic dimensions to the boats of the major heroes, calling them *wangkang tana* ('boats as big as lands'). This may mean that these craft symbolically represented the whole land of the royal heroes, brought with them as they travelled; but this tradition of the existence of huge ships, which survived even in the nineteenth century (in 1857 Wallace's informants in Aru still thought that the country where the Bugis and Chinamen went to sell their wares was a great ship called 'Jong' which stayed in the great sea), may echo some past reality. It reminds us, indeed, of the famous 'supernatural ships' built in south China at the end of the eleventh century which were 100 metres long with a capacity of 1,250 tons and could carry up to 1,000 passengers (Dars, 'Jonques chinoises': 43–6); and the existence of Insulindian (Malay or Javanese) ships of that size at that time is far from impossible (Manguin, 'Southeast Asian Ship'; 'Vanishing Jong'). However, this is unlikely to have been the case with contemporary Bugis ships.

In spite of, or because of, their dimensions, the Bugis boats of the *La Galigo* texts appear to be difficult to operate and also, from the time spans indicated even for direct journeys between identifiable points, to move incredibly slowly. This is the more surprising since one would expect an epic work to over-rate the speed of the heroes' ships. Also strange is the fact that these texts seem to record no regular Bugis travel outside eastern Indonesia; the only exceptions are a few expeditions to mythical lands somewhere in the western seas – whither, curiously, the route goes via 'Gima' (Sumbawa), not via Bali, Java, Sumatra or the Malaka strait. However, wares from the west are regularly brought to Sulawesi by foreign, mostly Sumatran, trading ships. It thus looks as if certain maritime routes were open and others closed to navigation from Sulawesi – or at least from Luwu' – as if to protect a monopoly.

---

fibres and the joints sealed with resin. This technique permitted the construction of very good sea-going boats, which could travel hundreds of miles without leaking.

In fact, a Chinese source of the end of the eleventh century states that 'in recent years, San-fo-ch'i [the Malay kingdom of Malayu, whose capital was then at Jambi] has established monopoly in sandalwood' (Wolters, 'Jottings': 59), and until the sixteenth century sandalwood was one of Sulawesi's important export commodities. Monopolies for this and other products, enforced either by Malayu or earlier by Srivijaya, Malayu's predecessor as the leading Sumatran power, may thus have been the reason why South Sulawesi navigators did not sail to the western part of the archipelago.

The great extent of the Sumatran kingdoms' sphere of influence in the archipelago has recently been emphasized by the discovery near Manila of a copper plate bearing an inscription in what appears to be old Malay, dated at AD 922 (Postma, 'Laguna Copperplate'). This was precisely the time of the Srivijayan hegemony whose reach during the tenth century can be imagined from the words of the Arab writer Mas'udi who said that it took a fast sailing boat two years to visit all the dependent islands.

Finds of Buddhist images at several points on the Sulawesi coast, and place-names like 'Waniaga', point to the possibility of very early visits from Sumatran Buddhists, connected by commercial, religious and diplomatic links with Tamils from south-east India and Sri Lanka. In view of the presence on the island of mineral products such as gold, iron and copper, and natural products such as sandalwood, tortoiseshell and resins, which were much sought after in foreign countries, visits from such traders would have not been out of the ordinary since they were also dealing within the archipelago and with China, India and the lands to the west of the Indian Ocean. Other indications of possible contacts with Sumatran Buddhism are offered by certain aspects of the pre-Islamic Bugis priests, the *bissu*. Although their lifestyle is far from monastic, a common interpretation of their name derives it from the Sanskrit word *bhiksu*, a term for Buddhist monks (Gonda, *Sanscrit in Indonesia*: 158). A few clues might even point to some influence from Tantrism, which we know was practised in ancient Sumatra and Java. For example, Tibetan Tantrism also knows the technique of producing a continuous high and sharp noise to facilitate the trance state by rubbing a finger round the edge of a ceramic bowl called in Bugis *gamaru*, from Sanskrit *damaru*. It is also interesting to note that the *La Galigo* texts mention high-ranking *bissu* bearing the title of *dapunta*, a title also bestowed on Javanese and Sumatran Buddhist religious dignitaries. It appears among other instances in the famous Srivijayan inscription of Kedukan Bukit in Palembang, which Professor Sarkar argues in an article on the origins of the Sailendra dynasty of Srivijaya has not a political or military but a religious signification (Sarkar, 'Sailendra Dynasty': 333–4). Sarkar takes the view that this strongly Buddhist dynasty, of which a branch established in central Java built the Borobudur, came from Srivijayapuri in the Andhra region of southeast India between AD 300 and 392. According to him, it was they who diffused specimens of the Amaravati school of art, to which the Buddha image found in Mandar has been related, and the Pallava type of script, which was used on the sacrificial columns of the fourth century found in east Borneo and to which the Batak, Old Malay and Bugis scripts are probably ultimately related. Although Sarkar's hypothesis is dismissed by many specialists in Insulindian history, the frequent references in *La Galigo* texts to 'Kelling' visitors, a name often associated with Jawa or Sunra, invites further consideration. 'Kling' in Malay does not simply denote people from Kaling but is generally used of Tamils from the Coromandel coast, and often also refers to traders from any part of India. This does not necessarily mean that many Kling traders visited Sulawesi at this time, though this is not impossible: the *La Galigo* texts speak of an island in the Moluccas called 'Kelling' which suggests the presence there of a Tamil settlement. Many wares brought to Sulawesi by 'Marangkabo' traders were also labelled 'Kelling': *patola* cloth, for example, also certain kinds of vessels (*balubu kelling*) and of steel (*bessi kelling*). The Tamils had a long-standing relationship with the Sumatran maritime kingdoms, and their Chola kings had especially close links, sometimes of friendship, sometimes of rivalry, with Srivijaya. As already noted, the Buddhist bronze statuettes found in Mandar and Bantaéng show striking affinities with those of Sri Lanka and southeastern India. Another indication of this link is perhaps to be seen in the ubiquitous presence in South Sulawesi of the palmyra (Malay *lontar*) palm tree (*Borassus flabelliformis*), called in Makassar *tala'*, in Bugis *ta'*, from the Sanskrit for 'palm tree' in general, *tala*. One of its major areas of exploitation, and its possible place of origin, is the Tamil regions of south-east India and north-west Sri Lanka, and it is said to have been brought by Tamil navigators to all important trading centres in Burma, Indochina and Insulindia to provide them with ready supplies of sugar for their journeys (Lubeigt, 'Palmier à sucre'); the leaves also provided material for writing on,

The *La Galigo* texts usually give the name of 'Marangkabo' (Minangkabau) to the Sumatran merchants trading with Sulawesi. Near Ussu', formerly the main outlet for Luwu' iron, there is a hill, said to have been an island in early times, which is also called Marangkabo, possibly echoing the existence of an ancient trading settlement. Another 'Marangkabo' island is visited by Sawérigading in his journeying to the Moluccas, and as late as the eighteenth century there was mention of a 'Namincabow' island near Buru. This identification of Minangkabau with sea traders coming to Sulawesi sounds a little strange, since this west Sumatran highland people, many of whom today migrate overseas and seek their living as traders, are, however, not mentioned anywhere else as a seafaring people. My hypothesis is that this name in fact refers to traders from the kingdom of Malayu, which around 1082 had taken over Srivijaya's leading position and at least part of its commercial role too (Wolters, *Early Indonesian Commerce*: 45, 90–3). While Malayu's main outlet was to the east coast of Sumatra, its power extended upriver to the west as far as the highlands of west Sumatra, where in the fourteenth century King Adityawarman established a capital city (Wolters, *Early Indonesian Commerce*: 58, 64). Before that time, the name Marangkabo/Minangkabau may have been applied not only to the highlanders but to the whole people of the kingdom of Malayu.

Many of the *La Galigo* protagonists belonging to kingdoms presumably located on the southern or western coasts of South Sulawesi and labelled 'to-Mangkasa' (Makassar) are simultaneously called 'to-Jawa' and sometimes also 'to-Sunra'; and indeed, several Javanese place-names, such as

Garassi' (=Gresik), Tuban, Jipang, Sorébaya (=Surabaya) are to be found on the south and south-western Makassar coasts between Ujung Pandang and Bantaéng. The *La Galigo* texts also label as 'Javanese' the Wolio people of Buton, another important post on the route to eastern Indonesia. This may point to the settlement and subsequent mixing with local people of Sundanese and Javanese traders; but their numbers were probably very small, since very little Javanese can be detected in Makassar and Bugis culture and language. Another sure sign of foreign settlement is the name 'Waniaga' given to the inhabitants of the small Bira peninsula, separated by a strait from Selayar Island. This strait has been on the sailing route from Java to eastern Indonesia up to the present day, and both places have retained oral traditions telling of Javanese contacts and settlements in ancient times. *Vaniyaga* is an old Malay and Javanese term of Indian origin for 'traders' (Gonda, *Sanscrit in Indonesia*: 443). In the Srivijayan inscription of Telaga Batu, where different social categories are listed, the members of the trading community include *vaniyaga*, merchants or traders, and *puhavam*, shippers (Casparis, *Prasasti Indonesia*: 19); this latter word may be the origin of the Bugis term of address *puwang*, meaning 'master' or 'lord'.

Another people marked by connections with western Indonesia and the southern Philippines are the Bajo, usually referred to in the *La Galigo* texts as 'Bajo Séreng' ('Moluccan Bajo'), apparently pointing to a specific role they may have played in the maritime relations between the Moluccas and Sulawesi. The traditions of those Bajo people now living in the Gulf of Boné link their origin as a nomadic maritime people with the construction of the *Wélenréng*, Sawérigading's giant flagship. *Wélenréng* was originally the name of a giant tree growing near Ussu'; all birds of the world nested in its branches, and when it was felled all the birds' eggs were broken and the ancestors of the Bajo who were living nearby in Bukira were washed away by a flood of egg yolk. That is why, they say, from that time on they have kept wandering on the seas. This myth aimed, of course, to link the South Sulawesi Bajo to Luwu', the dominant regional power, as other stories of later origin link them to its successors, Goa and Boné; but their association with Sawérigading's ship may also have the purpose of stressing their role in the development of navigation in successive leading South Sulawesi kingdoms, as Reid has suggested for Makassar (Reid, 'Rise of Makassar': 128–9; Bulbeck, 'Historical Archaeology': 436). As for Bukira, the hill, said to have been an island, like Marangkabo, with which it is associated in local tradition, may formerly have been another trading settlement. As is well known, 'sea peoples' (Orang Laut) had special connections with the Malay kingdoms (Sopher, *Sea Nomads*: 151; Andaya, 'Aquatic Populations': 39–43), and their dispersal in the archipelago between the eighth and ninth centuries, including that of the Sama–Bajo groups (Pallesen, *Culture Contact*: 246–7, 261–6), far from being the result of mere nomadism, may have been linked with the maritime commercial activity of Srivijaya and Malayu.

The *La Galigo* texts offer only sketchy or fantastic ideas of the western seas; this clearly shows that at the time they were composed the Bugis had only indirect knowledge of these parts. In these texts the western seas are portrayed as an immense expanse of water where travellers are at risk from dangerous whirlpools and sea monsters. In the far west lay the island of the 'Pao Jengki' (the 'mango tree from Jengki'). The Bugis name 'Jengki', like the Javanese and Malay 'Janggi', corresponds to the Arabic 'Zanj', which points to the lands west of the Indian Ocean. This giant tree is said to be full of gigantic beings and to reach the sky; stones supposed to come from its giant fruit are still kept as betel boxes and prized as treasures by princely Bugis families. They are in fact shells from the Seychelles double coconut (*Lodoicea maldivica*), which grows only in the small island of Praslin and is thus indeed a product of Zanj. Beyond the Pao Jengki' island in the 'Country of the Darkness' ('Marapettang') is the island of the dead, 'Pamessareng' or 'Waliala', where the china wares and *patola* silks with which the noble dead had to be provided at their funerals were traded in the afterworld to buy a passage to the abode of eternal rest. Similar ideas about the dangers of the Southern Sea (the Indian Ocean), with its fatal whirlpools and the danger of drifting to the 'Country of Darkness', were still common among Western navigators of the sixteenth century.

4

Early Civilization

In the *La Galigo* texts, trade is not merely an economic activity; by procuring precious goods, it enables rituals to be conducted at the highest levels and thus enhances the status of the people allowed to perform them by virtue of their divine blood. Even so, although these texts contain more information about aspects of ritual than about everyday life and economic activity, thorough examination of them can nevertheless reveal more details about these more mundane areas. Objects named may not be described, yet it is possible to gain a good idea of them thanks to the conservatism of the Bugis nobility, who cling to the ancient models, especially in princely rituals.

La Galigo Culture

Material Culture

It is possible to form a picture of the clothes worn by the *La Galigo* heroes by looking at the very conservative bridal attire of the present-day high nobility, which purports to reproduce it. Both men and women wore an ample ankle-length skirt similar to the *awi'* worn today by the bridegroom, tied at the waist for the women with a metallic belt, for the men with a long, card-woven[1] belt (*tali bennang*) which was wound round

---

[1] Card-weaving is a band-weaving process, known from many parts of the ancient world, 'in which warps are threaded through holes punched in cards

several times and into which a kriss was stuck. The men went bare-breasted but wore shoulder-belts and armbands of cloth, as well as golden necklaces and bracelets; they also wore a headdress (*sigera'*) made from a long, narrow, intricately wound band. We cannot be sure whether the blouse (*waju*) worn by noble women was already the typical chasuble-like garment now better known by its Makassar name *baju bodo*; *baju* is admittedly a word of Persian origin, meaning sleeves, but it may have been in use even before islamization, for Persian traders were travelling to the East Indies and even to China as early as the eighth century. Besides their anklets, necklaces, armbands and bracelets, noble women also wore over the shoulder a scarf on to one corner of which decorative golden objects were sewn. They went bareheaded, but wore ornamental pins and combs in their hair.

As material for these garments the texts mention a great number of types of precious imported cloth, including *patola* (silk double ikats[2] from Gujarat), particularly of the *patola uleng* ('moon' patola) and *patimanangi* types, which, as in many other Indonesian cultures, held a prominent place in the rituals, as did other, unidentified, types of fabric.

Such was, of course, the apparel only of the nobility: the clothing of commoners and slaves was probably not much different from that of their proto-historic ancestors.

Both nobles and commoners lived in houses built on piles. The palaces (*langkana*) were of the same type as ordinary dwellings, but larger: they were at least twelve pillars in length and nine in width, as compared to the four by four pillars of the average house of today.[3] They were also better built, using

which are turned to create shed openings for the weft to pass through' (Maxwell, *Textiles*: 418).

[2] Double ikat is a 'resist dyeing process applied separately to both warp and weft threads' (Maxwell, *Textiles*: 416).

[3] Although the number of pillars has consistently been used by the Bugis to place houses in different categories, and for any particular house the space between pillars is constant lengthways as well as widthways, there are very large variations from one house to another, depending on the availability of appropriate timber as well, of course as on the wealth of the owner. A rough estimate might set the distance between pillars from 3 to 6 metres lengthways and from 2 to 4 metres widthways.

better materials, and more lavishly ornamented, displaying distinct insignia showing the rank of their inhabitants. This type of house is obviously different from the Toraja *tongkonan* with its saddle-shaped roof; it prefigures instead the old Bugis houses of which a few examples still survive and which, like the more modern versions, belong in Dumarçay's terminology to the 'Malay type', with a roof 'not constructed on beamwork but simply on the piles which go through the inside of the house to the roof' (Dumarçay, *House*: 27, 30). One may surmise that the style of the *La Galigo* house resulted from the influence of coastal Sumatra, either directly or via Borneo, where it is also found.

In the *La Galigo* texts these houses seem to have had no furniture except for some kind of wide, curtained divans (*lamming*), on which people of high rank could sit in the daytime, with the curtains open, and sleep at night, with the curtains closed. There may have been up to seven layers of curtains, made from colourful cloth, often brocaded, embroidered or decorated with appliqué motifs. Present-day nuptial seats at princely weddings purport to reproduce this model, although they are usually based on modern beds. A better representation is probably given by the modern reconstruction in the rebuilt Minangkabau palace of Pagarruyng (west Sumatra) of the *pelaminan* on which princesses of ancient times used to take their rest. In view of the striking similarities between such resting couches/nuptial seats in a great number of coastal Indonesian peoples, the very archetype of such *pelaminan/lamming* may well be of one and the same Sumatran origin. Other domestic implements of foreign origin in these houses include mirrors, jars, china plates and metallic vessels used for various purposes, not forgetting the cuspidors necessary for betel chewing.

Settlements were established on hilltops above either a river or an estuary with a landing-stage, where people took their daily baths and where women did the washing; consequently, nearly all journeys were made by boat. For short inland trips, however, high-ranking travellers were carried in palanquins, the women behind closed curtains. Horses were unknown; the buffalo was important, but not, apparently for either ploughing or transport but essentially as a sacrificial victim and a source of meat. Pigs are not mentioned; they may have been associated with people of lower rank, or hunted rather than raised domestically. The main protein-rich food eaten to accompany rice and other staples, such as sago and tubers, seems to have been fish. Palm beer (*tua'*) was usually drunk at meals, and at feasts there was occasionally drunkenness.

Entertainments

After feasts, the guests sang and danced, sometimes 'Moluccan dances'. There is, however, no mention of the public reading of manuscript works, so popular in noble circles on such occasions right up to the twentieth century. Writing was known, but seems to have been used only for the exchange of messages, never to record longer texts, whether for practical, literary or historiographical purposes. The main entertainment was cockfighting: near every palace under a tamarind tree stood a cockpit, roofed but with no walls, where the men

Plate 11   Bugis dance at a princely wedding in Sidénréng

watched and gambled on the sport; women looked on from the house. Another popular entertainment was *raga*, a game played by men in a circle with a plaited rattan ball which must neither fall to the ground nor be touched by hand; the winner was the man who could juggle with the ball longest and send it highest in the air.

Warfare

War was in many ways another kind of entertainment for men, as well as a test of masculinity. In assertion of their virility, noble men bore names such as La Patau' ('Instiller of Fear'), La Tenriwéwang, La Tenrigégo' ('Not Shaken'), La Tenritatta' ('Not Struck') or La Pammusureng ('War Prone'). Blowpipes with poisoned darts, spears, short swords and krisses were all used. The kriss was presumably introduced at a relatively late date from Sumatra; South Sulawesi krisses are more similar to the Malay than to the Javanese version of the weapon, except for the golden pommels on the more precious ones.

The reasons for war given in the *La Galigo* texts are, in accordance with the epic style, apparently trivial or grounded

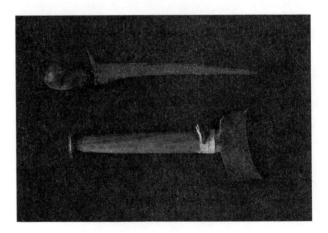

Plate 12 A Bugis heirloom kriss

in individual resentment towards an enemy, arising perhaps from the abduction of women, affronts received (particularly in the course of marriage negotiations), disputes over cock-fights, etc. Political concerns are never mentioned, although there are faint hints in personal names like La Ma'panyompa' ('The Submitter') or La Tenrisompa' ('The Never Submitted') of the submission of a vanquished lord to a more powerful noble, and the distribution among the three main South Sulawesi kingdoms of the various strategic points of the region implies political rivalry among them as well. The emphasis on naval battles, either between Bugis princes or against so-called 'pirates', highlights the importance of supremacy at sea in controlling trade. In the time of *La Galigo*, tribal wars with the aim of ritual headhunting (as perpetuated in the Toraja mountains until the early twentieth century) were no longer conducted, although enemies killed were still beheaded to ensure their 'definitive death' – perhaps as a protection against their ghosts.

In war there seems to have been more bravery than strategy: there were more frontal battles than ambushes. However, though single combat is sometimes mentioned, the princely war leader rarely participated personally in the actual fighting, usually sitting under his state umbrella on a point of vantage at the rear to observe the operations. Should he be encircled and his umbrella taken by the enemy, this would be disastrous for his realm; the last recourse against such a threat was retreat on to the ships which would be moored offshore.

La Galigo Society

The society depicted in the *La Galigo* texts is strongly hierarchical. The person of the Datu, the ruler, was the most precious in the kingdom: he guaranteed both natural and social order, and perpetuated the lineage of the gods on Earth. Should the Datu infringe the prohibitions instituted by the divine law (for instance by committing incest, or by spoiling cooked rice), disaster could overtake his realm. In fact, not only the Datu but the whole nobility participated to some extent in this sacred status, since they all claimed descent from the gods: all were said to possess 'white blood'. There were nevertheless several degrees of nobility, whose importance was stressed on important occasions such as marriage proposals, when individuals would list their genealogy from its divine beginnings. Noble women were never permitted to marry, or to have sexual relations with, a commoner, let alone a slave; this would have been sacrilege. The story of La Bulisa' in the *La Galigo* cycle tells of such a case in which the man incurred divine punishment, dying of a swollen belly.

In the ancient Bugis world, commoners with their red blood are seen as fundamentally different from the white-blooded nobility, with whom some of the divine essence has come down to Earth. Little is said in the texts about the common people; they are assumed to have descended from the servants of the divine dynastic founders who came with their masters from heaven or the abyss. However, from scattered popular traditions widely known around South Sulawesi, it seems that there was a myth accounting for their origin, of which only fragments are now available. In the beginning water covered the Earth; then a few pieces of land emerged, which were to become Mt Latimojong (west of Luwu'), Mt Bawakaraéng (north of Bantaéng), the hill of Tombolo' in Kajang and the hill of Gojéng in Sinjai. Man sprang up on top of these heights and then came downhill to people the plains. A more detailed myth may be found among those Makassar highlanders who adhere to the *patuntung* religious system (Rössler, 'Striving').

As for the origin of the slaves, no known myth is available. Batara Guru descended to Earth with Oro slaves, and Sawérigading took slaves on his ship as he journeyed. When danger threatened, a slave was offered in sacrifice: skinned, split in two, beheaded and thrown into the sea. Albinos, cripples, hunchbacks and dwarfs all became slaves.

La Galigo Religion

The Bissu *and their Ritual*

In a way, the *bissu* clergy of the *La Galigo* times were outside the social system: as priests, shamans and specialists in trance

Plate 13 Bissu *priests*

rituals they mediated between humankind and the world of the gods, and they had heavenly beings as mystic spouses. Portuguese sources tell us that, from the sixteenth century at least, they were – as they are today – for the most part transvestites and very often homosexuals. The *La Galigo* texts offer no clue as to whether this has always been the case. There is no way of telling from the names they bore whether they were by birth male or female; in a few cases, however, we do know of high-ranking ladies who became *bissu*, for example Sawérigading's twin sister, Wé Tenriabéng, and one of his daughters, Wé Tenridio.

Becoming *bissu* was often not a matter of free choice but the result of a call by a supernatural being, who became the mystic spouse of the new *bissu*. Even today male transvestite *bissu*, who can be considered both male and female, even when in ordinary life they have a male husband, have two supernatural spouses, one male and one female. The call is often marked by a psychosomatic phenomenon (sudden mutism, catalepsy) requiring a ritual cure (Hamonic, *Langage des dieux*: 174–5); it must be followed by a period of initiation with a *bissu* master concluded by consecration rites extensively described in some *La Galigo* texts, many of them still performed by present-day *bissu*.

Many rituals led by *bissu* are described in the *La Galigo* texts. Those surrounding childbirth and weddings receive the most extensive treatment; this is probably no accident, since it is precisely through marriage and childbearing that the 'white blood' received from the gods is kept pure, perpetuated and propagated on Earth. These are not just literary descriptions, therefore; right up to the present the Bugis nobility use them as a reference manual, setting the canon of ceremonies for the highest ranks. It seems reasonable to assume that they were composed for just that purpose, while other rituals, including those applicable to the common people, were for the most part left to be handed down by oral tradition. The *La Galigo* texts provide information on many religious practices, such as the gestures to accompany prayers or the details of sacrifices and offerings; but neither temples nor ritual grounds are ever mentioned, and there are no allusions to any material representation of either gods or ancestors.

Particularly striking is the paucity of information on funerals, which may be explained by the fact that the major heroes of the *La Galigo* cycle are immortal: those few protagonists who do die are the exceptions. There is a description of the afterworld where the souls of the departed have to remain in an outer area while back on Earth a long cycle of ceremonies and offerings is performed, sometimes including 'purification through fire'. As there seems to have been no primary cremation of corpses, this may refer to a superficial cremation of the bones after maceration, such as has been found in a number of excavated burials dated to between *c.*2000 and *c.*1000 BP (Bulbeck, 'Historical Archaeology': 446) and was practised up to the twentieth century by a number of Bornean peoples such as the Ngaju and the Maanyan. The texts also allude to two kinds of burials, both named *gosali*, a Sanskrit word meaning originally 'cow-stall' and by derivation 'holy dwelling' (Gonda, *Sanscrit in Indonesia*: 548): these took the form of tombs surmounted by wooden posts which had to be ceremonially renewed at certain periods, and house burials in the former residence of the deceased person, where no one was allowed to live.

Theology and Cosmology

Nowhere in the *La Galigo* texts is an exposition of the ancient Bugis religious system to be found, but it is possible to make a reconstruction from a thorough analysis of these and a few later texts.

Above everything is an eternal spiritual entity referred to as Déwata Sisiné, 'the one God'. From this entity, after the seven levels of heaven (*Langi'*), Earth (*Tana*) and the seven layers of underworld (*Pérétiwi*) had been created, emanated a divine couple associated with the sun and moon; with them the stars were created. From their encounter on the occasion of an eclipse another couple of gods is born, into whom Déwata Sisiné blows its breath. The male of this pair, again a solar god, is called La Patigana, a name which, although the Bugis myth is far from Sivaism, is reminiscent of the Sanskrit Ganapati, 'Ruler of the Categories', a title borne in Hinduism by Siva's son. From the sexual intercourse of this couple eighteen (or, according to other texts, fourteen) gods are born, in nine (or seven) sets of twins. This generation of gods marry each other, though pairs of twins do not marry each other as this would be incestuous; non-twins are called 'cousins'.

It is this generation of gods who intervene in the *La Galigo* texts: among them, six couples are particularly distinguished as the ancestors of the various dynasties in Luwu', Cina, Tompo'tikka, Wadeng, Senrijawa, Wéwang Nriwu', Gima and Jawa. Three of them belong to the underworld, seen as an abyss beneath the sea; of these the major god is entitled Guru ri Selle' ('Master of the Straits'). Three other couples of gods belong to heaven; the major pair, who also rule over the whole pantheon, are Datu Patoto' ('the Prince Who Allocates Destinies') and his spouse Datu Palingé ('the Begetting Princess'). Their abode is called Senrijawa or Boting Langi' ('the Highest of Heavens').

Each of these pairs of gods begot nine children, and these in turn begot further children and grandchildren, only some of whom are named in the available texts. Of Datu Patoto's nine children, seven rule the seven levels of heaven, each with specific tasks. These include, for the god ruling over the first level, opening the day, closing the night, making the rain pour, producing thunder, banging thunderbolts together and lighting lightnings ('gods' fire'); for the goddess ruling over the second level, making iron and gold grow in the mountains; for the god of the third level, ruling on war and cockfighting; and for that of the fifth, putting the constellations in order. The remaining two couples were sent down to Earth: the eldest son, Batara Guru, to put the Middle World (which includes the world in which humans live) in order and rule over Luwu'; the youngest to rule over the Navel of the Earth, located far away beyond the western seas. Of Guru ri Selle's children, seven rule over the seven layers of the underworld, again each with a different task, such as bringing man's offerings down to the gods of the abyss, producing storms and drowning the ships of impious people. The eldest child, a girl called Wé Nyili' Timo' ('Eastern Wink') is sent up to marry Batara Guru; the second eldest, La Punna Liung, who has the appearance of a monstrous sea crocodile, acts as a messenger between the abyss and the surface of the Earth.

No text has yet been discovered which accounts for the creation of the intermediate world. At the beginning of the *La Galigo* cycle, the intervention of the gods is required only to impose order on this world and people it, which is achieved by the descent of Batara Guru, the eldest son of Datu Patoto', to marry Wé Nyili' Timo' from the underworld and establish the first human dynasty in Luwu'. This couple constitute the archetypes of the *to-manurung* and *to-tompo'*, the beings of divine origin who are said to have respectively descended from heaven or arisen from the underworld to be the founding rulers not only of the kingdoms mentioned in the *La Galigo* texts but also of later historical kingdoms and seignories. Here again the *La Galigo* myth is used as a model with political and social significance, for it asserts the divine origin of the nobility, giving it the exclusive right to political power and fundamentally distinguishing it from the common people. This is why it has survived, notwithstanding the arrival of Islam, up to the twentieth century, and is still adhered to by a significant number of contemporary Bugis, not only among the nobility but also among traditionally minded commoners.

Other myths strong enough to survive islamization are those concerning Sawérigading, the Bugis culture hero, and Sangiang Serri, the rice deity.

Sawérigading, the Bugis Culture Hero

Batara Guru's grandson Sawérigading is not only the main hero of the *La Galigo* cycle; many Bugis, as well as those peoples who acknowledge former Luwu' suzerainty in central and south-east Sulawesi, consider him to be a charismatic historical figure; some, supported by certain oral, mostly

Plate 14 A kernel purported to be from the mythical pao jengki *mango tree*

esoteric traditions, even see him as a kind of prophet and messiah.

Sawérigading's mother Wé Opu Seng'eng had an 'adopted' sister called Wé Tenriabang, who had been carried in Wé Opu Seng'eng's mother's womb as a foetus and was later taken away to Cina in the heart of the Bugis country to marry its *to-manurung* ruler La Sattumpogi'. Each of the 'sisters' had promised the other that should one of them have a daughter and the other a son, they would marry the offspring to each other; Wé Opu Seng'eng gave birth to Sawérigading, and Wé Tenriabang to a girl, called Wé Cudai'.

Sawérigading is himself born as the twin brother of a girl called Wé Tenriabéng, who is brought up in a separate part of their parents' palace without his knowledge, for fear of a prophecy saying that should he meet his sister he will fall in love with her. Once grown to adulthood, he sails away on a journey to Taranati (Ternaté) to represent Luwu' at a gathering of princes held on the occasion of the ceremonial tattooing of Taranati's ruler. In fact, he has been sent away from Luwu' because his twin sister is to be ordained as a *bissu* in a public ceremony which he must not attend lest the prophecy be fulfilled. During his journey, however, he is told about his twin sister, and once back home he manages to see her through a hole in the loft of the palace: he falls in love with her and decides to marry her. No one can persuade him to give up this intention, even when he is told of the cataclysms which will surely result if he realizes his wish. Finally, Wé Tenriabéng tells Sawérigading of the existence in Cina of their cousin Wé Cudai': she is, says Wé Tenriabéng, her own exact likeness, and as proof she gives her twin brother one of her hairs, one of her bracelets and one of her rings so that he can verify her assertion. Should Wé Cudai's hair not be as long as her own, and should the bracelet and ring not fit her wrist and finger, she, Wé Tenriabéng, will accept marriage with her brother.

During the journey to find his cousin, Sawérigading meets several of Wé Cudai''s suitors at sea and defeats them. Arriving in Cina, he goes to the palace in the disguise of an Oro pedlar; having discreetly ascertained that Wé Cudai' really does resemble his sister, he asks for her hand in marriage. The match does not, however, proceed smoothly. The Cina rulers have accepted Sawérigading's proposal, but Wé Cudai' herself, having heard that her suitor is a savage Oro, refuses him and the bride price is returned. Sawérigading takes this as a *casus belli* and conquers Cina by force of arms. All sorts of incidents follow before Wé Cudai' eventually accepts Sawérigading as her husband and a son is born to them, named La Galigo.

Many episodes then occur in which Sawérigading, while remaining the most honoured figure, stays in the background. He re-emerges as the major protagonist at the end of the cycle, after La Galigo's son has been installed as the new ruler of Luwu'. On this occasion all the main figures of the cycle convene in Luwu' – including Sawérigading, despite his vow never to set foot there again. Setting sail after the feast to return to Cina with Wé Cudai', his ship is engulfed by the sea near Ussu'; but, far from being drowned, the couple become the new rulers of the underworld, while Sawérigading's twin sister Wé Tenriabéng and her heavenly spouse become the new rulers of heaven. They beget more children, Sawérigading a daughter, Wé Tenriabéng a son, who are married and themselves produce a child for whom a great feast is given in Luwu', again in the presence of all the main participants in the cycle. On this occasion the gods inform them that they are all to leave this world for either heaven or the underworld. Only the new ruling couple of Luwu' and their offspring will remain; and the rainbow will no longer permit passage between the divine and human worlds.

In addition to what is told of him in the *La Galigo* texts, there are many oral traditions concerning Sawérigading. Local folklore attributes to him features of the natural landscape: for example, hills are considered to be his upturned ship, springs to have sprung where his stick has stabbed. This occurs not only in the Bugis country but also in places which seem to have been under Bugis or Luwu' influence in ancient times: around Palu and Poso, in Gorontalo, in the eastern peninsula and Banggai, and in Buton, but not in the Makassar country, with the exception of Ara, Bira and Selayar (Zainal Abidin Farid, 'La Galigo'; Mattulada et al., *Sawérigading*). More or less esoteric traditions also make Sawérigading a mystic figure, said to have been in quest of eternal youth or to have tried to see God (Déwata Sisiné) face to face and to have been punished for the attempt. Messianic ideas are centred on him: unlike the sun, he was engulfed in the east, so he will rise again in the west, and when his coming is near the great tree Wélenréng will grow again. Some people say it has already begun growing and bears several leaves.

Sangiang Serri, the Multiform Rice Goddess

Sangiang Serri is the name given to the rice deity, who is thought of as a young and beautiful woman. There are several traditions concerning her which at first sight may seem contradictory. The best-known of them is the *La Galigo* story about Batara Guru's descent to Earth. His first child is a girl named Wé Oddang Riwu', who dies shortly after her birth and is buried; this is the first death on Earth. A few days later, when Batara Guru visits his daughter's tomb, he discovers that it has been overgrown by strange kinds of grass: these are in fact different kinds of rice. He is later told by Datu Patoto' that his child has been given to humankind, in the form of Sangiang Serri, for its subsistence; he himself does not have to eat the new crop and can content himself with sago, millet and Job's tears. Much later, on his visit to the afterworld, Sawérigading sees Sangiang Serri's house there and is told by his guide that while her body (rice) has remained on Earth, her soul (*banappati*) reigns here on over those children who have died in their infancy.

Another story, unpublished until now, takes place in heaven before the gods have taken the decision to people the Middle World. Datu Patoto' and Datu Palingé have a daughter called Wé Oddang Riwu' whose shining beauty drives all the male inhabitants of heaven wild, including her own brothers. A first attempt to send her down to the Middle World has to be given up because all heavenly beings want to follow her there, which would leave heaven empty. Datu Patoto' therefore decides to transform her body into something which everybody will be free to love: rice. Until then, the heavenly beings have eaten only sago. Wé Oddang Riwu's body is then finely chopped and put into a jar; after seventy days and seventy nights the jar is opened to reveal a rice stalk which is then solemnly taken from heaven to be planted at the Navel of the Earth. Not only has her body turned into rice; the golden sheaths of her fingernails have become the flying fish, her long, plaited hair has become the coconut tree, 'whose fruit is good to eat and whose beer is good to drink', and pieces of her clothes have become millet, Job's tears and all sorts of vegetables. Meanwhile, various members of her entourage have become the pests that attack rice, as well as rice's champion, the 'three-coloured cat', which protects it from rats. Her numerous cousins of lower rank have become devastating downpours, and her seven cousins of equal rank have become the seven constellations which bring forth good rains. At a great feast in heaven where the gods taste the unequalled food for the first time, Datu Patoto' announces that he will populate Earth so that there will be worldly beings to enjoy rice. But should humankind neglect the proper rites, fail to follow the constellations and not honour the gods, then rice will not bear fruit (Pelras, 'Mitos').

A third esoteric story which takes place still earlier in the mythic past tells that when Datu Patoto' and his brothers and sisters were born from the Sun – Moon divine couple they had a younger brother without bones who was called 'the one like rice porridge' and also 'heavenly rice'. He was later to become the ancestor of the *to-manurung* (Hamonic, 'Cosmogonies'; Pelras, 'Panthéon': 66).

These three versions of the rice story seem in fact to belong to one and the same system, as can be seen from the formulas recited during agricultural rituals, in which rice is called by different personal names corresponding to those given in the three stories. In systematic terms, there are several levels of reality for rice: first, the idea of rice in heaven; second, the prototype of rice planted at the Navel of the Earth, not a great distance from the country of the dead; and third, real rice, which descends from Batara Guru's daughter.

The Various Components of Early Bugis Religion

The basic, pre-Islamic religious system of the Bugis was essentially autochthonous, even if it is possible to detect in it ideas

Plate 15   A sanro *or popular practitioner*

which can also be found in the Indian – Hindu as well as Buddhist – world. The idea of heaven being related to the mountains and the underworld to the sea, and the myth of cultivated plants being born from the body of a sacrificed virgin, are found throughout the Austronesian world, including regions which had no contact with India; any similarity is therefore probably attributable to a common human heritage. However, other close similarities with the rice myths and rituals of mainland south-east Asian and western Insulindian peoples, who were formerly under Indic influences, such as the name Sri given to the rice goddess, suggest the diffusion at some period in the past of a whole integrated body of beliefs and rites. This may have accompanied the diffusion of certain cultivation techniques, such as ploughing, since the plough has a name of Indian origin throughout this area. Indian influence may also have been at work in the development of ideas about the gods as the masters of astronomical and climatic phenomena, as well as about the existence of three superposed worlds:

heaven with its seven levels, the underworld with its seven layers, and this world in between. A faint syncretism may also have been responsible for the few traces of borrowed terms and names pointing to both Buddhist and Sivaite influence, presumably due to indirect contacts mainly with Sumatra but perhaps also Java.

As Hamonic has shown (*Langage des dieux*), the *bissu* clergy itself seems to incorporate three series of elements, of which only one is purely Austronesian. Worship of the sun and moon, and a particular stress on sacred trees, seem to be linked to that primordial layer, as does their role as officiants of rituals directed towards the worlds of Above and Beneath, as organizers of the life-cycle ceremonies, as presenters of offerings to local spirits and noble ancestors, and as keepers of the regalia. In these activities, they do not differ much from the *sanro*, the ordinary officiants for the commoners. The second series of elements includes the sexual ambivalence of the *bissu*, a common trait in intermediaries with the spirit realm all over the Austronesian world – in Polynesia, among the Taiwan aborigines, in Borneo and formerly also in Java and Bali – but also shared by Siberian and Amerindian shamans and thus not purely Austronesian. Shamanistic elements, too, are in these regions characterized by similar forms of trance, possession and voyage to the other, spiritual world. A third series of elements, particularly related to their role as priests to the ruling elite, links the *bissu* to the Indian world, and seems to represent the main legacy of the *La Galigo* period, characterized by the assertion of a relation between a new ruling class and a pantheon of individualized gods.

5

The Rise of the Kingdoms

Myth and History in the Origins of Dynasties

Were the founders of the older Bugis dynasties mentioned in the *La Galigo* texts of foreign, more specifically Indian, origin? Such suggestions were made by some Dutch scholars before the Second World War, when there was a tendency to play down the possibility of autochthonous states emerging in the absence of any Indian influence. We now know, however, that such developments did indeed occur in south-east Asia before the very beginnings of indianization. Had the founders of those dynasties in Sulawesi been Indian or strongly indianized princes, the Indic elements in local cultures would have been much more conspicuous. It seems, on the contrary, that the sparse traces of Hindu and Buddhist elements in South Sulawesi cultures, and the noticeable number of words and personal names of Sanskrit origin – as well as their writing system, which all specialists consider as ultimately of Indian origin – may be accounted for by the existence of early regular trading connections with the western part of the archipelago.

The development of inter-insular trade and its growing integration with international trade was probably one of the major factors in the economic progress of certain prominent South Sulawesi communities, which thus became the main principalities of the *La Galigo* texts. This hypothesis raises several questions. For example, why did this process take place at precisely this juncture, and not earlier, particularly if we accept that the very establishment of the proto-South

Sulawesi peoples was linked with commerce from the start? Further, why did prolonged contacts with traders or even settlers of Indian or indianized culture and Buddhist or Hindu religion not result in the emergence here, as in Sumatra, Java and Bali, of indianized states?

Answers to these questions can only be conjectural; but it seems clear that South Sulawesi societies, while taking advantage of these contacts, were already strong enough to resist assimilation. Useful comparisons can be made with the process of islamization centuries later, a process which took place a long time after the first contacts with Muslim traders and even then not without resistance.

If we accept that the portrayal of Bugis civilization at the early period referred to by the *La Galigo* texts has a basis in some reality, we have then to account for the tremendous cultural and social differences between this civilization and that of the early historical period. Although the *La Galigo* texts and the early historical accounts are quite different in

Plate 16   The Soppéng regalia

nature and style, they share the common myth according to which the descendants of the dynasties of divine origin all disappeared at the end of the first period, excepting only the last representatives of the Luwu', Wéwang Nriwu', Tompo'tikka and Cina dynasties. Both oral tradition and chronicles also insist that this disappearance was followed by serious disorders, to which the appearance of new dynasties put an end. Little more is said of that intermediate period.

The opening sections of Bugis chronicles are usually of a mythical rather than historical nature and often follow a similar pattern. They begin with a story about the appearance of the first rulers, sometimes preceded by an account of the opening up of the domain (*wanua*) by roaming pioneers; then comes a description of the circumstances and terms of the agreement reached between the new rulers and the earlier inhabitants of the *wanua*, represented by their commoner leaders (*matoa*), sometimes with details of how the new government is organized; then follows a list of the subsequent first rulers, usually with very few other details.

From his detailed examination of the opening sections of the chronicles of the four important Bugis kingdoms of Luwu', Pammana (formerly Cina), Soppéng and Sidénréng, Ian Caldwell ('Bugis Texts': 169) has clearly established that the historicity of the rulers before AD 1400 is much less certain than that of those who are recorded after 1400. He concludes that this date corresponds to the first development of writing in South Sulawesi. One can readily agree with this if it is taken to mean not the first *introduction* of writing, which may be of much greater antiquity in South Sulawesi as a means of exchanging messages on perishable materials, but the first development of its generalized use as a means of recording events, genealogies, agreements or treaties in the form of documents that were then carefully preserved. However, I do not agree with his attribution of the terseness of these sources to a genealogical amnesia common, he says, to certain Indonesian societies. As experience with contemporary Bugis shows, they can remember long and complex genealogies even with a bilateral kinship system where one has to take into account every branching in every generation. Nor is the fact that dead rulers were to be named not by their own names but by their 'death names' a problem, since it does not prevent their filiation being stated. If we recognize that the *La Galigo* cycle, with its thousands of verses, existed first in oral form; if we consider its complex interlocking genealogies, involving hundreds of individuals and extending, when two generations of gods are included, over seven generations of protagonists; and if we further consider the capacity for memory still displayed by storytellers who memorize scores of narratives and recount them the whole night long; we should not find it unthinkable that fifteenth-century writers were able to record local genealogies and to recall historical events of one or two centuries earlier.

Nevertheless, the fact is that detailed records dating from before the fourteenth century are not available. This lack of information is unlikely to be accidental; indeed, bearing in mind the mainly mythical character of the opening parts of the chronicles, it probably has a particular meaning. Such a significant 'change of orientation', as noted by Macknight ('Emergence of Civilization': 6), and so many and such great differences can be perceived between the older state of civilization described in the *La Galigo* texts and that of the fifteenth century described in the chronicles, that we may suspect that fourteenth-century South Sulawesi was the site of major upheavals.

South Sulawesi on the Threshold of Historical Times

The images of South Sulawesi presented by the two series of texts contrast on many points. One area of major difference concerns the types of settlement described and the political map of South Sulawesi. In the *La Galigo* texts the population appears sparse: nearly all the settlements mentioned are established near the sea or on an estuary; a few others are on river banks, but all can be reached by seagoing boats. The hinterland appears almost devoid of inhabitants, except for the mountains in the north, where the Toraja live, and the southeastern peninsula, inhabited by the Mingkoka. Although all the settlements are dependent on one of the three major overlords (Wéwang Nriwu', Luwu' and Tompo'tikka), the latters' overlordship, presumably limited to control of the sea trade, does not seem very onerous and looks more like a hierarchical alliance. The fifteenth-century chronicles, by contrast, show a 'perceptible growth in the population away from the coast' (Macknight, 'Emergence of Civilization': 6); new settlements are being founded all over the peninsula, including far into the interior where no access can be gained by boat. Among the tales of origin of various Bugis domains are many of the migration of small groups of people looking for land and founding new settlements as they found convenient places. This trend has many implications, of which population increase is just one.

Physical Differences

One immediate implication of the proliferation of settlements in the hinterland is the occurrence of important physical changes in the natural landscape. We noted in chapter 4 the

Plate 17   A new settlers' hut in Luwu' tidal swamps

many details that lead to the conclusion that parts of the present lowlands were formerly under water, and it is precisely in these areas that at some time around the fourteenth century new settlements began to appear. This can be explained by a progressive drying up which has continued until the twentieth century.

Technical and Economic Differences

The second implication of increasing settlement concerns the intensive clearing of the hinterland's forest, another process which has continued up to the twentieth century – to such an extent, indeed, that the entire peninsula is now almost completely deforested. The consequences have included gullying of slopes and silting up of rivers and lakes. Place-names like Sumpang Ale' ('edge of the forest'), Ajang Ale', ('west of the forest') or Ongko ('princely parcel of forest') well away from any existing woodland bear witness to this vanished forest, which is still strongly present in the collective memory. Small, protected remnants are often considered as sacred places, the most famous of these in South Sulawesi being the sacred wood of Tombolo' in Tana Toa (Kajang). Forest also retains an important role in oral tales, where ancient Bugis settlements are often described as established in large clearings surrounded by wide tracts of virgin forest (Pelras, 'Mer et forêt').

This intensive clearing activity must have been accompanied by the expansion of iron working to produce the necessary tools: felling axes, wedges, crowbars and hoes. It may be no coincidence that one of the first historical rulers of Boné in the fifteenth century bore the title Panré Bessi, 'the smith'. There has been a long-standing tradition, too, of close ties between the Sidénréng rulers and the village of Massépé, which is still the main Bugis centre of iron working and where a sacred anvil is kept that is said to have descended from heaven together with Panré Baka, the first smith – according to another tradition, is said to have come from the land of the Toraja.

Another innovation that probably occurred around the same time is the introduction of horses: the *La Galigo* texts make no mention of this animal, while Portuguese sources of the

*Plate 18 A South Sulawesi pack-horse; these were probably
introduced around the fifteenth century*

sixteenth century refer to the 'many horses they use in the
mountains of the interior' (Sà, *Insulindia*, vol. 2: 348). They
must therefore have been introduced between the thirteenth and
sixteenth centuries. As horses are called *jarang* in Makassar and
anyarang in Bugis, a word obviously derived from the Javanese
jaran (as opposed to the Malay *kuda*), this seems to point,
unusually for South Sulawesi, to Javanese rather than Malay
influence, presumably from fourteenth-century Majapahit.

   The increase in population further implies a probable shift
from generalized slash-and-burn activity to wet rice cultivation and plough tillage. These innovations were clearly imported: the Bugis words for 'plough' (*rakkala*) and for
'ploughing' (*maréngala*) come from the word *langala* common
in south-east Asia among many indianized peoples in various
forms, for example Cam *langal*, Khmer *angal*, Malay *tengala*.
The plough itself is of a model called by Haudricourt the
'stock-handle plough' which is present in India and parts of

Plate 19   The Bugis plough

south-east Asia, while in other parts of the archipelago its place is taken by the Chinese model (Haudricourt and Delamarre, *Homme et charrue*: 259–65). Here again we find evidence of connections between South Sulawesi and areas of western south-east Asia other than Java. This is confirmed by the Bugis vocabulary to do with rice cultivation, where no trace of Javanese influence is discernible.

This is not to say that wet rice cultivation in some simpler form did not previously exist at all, but that the use of the plough, and perhaps the technique of bedding out seedlings previously sown in nurseries, became common at that time and that wet rice became the main crop in the newly opened lands, mainly in the basins of the Cénrana and Walennaé rivers, in the lake area and in the plains of Boné. Indeed, there must have been many transitional forms between the cultivation of rice on swiddens and classic wet agriculture. These methods can still be observed in some places in South Sulawesi, and the soil scientist Hisao Furukawa has described them very well (Furukawa, 'Rice Culture'). One such is the technique of tidal swamp fields still practised by new migrants in the lower Luwu' plain, by traditional inhabitants of the tidal swamps at the mouth of the Cénrana river and by Bugis settlers along the swampy coast of Jambi in Sumatra. Their fields are irrigated by river water which enters them at high tide, and are planted with appropriate varieties of 'floating' rice whose stalks grow fast enough to escape drowning in case of very high tides; harvesting is often done from canoes. Along the lower course of the Cénrana river, where the salt-tolerant *asé sawé* variety is cultivated, the people prepare the fields neither by ploughing nor by hoeing but by trampling the inundated fields with their own feet, a technique also used in Bantimurung near Makassar in small plots with very soft and deep mud. Another technique still used in the Luwu' plain further inland from the swampy coast, in the Toraja country and in some places in the Makassar country – and also known in Madagascar and Timor – is to use cattle to trample the ricefields. These techniques may have been the first used in the newly opened lands in areas formerly under water.

There is much evidence pointing to an association between the founders of historical Bugis domains, or their first rulers, and wet rice cultivation with plough tillage; among the regalia usually kept in many Bugis domains are ploughs said to have descended from heaven together with the first ruler. Moreover, every domain had its *arajang* ricefield, used for the yearly communal agricultural rites which included the first ceremonial ploughing, presided over by the ruler. The geomorphologist Yoshikazu Takaya has shown that in Bantimurung, where oral tradition explicitly attributes the introduction of wet rice cultivation to the first ruler, the ceremonial field originally consisted of a small parcel of land, surrounded by thick forest, which had been established on the lower part of a colluvial fan, beneath a spring. This location 'provides optimum conditions for wet rice growing, since the ground is saturated and it is only necessary to build bunds and clear the plot' (Takaya, 'Land Use'). This plot was presumably the first opened in that domain for wet rice agriculture. The varieties cultivated could be grown on both wet and dry land and were planted also on the upper part of the colluvial fan, where they merged with the upland rice which was grown under a slash- and-burn regime. Macknight has also noted in the chronicles the 'surprising number of indications of the importance of agriculture' at the early stages of development of the South Sulawesi states (Macknight, 'Emergence of Civilization').

Important changes in the economy are connected with the increased number of inland settlements. Previously, the majority of the Bugis population practised a subsistence economy in which rice was grown as just one, albeit the most important, of the staple foods, alongside sago, yams, taro, Job's tears and millet. An elite controlled the use of natural products from the forest, from mining and from the sea – products made precious by a demand from overseas which provided the elite with access to a number of luxury goods of foreign origin, such as Chinese ceramics, Indian silks, mirrors and perhaps damascened weapons. In early historical times, by contrast, although trade in natural products appears still to be very important, the control of agricultural products, especially rice, assumes a major role.

Socio-political Differences

The final implication of this spread of the population is political change. Alongside surviving older polities, such as Luwu', Cina (later renamed Pammana), Sidénréng, Soppéng and Lamuru, possibly governed by new or renewed noble dynasties, small autonomous domains (*wanua*) emerged from many of the new settlements which were created in the peninsula, placed under the authority either of 'elders' (*matoa*) or of noble rulers (*arung*); a number of these, such as Boné, Wajo' or Goa, unheard of in the *La Galigo* texts, were to become major kingdoms.

Other important kingdoms of the *La Galigo* cycle, notably Wéwang Nriwu' and Tompo'tikka, are completely absent from historical texts, and this has led some scholars to doubt that they ever existed. In my view that part of Tompo'tikka's zone of influence bordering the Gulf of Boné's eastern coast was taken over by Luwu', while Sulawesi's eastern coast and islands, including Tobungku and Banggai, fell into Ternaté's sphere of influence. On the western and south-western coasts of Sulawesi, three other polities seem to have played a significant role for a short period. Suppa', the only one cited in the *La Galigo* texts, perpetuated Wéwang Nriwu's control of the western access to the Saddang valley and to the Bugis central plains; Siang, near present-day Pangkajé'né, seems – if we are to give credence to local oral tradition – to have extended its sphere of influence, like *La Galigo*'s Pujananti/Sunra, both on the peninsula's south-western coast (later under Goa) and on the country yielding sandalwood around Palu in north-western Sulawesi; and Bantaéng may have had special connections with Java, as is suggested by its appearance in the *Nagarakertagama* and the location on that coast of place-names with a Javanese flavour (Reid, 'Rise of Makassar': 123).

Most of the newly founded small polities in the Bugis country, having been created in areas formerly claimed by Luwu', seem initially to have recognized the latter's suzerainty, while a few older domains such as Cina/Pammana or Soppéng may have played the role of intermediary powers. However, from their very foundation a dynamic seems to have been at work driving the stronger seignories to attempt to dominate the others, either through alliance or by conquest, thus creating round them a constellation of more or less loosely connected domains, embryos of the hierarchically confederated states of the future, which would soon be trying to free themselves from Luwu's suzerainty.

This, at least, is one possible reading of the available evidence. David Bulbeck, who does not take into account evidence provided by the many chronicles which exist for all the smaller polities, offers a different interpretation. He does not believe that Siang 'ever enjoyed a glorious period of suzerainty over the peninsula's west coast' (Bulbeck, 'Historical Archaeology': 125). He attributes the greatest antiquity to the dynasty of Soppéng, dating it to the late fourteenth century and asserting that it then ruled over Suppa' as well, and perhaps also that of Pammana. He also thinks that the local portrayal of Luwu' as the oldest Bugis kingdom is a legend, and would not date its rise to prominence to before the fifteenth century, although he acknowledges that in the early sixteenth century it 'could claim its vassals and dependencies over a vast area which included the Gulf of Boné from the Chenrana [Cénrana] northwards, the peninsula's southeast corner and south coast, and possibly Maros' (Bulbeck, 'Historical Archaeology': 473–85). His reasoning is of course commendably cautious, but the lack of conclusive proof of Luwu's antiquity is not proof against it. Local traditions and, admittedly, mythical texts such as *La Galigo* as well as the opening parts of many chronicles appear to have been of such importance to the people who produced them that there is a strong chance that they retain significant traces of the truth.

Other notable differences between *La Galigo* texts and early Bugis historical chronicles concern their depictions of social structures. *La Galigo* describes very clearcut, caste-like distinctions between the nobility, the commoners and the slaves; there is never any question of marriage across these class boundaries. Moreover, the power exercised by the ruler seems to be absolute: there is no mention of any kind of representative of the people, nor even of a constituted body of noble councillors or ministers, only of informal personal advisers. As for the commoners themselves, nowhere in these texts are they depicted as forming village communities with an organization of their own.

By contrast, striking socio-political innovations are to be found in the early historical texts, including a kind of contractual partnership between the rulers and the *pa'banua*, the 'people of the land', the ordinary members of the local community, and the presence everywhere of intermediate governing bodies. The opening section of most chronicles includes a passage in which a social pact is concluded between the ruler and the people, whose leaders declare in a formula mirrored in many texts: 'It is you that we take as our lord. Protect us from sparrows, that we be not plundered; bind [us like] rice sheaves that we be not empty; put your blanket on us that we be not cold; call us and we will come; lead us near and far. And should you hate our wives and children, we will hate them too.' This is followed by a statement about reciprocal rights and duties, in which the ruler is warned about the consequences of his possible misdeeds, be they actually witnessed or surmised from their consequences – plagues, bad harvest, natural disasters and so forth.

In this system the people's security and prosperity are still seen as issuing from the ruler, and this is still the case, as in the *La Galigo* texts, because of his or her divine origin. On the other hand, the ruler owes his or her power not only to that divine origin but also to the people, who take the responsibility of providing him or her with a house, specific sources of income and other goods. This is a contractual relationship and can be deemed void should either side fail to observe its obligations, and is thus very different from the situation described in the *La Galigo* cycle, where the ruler owes nothing to the people and the people owe everything to the ruler.

Religious Differences

Continuity is more apparent in the field of religious practice. The *bissu* remain as a permanent element in the pre-Islamic religion of the Bugis, although a significantly greater role now seems to be played by male transvestite *bissu* rather than female *bissu*. Those differences that are noticeable do not, by and large, concern the ritual, but one important innovation must be noted, namely cremation of the dead and ash burial in urns for important persons. This practice is frequently referred to in historical texts and is confirmed both by toponymy – *Patunuang* or 'place of cremation' is still a common place-name – and archaeology, which should soon provide reliable dating for this innovation. Cremation, however, was limited to the Bugis areas; both archaeological evidence and Portuguese reports show that the Makassar retained their practice of inhumation (Macknight, *Early History*: 38) or, like the Toraja up to the early twentieth century, disposal in caves.

The earliest rulers mentioned in the chronicles, however, are said to have been neither buried nor cremated but to have 'disappeared'. This is usually understood to signify a mythical return to heaven, but some informants say that it means that the corpses were leant against a tree until no flesh was left on the bones (Adriani and Kruyt, *Bare'e Toradja's*: 121). This suggests a system of exposure similar to that used by the Bali Aga of Trunyan in central Bali or to the practice of burial in hollowed trees formerly followed by some Bornean peoples as well as by the Toraja for babies. There is also information about stillborn babies or dead infants being sunk in the sea or in rivers. The *bissu* allude to all four kinds of funerals by speaking of a return to the four elements: air, earth, fire and water.

There are recurrent allusions (e.g. Raffles, *History of Java*, 1817, appendix 5, 'Celebes': CLXLIV) up to the beginning of the nineteenth century of the custom described in the *La Galigo* texts of eating an enemy's liver and heart in a raw preparation called *lawa'* (cf. the Balinese *lawar*). However, even the earliest historical texts present no traces of the bloody sacrifices depicted in many *La Galigo* episodes, such as the slaughter of slaves, or of the fights to the death between two groups of people, sometimes involving *bissu*, presumably representing the two parts of society.

The Possible Context for Change in South Sulawesi in the Fourteenth Century

All the evidence cited above supports the hypothesis that a multi-faceted upheaval occurred in Bugis society some time around the fourteenth century. But what actually happened? And what were the causes of change? At this stage, precise answers to these questions can only be speculative. My own intuition is that the changes we can assume to have taken place in the natural environment of South Sulawesi were crucial, in that places like Suppa' and Cina lost their strategic positions, and the expansion of agriculture they enabled had far-reaching social effects; but also that these factors were compounded by concomitant external developments. This very period witnessed significant upheavals elsewhere in the east, which were likely to have had consequences for the kingdoms of South Sulawesi, especially if, as I assume, their wealth was based mainly on overseas trade.

In Sumatra after the twelfth century the kingdom of Malayu/Jambi assumed Srivijaya's mantle as the major trading power of the archipelago. However, after succumbing to attack in 1275 by the Javanese of Singasari this and other Sumatran coastal kingdoms were considered by the successive

Javanese dynasties as belonging to their sphere of influence. In 1377, after the Jambi ruler had asked the Ming court to recognize his independence from Majapahit, the Javanese attacked the Chinese mission on its way to Sumatra and killed the envoys, presumably in order to prevent the revival of the Sumatran 'tributary trade' to China leading to the re-emergence of a rival Malay kingdom. Around 1395 Palembang was again attacked by the Javanese, and its ruler, forced to flee, founded the Malay kingdom of Malaka on the other side of the straits. This was a turning point in the history of the archipelago, for Malaka was to play a major role not only as a political and economic force but also, later, in the propagation of Islam, which it officially adopted around 1415 (Wolters, *Fall of Srivijaya*: 35–7).

Singasari rulers pursued an expansion of their influence in other areas too (Vlekke, *Nusantara*: 61), a policy continued after 1292 by the successor kingdom of Majapahit. Under King Hayam Wuruk (1328–89), it extended its direct rule over Sunda (West Java), Madura and Bali, and claimed overlordship over the Sumatran kingdom of Malayu and its vassals, Borneo's western, southern and eastern coasts, several islands in the south-east of the archipelago (Lombok, Sumbawa, Timor), other places in the Moluccas up to the western coast of New Guinea, and parts of Sulawesi (Vlekke, *Nusantara*: 70), including Luwu', Selayar, Buton and Banggai. Probably only a few of these claims reflected a real exercise of suzerainty, but they nevertheless bear witness to the existence of Javanese political interest in the 'outer islands' and their will to exert control over the region's trade.

To the north, China under the Mongol dynasty had asserted its authority over the 'southern barbarians' by attacking Campa in 1281, Pagan in 1287 and Java in 1292; but Chinese authority declined after 1323 as the country slid into a period of internal faction-fighting, natural disasters, economic troubles and peasant revolts. After the overthrow of the Mongols in 1368 the first Ming emperor prohibited his subjects to trade overseas and restored the system whereby the only permitted commerce with the outside world was that performed through official contacts with the envoys of 'tributary' states. Some illegal private trade nevertheless went on through a few

Chinese colonies in the southern seas, for instance Palembang; but Chinese trade with the Moluccas through the Sulu and Celebes sea was completely halted between 1368 and 1400. The clove trade was diverted south to the Java route, a development attributed both to the growing influence of Majapahit and to political disturbance in the Sulu – Borneo area. Whatever its causes, the hiatus in trade with China in the archipelago after about 1325, especially in the Sulu sea and the Moluccas, must have had an impact on the prosperity of a region such as South Sulawesi for which trade was vital.

An Attempt at Interpretation

If, as assumed in previous chapters, Sulawesi's main trade links had been with Sumatra and the Moluccas, the series of events which occurred there between the last quarter of the thirteenth century and the end of the fourteenth would have had significant consequences for its economic situation. From the eleventh to the thirteenth century trade in local mineral and vegetable products had brought increasing prosperity to South Sulawesi. Goods also arrived from India and China, probably via Srivijaya in the first instance and later via Malayu and transshipment harbours in the southern Philippines. Malayu continued to trade with eastern Indonesia in the fourteenth century: its first tribute to the Ming emperor in 1377 as a state independent of Srivijaya included cloves from the Moluccas, for which the most direct route from Sumatra was through the Selayar and Buton straits. It may be inferred from references in the *La Galigo* texts to 'Javanese pirates' and to naval battles that the Javanese tried to intercept this trade, which would not be surprising considering the importance to Java of Sulawesi iron; however, we do not know whether Java ever launched military expeditions against territories formerly under the suzerainty of leading South Sulawesi kingdoms. There is a tradition in Buton about the coming of troops led by Hayam Wuruk's chief minister Gajah Mada, and even the existence of graves said to be those of Gajah Mada's warriors. One place called Mancapai' (Majapahit) has been found on the east coast of the Gulf of Boné, not far from Malili, and Javanese toponyms also exist near Bantaéng, which may have become a main port of call on the route to the Gulf of Boné as well as to Banggai island (also an iron producer, named in the *Nagarakertagama*) and to the Moluccas. But even if Java did exert some influence over part of South Sulawesi in general or Luwu' in particular, this cannot have been prolonged for there is little trace of it. The name of one Luwu' ruler, Dewaraja, displays a Sanskrit influence which may have come through Malay as easily as through Javanese.

Assuming that the kingdoms named in the *La Galigo* texts really existed in the thirteenth century, we can imagine how the economic pre-eminence of their rulers was shattered by these changes in the archipelago's balance of power. Difficulties in trade with the western parts of the archipelago are also likely to have caused some disruption for trading centres on South Sulawesi's western coast (Wéwang Nriwu's domain in the *La Galigo* texts), which relied on this trade for their very existence. An economic crisis, occurring after a long period of prosperity which had produced an increased population and a great demand, now unsatisfied, for foreign commodities, may have sparked off political and social turmoil. In the coastal areas, the concomitant changes in natural conditions, such as the silting up of waterways, estuaries and bays or the drying up of large tracts of land formerly under water, added to the difficulties of trade and consequently of the aristocratic trading class. In these circumstances people in search of new opportunities to make a living moved to the newly accessible fertile lands left behind by retreating water and established new settlements. The numerous migrations and opening up of new domains which took place in the fourteenth and fifteenth centuries created new economic, social and political conditions, and the tremendous shifts at work may have given to the more conservative sections of the population an impression of instability which the chronicles expressed in the formula 'people ate each other like fish'. This is generally understood to refer to the law of the jungle; but I would suggest that in fact it reflects a hierarchical ideology and the regret of the writer for a past state of society which rested solely on an accepted hierarchy founded on the divine origin of the nobility.

South Sulawesi's traditional economy had previously been based on the export of rare products, a trade easily controlled by a closed ruling class which occupied strategic points and had little need to mollify the common people, a small number of whom was sufficient to provide them with food, labour and enough warriors to maintain their independence. By the fifteenth century the economy had become largely agrarian: to exercise power now, the ruling class had to control increasingly large rice-producing domains and growing numbers of people. To do this it needed new intermediaries and new systems of relationship.

Trade nevertheless remained important for South Sulawesi, and must have undergone a marked recovery after Malaka assumed the Sumatran Malay trading heritage in the early fifteenth century. This revival would have boosted the prosperity of the ruling class, even though trade was no longer its sole source of wealth. The effects were probably more pronounced on the western coast, where the main points of settlement of the Malay traders were located. The growing importance of the west coast explains why first Soppéng and then Sidénréng, no longer having a waterway to the Gulf of Boné, tried to incorporate it into their spheres of influence. On the eastern coast (the domain of Tompo'tikka in the *La Galigo* texts) a shift of gravity can be discerned from the area around Lake Matano to Ternaté in the Moluccas. Ternaté, which was becoming increasingly involved with traders from eastern Java, still retained close links with 'Tobungku' and its sphere of influence included north-east, central eastern and southeast Sulawesi. In 1580 the Sultan of Ternaté, Babullah, and the ruler of Makassar, Karaéng Tunipalangga, arrived at a precise definition of these spheres: from this point on, Selayar would remain under Goa and Buton under Ternaté. By this treaty, the Moluccan kingdom, as it were, assumed the heritage of Tompo'tikka (Andaya, *Maluku*: 86–8, 136).

Contesting Luwu's Heritage

At the end of the fifteenth century Luwu' was still the dominant power in most of the Bugis country, including the banks of the

Great Lake, the basin of the Walennaé river, the eastern plains and the coast along the Gulf of Boné, the Bira peninsula, the island of Selayar and the bay of Bataéng. However, challenges to its hegemony were already beginning to take shape.

South Sulawesi's Political Situation at the End of the Fifteenth Century

In the early fifteenth century Luwu' had still been in command of the Cénrana river, via which fairly large craft could reach the Great Lake. At the mouth of the river, the settlement of Cénrana was a favourite residence of the Luwu' Datu, while upstream were a number of riverine polities. Luwu' was trying to assert its authority further west, on the old transpeninsular route linking the Cénrana river through the Great Lake to the Makassar strait at Suppa', in order to gain control of the western outlet for natural and mineral products from the Toraja mountains, now also the outlet for agricultural products from the Walennaé basin. But Sidénréng, on the western bank of the lake, which had earlier been a tributary seignory under Soppéng, had been growing in importance and seemed unwilling to accept Luwu's pretensions any longer. Together with Sawitto', Alitta, Suppa' and Bacukiki', all located on the western coast, and Rappang, which commanded the lower course of the Saddang, it had formed the loose confederation of 'the lands west of the lake' ('Aja'tappareng'), an alliance constantly reinforced through marriage between the ruling dynasties of the members.

Other Bugis seignories, too, were no longer entirely reliable in their subordination to Luwu'. Upstream from Cénrana, the small domain of Wajo' was already nurturing desires for autonomy and beginning to extend its own authority over surrounding settlements. Its lords had already taken the title Arung Matoa, meaning 'chief lord'. Around 1490, one of them had secured a treaty whereby Wajo' would henceforth be considered Luwu's 'child' and no longer its 'servant'; his successor continued Wajo's expansion. Around 1498 the Wajorese chose as their new Arung Matoa Puang ri Ma'galatung, who was to become one of the most respected Bugis rulers of all, and the one who succeeded in making Wajo' one of the major Bugis states.

Further south, Boné, under the long reign of King Kerrampélua' (*c*.1433–83) had been similarly busy, occupying the vital agricultural plains lying around its inner core and thus enhancing its economic potential, labour power and military power (Macknight, 'Emergence of Civilization'). An outer circle of small domains were then taken into vassalage. Thus it came to control a large part of the territory over which it was to rule two centuries later, roughly delimited by the Walennaé valley to the west, the Tangka' river to the south, the Gulf of Boné to the east and the Cénrana river to the north. This expansion took it into areas more directly under Luwu', a confrontation with which therefore loomed.

Of the Bugis seignories mentioned in the *La Galigo* texts, Pammana (formerly Cina), Lamuru, Témpé and Suppa' had by now become the vassals of stronger, sometimes newer, seignories. Soppéng, trapped between Sidénréng, Wajo', Boné and the mountains to the west and south, was at pains to escape Luwu's authority without falling prey to the ambitions of the new emergent forces, since its only outlets to the outer world for its agricultural products were via Suppa' to the north-west and Cénrana to the north-east.

Luwu's Decadence

The period between about 1500 and 1530 saw the end of Luwu's supremacy in South Sulawesi in years of unceasing turmoil. Luwu' was ruled at this time by its last great warrior king, Déwaraja (*c*.1505–30). When his predecessor had died, Wajo' had refused to participate in the mourning, instead attacking and forcing into submission Luwu' vassals on the banks of the Great Lake. This gave Wajo' control over an area of great strategic significance. In a meeting held in about 1508 between Puang ri Ma'galatung and Déwaraja, the latter conceded to Wajo' its suzerainty over its former small vassals 'along the river', bestowed on it the northern territory of Larompong, acknowledged it as 'younger brother' and, in return, asked Wajo's help in overcoming Sidénréng. Defeated by this coalition, Sidénréng had to accept its vassal status as a 'child' of Luwu' and give up to Wajo' domains to the north and north-east of the lake.

In the following year, 1509, Luwu' attacked Boné in a desperate attempt to hold in check this new major force emerging in South Sulawesi; but Boné's strength was by now too great to be quelled, and Luwu's army was routed. Déwaraja himself narrowly escaped capture and might have been killed had the king of Boné not forbidden his soldiers to touch the person of the enemy king. Luwu's sacred red umbrella, however, the very emblem of its paramount overlordship, was taken by the Boné ruler, who at the conclusion of the peace treaty retained it, thus symbolically marking the end of Luwu's supremacy over the other Bugis states.

Despite their loss of temporal power, right up to the twentieth century the Luwu' rulers were considered by other rulers to be the highest-ranking princes in South Sulawesi.

The Rise of Makassar

Equally important events had also been taking place at this time on the western and southern coasts of the peninsula. The main Makassar powers were probably still Siang on the western coast and Bantaéng (which may still have been nominally under Luwu' suzerainty) on the southern coast, but the small twin Makassar seignories of Goa and Tallo' were growing in importance.

According to a possibly apocryphal tradition later recorded in both their chronicles, Goa and Tallo' had originally been one and the same domain; then, at some time in the fifteenth century, King Tunatangka'lopi had divided his heritage between his two sons. The chronicles, which were composed much later, say that under King Daéng Matanré (1510–47) a treaty concluding a war between Goa and Tallo' stated that they would henceforth be united as twin kingdoms 'with two lords but one people': anyone who attempted to set one against the other would be punished by the gods. According to Bulbeck ('Historical Archaeology': 117), this event took place no earlier than 1535. The first Portuguese map of Sulawesi,

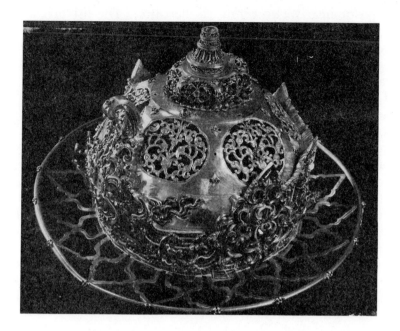

Plate 20   The crown of the king of Goa

drawn up in 1534, makes no mention of Goa and gives only the locations of 'Siom' (Siang), 'Tello' (Tallo') and 'Agaçim' (Garassi'). In his account written in 1544 Antonio de Paiva says that Goa, which he terms a 'great city' and which from then on appears on Portuguese maps, had previously been subject to 'one of Siang's vassals' but that at the time he was writing was no longer under such authority. This former vassal of Siang and suzerain of Goa may have been Tallo'. Goa also conquered Garassi', a trading harbour with possible Javanese connections at the mouth of the Jé'né'bérang river, controlling Goa's access to the sea, which became Goa's main trading outlet and the site of the palace of its rulers at Somba Opu.

Although the dynastic chronologies of Goa and Tallo' are fairly well established from the end of the fifteenth century, the exact sequence of events reported for each reign is still uncertain. It seems that King Daéng Matanré of Goa began the policy of expansion which the state was to pursue consistently for nearly two centuries thereafter. The list of Daéng Matanré's conquests includes Bajéng, Tallo's former ally and Bantaéng's vassal, and Gantarang, one of the best rice-growing areas east of Bantaéng. In making these acquisitions Goa was challenging the authority of Bantaéng in the southern tip of the peninsula, both over agricultural production and over the harbours used as trading posts for craft navigating from east Java to the eastern parts of the archipelago, as well as into the Gulf of Boné. It was also challenging the suzerainty of Luwu' over Bantaéng and threatening one of the latter's main strategic routes.

It seems that the later success of the twin states of Goa and Tallo', better known to foreigners as a single entity under the name Makassar, was founded on a wise division of tasks: the Tallo' rulers, who were usually chief ministers of Goa, oversaw the organization of trade and contacts with the outside world, while the Goa rulers ran the armed forces and led the land wars. This arrangement was soon to make Makassar one of the leading powers in South Sulawesi.

The death, probably in 1530, of the Luwu' ruler Rajadéwa had been followed by a dynastic dispute. Taking the side of an ousted pretender who had fled to Goa, Daéng Matanré sent Makassar forces to back up the king of Boné in a successful attack on Cénrana, which was at that time held by the other claimant to the throne of Luwu', Sanggaria. In about 1535 Sanggaria was finally overthrown and took refuge in Wajo'. Boné and Goa grasped this opportunity to strike a decisive blow at Luwu', which was then compelled to sign a treaty with Goa recognizing its defeat, and as a token of this to participate alongside Goa, Boné and Soppéng in an expedition against Wajo' as punishment for the latter's neutrality during the recent military operations. As a result of this campaign, Wajo' had to shift its allegiance from Luwu' to Goa, which thus gained a foothold in the Bugis heartland. Sanggaria was reinstated on his throne, but no longer had the power to restore Luwu's hegemony on the peninsula.

6

Contests of Powers and Faiths

The Immediately Pre-Islamic Bugis World

South Sulawesi's physical setting and coastline in the sixteenth century were not very different from their present form, except that the Saddang river still had its outlet into the

Plate 21 Témpé, at the outlet of the lake into the Cénrana river: an example of a riverine Bugis settlement

Makassar strait between Sawitto' and Suppa', while a single vast lake stretched between Sidénréng and Témpé, criss-crossed by scores of seagoing craft which linked it with the Gulf of Boné via the Cénrana river and the fortified settlement of Cénrana, now in the hands of the Boné kingdom (Wicki, *Documenta Indica*, II: 420–2). The country's economy now rested on a productive agrarian base; exports of a number of these products contributed to the prosperity of the newly developing kingdoms.

Commodities and Trade

The main product exported from the central plains of the Bugis as well as from the area around Makassar was rice. The reports of the first European visitors ceaselessly praise the land's fertility (Pelras, 'Témoignages étrangers': 156; Wicki, *Documenta Indica*, II: 428), and the Portuguese Pinto said that rice, which was exported from South Sulawesi as early as 1511, albeit in limited quantities, could provide all the needs of their Malakan fortress. In 1607 the Sultan of Johor, an enemy of the Portuguese, vainly tried to prevent these imports. Other agricultural products included coconuts, fruit such as mangoes and bananas, and vegetables. Domestic animals included buffaloes (sometimes in herds of fifty to sixty), pigs (of which great numbers were consumed in South Sulawesi), goats, chicken and ducks. Cows were still unknown but horses had become common, especially as beasts of burden. Game included deer, boar, partridges, pheasant, heron, wild duck and pigeon. Other natural products obtained by the Bugis from neighbouring places and then re-exported were sandal-wood from around Kaili and Palu and possibly also from Bima, sappanwood from Sumba, aguilawood, resins, mother-of-pearl and tortoiseshell (Pelras, 'Témoignages étrangers': 156–63).

According to Pinto, in 1544 six Portuguese Malakan *cruzados* (1,800 Portuguese *reis*) would buy three buffaloes or twenty pigs or thirty goats or 360 chickens or the equivalent of 2,400 litres of rice. Textiles, which were to make South Sulawesi famous in the nineteenth century, were in 1544 already sold at a price of about 200 *rials* for a large piece of white, probably cotton, cloth.[1] This information is interesting because it indicates that South Sulawesi had already entered an international monetary system based on the use of metallic (silver or brass) money, with the Portuguese *real* being used as one of the main standards. What system of exchange was used before this time, besides simple barter, is not quite clear. Gold coinage, which was in use in Java from the tenth century at least, does not seem to have been current here; nor were Chinese cash coins, which had been used for some time in Java and Bali, or the small tin ingots used as money in Malaya. Buffaloes may have been used as an abstract unit of value, as they sometimes still are in the Toraja country; and there may have been nonmetallic special-purpose currencies such as cloth, still used in Buton in the nineteenth century, and more probably cowrie shells, which have been used all around the Indian Ocean for centuries.

One apparently new commodity in the sixteenth century was slaves. These were prisoners of war, which could mean anyone taken in a conquered place, man, woman or child; the Portuguese accounts say that many of them were trained as galley slaves from childhood. A slave fetched 1,000 *rials*, a good bargain according to the Portuguese. The slave trade in South Sulawesi seems to have been largely prompted by out-side demand from the fifteenth century on, and it persisted for centuries. In 1680 the French ambassador in Siam bought a Toraja slave from a group brought there by Makassar traders, and shiploads of slaves were still arriving in Singapore on Bugis boats in the early 1820s. This commerce was conducted by a circumscribed group of people close to the high nobility and major war leaders; it seems to have taken place inde-pendently of the normal course of social life, which probably was little affected by it.

Another export commodity – the first, in fact, to attract the interest of the Portuguese – was gold. This came mainly from the Toraja mountains and from Luwu'; gold from North Sulawesi seems to have been under the control of Makassar

---

[1] The Portuguese currency unit *real* (pl. *reis*) has become in Malay the *rial* (pl. *rial*).

people, who brought it to Ternaté. In 1544 Antonio de Paiva had been much impressed in Suppa' by a procession of thirty noblewomen all wearing numerous gold bracelets (Jacobs, 'First Christianity': 285). De Paiva also speaks of the sacrifice of buffaloes whose horns had been gilded with gold leaf, a custom mentioned in the *La Galigo* texts. Other mineral exports included iron from Luwu' and Banggai, copper and lead, which may have existed in small quantities in the same sites as copper. More lead, indeed, could also have been imported from elsewhere, but it is not known from where: the only significant south-east Asian sources were Burma, Siam and Vietnam (Reid, *Age of Commerce*: 116).

Navigation, Boats and Warfare

Although the coastal peoples of South Sulawesi had already made considerable progress in nautical matters by the sixteenth century, at that time most of their exports still seem to have been carried on Malay and Javanese ships. Bugis and Makassar navigation was still not significant enough in the eyes of external observers to deserve more than cursory mention. However, what is important is that the South Sulawesi states now sent their trading boats not only, as before, to the eastern parts of the archipelago but also to the west, which seems to have been a new destination for them. As they were situated midway between Malaka and the Moluccas, with half their coastline facing west and the other half facing east, they were ideal intermediaries on this sea route. Bugis and Makassar rulers thus began progressively to develop their skills as ship owners and managers by entering into joint ventures with Malay traders. There were no roads worthy of the name; with the help of pack horses it was just possible to cross the mountains on a few paths, such as that from Makassar to Boné through the Camba pass and Lamuru, but most travel remained waterborne.

From the few jottings available in scattered sources, we can gather that the South Sulawesi peoples mention several types of craft, for which the Portuguese had four names (Couto, *Decadas*: 87). The term *pelang* describes a big decked canoe with

Plate 22 Indonesian ships and canoes of the early seventeenth century

double outriggers, constructed on a dugout base with supplementary side planking; these boats were still in use in the 1950s in Mandar and on the western Bugis coasts. *Lopi* is the general word for 'boat' in Bugis, but Couto uses it to designate small trading ships. It might correspond to the normal type of planked boat still in use on the Makassar coasts under the name of *biséang*, sometimes as freight craft but mainly for fishing. *Jojoga* obviously corresponds to the Makassar *joncongang* and Bugis *joncongeng*, a word that appears as early as the *La Galigo* texts and was still in use in the nineteenth century, at which time it referred to large trading ships, probably similar to the *lopi* but bigger. Finally, there were the *pangajavas*, probably the Bugis *pencaja'*, Makassar *pancaja'* and Malay *penjajap*; in the nineteenth century these were the light, long and narrow ships used by the Sulu and west Borneo pirates; their two masts were supplemented by twenty to thirty rowers. They recall Paiva's depiction of the Suppa' Datu''s war fleet of about twenty proas,[2] each with seventy to eighty rowers; this means that they must have been at least 25–30 metres long and that the total crew of the fleet numbered around 2,300. A similar picture emerges for the following century, when in 1640 the flagship of Sultan Malikussaid of Makassar was said to be 40 metres long and the second one 30 metres long, each with 200 rowers in three ranks; the other vessels were 26 metres long (Side', 'Expansion de Goa': 160).

Firearms came into common use about this time: muskets, culverins or cannons, of which the lighter ones were carried on board the warships. Many of these were made, of brass, in Brunei; and, of course, Portuguese artillery pieces were also much in demand. For protection, the coats of mail and breast armour made of metal plates that were still being worn in the nineteenth century may have come into use at this period. The new weapons did not, however, displace the traditional shields, krisses, blowpipes with poisoned darts and the short swords used to cut off the heads of dead enemies.

Other Aspects of Material Culture

Bugis life in the sixteenth century, as compared to the picture conveyed by the *La Galigo* texts, is characterized by a growing openness to outside influences, with imported goods no longer the exclusive preserve of the ruling class but reaching common people as well. The form and construction of housing remained essentially unaltered: the few western sketches we have from the first half of the seventeenth century show high and strong wooden houses raised on piles which accord as much with *La Galigo* as with nineteenth-century descriptions. Inside the richer houses, however, a few pieces of furniture of foreign type such as chairs and tables began to appear, and simple openings in the outer walls sometimes became real windows, with shutters. The Bugis names of these innovations

[2] *Proa* and *prau* are alternative forms of the term *prahu* (a type of boat) commonly used in writings in English about the Insulindian world.

*Plate 23   The old house at Karampuang (west Sinjai), representative
of the architecture of pre-Islamic times*

clearly indicate their Portuguese origin: for example, *kadéra*
(chair) from *cadeira*; *méjang* (table) from *mesa*; *jandéla* (win-
dow) from *janela*. New domestic implements included glasses
and Iberian-style jugs and trays. Some Portuguese games were
also adopted: dice, the card game *hombre* and marbles.

Consumption of food and stimulants was also affected by
innovations, mainly the introduction by the Portuguese and
Spaniards of a number of South American plants: sweet potato and tobacco are specifically mentioned in contemporary
sources, but many other items that were to become essential
elements of the Bugis diet probably also arrived at the same
time: manioc, maize and chillies, for example, though not yet
tomatoes. Another new arrival, now fortunately fallen into
disuse, was opium, which became an indispensable requisite
for warriors before battle, and to which a number of high-
ranking people became addicted.

Innovation could also be seen in clothing. Women were now
wearing baggy trousers or pants, and while slave women still

went bare-breasted, free married women wore short tunics with sleeves. Western visitors were amazed to see that in this still unislamized country men and women bathed together naked. Adult men are described at this period still wearing only loincloths, but this must have applied only to the common people. The more affluent were developing a taste for western shirts, hats, sometimes adorned with a plume, and jackets. Large sarongs, described as 'large sashes covering from the feet to the top of the head', were used by men and women sleeping together. In Bugis poetry, indeed, 'to sleep together in one sarong' is the wish of lovers. Men often had small ivory balls inserted in the penis around the base of the glans, a custom intended to increase women's pleasure during intercourse and attested to in ancient times all over south-east Asia, including Java and Bali.

A Century of Upheavals: From the First Western Visitors to Islamization

In 1511 the Portuguese conquered Malaka, bringing with them Western Christianity and a potential disruption of the smooth-running Insulindian trading networks. In 1611, after five years of the so-called 'Islamic wars' led by the Makassar kingdom, Boné became the last kingdom to adopt Islam as its state religion. These two milestones mark either end of the series of events in the sixteenth century which produced drastic changes in South Sulawesi.

The fall to the Portuguese of Malaka, heir to the Sumatran Malay maritime empires and one of the major ports of call on the trade routes between eastern Asia and the West, forcing the Malaka Sultan to withdraw to Johor, must have created a considerable stir in South Sulawesi. We know from the testimony of Tomé Pires that a few traders from 'the Macassar islands', including Bugis and Bajo, were at that time among the many peoples who came there to trade, albeit in small numbers (Pires, *Suma Oriental*: 326–7). Antonio de Paiva, too, tells us that Muslim Malay traders from Patani, Pahang and Ujung Tanah in the Malay peninsula and from Minangkabau in Sumatra had been established in Siang since about

1490 (Jacobs, 'First Christianity': 295). The South Sulawesi people were thus well informed of the political and religious developments taking place in the western parts of the archipelago, and they presumably soon gained some knowledge of the Portuguese – their customs, religion, attitudes, trade policy, political behaviour and military power.

We can deduce from various sources that, as a consequence of the fall of Malaka, maritime relations intensified between South Sulawesi and other trading states such as Acheh in Sumatra, Patani and Johor in the Malay peninsula, Banjarmasin in Borneo and Demak in Java – all centres of Islamic belief. Yet by the middle of the sixteenth century South Sulawesi remained one of the very few important places in the inter-insular native trading network where Islam had not yet taken hold. The anomaly must have been keenly felt, by local Muslim settlers as well as by the Muslim communities in the archipelago.

It took the Portuguese quite a while to become really interested in South Sulawesi. Their first maps ignored the island: in its place were a few small archipelagoes, including the 'Macaçares' in the south, the 'Celebes' in the north and a big empty space in between. Their main concern at this time was the attempt to secure a major role in the spice trade from the Moluccas, and this led them to focus on the route along the Javanese north coast and via the Lesser Sunda Islands. In 1533, however, it seems that the Portuguese in Ternaté heard from a captain of their own nationality who had by chance touched land there that much gold was to be found in the 'Macaçares', close to the 'Celebes'. The governor of the Moluccas then sent a reconnaissance expedition. From the maps made after that voyage, it seems that the expedition sailed from harbour to harbour along the northern peninsula and then along the whole of the western coast of Sulawesi, calling at Manado, Toli-Toli, Mamuju, Siang, Tallo' and Garassi' (Pelras, 'Premières données').

Aborted Christianization

In 1540 two noblemen from 'Macaçar' visiting Ternaté were baptized; the following year they came again, bringing with

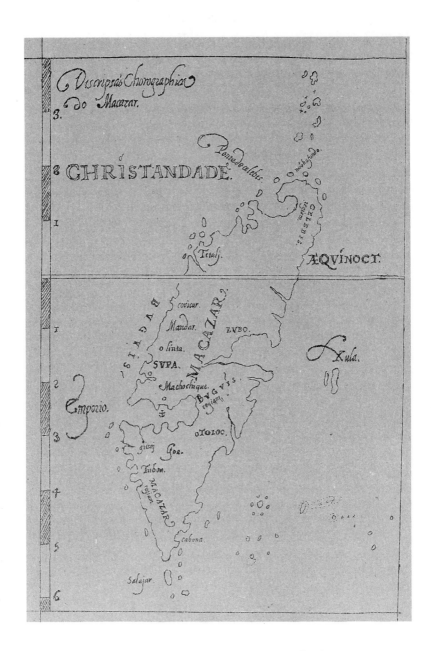

Plate 24 One of the first Portuguese maps of Sulawesi, c.1540

them gold, sandalwood and iron weapons as representatives of the island's most highly prized products. In 1542 the Portuguese trader Antonio de Paiva, perhaps prompted by this evidence of potential wealth, left Malaka for Sulawesi to trade for sandalwood in 'Durate', in north-west Sulawesi between Toli-Toli and Dampelas, where an eighteenth-century map still shows a 'Kingdom' of Toerate (de Lat and Keizer, *Atlas*). On his outward voyage he called at Siang; on his return trip he again stopped there, but this time was forced to stay by illness, and remained as a guest of the king for several months. In 1544 he travelled once more to trade in Suppa' and Siang (he could not get to 'Durate', which was in revolt against Siang), and after what seems to have been a passionate theological debate was asked to baptize both rulers. He brought back with him not only official gifts for the Portuguese Crown but also four young men who later went to Indian Goa to be educated at the Jesuit college and envoys from the two rulers to ask the Malaka governor to send them priests, and possibly also military support. The two kings had also taken the opportunity offered by their common baptism to conclude a military alliance, probably against the growing danger represented by Goa and Tallo'.

From Paiva's writings we learn that Siang had recently been at war with, and had defeated, rebel seignories and that it still held sway over the Mandar coast, the Gulf of Kaili and, further, the north-west coast of Sulawesi, then rich in sandalwood and gold. The ruler of Siang had long been on good terms with his counterpart in Suppa', himself a close relative of the ruler of Sidénréng and, in spite of his age (about seventy) still a great warrior. We owe these and other details to a letter written by Paiva to the bishop of Indian Goa to apologize for his uncommissioned initiative in baptizing the two rulers (Jacobs, 'First Christianity': 282–303). The news of these conversions prompted the illustrious Jesuit missionary Francis Xavier to travel to Malaka, from where he planned to go to Siang and Suppa'; however, the outbreak of war prevented him from carrying out this plan.

In response to requests from the South Sulawesi rulers, one of the Portuguese ships that visited the island in 1545 brought a priest, Father Vicente Viegas. During this expedition, which lasted a year and a half, further baptisms took place, including those of the rulers of Alitta and Bacukiki', allies of Suppa', and, if my reading is correct, of the Tallo' ruler, who presumably sought by this means to counter Siang's policy of friendship with the Portuguese. Admittedly this event is reported in neither the Tallo' nor the Goa chronicles, which were written after islamization; but one Bugis chronicle did record the fact that two young Goa princes were entrusted to the Portuguese for their education (Pelras, 'Dynamics of Islamization': 115). The prospects for the Portuguese looked very good – until the untimely elopement of a Portuguese officer with a daughter of the Suppa' ruler. The fleet had to weigh anchor hastily to avoid bloodshed and no Portuguese dared to return until 1559. Meanwhile the Bugis princess was legitimately married to the officer in Malaka; one of their children was Manuel Godinho de Eredia, the writer and geographer who was the first to mention the existence to the south of Timor of the land which would later be named Australia. The story of the 1545 expedition to Suppa' is also related in one of his writings (Eredia, 'Description of Malacca': 54–7).

One member of this expedition, Manuel Pinto, did not sail back with the other Portuguese. In a letter written to the bishop of Goa after his eventual return he tells of his experiences in South Sulawesi (Wicki, *Documenta Indica*, II: 422–3). After some time in Suppa' he spent eight months in Sidénréng, whose king, he said, also wanted to receive Portuguese priests. Pinto called the king 'emperor' and said that he ruled over 300,000 people: this figure might include the whole Aja'tappareng confederation, which then included Sidénréng, Suppa', Bacukiki', Alitta, Sawitto' and Rappang. In comparison, its population in 1827 was estimated at about 180,000 (Nahuijs, *Brieven*: 49) and in 1884 at about 236,000 (Staden ten Brink, *Zuid-Celebes*: 40).

From Sidénréng, Pinto went to Siang, whose population he estimated at about 40,000. He stayed here for a while, and probably also in Tallo'; both rulers expressed their desire for an alliance with the Portuguese, each probably as a weapon against the other. But Siang was now in decline, not only for political but also for physical reasons: in 1544 Paiva's ship had had to leave Siang to take shelter from the western winds in the Goa harbour, and Siang's river, nowadays a small stream, must already have been silting up, rendering it unfit as an anchorage and leading to the diversion of trade to better ports. On his return to Malaka, Pinto brought the news that the Bugis kings were at war with each other. This was probably the war being waged by Sidénréng, with the help of Goa, against Wajo'; in any event, it was this news that prevented Francis Xavier from making his planned voyage.

Pinto's return journey to Malaka took him first to Java, probably to Demak, then the leading north-east Javanese Muslim state. Here he was received by the Sultan, who told his visitor that he was contemplating a military expedition to islamize Makassar; however, he was prevented from carrying out this project by his untimely death the following year while engaged in a campaign against the Hindus of east Java.

The flirtation of some of the petty states of South Sulawesi with the Portuguese would inevitably have upset their Muslim trading partners, as well as the local Malay settlers whom the Portuguese described as fiercely hostile to these conversions – a hostility probably rooted as much in economic as in religious grounds. They had themselves been pressing the rulers to adopt Islam, but to no avail. The latters' reluctance may have been related to the egalitarian tendencies of these commoner Muslim traders, and to the Islamic stress on God's oneness and absolute transcendence which could threaten the power of the rulers, based as it was on the myth of the divine descent of the nobility. Conversely, information gleaned about Catholic teachings, perhaps in part through polemics put forward by the Muslims themselves, may have given the rulers the impression that Catholic Christianity was a more flexible faith and led them to the view that, if they were to adopt one or other of the world religions, Christianity would more probably permit them to retain their semi-divine status (Pelras, 'Dynamics of Islamization'). It is significant that the matters raised by the ruler of Siang before deciding to receive baptism included questions about the ascent to heaven of Christ the Son of God, which may have recalled that of Batara Guru, Datu Patoto''s son, at the end of the *La Galigo* cycle; about the cult of saints, who as intercessors may have been seen in a similar relationship with God as the *déwata*; and about St James, the patron saint of Iberian countries, whose protection may have been compared with that bestowed on the Bugis states by their founding *to-manurung*, and whose banner brandished in battle may have been equated with the sacred *arajang* banners. There may also have been an assumption that the Catholic priests, with their elaborate rituals, could fulfil more or less the same function for the rulers as the *bissu* had done. There must also, of course, have been political considerations. Competition was intense, not only among the South Sulawesi states themselves for political leadership and for the control of the important overseas trade, but also more widely, between two trading networks, one mainly Muslim and the other connected with Portuguese Malaka. The choice of one religion over another would necessarily have political and economic consequences.

Strangely enough, the Portuguese let their chance escape them. After the resumption of trade with Malaka in 1559, the South Sulawesi rulers several times repeated their request for priests, but few were available and the Portuguese did not consider Makassar a priority. Only in about 1584 were four Franciscan fathers sent there, and their stay was a short one; thereafter no further attempt was made to christianize Sulawesi, although from that time on many Portuguese settled in Makassar, where they numbered about 500 by the end of the century. It seems that the Franciscan mission discovered that the declared sympathy of the South Sulawesi rulers towards Christianity was based on serious misunderstandings about dogma, and that major compromises with native beliefs would have to be made if the faith were to be adopted there; moreover, no mass conversion of the people was possible without the acceptance and prior conversion of the rulers. The Franciscans were certainly not prepared simply to become substitutes for the *bissu*, for whom they were often taken in an error which certainly contributed greatly to their decision to leave.

Goa versus Boné

By the time the Portuguese resumed relations with South Sulawesi in 1559 the political situation had changed dramatically. After Daéng Matanré's death in 1547, Goa had conti-

Plate 25 Guruda-é, one of Boné's state banners

nued his policy of expansion. It had subdued Portugal's friends and Sidénréng's allies on the west coast – Siang, Suppa', Alitta, Sawitto' and Bacukiki' – and had probably also gained the submission of Siang's former vassals in Mandar and near the Gulf of Kaili. In the south and south-east Goa was advancing through Bulukumba, Héro, Bira and Selayar island, and northwards from Bira on to the south-west coast of the Gulf of Boné. Kajang, Bulo-Bulo and Lamatti, Luwu's former vassals on the right (south) bank of the Tangka' river, were conquered in their turn.

At the same time Boné, under King La Tenrirawé Bongkang-é (1535–84) had been pursuing its own advance southwards and had already reached the left (north) bank of the Tangka'. Here Goa and Boné came into direct contact, both striving to establish ascendancy over the whole peninsula. At stake in their dispute over the area was not only prestige but the all-important trade routes. Selayar was still an important stage on the route between the west of the archipelago and the Moluccas; Bira remained until the twentieth century a major point of embarkation for voyages to eastern Indonesia, and also commands the entrance into the Gulf of Boné; and off Lamatti and Bulo-Bulo lay the Nine Islands archipelago, a strategic point from which it is possible to intercept any fleet sailing into or out of the Gulf. War between the two kingdoms had become inevitable, and it broke out in 1562 after the king of Boné had incited the seignories of Tondong, Lamatti and Bulo-Bulo, Goa's recently acquired vassals, to form an alliance with him against their new suzerain.

Goa was aided in its struggle against Boné by Luwu', obviously eager to check its challenger in the Bugis lands, and also by Wajo' and Soppéng, which probably preferred a remote suzerain like Luwu' or Goa, which would leave them a larger measure of autonomy, over a nearby one like Boné, which would be likely to dominate them. In 1563 Goanese troops landed in Cénrana, then still under Luwu', and proceeded to attack Boné; but the king of Goa, Manrio Gau', was wounded and had to return home. Two years later he attacked again, but this time fell ill and once more had to be taken back to Goa, where he died. He was succeeded by his younger brother, who returned to the attack on Boné, this time through Soppéng; but after three weeks of campaigning the new ruler was killed on the battlefield and beheaded. Peace negotiations followed, and the two kingdoms agreed at the Treaty of Caleppa to recognize the Tangka' river as marking the limit between their respective spheres of influence. Boné was recognized as the suzerain power on all the lands east of the Walennaé and on Cénrana; and Boné and Goa citizens were afforded equal rights within each other's jurisdiction. The new Goa king chosen from among the late king's sons, Daéng Mamméta, had the support of Boné, where he had lived for several years.

The Emergence of a Makassar 'Empire'

Having succeeded in acquiring both vital agricultural land and strategic coastal points in South Sulawesi, Goa – now increasingly known to outsiders as Makassar – began from the mid-sixteenth century to develop its maritime activities. In this it had the strong support of the Malay community, which had moved there from Siang around 1550, and of the Portuguese community, which began to settle there after 1580. It also strengthened its links with various overseas kingdoms in the region, including Johor in Malaya, Banjarmasin in Borneo, Demak in Java, Timor and, especially, Ternaté in the Moluccas. In 1580 the Sultan of Ternaté, Babullah, the 'Lord of Seventy-Two Islands', whose influence extended over most of the Moluccas and the surrounding lands, concluded an agreement with Daéng Mamméta whereby Selayar was recognized as belonging to the sphere of Makassar and Buton to that of Ternaté.

This maritime policy was pursued alongside a continued drive for hegemony on South Sulawesi. Between 1570 and 1591 several campaigns were mounted in which Luwu' often sided with Goa; no further advantage to either Goa or Boné resulted. Although a distant suzerain, Goa had unwisely been excessively harsh towards its Bugis vassals Wajo' and Soppéng, and this made them susceptible to promptings from Boné to try to regain their autonomy. With that end in view, in 1582 the three kingdoms entered into a triple alliance called *Tellumpocco'é*, 'the Three Summits' – i.e. 'the Big Three'. In 1590 Daéng Mamméta launched another expedition to conquer Wajo', but while sailing along the west coast he fell victim to an amok and was killed.[3] A truce followed, and in 1591 the Treaty of Caleppa was renewed. Among the peace negotiators for Makassar was I Malingkaang Daéng Nyonri', the young crown prince of Tallo', then aged only eighteen. Two years later he was to succeed his father and reign over Tallo' until 1636. Later, he would be known as one of the most respected figures in South Sulawesi history under the name of Karaéng Matoaya, 'the Old Lord'. It was he who made Islam the state religion in Makassar and imposed it on the rest of South Sulawesi.

The Adoption of Islam

During the second half of the sixteenth century competition between Christianity and Islam in South Sulawesi was incon-

---

[3] An 'amok' is a fit of murderous rage which seizes a man, usually when his honour is at stake, which drives him to kill not only the person he thinks has brought disgrace on him but also everybody he meets, until he himself is killed. It has passed into general usage in the phrase 'to run amok', sometimes spelt 'amuck'.

Plate 26   The great mosque of Palopo, said to be the oldest in South Sulawesi

clusive. Kingdoms elsewhere in Sulawesi had already become Muslim under the influence of Ternaté – Gorontalo in 1525 and Buton in 1542 – and already there were individual converts in South Sulawesi. Around 1550 the ruler of Goa, Manrio Gau', bestowed special privileges on the Malay Muslims of Makasar; but when, around 1575, one of the Minangkabau proselytizers of Islam, Abdul Makmur, visited South Sulawesi for the first time to try to make conversions, he encountered several obstacles, among them the people's excessive fondness of dried boar flesh, raw deer liver chopped with blood (*lawa'*) and palm beer. He moved on to Kutei, where he was more successful. In 1580 the Sultan of Ternaté, Babullah, an implacable enemy of the Portuguese, in turn urged Manrio Gau''s successor, Daéng Mamméta, to adopt Islam; the king declined, but in a gesture of benevolence gave the Makassar Malay community permission to build a mosque.

The fact that the competition between Christianity and Islam had been indecisive up to this point is probably at the origin of a story which was told repeatedly to foreign visitors all through the seventeenth century. According to this story, the king of Makassar, unable to take a decision in favour of one of the two religions, decided to resort to chance. He sent messengers at the same time to Portuguese Malaka to ask for priests and to the Aceh ruler (or Mecca mufti) to ask for *ulama*, and took an oath that he would embrace the religion of the first to arrive; the Muslims arrived first and so won. It is indeed the case that around 1620 Sultan Abdullah Karaéng Matoaya told a Portuguese priest that he had repeatedly asked for Catholic missionaries without result, and that he had eventually become a Muslim under pressure from the Johor Sultan. But although he does seem to have been genuinely concerned about theological issues, leaving little doubt as to his strong religious motivation, he also clearly gave his visitors to understand that his decision had been reinforced by equally strong political considerations.

By 1600 the Portuguese had already considered Karaéng Matoaya lost to Christianity, but it seems that he had not then definitively made up his mind. Then Abdul Makmur (Dato' ri Bandang) revisited Makassar, with two companions, Sulaiman (Dato' ri Pa'timang) and Abdul Jawad (Dato' ri Tiro). All three were Minangkabau, but had probably been educated in Aceh and may have come on the recommendation of the Sultan of Johor. When their attempts at proselytization once more met resistance, they left Makassar for Luwu' in a move which proved decisive. In Luwu' they succeeded in converting the ruler, who in February 1605 officially uttered the Islamic profession of faith and took the name of Sultan Muhammad. The visitors then returned to Makassar, where only eight months later Karaéng Matoaya adopted Islam as his religion and then persuaded his nephew and pupil, the young ruler of Goa, to become a Muslim under the name of Sultan Ala'uddin. In November 1607 the first solemn public prayers were said at the newly built Tallo' mosque (Noorduyn, 'Islamisiering van Makasar').

The suddenness of this major religious change, with such important consequences and after such lengthy hesitation, is extraordinary. Makassar and Bugis traditions explain it by attributing many miraculous deeds to the three Dato'. My own hypothesis is that the three had finally discovered that the main point of incompatibility with Islam for the South Sulawesi rulers was the myth of the divine descent of the nobility. One Wajo' chronicle says that they moved from Makassar to Luwu' when they came to understand that 'if power is in Goa, majesty is in Luwu''. In other words, the Luwu' ruler had to be converted first, not just because of the political prestige associated with his former suzerainty over other South Sulawesi kingdoms, but because Luwu' was the mythical navel of South Sulawesi.

The conversion of the Luwu' ruler was attributable in large part to Dato' ri Pa'timang's ability to transmit theological dogma, basing his teaching on Bugis tradition about the 'one God' and beliefs about Sawérigading. One might even trace back to his teachings certain esoteric and highly respected *lôntara'* still to be found in Luwu' which mix the original Bugis creation myth with Muslim mysticism, equate Adam and Eve with the primordial divine couple from whom the gods of the *La Galigo* cycle are said to be descended, and describe Sawérigading as a prophet *avant la lettre* who before leaving this world announced the descent of the Qur'an. It is my view that the three Dato', in order not to lose the contest of religions to the Portuguese Christians, deliberately chose the path of syncretism as the only one which would enable most of the Bugis and Makassar nobility to accept the new faith. They probably counted on later religious teaching and proselytism in the long term annihilating those beliefs and practices which were not compatible with true Islam. After the conversion of the Luwu' ruler, indeed, it took them only a few months to overcome the resistance of the Makassar nobility; but the struggle for thorough islamization was to prove a longer task than may have been expected, and despite the consistent spread of orthodoxy some lingering remnants of paganism are still to be found in the Bugis country.

The rulers of Goa and Tallo' felt that their adoption of Islam enhanced their entitlement to the leadership of the whole peninsula at which they had been aiming. No sooner had their twin kingdoms officially become Muslim than they invited the other South Sulawesi rulers to follow suit. When this invitation was refused, they decided to resort to arms and launched a series of campaigns known in Bugis as 'the Islamic wars'. In 1608 Bacukiki', Suppa', Sawitto' and Mandar on the west coast, and Akkoténgeng and Sakkoli' on the east coast, submitted; in 1609 Sidénréng and Soppéng were subdued; and in 1610 Wajo' fell into line. In 1611, with the final submission of Boné, all of South Sulawesi except the Toraja had embraced Islam.

The Enforcement of Islamic Law

Surprisingly enough, after such resistance, it took relatively few years to entrench Islamic law (*shari'a*) and to integrate Islam into Makassar, Bugis and Mandar cultures. Dato' ri Bandang concentrated first on establishing the *shari'a*, stressing the performance of religious services and the correct celebration of Islamic rites at circumcisions, marriages and funerals. However, except for the funeral rituals, which were

Plate 27   An old Muslim princely grave

completely islamicized, in other rites of passage Islamic elements were simply added on to the traditional practices. As for prohibitions, those on the consumption of pork and on adultery were among the most rigorously enforced; other proscribed behaviour, such as consumption of alcohol and opium, lending money at interest, gambling, and even bringing offerings to sacred places and worshipping the regalia, although condemned, do not seem to have been very energetically fought from the start. The organizational aspects of the *shari'a* were then incorporated into the customary set of laws and norms. In each kingdom or seignory a mosque was built and appointments made to the offices of *qadi*, *imam* and *khatib*, usually from among the nobility. Many of the nobles, anxious to maintain or even improve their position in society, were now trying to combine the advantages of both the old and the new religious systems by monopolizing the new Islamic offices and at the same time maintaining those elements of the old system on which their political power had rested. Meanwhile, however, Islamic teaching was developing and *sufi* brotherhoods were being introduced. Besides purely 'social' religion, true Islam was increasingly taking root in society at large.

Islamization did not prevent the successive rulers of Goa, devout Muslims as they were, from maintaining a particularly friendly attitude towards Christianity and the Portuguese, the numbers of whom in Makassar continued to grow. In 1614 Sultan Ala'uddin even wrote to Manila to invite the Franciscans there to come and establish a house in his kingdom. His son Karaéng Pa'tingalloang, who spoke Portuguese and read Latin fluently, had a deep knowledge of the works of contemporary Catholic theologians and even used to participate in church services and processions. Nonetheless, the choice of Islam was definitive: any attempt by a Makassar or Bugis to become a Christian was punishable by death.

The End of the Competition for Hegemony in South Sulawesi

Between the end of the seventeenth century and the beginning of the nineteenth, the peoples of South Sulawesi were to experience a succession of political vicissitudes including the conquest of Makassar by the Dutch, political division, internal struggles and exposure to increasing indirect influences from Western material culture. However, over the same period they experienced something of a new golden age in the cultural field: most of their post-*La Galigo* literary production, for example, dates from these years. After the fall of Makassar, too, they began their daring overseas enterprises in the western parts of the archipelago, particularly Malaya. With the integration of Islam and Islamic values on the one hand, and their confirmation as one of the major Insulindian maritime peoples on the other, two important constituents had been added to an identity which would then remain virtually unchanged until the Dutch takeover of 1906.

The Apogee and Fall of Makassar

In the first decades of the seventeenth century Makassar had not only extended its authority throughout South Sulawesi, but had also become one of the leading maritime powers of the archipelago. To achieve this latter end it had taken advantage of its mastery of both the western and eastern coasts of South Sulawesi, thus securing its position as an essential staging post on the most direct route from the strait of Malaka to the Moluccas. This route was becoming ever more important for those traders who wanted to escape the increasing control exercised by the Dutch over the southern route, which called first at Javanese harbours and then joined the Moluccas either via Buton or via the Lesser Sunda Islands. Even on this southern route, the Makassar tried to secure bases from which they could operate freely, mounting successive expeditions against Sumbawa in 1617, 1619, 1621 and 1632; against Lombok in 1624; against Buton in 1624, 1633 and 1639; and against Timor in 1640. Meanwhile they maintained close links with Ternaté and the Banda people. The main commodities on both routes were the expensive Moluccan spices (cloves and nutmeg), in which Makassar had by now established an important open market, with prices sometimes cheaper than in the Moluccas themselves. Other commodities traded in Makassar

Plate 28   A shrine in honour of Arung Palakka at the Boné Museum

included local rice and cloth, pepper from Banjarmasin and
Jambi, and slaves.

   The Malay community contributed a great deal to these
developments. Their fleet, together with the Bandanese and
Javanese, dominated the spice trade to and from Makassar.
Only following the demise of the once important Javanese
fleet, as a result both of the Dutch action and of the Javanese
turn to land-based activities under the influence of the Mata-
ram sultanate, did the Makassar fleet itself become a progressively more important player. Bugis traders, too, became
increasingly involved in Makassar-centred commercial ventures. In the first half of the seventeenth century marriages
between Makassar and Bugis aristocrats led an increasing
number of the latter to live in Goa. Likewise, the alliance
concluded between Goa and Wajo' was followed by the estab-

lishment in Makassar of a thriving Wajo' Bugis community, whose main activity was maritime trade. This commercial expansion paralleled the development of shipping based on the eastern and southern coasts of Lake Témpé, from where access to the Gulf of Boné through Cénrana was now under Goanese control.

Another thriving trading community in Goa was that of the Portuguese and *mestizos* who had flourished there, independent of any interference from the Portuguese Crown or the Malaka authorities, since the end of the sixteenth century. After Malaka's conquest by the Dutch in 1641 many more arrived as refugees, swelling their number to about 3,000 (Jacobs, *Portuguese Presence*). They had their own neighbourhood in Barôbboso', with their own churches and priests, and lived on quite good terms with the local people; they even conducted joint ventures with Makassar traders, generally of the high-ranking nobility. The Portuguese merchant Francisco Vieira de Figuereido was a key figure in the city (Boxer, *Francisco Vieira*). The Portuguese were both Makassar's main providers of arms and gunpowder and also the main agents of diffusion of Western written works on such various subjects as fort building, artillery, mathematics, astronomy, geography and cartography, some of which were translated into Makassar and Bugis. Many of the Makassar nobility, including the chief minister Karaéng Pa'tingalloang, could read and speak Portuguese. Other Portuguese borrowings, in games, dance and music, have survived in the Makassar and Bugis cultures up to the present day.

There were other nationalities living in Makassar too. The British East India Company had opened a trading post there in 1613; the Danish India Company opened theirs in 1618, and even the French had one from 1622 to 1625. The Dutch, in the beginning, had been as well received as any (Villiers, 'Makassar'), and in 1607 Sultan Ala'uddin told them: 'My country stands open to all nations and what I have is for you as well as for the Portuguese.' However, when in 1615 they asked for a trade monopoly, he was less accommodating: 'God made the land and the sea; the land He divided among men and the sea He gave them in common. It is unheard of that anyone should be forbidden to sail the seas.' This was precisely what the Dutch were setting out to do in the Moluccas, especially after 1621 with their conquest and destruction of Banda; Makassar did not acknowledge the trade ban imposed by the Dutch, and it became clear that coexistence between them was impossible. Together with Ternaté, the Makassar attacked Dutch settlements in the Moluccas, and in 1634 they supported the revolt of the Ambonese. The Dutch responded by trying – unsuccessfully – to blockade Makassar, and Makassar mounted several attacks on the Dutch fort in Buton. From 1637 to 1653 a precarious maritime truce persisted, while Makassar waged war on land against Boné. Then in the latter year Makassar once more went to the aid of the Ambonese of Hitu and Ceram, and in 1655 the Dutch retaliated with a limited attack on Makassar, which was only partially successful. A following spell of peace was short-lived: hostilities resumed in 1660 with a new and successful Dutch attack on Makassar during which the Portuguese ships at anchor there were destroyed. This time the balance of power had changed, to the detriment of Makassar, for the Bugis of Boné, under the leadership of the famous Arung Palakka (Andaya, *Arung Palakka*), had become involved in the war.

Nearly twenty years previously, the century-long competition between Goa and Boné for hegemony on the peninsula had led to another war, from which Goa had emerged the victor. It had begun as an internal affair in Boné, whose ruler from 1631 to 1634, La Ma'daremmeng, had antagonized his nobles with measures based on his strong Islamic convictions, such as discarding the *bissu* and forbidding gambling, drinking of palm beer, and any kind of superstition. The last straw had been his decision to free the slaves: this sparked a rebellion led by his own mother, who sought refuge and assistance in Goa. The Makassar could not have hoped for a better opportunity for military intervention: they achieved a resounding success and took more than 30,000 Bugis prisoners, including La Ma'daremmeng himself. But then, instead of contenting themselves with a demand for substantial war tribute and the signing of a treaty putting the vanquished in a position of mild dependence, they replaced the deposed Boné ruler with a Makassar proconsul supported by a Bugis regent; after a subsequent revolt, Boné was made a fully fledged colony. Thus a desire for revenge became entrenched among the Boné people and nobility.

Their chance came after the successful Dutch attack of 1660. Obliged to sign a disadvantageous truce, the Makassar set 10,000 Boné people to forced labour digging a ditch as protection against possible attacks from inland. Their revolt was once more harshly repressed. A number of Boné noblemen, including the young Arung Palakka, took refuge in Buton and proposed an alliance to the Dutch there in order to take their revenge on Makassar. The following war was inconclusive until 1666, when a joint Dutch–Bugis force under Admiral Speelman, with the help of troops from Ternaté, Ambon and Buton, besieged Makassar, the Dutch at sea and the Bugis on land. After a fierce and protracted battle, in which Makassar's only true allies were the Wajo' Bugis and the Malay community, Sultan Hasanuddin signed the treaty of Bongaya on 18 November 1667. This obliged Makassar to dismantle most of its fortifications, give up any trade in spices, stop importing foreign goods from any source other than the Dutch East India Company, expel the Portuguese and renounce any kind of suzerainty, either over other parts of the archipelago or over Bugis lands. In 1669, Sultan Hasanuddin of Goa abdicated.

The New Situation of the Bugis

There is no need to describe subsequent historical developments in great detail; an outline of a few important points will suffice. The Dutch had achieved their goal, but they were not the only winners: another was Boné, which, although limited in its scope for action by the treaty which it also had signed, would maintain its virtual independence until the nineteenth century. This is why, in Boné tradition, the national hero is not Hasanuddin and the villain Arung Palakka, but vice versa. Once rid of Makassar's rivalry, Boné could claim an undisputed pre-eminence in the entire peninsula. The movement towards unification of the Bugis under a single leader, however, was frozen by the presence of the Dutch, and they remained in a patchwork of larger and smaller confederated,

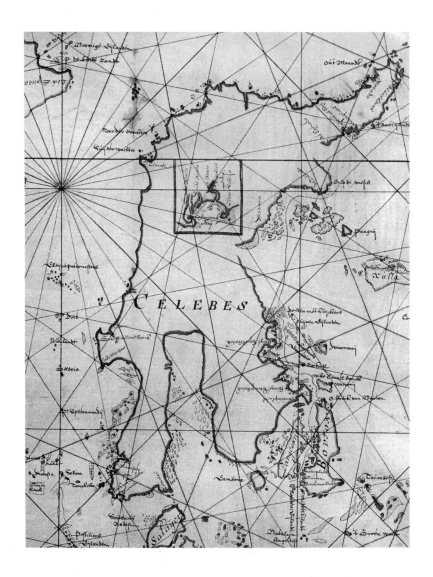

Plate 29   Johannes Bleau's map of Sulawesi, dated 1688

federated or unified polities all of which more or less maintained their autonomy. The Wajo' Bugis, for one, never accepted Boné's suzerainty, although after an armed rebellion

was put down by a joint Boné–Dutch force, they were seemingly content to express their wish for freedom through successful trading enterprises overseas.

A side-effect of the fall of Makassar was an important change in the patterns of navigation and emigration among the South Sulawesi peoples. A number of Makassar noblemen left for Java, where they joined the struggle against the Dutch and their Boné allies, fighting either with Prince Trunajaya of Madura in east and central Java (1674–8) or with Banten's Sultan Agung Tirtajasa (1682–4) in west Java. Other Makassar emigrated to Sumatra and even to Siam. In Makassar City, Bugis communities, not only from Wajo' but also from Boné, whose ruler by now had a residence there in the Bontoala' neighbourhood, became increasingly prominent. Thus Makassar became the major point of embarkation not only for its own fleet but also for the Bugis fleets and the Bugis adventurers who set off in search of wealth and fame for the western parts of the archipelago, now their main area of maritime activity since the Dutch had restricted their access to the eastern islands. From the Riau archipelago, where many of them had settled in the vicinity of the Johor court, at a strategic meeting point of the local and international trade routes, they extended their activity in various directions, including that of the Malay peninsula. Here they established themselves at a number of strategic river mouths to compete with the Dutch for control of exports of the tin mined upstream. They also began intervening in dynastic quarrels among Malay rulers, and through armed action and strategic marriage they succeeded in becoming one of the major political forces in the Riau–Johor sultanate and in the peninsula as a whole.

Part Two

Society and Culture:
Survivals and Transformations

7

Society

From Traditional to Modern

It should be obvious from the preceding chapters that it would make no sense to try to define a particular 'traditional' state of Bugis society and culture, where 'traditional' would mean 'untouched by external influences'. Any specific culture at any specific time contains elements of maintained tradition, independent innovation and borrowing; and while some societies are keener than others on novelties from outside, the Bugis seem to have been one of the more receptive, especially when they deemed such importations advantageous to themselves. External contacts and trade have thus been among the main factors at work in the shaping of Bugis identity. Although there is clear continuity in a number of particular aspects which have preserved elements of that identity over the ages, Bugis society and culture have been in a state of constant change that continues up to the present day.

Descriptions of the Bugis set down between the middle of the nineteenth century and the beginning of the twentieth, by such scholars as the Dutch orientalist B. F. Matthes or successive visitors including the British gentleman adventurer James Brooke, the Austrian lady traveller Ida Pfeiffer and the Swiss naturalists Paul and Fritz Sarasin, thus depict a traditional Bugis society not in the sense of an undisturbed, ageless state of things but rather in the sense of a situation applicable at a particular date produced through a continuous process of change. Many external elements had been incorporated over the years in almost every area of Bugis life – customary law, socio-political rules, customs, rites and creeds, models of behaviour, daily occupations, technology, knowledge, folklore, entertainment, literature – but these importations had been so well digested that they could be seen by outside observers as well as by the indigenous people themselves as integral elements of a coherent tradition. From this perspective, interaction with Westerners may initially have been considered not so very different from interaction with the Malays, the Javanese or the Chinese. Even the conquest of Makassar by the Dutch could easily be viewed as just one more episode in the continuing struggle for hegemony on South Sulawesi and for control over its trading activities, with the Java-based foreign power playing much the same role towards Goa as that previously played by Goa towards Boné, or by Boné towards Luwu'.

However, this continuity in the pattern of external relations was broken from the beginning of the nineteenth century as the whole area, and especially the trading peoples within it, became involved in the new global world economy driven by Western industrial capitalism. This new commercial environment gave an increasing prominence to cheap, imported, mass-produced industrial goods which in many cases progressively replaced the output of cottage industry and domestic production; and the local development of cash crops such as maize, coffee, copra and cocoa, mostly intended for the Western market, completely upset the economic balance. These changes in turn had consequences for social structures. The broadening of people's social and mental spaces beyond the area within which they had hitherto functioned to a global horizon, which is one of the main distinguishing features of modernity as contrasted with traditionality, and the associated improvements and developments in transportation, communications, literacy and education, had their effect in the fields of religion and general knowledge.

A key point in the Bugis' transition to modernity was the founding in 1819 of Singapore, in which they were specifically involved. This south-east Asian entrepôt was to remain the pivot of their trading operations in the archipelago up to the 1950s: a springboard for their enterprises in Malaya, Sumatra and Borneo, a staging post for their pilgrims en route to

Mecca, and an important centre for the dissemination of knowledge and information. Five years after the foundation of Singapore, the treaty signed in 1824 between Britain and the Netherlands to delimit their respective zones of influence in maritime south-east Asia formed a basis for new political developments whose consequences are still felt today: the creation of British Malaya, the progressive extension of Dutch authority in the Indies and the eventual emergence of the contemporary states of Malaysia and Indonesia. The Bugis world, straddling the two zones, was inevitably affected by all these changes. From 1824 to the beginning of the twentieth century the Dutch endeavoured to establish their authority on those parts of South Sulawesi where their control had hitherto been purely nominal, as well as on those which had remained more or less independent. In the later colonial period, between 1906 and 1942, the Dutch introduced radical changes in the political organization of South Sulawesi societies under the rubric of so-called 'indirect rule'.

During periods like the second half of the twentieth century, when tremendous changes are taking place throughout the world, native intellectuals as well as Western anthropologists are prone to take an idealized view of the past as an image of how things had been for centuries and should have remained. The Bugis have always been very conscious of their own past and accord great importance to writings dealing with 'the people of yesterdays' (*to-riolo*) and with 'precedents' (*ade' pura onro*). It is no wonder, then, if in the contemporary context local intellectuals are keen to extol traditional values to the younger generation, prominent members of society are organizing lavish weddings which revive the old princely ceremonials and local government is helping to establish ethnographic and open-air museums, while anthropologists, archaeologists and historians are invited to 'dig up' ancient culture.

For the Bugis, the transition from traditionality to modernity has been a long and complex process. Many specific cultural elements inherited from the past are still alive; others have in the past century undergone a slow process of transformation into new ones, which however retain indubitable signs of continuity and have become part of a modern Bugis culture; yet others have disappeared entirely; and completely new objects, norms and patterns of behaviour have successively appeared, most of which have nothing to do with a specifically Bugis identity and represent at most the South Sulawesi, Indonesian or south-east Asian manifestations of elements of a world culture. All these heterogeneous threads have become interwoven to make up the global environment of today's Bugis.

In the following pages, in reviewing the main aspects of the Bugis' social, spiritual, mental and material life I will present an image of the state of things as it existed around the end of the nineteenth century and examine what remains of it today, despite the many changes which have occurred since. The word 'traditional' as used in the following chapters refers to that dated reality. In the final pages of the book, I will address myself to the contemporary transformations and innovations that have been at work to create the Bugis world of tomorrow.

Kinship, Gender and Marriage

Kinship is a key aspect of all societies, both because it is of major concern to the members of any society and because it is the basic structure upon which the social fabric rests. In the case of the Bugis, a sound knowledge of kinship principles is essential if one is to understand how those inextricably interlinked aspects of their society which matter most to the people – marriage, social hierarchy, power and personal influence – really work.

The Kinship System

Like many other Austronesian, specifically Insulindian, societies, such as the Malays, the Javanese, and the peoples of Borneo and the Philippines, the Bugis have a bilateral or cognatic kinship system. This means that a person's kindred is reckoned through both the father's and the mother's side. This principle is shared by European peoples, but is not a universal feature; on the contrary, most of the kinship systems which have been studied by anthropologists in non-European societies are based on either patrilineal or matrilineal descent.

Bugis kinship terminology is quite simple and is of the 'generational' type. All your relatives of the same generation as yourself, be they male or female, brothers, sisters or cousins, fall into the single category of 'sibling' (*séajing*, 'of one origin'); the most important thing to know about each is whether he or she is your elder sibling (*kaka'*) or younger sibling (*anri'*). Similarly, in the generation following your own you can call everyone, including your own children, nephews, nieces and cousins' children *ana'* (child), although there is a special term (*ana-uré*) for nephews and nieces. All their children – whether of *ana'* or *ana-uré* – are your *eppo'* (grandchildren). You will call all your relatives in the same generation as your parents either uncles (*ama-uré*) or aunts *ina-(uré)*, and all of their parents, grandparents (*néné*). It is of course always possible to state through precisely which kind of links one is related to a particular individual by using additional specifying terms; but more often it is difficult to be sure whether a person to whom someone refers using the terminology described above is a relative at all, since there is a common tendency to extend immediate kin terms to close but unrelated friends of the appropriate generation.

In such a system, where descent is acknowledged from the mother's as well as the father's side, the most important concept is not 'lineage', which is an unknown term among the Bugis, but 'branching off', which is reckoned from each pair of each person's ancestors and produces successive circles of cousins who descend from both parents' parents', from the four couples of parents' grandparents, from the eight couples of grandparents' grandparents, and the sixteen couples of grandparents' grandparents' parents. These are, respectively, one's 'first', 'second', 'third' and 'fourth' cousins (*sappo siseng, sappo wékka dua, wékka tellu* and *wékka eppa'*).

Thus an individual is surrounded, both on his father's and on his mother's side, by successive layers of collateral kin, from the closest, branching off from his parents (brothers, sisters, nephews, grandnephews), to the most remote, branching off from his fifth-generation ancestors downwards. These nested kinship units are usually called *a'séajingeng* ('those having the same origin'), and are given more or less importance according to which common ancestor is the point of connection. This set of ancestor-based units on both the father's and the mother's side constitutes a person's kindred as opposed to 'other people' (*tau laéng*). The Bugis do not have the kind of discrete cognatic groups that include all the descendants of a single pair of common ancestors, such as the groups centred on a common family house of origin among their Toraja neighbours. Of much greater importance to the Bugis is the level they occupy in the hierarchical system of social stratification.

Marriage

For the Bugis, to marry is *siala*, 'to take each other'. It is thus a reciprocal act, which means that even if they are of different ranks, the man and the woman are partners. But marriage does not involve the bride and bridegroom alone; it is the celebration of an alliance and an act of partnership between two sides which are often already related but wish thus to renew and enhance their relationship (Millar, *Bugis Weddings*: 26–8). Among the commoner inhabitants of the villages, marriages often take place in the vicinity or among the same clientele group (see section on 'Clienteles' below), so that existing kin relationships are already well known by all concerned. Migrants from other regions tend to seek alliance by marriage with people with whom they have already entered into a close relation of some kind, who may be more or less close kin or relations by marriage. Marriage is the best way of making non-kin into 'not other people' (*tennia tau laéng*), as is the intention also when two friends or business partners decide in advance to marry their future offspring, or betrothe their young children, to one another.

Marriage should ideally take place within the individual's kindred. Marriage between cousins, be they parallel cousins or cross cousins (i.e. one from the mother's and one from the father's side), is considered the best arrangement. Opinions differ from one family to another among the Bugis themselves as to which degrees of cousinhood are propitious and which should be avoided. Many think that the relationship between first cousins is 'too hot', and marriage between first cousins seems to be rare except among the highest-ranking nobility, whose 'white blood' allows them to act in ways similar to the *La Galigo* heroes. Most lower-ranking people prefer to stick to marriage between second or third cousins.

It is important that the couple to be married are not of different degrees of descent from one common ancestor; that is, they must be of the same generation. Marriage between uncle and niece, or between aunt and nephew, is prohibited, and sexual intercourse between such couples would be considered *salîmara'* (incest). Marriage with the child of a cousin, at any degree, should likewise be avoided. Genealogies show that this rule was quite strictly followed, with exceptions being relatively rare. The numerous marriages of noble men with women much younger than themselves, and the great number of their children, resulted in many individuals in the same age class as those who were classified as their uncles and aunts; however, despite the similarity of age, there were no marriages between these uncles/aunts and their nephews nieces.

For the nobility, another point to be considered – in fact, the most important – is the respective ranks of the man and the woman. The general rule is that while a man may marry beneath his rank, a woman may not. The higher the rank, the more strictly the rule is applied, even now; among the lower ranks, however, compromises were possible, and tend to be made more frequently today. Usually, a high-ranking man's primary wife (not necessarily the first married) was of the same rank as him, while his other wives could be of lesser rank, or even commoners. This principle held for as long as the traditional Bugis political system remained in force, because it had consequences for the rank inherited by the children and *ipso facto* for their succession rights. (This point is discussed in more detail later in the chapter.) However, the strict principle of relative ranks could on occasion be waived where wealth was involved; in former times, particularly among the Wajo'people, the son of a wealthy family was sometimes permitted to marry a bride of a higher rank than his, in a practice called *mang'elli dara* or 'blood buying', that is, buying rank.

A marriage is accompanied by the presentation of a dowry by the man's side to the woman's side (the term 'bride price' common in anthropological literature seems inappropriate, as conveying the unwarranted idea of a purchase of the woman). There are two parts to this dowry: the *sompa* ('homage'), a now symbolic sum of money expressed in *rella'* (*rials*, the former currency of, among other places, Portuguese Malaka), proportional to the woman's rank and intended for the bride herself, and the *dui' ménré* (literally, 'ascending money'), which is the contribution of the groom's side to the expenses of the wedding feast, which is organized by the bride's side. To this is added the *lise' kawing* ('wedding's substance'), the Islamic *mahr* or bridal gift: usually a small sum of money, it now sometimes takes the form of a printed copy of the Qur'an. In former times, before colonization by the Dutch, men coming from another polity also had to pay to the ruler a tax or *pa'lawa tana* (literally, 'the country's obstacle') proportional to the *sompa*.

Weddings

There are long preliminaries before a Bugis wedding occurs. First, if no promise of marriage has already been concluded during the boy's childhood – or even before his birth – people from the young man's side begin discussing desirable alliances and evaluating prospective brides from among young women they know or of whom they have heard. Among the nobility, genealogies are studied in order to ascertain the respective ranks of the intended groom and possible brides. The first stage of the preliminaries is completed by older women who make informal visits to the families of the latter to get a better idea of what the girls are like. Then comes the first open contact, with questions asked in indirect and allusive terms, in order to save face on either side should an approach be rebuffed. If the girl's parents are open to further conversation, a day is fixed for the first formal move, 'to come in embassy' (*ma'duta*). At this meeting the genealogy, rank, kinship and assets of each of the prospective spouses are further scrutinized, while negotiations are opened on the *sompa* as well as on the amount of money to be paid by the bridegroom's party in contribution to the wedding expenses and on the gifts to be made to the bride

Plate 30   A peasant bride in full attire

and her family. When agreement on these points is reached, a
day is fixed for its solemn ratification. The betrothal gifts to
the future bride are brought to this ceremony, sometimes in
procession. They include a ring, and also a number of presents
of symbolic significance. The bridegroom is represented by a
delegation of relatives or honoured friends of his parents'
generation, but his mother and father, and the bridegroom
himself, are not present. A spokesman for the bridegroom's
party makes a speech recalling the points of the agreement; he
is answered by a spokesman for the bride's party, and the date
for the wedding itself is definitively set. Then the gifts are
passed round to be examined, first by the men, then by the
women, after which they are taken to the future bride's room.

Wedding ceremonies take place in two stages: first the wedding proper (*ma'pabotting*), which is organized at the bride's

house and which the groom's father and mother do not attend; then, later – sometimes several days later – the *ma'parola* ('having' the bride 'follow' to the house of her parents-in-law), which the bride's father and mother do not attend. On the day of the wedding the bridegroom comes in procession accompanied by a delegation and preceded by the bearers of the *sompa*; in former times he had to overcome a number of symbolic obstacles, such as staged resistance by horsemen or demonstrations of martial arts, and had to gain his way through by dispensing small gifts to the defenders. For men of the highest nobility a special ritual was observed, the central element of which was the *ma'lawolo*, a dialogue between the bridegroom's party and a *bissu* representing the bride's party. Speaking from the elevated entrance platform of the house, the *bissu* asked the newcomers whether the bridegroom really was a descendant of 'those who are paid homage with both hands', that is, of the highest nobility, who by their pure 'white' blood are nearest to the gods. During the ensuing dialogue, the *bissu* and the bridegroom each held one end of the *lawolo*, a braid made from a *patola* cloth and a white cloth twisted together, symbolizing the rainbow of *La Galigo* times as well as the mythic Wélenréng tree which linked the Earth, here represented by the groom's party, to heaven, represented by the bride's house. Once convinced that the bridegroom was indeed a descendant of Tompo'tikka, Wéwang Nriwu' and Luwu', representing the east, west and centre of the world respectively, the *bissu*, gently pulling on the *lawolo*, drew the bridegroom upstairs under a shower of scattered puffed rice. This ceremony was in most respects similar to that performed for the enthronement of a ruler (Hamonic, '*Mallawolo*').

Once in the bride's house, the bridegroom still has several physical and symbolic barriers to overcome before he reaches his bride and performs both the Islamic and customary rites which make them legally husband and wife.[1] For example,

---

[1] Among traditionally minded Bugis, both Islamic and customary rites are deemed necessary for a marriage to be considered contracted. Among Bugis of the Muslim reformist trend, however, only Islamic rites are performed, while among the To-Lotang (non-Muslim) group of Bugis, only customary rites are performed.

sometimes he has to pay a symbolic fee to the women who guard the door of the room where the bride is awaiting him; always he has to touch the bride's hand or wrist; sometimes bride and groom are symbolically 'sewn' into the same sarong. After the rites have been performed, the marriage has then to be made public and official; to achieve this the bride and groom sit together in state for a period of some hours – formerly, in the case of princely weddings, even for days, in front of the hundreds or sometimes thousands of guests invited to the ceremony, just like a king and queen on their thrones, with only very short intervals for the couple to take food and change clothes.

The young man then has to go through a series of stages on that night and the following nights to win his new wife's goodwill: first to gain her acceptance of him sleeping in the same room as her, then to unveil her face before him and address a few words to him, then letting him come closer, until finally she agrees to sleep with him. This lengthy process, recalling the approach of Sáwerigading to Wé Cudai' in the *La Galigo* texts, could sometimes go on for months before the marriage was consummated; sometimes the bride persisted in refusing herself, in which case the marriage had to be dissolved by divorce. Even today the process may take some weeks, and if unsuccessful can still culminate in divorce.

The public wedding ceremonies are the main means by which the Bugis demonstrate their place in society. By performing the appropriate rites and displaying the garments, ornaments and other accoutrements to which they are entitled, they assert their rank; the identity, rank and number of guests bear witness to their social connections and influence; and the wedding feast is an opportunity for both the bride's and the bridegroom's families to display their wealth, the latter by the amount of *dui' ménré* contributed (Millar, *Bugis Weddings*: 105–8).

At the end of the nineteenth century the size of the dowry was specified according to rank, in units called *kati* ('pounds' of 'old money'): one *kati* was worth 88 *rial*, and to each *kati* was added one slave (worth 40 *rial*) and one buffalo (25 *rial*). The *sompa* for a noblewoman of the highest rank amounted to 14 *kati*, while for a noblewoman of the lowest rank it was one *kati* only, and for a commoner one-quarter of one *kati*. Similar computations are still made, but since Indonesian independence the *ringgit* (originally worth 2.5 *rupiah* or Dutch guilders) has been used as the unit of account. Figures recorded in 1975 by Susan Millar for her study of Bugis weddings show that the actual sums were rounded off, while the *dui ménré* ranged from 2,000 to 500,000 *rupiah* (Millar, *Bugis Weddings*: 105–7). Since the abolition of traditional political power in the present century, no one has the authority to enforce the customary rules, and so some wealthy commoner families who are prepared to brave the resulting gossip have started to use social symbols in weddings which were formerly reserved for the nobility.

Gender and Gender Roles

In Bugis society, as in most societies in the world, men and women have their own respective domains of activity. However, neither gender is considered intrinsically dominant over the other, and the criteria on which gender roles are distinguished are not so much physical as based on socially recognized trends in individual behaviour (Hamzah, 'Femmes Bugis'). In fact, the Bugis take the principle of non-differentiation between genders, enshrined in their bilateral kinship system, to its logical conclusion: just as the mother's side and the father's side play equivalent roles in determining kinship, so women and men have equal, though different, roles in society. The difference in roles is the basis of their partnership in caring for each other's concerns. Although islamization has enhanced and in some cases introduced behaviour which appears to place men in the foreground and women in the background, these practices do not represent any idea of male dominance or female subjection (Millar, 'Interpreting Gender'). On the contrary, the freedom enjoyed by Bugis women, and the responsibilities they sometimes bore, amazed Western commentators. Sir Stamford Raffles, for example, noted in 1817 that in South Sulawesi the women 'are held in more esteem than could be expected from the state of civilization in general, and undergo none of the severe hardships, privations, or labours, that restrict fecundity in other parts of the world' (Raffles, *History of Java*, appendix F, 'Celebes': CLXXIX), while Crawfurd wrote that 'the women appear in public without any scandal; they take active concern in all the business of life; they are consulted by the men on all public affairs, and frequently raised to the throne, and that too when the monarchy is elective' (Crawfurd, *History*: 74).

At the beginning of their married life the young couple usually live with the wife's parents; this certainly does not favour dominant behaviour by the husband. The space within the house is divided according to gender: the front part is considered the men's portion and the back part the women's. Each part has its own entrance, but in practice the women of the house, their female kin and other women commonly use the front as well as the rear entrance, while the back entrance is seldom used by men of the family and never by male outsiders. The women quite often spend time in the front part of the house, but avoid it when unrelated male guests are visiting; similarly, although the kitchen in the back part of the house is the women's realm, the men of the family do come into it sometimes, most often to take their daily meals. Another female part of the house is the loft where rice is stored; even men of the family rarely go here, and it used to be a favourite sleeping place for unmarried girls, especially if male guests were staying overnight. The division of space according to gender is most apparent when formal meals are being taken or when male visitors who are not kin are in the house; these occasions take place in the front part of the house, with only men present, the women entering only to bring food or other refreshments. Rather than a strict and permanent division of space by gender, it would be more accurate to speak of a flexible arrangement whereby women benefit from areas protected from the intrusion of male outsiders, who are normally confined to the 'male' portion of other people's houses. On a more general level, one can say that the house is basically woman's, not man's domain – and indeed, it is usually inherited by the youngest daughter.

According to a Bugis saying, the woman's domain is around the house, the man's domain reaches 'the borders of the sky' (the horizon). This formulation also defines the respective roles of man and woman in domestic life. Whether as a peasant, a fisherman, an artisan or a trader, the man's main field of activity is outside the house, and he is the main income provider; the woman, in taking care of the children, pounding rice, cooking, washing, tending vegetables and making purchases for the family, is occupied mainly in the house or not too far from it and is the main income spender. However, this is not the whole picture. Many women play a part in providing an income for the family by practising domestic crafts such as weaving, embroidery, making mats or baskets, or preparing cakes or snacks for sale, sometimes selling them themselves in the market or from a small stall near the house. The wives of sailors are actually responsible for providing a regular income to support their families while their husbands are at sea; for months at a time, during these absences, the men provide only for their own needs, giving their family the surplus when they come ashore – sometimes, though rarely, in cash; more often in the form of clothes, ornaments, furniture or luxury items. Women also take part in some of the work in the fields, especially when collective labour is necessary, for example when planting or harvesting, or in delicate tasks such as weeding. Likewise, there is no strict prohibition on men performing domestic tasks usually the province of women; a man can cook, for instance, when he is alone in a field hut, or when his wife is ill, or on the occasion of a feast, when fires are lit outside and huge quantities of rice or meat are cooked for hundreds of guests.

There are, however, some tasks that are restricted to either men or women. The specifically masculine activities include tillage, sowing, fishing from a boat (although women do sometimes fish with a line from the coast, or catch fish with a landing net), looking after cattle, gathering in the forest, tapping palm sap to make palm beer, hunting, carpentry, house- and boat-building, and working iron, gold or silver. Tasks reserved for women include pounding rice, weaving and all other textile work, and pottery-making. Despite appearances, this does not amount to a simple division of labour whereby men do the hard work, women the light work: pounding rice needs a lot of strength, and few jobs are more delicate than that of the goldsmith.

Gender distinctions are also manifested in clothing, physical attitudes and gestures, and general behaviour, but in these areas there is a large measure of overlap and flexibility. In contrast to other Insulindian peoples, among whom men wear the tubular sarong while women wear the open, draped skirt, Bugis men and women alike wear the sarong, differing only in the way of knotting it. On formal occasions, Bugis women do not knot their sarong, but hold the unknotted part over their right forearm, which is elegant but not very practical. Even when they wear no upper garment men normally knot their sarong at the waist, while since islamization women wear theirs higher, secured under the armpits or over one shoulder (although in some villages in the 1960s some women, and not only elderly ones, still went bare-breasted in the privacy of their homes). Outside the home, women sometimes used to wear a second sarong pulled over their head; this habit was particularly prevalent where Islam had a strong influence, but was not an Islamic innovation, being alluded to in the *La Galigo* texts.

Posture and bearing also differ: seated on the floor or on mats, men sit cross-legged while women usually sit with both legs bent to one side or, on formal occasions, with one leg bent to the side and the other bent with knee raised. Men carry burdens on a carrying pole held over the shoulder, while women carry them on their heads. In general attitude women are expected to observe a certain restraint, while some degree of aggression seems normal among men, most of whom probably wear the small dagger with a pistol-shaped handle, called *kawali*, under their clothes; quarrels can therefore end in bloodshed. However, quite a number of women also carry the *kawali* when travelling, albeit for protection only.

The flexibility of Bugis behavioural gender distinctions is well expressed in the saying 'Whoever, although a man, has female qualities, is a woman; and although a woman, has male qualities, is a man.' A partial application of this principle is to be found in the appointment of women as political or war leaders. Such figures are quite common in Bugis literature, but there have also been historical examples of female warriors. A striking case is cited by Crawfurd, concerning a Makassar woman (in this respect the Makassar resemble the Bugis) who in 1814 was sovereign of the little state of Lipukasi:

Not many days before I saw her, she had presented herself among the warriors of her party drawn out before the enemy, upbraided them for their tardiness in the attack, in lofty terms, and demanded a spear, that she might show them an example. Encouraged by her exhortations, it appears they went forth, and gained an advantage. (Crawfurd, *History*: 74)

More recently, women participated in the struggle for Indonesian independence, and female squads could be seen among Bugis rebel troops in both Kahar Muzakkar's Tentara Islam Indonesia (Indonesian Islamic Army) and Usman Balo's Tentara Keamanan Rakyat (People's Safety Army). Nor were female rulers uncommon in Bugis history, a fact which caused Crawfurd further amazement:

The women . . . are consulted by the men on all public affairs, and frequently raised to the throne, and that too when the monarchy is elective . . . At public festivals, women appear among the men; and those invested with authority sit in their councils when affairs of state are discussed, possessing, it is often alleged, even more than their due share in the deliberations. The present sovereign of the Bugis state of Luwu in Celebes, is wife to the king of Sopeng, another Bugis state, but the king of Sopeng does not presume to interfere in the affairs of the state of Luwu, which are administered by his wife, his proper queen. (Crawfurd, *History*: 74)

A few years later, Brooke wrote in similar vein:

All the offices of state, including even that of *aru matoah*, are open to women; and they actually fill the important posts of government, four out of the six great chiefs of Wajo being at present females. These ladies appear in public like the men; ride, rule, and visit even foreigners, without the knowledge or consent of their husbands. (Brooke, *Narrative of Events*: 75)

However, at the village level, the informal community leaders are all men; and yet, because of the maternal qualities they display towards the villagers, they are often called *ina tau*, 'mothers of the people'. The reason why it was possible for high-ranking women to occupy public office is probably related to the principles which underlie the rules of social interaction between genders among the Bugis, which result from the converging requirements of Islam and pre-Islamic *adat*. In the same way as a Muslim woman is permitted to stay only with men whom she is forbidden to marry, such as her direct forebears, uncles or brothers, a high-ranking woman is permitted to have in her service a man of lower rank with whom marriage is prohibited and sexual intercourse would be as grave a crime as incest, in both social and religious terms.

Transvestism: calabai' *and* bissu

One cannot conclude a discussion of gender among the Bugis without reference to the existence and importance of an, as it were, third gender, the *calabai'*, and a less well-known fourth one, the *calalai'*. The *calabai'*, etymologically 'false women', are male transvestites and the *calalai'*, 'false men', female ones. Very little has been written on this subject, apart from a little embarrassed explanation by Matthes in 1872 (*Bissoe's*) and some recent research by Hamonic ('Travestissement et bisexualité'; 'Fausse femmes'; *Langage des dieux*: 40–8) since the allusion made by James Brooke in the journal of his visit to Wajo in 1840:

The strangest custom I have observed is, that some men dress like women, and some women like men; not occasionally, but all their lives, devoting themselves to the occupations and pursuits of their adopted sex. In the case of the males, it seems that the parents of a boy, upon perceiving in him certain effeminacies of habit and appearance, are induced thereby to present him to one of the rajahs, by whom he is received. These youths often acquire much influence over their masters. (Brooke, *Narrative of Events*: 88)

The *calabai'* are a common sight in almost all Bugis villages: clad either completely or partially in women's clothes, they can be seen engaging in all kinds of women's tasks, such as cooking, pounding rice or washing clothes. Even though, in speaking of them, some Bugis youths smile and some strict *ulama* frown, to the Western eye they appear to be surprisingly well accepted and integrated into a society where their status is considered by most to be perfectly honourable. Some live with their parents or with a married sister; others live by

Plate 31   A transvestite

themselves. Others live in partnership with another young
man, and although there is some restraint among the Bugis in
speaking of sexual matters, there seems to be no doubt that
these are homosexual couples; yet the companions of the
calabaï seem to be considered as sexually normal, and some
of them even marry women later and have children. Other
calabaï who live alone are said to be impotent; this might be
understood as a choice of sexual abstinence, either in order to
avoid engaging in behaviour considered sinful under Islamic
prescriptions, or in order to obtain enhanced magical powers
through asceticism. (This latter reason for abstinence is also
cited by some middle-aged heterosexual men.)

The first Western report on *bissu*, written by the Portuguese
Paiva in 1545 (Jacobs, 'First Christianity'), explicitly stresses
their – to him, repulsive – homosexuality. From his obscure

and embarrassed circumlocutions it is possible to glean that they were said to practise both sodomy and fellatio. Sacred homosexuality is attested for Java at the same period, and it was common practice among the shamans of the Baré'é of Central Sulawesi, in Bali, among certain Dayak and Formosan peoples, in the Philippines and in Polynesia (Kroef, 'Transvestism in Indonesia'). Not all Bugis *bissu* were *calabai*', and only some of the *calabai*' became *bissu*; but the ambivalence of the *calabai*' probably placed them in the sacred sphere. Now that the genuine *bissu* have nearly disappeared, many of the ordinary *calabai*' have taken on aspects of their former role in the organization and celebration of weddings. They take charge of practical matters such as the decoration of the house, the cooking, the make-up and costumes of the bride and bridegroom and the hire of ornaments and accessories for the couple and their retinue; often they also conduct the traditional ritual ceremonies. For most *calabai*', these activities represent their main source of income, and some become fairly well off. This prospect may explain why, when a young boy begins to show a propensity to adopt feminine behaviour, playing girls' games or dressing up as a girl, many parents do not oppose the development.

Calabai' insist that they are not just men turned into women, and few of them would wish to become physical women through transsexual surgery. Most say that they enjoy being able to combine the masculinity with which they were born and the femininity of which they have progressively become aware during adolescence, and insist that they possess masculine strength and aggression alongside their feminine qualities. They interact freely with both men and women, but must beware of sexual prohibitions: in the sixteenth century, *calabai*' *bissu* convicted of sexual intercourse with women were put to death by boiling in pitch.

Some of the *calalai*' also live in homosexual couples; they are said to perform sex with the aid of dildoes made from animal guts filled with wax. They seem to be much less numerous, and to enjoy a much lower degree of tolerance from the public. Most of the *calabai*', too, do not like them. Theirs is only an individual status, and accords them no social or ritual role, although there have until relatively recently been cases of *calalai*' rulers.

Social Stratification

The Principles of Hierarchy by Birth

The principles on which the traditional hierarchy of the Bugis is established are quite simple. According to both the *La Galigo* texts and the origin myths, there were originally two kinds of humans: 'white-blooded' people of divine ancestry, and 'red-blooded', ordinary, people, who were either commoners or slaves. In these texts the division between the two categories is absolute and unbridgeable. However, in the actual system as it operated in historical times, intermarriage between the categories appears to have been not only possible but even frequent, giving rise to the many intermediate ranks between the highest nobility and the lowliest slaves.

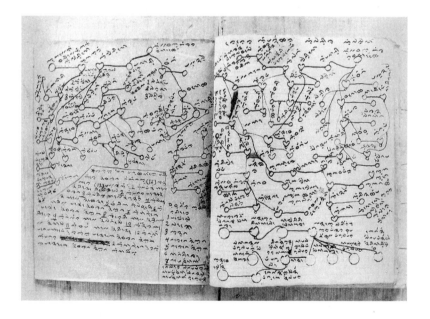

Plate 32   The genealogy of a noble Sinjai family

According to the *La Galigo* texts, the divine ancestors of the
nobility were sent to Earth to become human beings precisely
because 'one is no god when there are no human beings'.
Batara Guru had to pass through desacralizing rites, including
a bath which changed his divine fragrance into the human
odour. However, he and the later *to-manurung*, as well
as their pure-blooded descendants, kept their 'white blood'.
Before a marriage between nobles was contracted, a cut in
one finger had to be made to demonstrate that the blood
which dripped out was really white; as late as the sixteenth
century Portuguese observers reported with awe that such a
marvel had occurred in the case of the Luwu' ruler (Eredia,
'Golden Khersonese': 246]. Nowadays, even those who still
believe in the divine origins of the nobility would acknowledge that by intermarriage with commoners even the highest-
ranking princes have lost the original purity of their white
blood.

Bugis Ranks

From the earliest historical times the only strict constraint on
marriage was that while a man could marry any woman of
equal or inferior status, he could not marry any woman of
superior rank to himself. In a system based on cognatic descent the question then arises: if a 'white-blooded' man marries a 'red-blooded' woman, what will be the rank of their
children? The Bugis have answered this question by establishing a system of ranks based on the idea of blood-blending,
sometimes compared with that of making an alloy between a
noble and a base metal. The situation as described below is
generally accepted by the specialist genealogists (Pelras, 'Hiérarchie et pouvoir').

The highest rank is called *ana' ma'tola*, that is, 'the children'
(*ana'*) able to 'succeed' (*ma'tola*) their parents as rulers of the
highest kingdoms. This level is subdivided into two sub-ranks,
the higher of which is called *ana' seng'eng*. The second highest
rank is that of the *ana' rajéng*, which is also divided into two
sub-ranks. A marriage between a man of any of these ranks
and a woman of a lower grade will produce children of a

Plate 33 The elderly Wajo' princess Andi' Ninnong with her retainers

degree intermediate between those of its parents. Thus, if an *ana' ma'tola* of either sub-rank marries a commoner wife, their children will be *ana' céra'* ('blood children') *siseng* ('of the first degree'). The marriage of a *céra siseng* with a commoner wife will produce a *céra' dua* ('*céra'* of the second degree'); the offspring of the latter and a commoner wife will be *céra' tellu* ('of the third degree'). These three ranks of *ana' céra'* can be considered as constituting the middle nobility. Successive further degrees of matches between the offspring of the lowest of these ranks and commoner wives produce the lower nobility: *ampo cinaga, anakarung ma'dara-dara* and *anang*. Below these come the commoners (*tau sama'*) or freemen (*tau maradéka*); even among these there is still a distinction between those who still count a noble among their ancestors, however far back, and those whose ancestry is exclusively common.

The pyramidal pattern of this system is reminiscent of both the kinship system, with its degrees of cousinhood reckoned from a more or less remote common ancestor, and the system of political organization, with its pyramidal structure of vassalage (discussed in more detail below). It is also clear that kinship links cross divisions between hierarchical ranks: a nobleman with wives of different ranks will have children of different degrees. Besides their wives of equal rank, who bore them children capable of succeeding to their own positions, Bugis rulers used also to marry wives of lower rank who offered the twin advantages of children who could fill relatively senior offices and the support of the influential commoners or lower-ranking noblemen who thus became their fathers-in-law. The latter in turn were attracted to such matches for their daughters by the prospects they offered for their descendants to climb in the social hierarchy. This trend towards intermarriage led to the gradual shrinking of the higher ranks; indeed, in some places the office of *arung* (lord) came to be held by nobles of relatively low rank who took advantage of the position to claim to be of higher degree than they actually were.

Flexibility in an Apparently Rigid System

The description given above of the rank system represents the view of specialists; most laymen have only a partial view of the structure. In order to ascertain someone's rank with absolute precision one would need to know who all his ancestors were since the first recorded *to-manurung*, twenty to twenty-five generations back. This is just not possible with a bilateral kinship system, for each individual's ancestors double in number at each generation. The high nobility, for whom rank is of the utmost importance, only pay real attention to ranks of *céra' tellu* and above. At the other end of the spectrum, most commoners and members of the lower nobility in practice use a much simplified system of classification based on title alone. At the village level, all persons of influence, be they lower noblemen, commoners with just a faint trace of noble ancestry, or complete commoners with some wealth, influence or expert knowledge, are known as *tau décéng* ('excellent people'). Since the 1920s a new title has come into use with the adoption by the Bugis and Makassar nobility at or above the level of *céra' tellu* of the titles 'Andi' and 'Andi' Bau' (only the very highest rank is entitled to use 'Andi' Bau', and even some of these content themselves with 'Andi'), while the lower noble ranks use their 'nobility name' preceded by the title 'Daéng'. Thus most commoners, ignoring the subtleties of hierarchy, distinguish simply between 'Andi' and 'Daéng'. Moreover, there has recently been an 'inflation of titles', with many people tending to use 'Andi' and 'Daéng' who would not be entitled to do so according to customary rules.

Thus the stratification of Bugis society is far from being an ossified system. Emigration can also be a means of gaining rank. Lower noblemen, leading small groups of followers abroad where little cross-checking of ancestry was possible, had a tendency to claim higher birth than that to which their genealogies would have entitled them; and their followers had an interest in backing such claims, since they enhanced the status of the whole group. Economic success, too, can contribute to a rise in status: when a person is wealthy, owns a lot of land and has a large and beautiful house, it is easily assumed that he has some – perhaps forgotten – traces of noble blood in his veins (Lineton, 'Study of the Bugis').

Outward Signs of Rank

The importance of hierarchy in traditional Bugis society was clearly demonstrated by the existence of a number of outward signs by which an individual could assert his rank and from which others would know the appropriate mode of behaviour towards him. These signs included details of clothing and also of architecture. Terms of address were precisely determined according to both rank and age, while there existed certain gestures and body positions to be adopted when sitting and when passing in front of or nearby a noble person, intended to express respect. Weddings, at which status is reaffirmed and passed on to the following generations, were – and remain – the foremost occasion for the manifestation of social rank among the Bugis.

Plate 34 The arrival of a princely bridegroom, under shelter of a state umbrella

The Origins of Social Stratification

Bugis myths of origin stress two interlinked elements: the divine origin of the nobility, and its extremely strong ties with the ancient kingdom of Luwu'. Thus from the beginning an unbreakable bond is affirmed between the sacred, power and wealth. My former hypothesis placed the birth of the Bugis nobility in the period when the historical polities emerged, around the fourteenth century. I took the view that economic changes had provoked an internal social mutation within

Luwu' (Pelras, 'Hiérarchie et pouvoir', 2: 214–16), with influential and newly wealthy individuals acquiring a noble status which had not previously existed and whose distinctive trait, as opposed to ordinary chiefdom, was its sacred character. The leading role of Luwu' would have ensured the spread of that nobility throughout the areas under its control. Now, however, I believe that the social stratification of the Bugis has its roots much further in the past, and that it coincided with the immigration in the first centuries of the Christian era, perhaps from south-east or east Borneo, of groups of migrants, each following its own leader. An alternative hypothesis might be that coastal communities, rather than originating from sizeable groups of migrants, evolved locally under the influence of a small number of merchant-leaders also coming from south-east or east Borneo, whose language and culture they adopted. In either case the result would have been the constitution of communities oriented towards overseas trade and with a different culture. These groups, impelled mainly by economic motives – the control and export of natural products and metallic ores – were better organized than their predecessors, the still scarce population of Austronesian villagers, let alone the remnants of a pre-Austronesian population living in the forests and along the shoreline. Connected as they were to inter-insular commercial networks which extended to Sumatra and the Malay peninsula, whose ports were themselves linked to India and other places around the Indian Ocean, the incomers probably had a richer culture than the existing inhabitants; their religion had already received a smattering of Indic influence, and their priests were the *bissu*. As they spread throughout the area, they progressively assumed a dominant status and imposed their social order and language. Thus they came to constitute an aristocracy, the magnified memory of which was conveyed to following generations much later by the *La Galigo* texts, after a common culture had emerged from the fusion of the respective heritages of the early settlers and the later arrivals, and some interbreeding had occurred in spite of the ideological division between the 'white-blooded' newcomers and the 'red-blooded' earlier settlers.

Similar processes presumably took place, against different backgrounds and in somewhat different conditions, in the

areas peopled by the Makassar, Toraja and Mandar, accounting for the similarities and differences between these groups.
However, for specific reasons – presumably economic factors
deriving from its strategic situation in control of the access
routes to the gold and iron ore of the interior – Luwu' became
the political centre of what we may call an 'early South
Sulawesi civilization', although it had no cities, places like
Ussu', Wotu and Ware' functioning as its cultural centres.

The upheavals that I presume to have occurred around the
fourteenth century were genuinely revolutionary, since they
fundamentally changed the relationship between the 'white-
blooded' and 'red-blooded' elements of society. Despite the
persistence of the myth of an original absolute heterogeneity,
the system which now came into being was based on a social
contract between the nobility, represented by the *to-manurung*, and the commoners, represented by their *matoa*, ex-
pressing their mutual need and regulating their mutual rights
and duties. These new relationships may have been linked to
a new economic context, with a greater emphasis than previously on agriculture, as a result of widespread land clearance and the multiplication of new settlements and peasant
communities at the initiative of commoner leaders. This period was later represented by the chronicles as one of anarchy,
which came to an end when the nobility succeeded in reassum-
ing the leadership of society, albeit under changed conditions.
However, Luwu', as the mythic point of origin of the Bugis
nobility and culture, remained the central point of reference,
and communities without leaders other than commoners even
asked, on their own initiative, for noble leaders to be sent to
them by the still prestigious Luwu' ruler. This interpretation
would account for the belief – still very widespread, although
it conflicts with the *to-manurung* stories – according to which
all Bugis nobility ultimately hails from Luwu'.

Lords, Domains and Kingdoms

Even if the hypothesis advanced above reflects the actual
reality, we cannot be sure that the Bugis ever in fact experienced the form of absolute monarchy depicted in the *La*

Galigo texts. Certainly it did not exist in the political system
experienced by the Bugis between pre-Islamic times and the
final conquest by the Dutch, as summarized by Crawfurd:

The people who speak the Bugis language are, at present, divided
into many small states, and seem never to have been united under
one government. Several of these little states are united into con-
federations for general purposes. Each state is under the government
of its own prince, elected by the chiefs of the tribe from the members
of a family in which the office is hereditary, and women are not
excluded from the choice. The princes so elected form a council,
which must be unanimous for the decision of all matters of common
concern. (Crawfurd, *Descriptive Dictionary*: 74, s.v. 'Bugis')

The Wanua: *Grouping and Internal Structure*

Crawfurd had gained a good grasp of the pyramidal structure
of the prevalent mode of organization. However, although
there were common schemes among the Bugis' individual political systems, they were by no means uniform. A good
example is the kingdom of Wajo', which in the nineteenth
century could be called a confederation of constituent polities
varying in both extent and importance (Crawfurd's 'little
states'). Each of these polities, called *wanua*, a word also
found in Srivijaya as well as in early Java, or sometimes also
a'karungeng, 'a place with an *arung*', had its own institutions,
subdivisions and sometimes even dependencies (*ana' wanua*,
'child *wanua*'), each with its own *arung*. The *wanua* should
not simply be identified with a 'village community'. Each one
was a territorial and political unit; they varied in size,
some being small and consisting of only one settlement,
others including many settlements and several territorial divisions. They were indeed self-governing social units, but their
governing bodies were not of the 'village democracy' type such
as those described, for instance, by Dutch scholars in Bali.

The relationships within the Wajo' confederation, between
the core *wanua* – later to be known as Tosora – and each other
wanua, were defined by written bilateral agreements concluded at various historical junctures (Andaya, 'Treaty Conceptions'). These agreements established the nature of the

Plate 35 The posi' tana *('Navel of the Earth') at the centre of the Kajang domain*

links between Wajo' and each of its vassals, and other *wanua* within the same alliance group, expressed in terms of subjection as of a dependant to a master, attachment as of a retainer to his leader, dependence as of a child on his mother, or alliance as between brothers of equal status or between an elder and a younger sibling. Each *wanua* retained its own jurisprudence (*bicara*) and its own customs (*ade'*), receiving protection and advice from the suzerain in exchange for fulfilment of a number of obligations as stipulated in the agreement, for example tributes in kind, particular named services or the provision of a specified number of armed men in case of war. In joining the Wajo' confederation, each member *wanua* was affiliated to one or three *limpo* or groupings of *wanua*, called Tuwa, Bettempola and Talotenreng. These were supposed to correspond to the original division of the Wajo' nucleus into three parts, each linked with a particular trade: Tuwa with fishing, Bettempola with agriculture and Talotenreng with palm tapping.

The confederation of Wajo' was itself involved in similar relationships with political entities on the same level as itself. In the sixteenth century it joined the pact of the 'Three Summits', with Boné as its elder sibling and Soppéng as its younger; and although political differences and even wars set one member of the trio against another, the relationship was never disavowed, even after Wajo' concluded an alliance of dependence with Goa, to which it remained faithful from the time of islamization to colonization.

The Kingdoms

At the level of the federal or confederal kingdoms, the institutions were similar to those of the smaller polities. In Wajo' the ruler, called Arung Matoa ('chief lord') – always a man – was assisted by a select council, the 'Six Lords', comprising three *ranreng* (regents), who could be men or women, one for each *limpo*, each assisted by one 'standard bearer'. In spite of their modest titles, these six officers held at least as much power as the Arung Matoa himself; together with the Arung Matoa they constituted the supreme ruling council of Wajo'. Each *limpo* had a 'herald' who was charged with transmitting messages from the central authority to the vassal *wanua*; four 'deliberating lords' whose task was to discuss cases of law and custom not solved at the level of the *wanua*; and six other councillors with a solely deliberative function. These forty officials, including the Arung Matoa, were called the 'Forty Lords of Wajo'' and constituted its main governing body, whose likeness to a parliament, combined with the existence of recognized rights conferred on all Wajo' freemen, gave nineteenth-century Wajo' its somewhat exaggerated reputation as an 'aristocratic democracy'.

In Boné, by contrast, a structure originally very similar to that in Wajo' had evolved along much more centralized and authoritarian lines, although the choice of the ruler (Arung Mangkau'-é), as well as that of the chief minister (To-marilaleng) was still made by a body called Arung Pitu (the 'Seven Lords'). The kingdom was also originally a confederation, but although the constitutive *wanua* had kept their own *arung* and internal organization and law, the central authority of the realm had become stronger than in any other Bugis state, with the possible exception of Luwu'. Indeed, upon visiting Boné, James Brooke observed that here

the constitution is a name rather than a reality at present: the country, as far as I observe, being reduced under the despotic sway of the patamankowé (Petta Mangkau'-é). The power of the monarch seems to have no limit: none can approach him on terms of equality, save the Aru matoah of Wajo and the datu of Soping. The authority delegated by him to his minister appears equally arbitrary and the aru [arung] pitu – the great council – is a mere tool in his hands. (Brooke, *Narrative of Events*: 133–4)

Officers, Lords and Rulers

No office in any Bugis kingdom was properly speaking hereditary, although it was not uncommon for a son or daughter to succeed a parent. Many offices were open to women; in the kingdoms of Luwu', Soppéng and Boné, these included the position of supreme ruler. When a post fell vacant, the new occupant was chosen by an ad hoc elective body on the basis of various criteria, including the candidate's ancestry, relationship to the previous occupant, personal qualities, and influence in terms of number and quality of followers, but not necessarily residence. No office, even that of lord or ruler, was conferred for life: the holder could after a variable period of time either retire or be dismissed, and an individual could move from one office to another as well as accumulate offices.

Even if it was somewhat of an exaggeration to speak of Wajo' as an 'aristocratic democracy', it is true that power there was properly speaking neither autocratic nor arbitrary. Brooke writes:

It will strike us that the government of Wajo, though ruled by feudal and arbitrary rajahs, though cumbersome and slow in its movements and defective in the administration of equal justice between man and man, yet possesses many claimes [*sic*] to our admiration, and bears a striking resemblance to the government of feudal times in Europe . . . I regret, however, my being compelled to give many details, which show that their practice is very much at variance with their written laws . . . Our judgement, however, of their faults must be mild, when we consider that, amid all the nations of the East . . . the Bugis alone have arrived at the threshold of recognised rights, and have alone emancipated themselves from the fetters of despotism. (Brooke, *Narrative of Events*: 65–6)

At each level from the common people to the ruler – and not only in Wajo' – mutual rights and duties were defined by the customary law, as written in the *lôntara'* and generally known. One text sets out the following principle: 'Should the decision of the lord be contested, that of the customary council should not be contested; should the decision of the customary council be contested, that of the people's leaders should not be contested; should the decision of the people's leaders be contested, that of the people should not be contested.' The role of the people's leaders was also observed by Brooke:

There is a general council of the people, composed of the heads of villages and all the respectable freemen, who are convened on extraordinary occasions, to state their opinions and discuss important questions, without, however, having the power of arriving at a decision. (Brooke, *Narrative of Events*: 63)

This again shows how the Bugis were always able to mitigate an apparently strictly organized system of government with a significant dose of flexibility and pragmatism. This was true not only of Wajo' but also of other kingdoms: the pyramidal structure linking the *wanua* with the centre by bilateral agreements existed in all Bugis kingdoms, as did intermediate bodies of noble councillors, the rule of election to office and the primacy of customary law. The main difference between kingdoms lay in the will or capacity of the successive rulers to enforce a more authoritarian and centralizing approach. In this respect Boné was the exact opposite of Wajo', which accounts for the mutual incompatibility of the two kingdoms through the centuries.

Clienteles

Alongside the system of social stratification which fixed everyone's status according to their birth, and the system of government which distributed everyone among a number of territorial units, each with its lord or ruler – systems which, by allocating every individual to a permanent subdivision of society, secured a high level of social stability – there also exists among the Bugis a system which has for centuries permitted social mobility, competition between equals, cooperation between social strata and integration into groups, often irrespective of territorial borders. This is the system of patronage and clientship (Pelras, 'Patron–Client'). Although referred to by several authors since the beginning of the nineteenth century (Kooreman, 'Feitelijke toestand'), its existence and importance in all South Sulawesi societies did not receive the scholarly treatment it merited until Chabot's book (Chabot, *Verwantschap*) on kinship, status and gender in Makassar society. More recent studies that deal with Bugis as well as Makassar milieux (Lineton, 'Study of the Bugis'; Hasan Walinono, *Tanété*) have demonstrated the durability of the same pattern in quite different political and historical contexts.

The Basic Pattern of Patron–Client Relationships

In the patron–client system, known from many other societies, including ancient Rome, modern Latin America and other Insulindian groups, leading individuals and their followers are linked to each other by a number of reciprocal duties and rights. In Makassar and Bugis hierarchical societies of precolonial times, every leading nobleman was at the centre of such a network or clientele. When a follower acknowledged a nobleman as his lord, he declared his willingness to comply with the latter's request when summoned, whether this was to go to war, hunting or travelling with him, to work in the lord's ricefields, or to do some kind of domestic service such as providing drinking water or firewood. If the lord organized a celebration, for instance a wedding, his followers would be ready to attend even if they lived some distance away: they took pride in their presence at such prominent occasions which displayed their patron's status and importance. They would contribute money or gifts and/or help with the preparations, and in return would be lodged, fed and entertained. Some of those followers who were still unmarried would voluntarily stay in their patron's house as domestic servants, receiving lodging, food and clothes but no wage. A position of such dependence for those who were very poor was not very far removed from a mild form of slavery, and might have been mistaken for that by casual observers. The big difference lay in the followers' legal status: for in spite of their dependent position, these commoners remained *to-maradéka* (freemen), and thus were always legally free to depart, could not be disposed of at will and enjoyed specific rights according to customary law (Pelras, 'Patron–Client').

The benefits of this relationship to the followers were not insignificant. The patron had to 'show goodness' to his clients, and would protect them; if they were badly treated he would defend them, and if they were offended against he would consider himself offended against likewise, and entitled to take revenge. If a follower suffered the theft of his cattle or horses, the patron would try to recover them and see to it that the thief was punished. Many noblemen took some responsibility for their clients' welfare, supplying them with land, cattle or tools as needed and helping them in cases of either domestic celebration or personal misfortune. If a client's crop failed, he would be provided with rice and other commodities; if he wanted to marry, his patron often organized the wedding and sometimes even looked for a bride or bridegroom from among his own followers. Once married, such a couple would probably live in a house near that of their patron, which made it easy for them to come and help him when needed, despite having their own fields to work.

The Foundations of the Patron–Client System

Several factors in Bugis society may have favoured the emergence of patron–client ties. One is the existence of a bilateral kinship system in which clienteles may to a certain extent represent a substitute for those corporate kinship groups, such as clans or lineages, which exist in societies with unilineal systems. Clienteles are usually reinforced by marriage between members, so that they progressively become indistinguishable from bilateral kin groups. Another contributory factor is the existence of a type of social stratification which permitted the involvement of the nobility in trade and in the redistribution of wealth. Yet another has been the hierarchical relationship existing in historical times between the lowest territorial units and the great kingdoms, and the need for noblemen to gain supporters to enable them to climb the ladder of political office.

The relationship between lord and follower, patron and client, was voluntary in nature and based on only an implicit contract. It could be ended at any time, and unless a client was in debt to his patron he could at any time shift allegiance to another lord. This aspect of the matter struck Western observers with some force. Raffles, for example, remarked:

The Bugis attach themselves to their chiefs principally for their own convenience, but in some cases they have evinced a devoted fidelity. They often change their chief, but scarcely any thing can induce them to betray the chief they have left . . . Their minor associations are held together by all the attachment and warmth which distinguished the clans of North Britain. (Raffles, *History of Java*, appendix F, 'Celebes': CLXXXIII–CLXXXIV)

The lord could also drop his follower if the latter did not meet his obligations. Both sides, however, tried to ensure that the relationship was not terminated in conflict.

If a follower of some rank felt strong enough to stand by himself without any protector, he could disengage himself from his patron and even become the protector of his own followers. For not only the high aristocracy but also the lower nobility, and even rich commoners, had followers. Having many followers enhanced a nobleman's own social status and also that of his kin group; and they constituted an important asset in competition with other nobles for honour, office or wealth. Conversely, the higher the honour or office, or the greater the wealth, attained by the patron, the greater also the pride, advantage and profit accruing to his followers. A patron who wanted to retain the loyalty of his followers and increase their number had to perform his role well and give them the maximum security, otherwise they would desert him.

In former times there were three main ways of acquiring followers. The first was by a kind of inheritance: on the death of their patron, followers would sometimes transfer their loyalty to one of his children, but this process was far from automatic. The second was to attract clients by personal charisma. In both cases three factors were important: the patron's rank, the political office he held, and his personality. The higher an individual's rank or office, the better his chances of attracting followers, so long as this status was supported by the personal qualities expected of a good leader: courage, eloquence, willingness to take the initiative, the ability to raise the morale of followers and, above all, personal sympathy. The third way of attracting followers was through marriage: alongside rank and degree of kinship, a factor in the choice of a bride for a nobleman was the degree of influence wielded by her father or brothers over a more or less large number of followers, who would then become indirectly her husband's followers. This was one particular reason why high-ranking noblemen, besides marrying a wife of equal rank who would bear them children to succeed them, also took wives of lower rank through whose fathers or brothers they could extend their influence to groups or areas hitherto beyond their reach.

Patronage and Clientship as Political Tools

As political offices in the Bugis system were not absolutely hereditary, and the only prerequisites for succession were rank and membership of a loose descent group stemming from a sometimes very remote common ancestor, the choice from among a group of candidates with more or less the same claims to a post was to a large extent based on the number and influence of their followers. A distinction has to be made here between two kinds of followers: commoners, who were directly at the service of a noble patron and could, for instance, serve under arms, and noble followers, perhaps better termed supporters, who themselves had followers, and through whom a kind of pyramidal structure could be formed, with several groups of followers united through their respective individual leaders under a common higher patron, and so on up the scale.

There are clear testimonies to the fact such a system was at the root of the immense influence possessed by such leaders as the famous Arung Palakka in the seventeenth century. Another example is the role played in Malaya and elsewhere in the eighteenth century by exiled Bugis chiefs and their groups of followers, so important in the changes that occurred in the Malay sultanates. The same system seems to have functioned, too, at the very beginning of the historical period, in those *wanua* whose foundation is credited to leaders who came from elsewhere at the head of small groups of retainers in search of new opportunities and virgin lands, and who, as a result of both their personal charisma and economic success, then attracted new settlers who also put themselves under their leadership. Such processes may have already been established when the ancestors of the present-day South Sulawesi peoples came from overseas to settle the lower course of the Saddang river. It is therefore somewhat puzzling to note that nothing of the kind seems to be described in the *La Galigo* texts. This may perhaps be explained on ideological grounds: in the *La Galigo* system, princes have to be obeyed by virtue of their divine blood, and not because of their individual qualities.

Economic Aspects of the Patron–Client Relationship

Although pride and power were prominent aspects of the patronage relationship, economic factors were no less important. As clearly shown by Lineton ('Study of the Bugis'), one of the main tasks of the traditional leaders was that of the redistribution of wealth. As late as the early 1950s, just before the traditional system of political organization in South Sulawesi was abolished, this role still underlay economic exchanges whereby goods received by members of the nobility, either as an income linked to offices they held or on the occasion of particular celebrations, were either immediately redistributed or put into store to be distributed later as needed. This kind of economic 'pumping' was particularly efficient in the heyday of the old South Sulawesi kingdoms when rulers added to the incomes they derived from agriculture those from inter-insular trade.

There was also a link between political power and control over (which does not necessarily imply ownership of) land. Despite a few exceptions, the Bugis nobility was not primarily a landed class. Its wealth came from collective access to political offices to which specific sources of income were attached: these included the products of certain lands, forest tracts and fisheries; percentages of the yields of other lands; and taxes on crops, markets and gambling, and goods entering harbours (Pelras, 'Patron–Client').

The burden on high-ranking noble families as a result of this system was quite heavy. They had to support in their houses a large number of people, including slaves, servants, dependent followers, pages, ladies-in-waiting, and kinsfolk either close or distant, all of whom had to be provided with food and sometimes clothes. Noble leaders also had to take care of those of their relatives who had lower incomes than themselves: the non-ruling noble ones who did not bring in enough to support their own followers decently, and the non-noble ones whom they would be ashamed to see in poverty. And of course they had to help their own needy dependants, be they poor commoners with little land or true slaves owning nothing – though even slaves could own land and other property, for the situation of 'slaves' among the Bugis, and more generally among south-east Asian peoples, was very different from that prevailing in Mediterranean antiquity or later among the African Americans in North American or the West Indies. Their status was indeed one of complete dependency, but in general they were subjected to neither hard labour nor corporal punishment; indeed, their position was hardly distinguishable in practice from that of other dependants, except for the fact that they were bound for life to their masters, who had the right to sell them and their children. But he also had to take care of them, and often would provide them with a house and some land.

8

Spiritual and Mental Life

Religion and Ritual

Religion is a vital element in the identity of any people. For the
Bugis, the passage from paganism to Islam was a determining
event. Their compatriots usually consider them, together with
the Acehnese, the Malays, the Banjar, the Sundanese, the
Madurese and of course the Makassar, as among the most
islamized of Indonesian peoples. Indeed, with the exception of
the relatively small group of pagan To-Lotang, probably not
numbering much over 20,000, whose main centre has since
the seventeenth century been Amparita in Sidénréng, and a
few hundreds of Bugis Christians, all Bugis strongly assert
their adherence to Islam. Alongside the sense of brotherhood
which links any Muslim to any other Muslim, they also have
a special sense of community with the other South Sulawesi
Mulsims among the Makassar, Mandar and Ma'sénrémpulu'
peoples, which may account for the increasing consciousness
of a supra-ethnic 'Bugis–Makassar' entity.

In reality, of course, the situation is much more complex
than this. Certainly Islam is omnipresent, in Muslim practice,
Muslim names and a growing number of mosques and Islamic
schools and other institutions. However, no one who has
prolonged contact with the various Bugis communities in
South Sulawesi could fail to notice, in both rural and urban,
aristocratic and popular milieux, the astonishing survival of
elements of pre-Islamic religion, manifested in popular rituals,
beliefs in pre-Islamic myths, the worshipping of regalia and

sacred places, and the active role still played by a number of the pagan transvestite priests, the *bissu* – all of which are radically incompatible with Islam.

Syncretic and Orthodox Islam

Two conflicting trends seem to have been present from the beginning in the process which led to the acceptance of Islam by the South Sulawesi elite: that tending towards orthodox Islam, probably stronger among traders and navigators, and that prevailing for the most part among the higher nobility and admitting a greater or lesser degree of syncretism. This dichotomy must not, however, be seen as a clear-cut opposition. From the outset a few aristocrats followed Islam to the letter, for example La Ma'daremmeng, the seventeenth-century Boné ruler who decided to apply the *shari'a* literally, forbidding superstitious practices, expelling the *bissu* and liberating the slaves. He was a *sufi* and a number of his writings are still in circulation among Bugis Muslim scholars. Indeed, the role of sufism and of the mystic brotherhoods in the establishment of Islam in South Sulawesi must not be underrated. Another good example is that of the famous Shaykh Yusuf, who was related to the ruling family of Goa. In 1645, at the age of nineteen, he left Makassar for Mecca and en route studied first in Aceh with the famous *sufi* master Nuruddin ar-Raniri, then in Yemen with two other masters. After spending some time in Mecca, again studying mysticism, he went to Damascus, where he was initiated into the Khalwatiyah order. On his return from the Holy Land around 1678 he is said to have been very much shocked by the poor state of Islamic observance in South Sulawesi, with gambling, palm-beer drinking, opium smoking and pagan cults still going on, freely tolerated by Muslim rulers. His attempts to suppress these practices were strongly opposed by the nobility, who still strongly held that kind of syncretism that left the previous traditional social order intact as far as possible. After a time Yusuf left Makassar for Banten in west Java, but via one of his disciples managed to introduce the Khalwatiyah order into South Sulawesi, which initially deliberately concentrated its proselytizing activity on aristocratic circles (Bruinessen, 'Khalwatiyya').

After islamization, South Sulawesi's connections with other parts of insular south-east Asia underwent further development, and it came to be increasingly involved in an intricate network of commercial, political and intellectual relationships with other Muslim kingdoms such as Aceh, Malaka, Sulu, Brunei, Banjarmasin, Banten, Buton and Ternaté. It also established links with other Asian countries, including Muslim states in India and the Middle East, and, of course, with Mecca, where some of its young men went to pursue their religious studies, returning as learned *ulama* to teach their compatriots. Consequently, the movement of ideas at work in the wider contemporary Muslim world sooner or later made its mark here too.

In the eighteenth century a new development in Islam in South Sulawesi was marked by the composition by an unknown Bugis writer of the *Book of Budi Istiharat Indra Bustanil Arifin*. Inspired by a Malayan – Indo-Persian tradition, this text was strongly akin to, if indeed not adapted from, the *Mahkota Segala Raja* (Malay) or *Taju's-Salatin* (Arabic) ('The Crown of the Princes'), written in Aceh in the previous century by Shaykh Bukhari of Johor. This and similar texts may have represented an attempt to replace the pagan myth of the descent of the rulers from heaven on which aristocratic power had formerly rested by an Islamic-based ideology in which the rulers appeared as the chosen representatives and instruments of God on Earth. That ideology was not new in the Malay world: the medieval Islamic idea of the ruler as the 'Shadow of God', influenced by Persian thought, had been one of the founding concepts of those Malay sultanates with which South Sulawesi aristocrats had been connected for centuries (Milner, 'Malay Kingship').

Islamic Law (sara') *and Customary Law* (ade')

In Bugis legal and historical texts alike, the concept of *ade'* (Malay *adat*) is central. In texts concerning pre-Islamic times, or in the wording of social contracts or treaties purported to originate in these ancient times, it has replaced older terms. Traditional Bugis society has been expressly based on *pang'ade'reng*, that is, '*adat*-hood', a corpus of interlinked ruling principles which, besides *ade'* proper, includes also *bicara* (jurisprudence), *rapang* (models of good behaviour which ensure the proper functioning of society), *wari'* (rules of descent and hierarchy) and *sara'* (Islamic law and institutions, from the Arabic *shari'a* (Mattulada, 'Kebudayaan Bugis Makassar': 275–7; *La Toa*).

The religious officials or 'instruments of the *sara*'' occupied the same footing in relation to the ruler as the civil officials. The *kali* (Arabic *kadhi*) was the chief religious official and counsellor to the ruler in the field of religious affairs. He presided over the enforcement of the *sara'* and intervened when there was need to resort to this code rather than to the provisions of customary law. His most specific field of competence was that of marriage, divorce and inheritance, as provided for according to the Islamic law. The *âmélé* was specifically in charge of collecting the alms laid down in law (*zakat fitrah*); he also represented the ruler at the main mosque of the *wanua* or kingdom.

Each parish community linked to a mosque was, and still is, provided with a set of officials each charged with specific duties. The main figure is the *imang* (Arabic *imam*), who is not a priest but a person chosen by the community to lead the communal prayers. He is usually well versed in religious knowledge and is often also the master of a locally established informal religious school (*ang'ajing*). Alongside him there is also a *katté* (Arabic *khatib*), who delivers the sermon at Friday prayers; he too is often a teacher of religion. Other mosque officials include one or two muezzins, here called *bîdala'* or *bîlala'*. Finally, there is the *doja*, who is in charge of maintaining the mosque and keeping it tidy, and for seeing that water is always available for the ritual ablutions.

These religious officials derived their income – as did the civil officials – from the yield of a number of ricefields tied to their posts and from various taxes or gifts, received for example on the occasion of a marriage or at the resolution of a legal case. They also received a percentage of the *zakat fitrah*. All were respected members of the community, often invited to family events where they would be expected to say prayers or to deliver the public reading, in Arabic, of the Book of Barzanji, which throughout Indonesia is one of the most popular narratives of the birth and life of the Prophet.

Islamic Practice in Traditional Bugis Society

On the face of it, the practice of Islam in South Sulawesi does not differ much from that which prevails in other parts of the archipelago. The people are all followers of *sunni* Islam and observe the prescriptions of the *shafi'i* rite while countenancing local customs in so far as they do not contradict the basic tenets of Islam. Until the nineteenth century mosques existed only at the level of political units (*wanua, a'karungeng*); at lower levels there were only *lânggara'*, small houses of prayer fit only for the daily observances, not for the solemn Friday assembly. Their number has considerably increased in the

Plate 36   The open air prayer of 'Idu'l Adha *celebration*

Plate 37   Pilgrims at a sacred grave in Soppéng

twentieth century, and nowadays there are also mosques in each settlement or neighbourhood. According to Islamic law, attendance at the mosque for Friday prayers is mandatory only for men, but women may also attend; those who do stay behind the men. A few, usually elderly, women do attend even on ordinary days (i.e. not on Fridays or special celebrations), especially for evening (*maghrib*) prayers. Women are usually present in larger numbers for the optional evening prayers of *tarawih* which take place at the mosque each night of the fasting month of Ramadan, and for the solemn *'id* prayers on the closing day of Ramadan (*'Idu'l-fitri*) and on the day commemorating Nabi Ibrahim's (Abraham's) sacrifice (*'Idu'l-adha*). On both these occasions people sacrifice fowls or goats, prepare the most exquisite possible food and delicacies and entertain each other all day long, visiting and receiving family members, friends and acquaintances to ask each other's forgiveness for any past offence; they also visit cemeteries and pray for their dead.

Another Muslim festival much celebrated in South Sulawesi is the commemoration of Nabi Muhammad's birth (*Maudu'*; Arabic *mawlud*). Although a specific date is allocated for this feast (the twelfth of the month of *rabi'u'l awwal*), the commemoration may be organized for any day of that month. The celebration usually takes place at the mosque, which is decorated in quite a festive way with painted eggs decorated with cut paper hanging from banana stems stuck with palm ribs. Those attending listen to sermons and sung excerpts from the Book of Barzanji and sing praises in honour of the Prophet.

The first day of the month of *muharram* (the first day of the Muslim year) is not celebrated: it is even considered an unlucky day, on which people avoid going too far from their homes. However, the tenth of that same month (*sura*; Arabic *ashura*), which commemorates, among other occasions, the exit of Noah from the Ark and the deaths of the Prophet's grandchildren Hassan and Hussein, is usually marked by the consumption of a ritual dish, called 'porridge of seven kinds' because it must include seven ingredients, which is first presented in offering to the ancestors of the family and then shared by all the household. On this day, too, people visit cemeteries. Another calendar rite, the 'Safar bath', takes place on the last Wednesday of the month of *safar*. This is a ritual bath of purification performed by certain people – members of a mystic order, disciples of a particular master, or regular patients of a healer – under the guidance of their master, who prays over the water or immerses in it pieces of paper bearing formulae in Arabic, ensuring that the bathers will be protected by that water from any calamity during the year to come. This practice, which is considered by many to depart from orthodox Islam, is of *sufi* origin.

Religious Instruction

Traditional religious instruction begins at the age of about five or six years, when the children, boys and girls alike, are entrusted to a teacher, who may be a man or a woman, who receives them at his or her home daily for one or two hours to each them the rudiments of daily religious practice and to

Plate 38 Learning how to read the Qur'an

train them in reading aloud the *surats* of the Qur'an. They begin not with the complete Qur'an but with a volume called the 'small Qur'an' which includes only one-thirtieth of the complete work. When they have learnt how to read it they change to the full version. Each stage in the study of the Qur'an may be marked by a small celebration which includes a feast meal of fowl, glutinous rice and various accompaniments, eaten at the house of the teacher or *guru* after he has recited a prayer and symbolically fed the pupil. The completion of this first stage of Islamic education is marked by a further celebration called *ma'panré temme'*, 'to have [the pupil] eat [the Qur'an] until it is finished', which is an occasion for the family to gather at the pupil's parents' house to see him or her demonstrate his or her newly acquired ability, and to feast together. Sometimes this celebration is postponed until the pupil's marriage, when it takes place on the eve of the wedding.

Those boys and girls who are to take their religious education further are usually sent to 'study the religious books' in a more or less prestigious school (*ang'ajing*) of the same type as those known in Java as *pesantrèn* or in Sumatra as *pondok*. The youngest students (*santari*) begin with the study of Arabic grammar and syntax and the elements of Islamic law; then they begin deeper studies in the various aspects of Islam such as law, theology or exegesis of the Qur'an. At a higher level, some of them are introduced to mysticism. The method followed is the successive study of selected books written by renowned *ulama* of the past, most of them in Arabic but some in Malay or Indonesian and some even in Bugis. These are read and commented on collectively under the guidance of either the master himself or one of his assistants, often a member of his family. When the students feel that they have learned enough with a particular master, they can move to

Plate 39   Master and disciples

another one or to another school in search of a different kind
or higher level of learning. During their stay at a particular
school, the students live in small huts that they have built themselves and do their own washing and cooking, having brought
rice and other ingredients from their homes. They may also tend
gardens, either for themselves or for the master. By the end of the
nineteenth century the most renowned South Sulawesi *ulama*
appear to have been centred around Maros and Pangkajé'né'
(including Salémo island), as well as around Rappang.

Islam and Pre-Islamic Traditions

Despite the deep and long-standing penetration of Islam in
South Sulawesi, a considerable degree of syncretism has prevailed among many traditionally minded Bugis. Two kinds
can be distinguished, which may be called 'esoteric syncretism'
and 'practical syncretism'. Esoteric syncretism involves teachings dating from the beginnings of islamization which have
since been passed on through esoteric texts by adepts among
the Luwu' nobility, sometimes associated with the sacred sites
of Ussu' or the To-Lotang Bénténg of Amparita. There are
also a number of esoteric texts, considered by those who know
them to be highly sacred, which aim at reconciling Islamic
mystic teachings with pre-Islamic Bugis cosmology and theo-
gony. However, few adepts were introduced to these manuscripts, which could not be read without prior rites and
sacrifices being conducted.

In one of these texts, Sawérigading is presented as 'the
foremost and the ultimate' prophet, designations which in
Islam should apply to the Prophet Muhammad alone. At the
last meeting in Luwu' of the main protagonists of the *La
Galigo* cycle, the news is broadcast that Heaven and the Abyss
have to be emptied because the Holy Book (*al-Furqan*, the
Qur'an) is to be sent down to Earth and humankind given
the *shahada* (the Muslim profession of faith). In accordance
with the will of the One Lord, Batara Guru and the other
heavenly beings will move towards the rising sun; Sawérigading and all the other beings living in the Abyss will move
towards the setting sun. From then on, only angels and genies

will inhabit Heaven and the Abyss, and humans will no longer
be permitted to worship Patoto' and Palingé'. God alone will
dwell in the highest. Later, Sawérigading's soul will be sent to
Mecca and 'introduced into a pure womb' to be reborn there.
This assimilation of the Bugis mythical hero to the Prophet
Muhammad, obviously unacceptable in orthodox Islam, seems
however to have been quite popular among the Bugis.

Practical syncretism, in spite of declared opposition from the
defenders of orthodoxy, remains widespread and openly practised all over South Sulawesi. However, it lacks precise formulations: one can only infer its underlying concepts by
observing the various manifestations of what can be called
Bugis 'practical religion' in most of the rites of passage and in
rituals to do with agriculture, houses, boats and fishing, as
well as in healing rituals. These practices imply, not always
very consciously, a basically un-Islamic appeal to 'spiritual'
entities (*to-âlusu'*) or 'invisible' entities (*to-tenrita*) which act
as intermediaries with God; some people identify them with
the *déwata* or divinities of old, while others prefer to view
them as *jinn* (genies) or *mala'ika* (angels): belief in genies and
angels, but not, of course, their worship, is part of orthodox
Islam. Only faint traces remain of the worship of ancestors
which must have been general before islamization, but pilgrimage to the graves of particular individuals is still quite
common; be they the mythical founders of dynasties, historical heroes, Muslim saints or local miracle-workers, they are
all considered as intermediaries with God in the same way as
purely spiritual entities.

Some traditional Bugis houses still have in their attics structures in the shape of miniature houses or beds, complete with
small mattresses, pillows and bed-curtains; these are provided
as temporary residences for spiritual beings who are summoned on the occasion of certain rites and to whom offerings
are brought. In traditional houses, too, the main post of the
house and the post supporting the front staircase are considered to be the permanent places of residence of its spirit
guardians. Outside the house, other places where offerings are
made include the seashore, river banks and certain boulders,
trees, cliffs or hilltops which are known either as the habitations of spiritual beings or as points of access to Heaven or the

Plate 40   A tabernacle for spirits in an attic

Abyss. Also important in this respect are the sacred graves of important figures of the past; indeed, a number of ancient sacred places have been turned into bogus graves, thus permitting those people who wish to maintain at least formal respect for Muslim orthodoxy to visit in pilgrimage without appearing to be indulging in spirit worship.

Some Bugis Muslims who regularly attend the mosque, however, indulge in these practices without any pretence or indeed any misgivings. When asked, they acknowledge their faith in the One Almighty God and would deny that they 'give Him seconds', as the more orthodox Muslims allege, by making offerings to other spiritual beings; they say only that, God being spiritual and far away from humankind, it is easier to reach Him through the aid of other spiritual creatures or the souls of certain deceased people. Moreover, they say, by doing so they are merely continuing what their forefathers, from whom they inherited their religion, had been doing for centuries before them; so they do not bother theorizing much about it.

Practical Religion: Rituals and Representations

One might define practical religion as the religion of the non-theologian. In the case of the Bugis, it is the religion of neither the *bissu* nor the *ulama*, although it partakes somewhat of both, as well as of a far older Austronesian heritage. Far from being confined to rural areas, to the peasantry, the poor, the illiterate or the lower-class, its manifestations are to be seen also in middle-sized or large cities and among the middle-class, the wealthy and the educated, with particular variants in evidence among the higher aristocracy.

As embodiments of practical religion, Bugis rituals are a mixture of pre-Islamic and Islamic elements which vary widely in their respective proportions from one case to another, since there is no pre-established canon: each *sanro* (officiant or regular ritual practitioner) or private individual performing a rite follows rules whose detail is defined by him or her alone; the idiosyncrasies of individual practice may be in part inherited from a master, in part innovations which are seen not as inventions but as resulting from a revelation, often received through a dream, and which are usually only variations on a common scheme. According to a view widespread among the Bugis, the main difference between traditional Bugis rites and Islamic rites is that the former address the divinity through offerings and the latter through prayers; these are seen as two techniques which can be used concurrently to obtain the same results.

The *sanro*, similar to the Javanese *dukun* or the Malay *pawang* or *bomoh*, usually specialize in certain areas. For example, the *sanro wanua* are in charge of the rituals for the territorial community, especially collective agricultural rites; the *sanro bola* are in charge of the rituals connected with the

Plate 41   Ritual for a new-born baby

construction and protection of houses; the *sanro ana'* are in charge of the rites of passage of children, from pregnancy to after the birth; and the *sanro pa 'bura* are in charge of healing and protective rituals. However, the specialists in marriage rituals, who act as 'wedding mothers', be they women or transvestites, are not called *sanro*; nor are those members of the family or friends who have the necessary knowledge to perform other rituals, for example those of a domestic or individual agricultural kind. Ritual conservatism is probably at its strongest among the Bugis in respect of the rites of passage which mark important steps in the life cycle, especially before and after birth. Although the Bugis do not theorize much about their rituals, the main idea underlying these particular practices seems to be that of conserving and strengthening the personal *sumange'*, the individual's vital energy (Errington, *Meaning and Power*: 51–7).

Full offerings essentially consist of a meal dedicated to spiritual entities, generally not deities but local figures or guardian spirits – with the notable exception, in agricultural rituals, of Sangiang Serri, the rice deity. These entities are deemed to consume the spiritual essence of the meal before the human participants consume its material substance. This ritual meal normally includes dishes of glutinous rice of four colours (white, red, yellow, black), symbols of the cosmic totality,[1] regularly accompanied by dishes of chicken, fish and shrimps, prepared according to age-old recipes; to these, specific varieties of bananas and unboiled water, or alternatively coconut water, are added. Offerings to spiritual entities of the world above should be taken to high cliffs or hilltops; however, the attic may be used as a symbolic substitute for these places, where the offerings are laid near either the front gable or the domestic tabernacle. If the house has no attic, the offerings can be put on top of a cupboard. Offerings to spiritual entities of the world beneath should be made at the water's edge – either the seashore, the edge of a pond, or a river bank – but this location too can be symbolically represented by a basin full of water (Pelras, 'Rituel populaire'). As in other Insulindian cultures, the world above (*Langi'*, the Heavens) seems to have been associated with mountains, upstream, the coconut, the sun, hornbill birds and male beings; offerings to its entities must include boiled eggs. The world beneath (*Buri' Liu*, the Abyss) seems conversely to be associated with the sea, downstream, the areca nut, the moon, crocodiles, lizards and female beings; offerings to its entities must include raw eggs.

In the course of fully fledged offering rituals (Pelras, 'Rituel populaire'), the attention of the spiritual entities is usually attracted by the burning of incense if they are from the world above, by a libation of fragrant oil or by dipping an iron blade into water if they are from the world beneath. They are then called to the meal by the scattering of puffed rice, thought to be their preferred delicacy, or puffed maize. When they are deemed to be present, cymbals or iron or bamboo noise-

---

[1] According to the traditional Bugis view, everything complete consists of four parts or elements: not only the world, but also the human body, the house, the boat, etc. The four colours represent completeness as a four-part whole. Sometimes each colour is linked with a particular element of the world, the body, etc., but opinions differ on which colour represents which element.

makers are sounded while candlenut candles are lit; the officiant, having smeared his or her fingers with fragrant oil, then presents a pinch of each kind of food to the spiritual guest, closing the meal by spilling some water as a final drink. This ritual meal is usually followed by a common thanksgiving meal, the participants in which share the left-overs of the spirits. Food offerings may be followed by betel offerings; in former times betel was presented as a means of honouring distinguished guests.

Betel juice is also used in healing or protective rituals. The officiant chews the betel, then squirts reddened saliva from his or her mouth on to the person for whom the ritual is performed, or smears it on to particular parts of the body, such as the fontanelle, the forehead, the temples, the hollows of both shoulders, the pit of the stomach, the navel or the thighs. Smearing with blood (*ma'céra'*) taken either from a cut in the crest of a live chicken or from a sacrificed animal is another rite regularly performed on either persons or objects which are to fulfil a sacred function. As with the smearing with betel juice, it seems to be a means of infusing or increasing the object with vital energy (*sumange'*); by contrast, smearing with fragrant oil is designed to protect against exposure to an excess of the same vital energy when dealing with spiritual beings. Another common basic rite is sprinkling with lustral water made by soaking ritual leaves, betel, betel nut, a whole egg, and various other ingredients. The bunch of ritual leaves used as a sprinkler must always include leaves of the *Cordyline fruticosa*, a shrub used for ritual purposes all over insular south-east Asia and the Pacific.

Even though the rites described above are of pre-Islamic origin, a few mutual influences with Islamic rites may be observed. For example, animal sacrifices are always performed in the Islamic manner by cutting the victim's throat after the uttering of the *bismillah*; complete food offerings often include a cone of white glutinous rice intended for the Prophet Muhammad; Muslim prayers are recited before thanksgiving meals, and incense is burned before public readings of Islamic works. Thanksgiving meals can in fact vary widely from one household to another according to the respective proportions of pre-Islamic and Islamic elements they display. Some, mainly featuring offerings such as those described above, with a menu of age-old Bugis dishes, are not very different from similar celebrations among the pagan To-Lotang; others, beginning with a reading from the Book of Barzanji and the recitation of a thanksgiving prayer, and including goat curry on the menu, are reminiscent of the purely Muslim Malay *kenduri*. A whole range of practice may be observed between the two extremes.

Most Bugis popular rites not of a purely Islamic nature are accompanied by the recitation of formulae which, in contrast to the hymns and prayers of the *bissu*, are not uttered aloud but repeated silently. Those which have been collected by local researchers, or which can be seen in Bugis manuscripts or heard in oral stories, usually display the presence, alongside age-old formulations and a few names of Sanskrit origin, of quite a few Muslim elements. As the Book of Barzanji was written in the eighteenth century (Kaptein, '*Berdiri Mawlid*': 126–7), it must have been in the late eighteenth or nineteenth century that these readings supplanted readings from the *La Galigo* texts, which still occur in traditional areas of Wajo', Boné and Soppéng but not, to my knowledge, any longer as part of complex rituals.

Mentalities and Norms

The mentality of the Bugis may be interpreted from the outsider's or the insider's viewpoint. Outside observers have, of course, propagated many, often contradictory, stereotypes, which may yet contain elements of reality, as the following examples show.

The Buggesses [*sic*] in general are a high-spirited people: they will not bear ill-usage . . . The Bold Buggess . . . deserve the character given of the Malays in general by Monsieur Poivre . . . fond of adventures, emigration, and capable of undertaking the most dangerous entreprizes. (Forrest, *Voyage from Calcutta*: 76–8)

They are said to be revengeful; but during the period of British government at Makasar, few, if any examples occurred to support such an assertion. Certain it is, that in no single instance, was the death of those who fell in a recent war between the two parties, avenged by their relations . . . Agreements once entered into are invariably observed, and a Bugis is never known to swerve from his bargain . . . On the other hand, they are throughout notorious thieves, and scarcely consider murder as a crime. (Raffles, *History of Java*, appendix F, 'Celebes')

The insider's view is, as might be expected, more complex, but nonetheless not free from its own stereotypes. How the Bugis themselves say a Bugis should behave, how they judge actual behaviour, and how they behave themselves, by no means always coincide.

The Recommendations of the Ancient Sages

Literary works of many kinds contain recommendations on good conduct. In verse, for example, there are the *élong to-matoa*, 'couplets for the old', and the *élong to-panrita*, 'couplets for *ulama*', which remain part of the chanted repertoire of the Bugis bards up to the present; and in prose, collections of instructions (*pa'paseng*), edifying stories with a religious (Muslim) theme and didactic works such as the *Budi Istihara* and the *La Toa*. The latter is a book of instructions for the prince's good conduct, the existence of many copies attesting to its great influence throughout the Bugis country in the past (Mattulada, *La Toa*). These works are still much praised and very often cited in sermons and the speeches delivered at weddings and on other social occasions. Literati or traditionally minded individuals also like to compose their own anthologies by copying from one another's manuscripts; one such an anthology of wise sayings by the sages of old features among the few Bugis books printed since the 1960s (Hasan Machmud, *Silasa*). The following are a few examples of the shorter formulae taken from this work, cited under the headings by which the editor has classified them.

On inner passions: 'To follow one's inner passions is like boarding a leaky boat.'
On uprightness: 'Uprightness is of four kinds: forgiving when one has been harmed; being firm in one's words; not being greedy for what belongs to others; not reneging on one's promises.'

On enterprise: 'If you want to catch an animal, follow its tracks; if you want to be successful, look where people's footprints are thickest.'
On man and woman: 'O woman, enclose yourself in your honour; O man, enclose yourself in your self-control.'
On social duties: 'Setting upright what is fallen down from each other; taking ashore what is adrift from each other; pulling each other uphill, not downhill; correcting each other when faulty, until successful.'
On honour [siri'] *and courage*: 'Two or three who had furiously fought died; later, the one who had remained quiet also died. If you fight furiously you die; if you don't fight furiously you die too. Better die in furious fight.'
On cautiousness: 'Don't use a single thread as a bridge.'
On wisdom: 'The signs of a wise man: he can follow and understand discussions; he can reply and convince; he knows how to speak precisely and in an orderly fashion; he acts reasonably.'
On greed: 'Greedy in the beginning, selfish in between, everything lost in the end.'
On good conduct: 'Three kinds of good in this world: avoiding doing bad actions, avoiding uttering bad words, avoiding having bad thoughts.'
On gratitude: 'Remember two things, forget two things: remember the good that others have done to you, in order to be grateful, and the evil that you have done to others, in order to repair it; forget the good that you have done to others, in order not to ask for thanks, and the evil that others have done to you, in order not to seek revenge.'
On a few good things: 'There are four good things which are really good: giving your love to people who never gave theirs to you; giving without being asked for and without awaiting thanks; helping people in difficulty as much as possible; having your sound advice reach their heart of hearts.'
On a few bad things: 'To eat like a sparrow and to shit like a buffalo.'

The title of this anthology, *Silasa*, which means 'fitting' or 'harmonious', and most of the sayings it records, clearly refer to an ideal society in which solidarity, justice, honesty and wisdom are the foundations of social relations among equals. The book of *La Toa*, on the other hand, describes how things should be – how rulers should behave towards people, and how the people should behave among themselves – in a state based on *ade'* (custom), *rapang* (civil law), *wari'* (the rules of inherited hierarchy), *bicara* (the deliberations of knowledgeable persons, constructing jurisprudence) and *sara'* (Islamic law). 'Custom', says the *La Toa*, 'basically consists in bringing harmony; deliberation, in bringing mutual improvements and mutual respect; civil law, in bringing equity; and the rules of inherited hierarchy, in knowing differences' (Hamid Abdullah, *Manusia Bugis-Makassar*: 24).

Valued Feelings: Siri' *and* Pessé'

As well as giving advice on good social conduct, many Bugis sayings praise types of behaviour which seem to contradict these precepts and which are based on *siri'*, that is, the sense of honour and shame. According to Hamid Abdullah,

In the life of the Bugis-Makassar people, the most basic element is *siri'*. For them, no other value merits to be more defended and preserved. *Siri'* is their life, their self-respect and their dignity. This is why, in order to uphold and to defend it when it has been stained or they consider it has been stained by somebody, the Bugis Makassar people are ready to sacrifice everything, including their most precious life, for the sake of its restoring. So says the saying . . . 'When one's honour is at stake, without any afterthought one fights.' (Hamid Abdullah, *Manusia Bugis-Makasar*: 37)

A matter in which *siri'* plays a most conspicuous role is marriage. If a marriage proposal is rejected, the suitor may feel offended ('his honour is dead') and resort to elopement (*silariang*) as a result. For the girl's family this is an even worse offence, and any male relation of hers will feel justified in killing the culprit in order to restore the family's honour, in the absence of a formal reconciliation only reached by long and difficult negotiation between the two families. Such situations can of course lead to real vendettas, lasting over generations. If the girl did not go with the young man willingly but was forced into the elopement, no reconciliation is possible: not only the suitor but all his male relatives are considered to have committed the offence, and all may be killed without compunction. This is not just theory: many such cases come before the courts in South Sulawesi every year; many people are willing to incur fairly harsh punishments where their *siri'* is at stake.

Similar results may follow when someone has been shamed by words or actions he considers improper, even though to an outsider they may seem trivial. The person's family, followers or retainers may also feel offended and act accordingly. In extreme cases the offended individual may run amok, killing anyone, even if they are completely unconcerned in the cause, who is unlucky enough to come across his path, and finally being killed himself – but dying satisfied that he has re-established his honour.

It is in fact a duty for a man to defend the honour of his relatives, especially of the women; for the members of a social group to defend the honour of their leader; and for a leader to defend the honour of his followers. Should someone fail to fulfil this duty, he would be considered a coward, without honour, and would forfeit any esteem from society. His only option would be to move to another place where he was unknown. On the other hand, exile and emigration, if resorted to immediately after someone has been shamed, may be an appropriate response when revenge would conflict with other social demands. *Siri'* is thus not based solely on individual, spontaneous feelings; it is much more a group feeling and a token of group solidarity. It can accordingly be considered an important motive force in Bugis social life and can be an incentive for social achievements. This is why many Bugis intellectuals tend to praise *siri'* as a virtue, and condemn only what they say are its mistaken extremes, insisting that *siri'* must, and usually does, go hand in hand with *pessé*.

Pessé, or in its complete form *pessé babua*, 'to feel pain [for somebody else] in one's stomach', indicates a deep feeling of compassion for one's neighbour, relative or fellow member of a social group; it signifies solidarity, not only with someone who has been shamed, but with anyone in the group who is in need, sorrowing, or suffering misfortune or serious illness. *Pessé* has of course to do with identity: mutual *pessé* is a token of common membership of the same group. This can include ethnic identity, especially for people such as navigators or migrants who live in contact with other ethnic groups. It lies at the root of the concept of *sempugi'*, 'partaking of a com-

mon Bugis-ness', 'to be fellow Bugis'. Hence the saying:
'Should my fellow Bugis [*sempugi'ku*] feel no *siri'* for me, at
least he will have *pessé*.' Mutual *pessé* between members of a
group is thus an important force of cohesion, for instance
between people who are subject to the same hardships in war
or emigration and who are ready to help each other whenever
need arises. The mutual promise of two individuals to be 'as
brothers' to each other, as well as the more general consciousness of being members of one and the same group, thus carries
implicit obligations which can never be disavowed for fear of
loss of honour. Hence the saying: 'Honour may cause your
death; compassion can bring you to the other world.' A balance should thus be kept between *siri'* and *pessé* so that each
neutralizes the extremes of the other (Nurdin Yatim, *Subsis-
tem Honorifik*: 33).

Norm and Practice: Valued and Actual Behaviour

Observation of Bugis social life shows that, although wise
sayings are certainly appreciated, they remain ideal images; on
the other hand, the concepts of *siri'* and *pessé* are real keys to
understanding many aspects of social behaviour, and especially
the apparent contradiction between competition and solidarity.

Group solidarity or *pessé* ensures the internal cohesion of
the family or social group. On particular occasions, a wedding
for example, all members of the family group will do their best
to maintain its prestige *vis-à-vis* other families of equal rank
by contributing to the feast. However, competition may also
take place between members of the same family or group of
followers: for example, if a man has achieved some notable
feat, his brother may for his own *siri'* try to achieve something
better. Competition of this kind is an important incentive to
enterprise in business and also to emigration as a means of
achieving economic success (Hamid Abdullah, *Manusia Bugis-
Makassar*: 60–2).

Without the hierarchical system, social competition might
become so fierce as to lead to the situation described by the
Bugis chroniclers as prevailing before the coming of the *to-
manurung* rulers, when 'people ate each other like fish'. But

Bugis hierarchy does not operate in isolation, raising the puzzling question of how this elaborate and seemingly rigid system coexists with a real and strong trend towards equality, particularly conspicuous among Bugis migrants overseas. Indeed, the popular etymology of the name of Samarinda city in eastern Kalimantan, founded in the eighteenth century by Bugis migrants, is *sama rendah*, that is, '[everybody] of the same low status'.

The contradiction is in fact more apparent than real. A hierarchy which differentiates among people according to their birth also confers equality on people of similar rank, whether among the few Bugis princes of the noblest birth, to whom the most important political offices were reserved, or among the ordinary people who form the bulk of society at large. And whereas the barriers between people of different rank endure for ever, between people of the same rank competition is open for other kinds of achieved status based on office, influence or wealth. Equality in this sense thus fosters instability, even, sometimes, conflict.

From the beginning of islamization, however, the Islamic ideal of a fundamental equality among all men has appealed to more and more Bugis. A few of them, like La Ma'darem-meng, the reformist Boné ruler who tried to abolish slavery in his kingdom, were of high birth; many more were common people and, not surprisingly, many were traders. Many of those who for various reasons felt uncomfortable in traditional Bugis society have, since the seventeenth century at least, resorted to emigration. In the new social context of their migrant community, they could pretend to be of higher rank than they really were, or, by escaping the hierarchical system, achieve a leading status of another kind; or, indeed reject the principles of hierarchy altogether.

The Valued Qualities of the Mythical and Fictional Heroes

It is interesting to look at the heroes of popular stories who, because they are imaginary, are not subject to the norms by which actual Bugis live, and to note which aspects of their behaviour arouse approval among listeners. An examination

Plate 42   Violins and lute accompanying the chanting of stories

of their behaviour produces a picture of Bugis mentality in which the four cardinal qualities loom large. These are the 'four sides' (*sulapa eppa'*) which according to the *lôntara* are essential in any good leader: besides being of appropriate descent, he should be brave (*warani*), clever (*macca*), rich (*sugi'*) and religious (*panrita*).

The foremost prototype of a brave man (*to-warani*) in Bugis literature is without doubt Sawérigading himself. In the *La Galigo* cycle, the first war he has to wage occurs during his first voyage to the western seas, when he has to fight his way against Letté Warani ('Brave Lightning'), the Lord of the Land of the Navel of the Earth. Their struggle is ended by a 'golden message' sent by the gods to inform the combatants that they are great-uncle and great-nephew. Later, on behalf of Letté Warani, Sawérigading vanquishes the Lord of the Land of the Setting Sun, who is not entitled to rule there, not being of pure divine blood. Sawérigading's next fight is with Daéng Lebbi', the Lord of the Land of the Dead, who is doubly at fault: first, he should not rule there, not being of pure divine blood; and secondly, he should not have married Wellé ri Cina, a princess of higher rank and moreover formerly betrothed to Sawérigading. Back in the country of the living, Sawérigading has to resort to arms once more to gain the hand of his future main wife, Wé Cudai' of Cina, first against seven other pretenders, then against his prospective father-in-law when at Wé Cudai's request his proposal is turned down at the last moment.

In all these episodes, Sawérigading fights with just cause. This is not so in the case of his son, La Galigo, a prince always described as a restless, quarrelsome and naughty youth; prone to taking other men's wives, by force if necessary, he is a frequent attender at cockfights and a bad loser, never willing to accept his defeats, which leads him into further fights. But although other characters in the stories criticize La Galigo's behaviour, neither the author nor the audience seem to take against him strongly. We may therefore see Sawérigading and La Galigo as the two faces of an ambiguous image, that of the Bugis nobleman of yesteryear who at times fights for his honour, for justice or for the protection of his people, but at other times indulges in war for war's sake, or to satisfy his personal ambition, greed or interest. Many historical figures could be taken as examples of the ambiguity of the *to-warani*, who have been admired for their qualities as fighters even when they are acting wrongly.

Another particular character among the *to-warani* in the *La Galigo* cycle deserves particular mention. This is Karaéng Tompo' of Pujananti, La Galigo's abandoned wife. Having had no news from him or from their son La Ma'pang'anro for years, she decides to set sail in pursuit of him in an armada 'manned' only by women disguised as men, as she herself is. Arriving in Cina, unrecognized by her husband, she challenges and beats him at a cockfight. Being a bad loser, he declares war on her, and only when he is defeated by her and her women warriors does he discover her real identity. Karaéng Tompo' can again be seen as a prototype for the warring noble ladies of South Sulawesi history: the Lady of Lipukasi, whose bravery before the enemy in 1814 was described by Crawfurd (see above); Wé Kambo, the female ruler of Luwu' who fought the Dutch when they conquered South Sulawesi in 1905; the women who took part in the struggle for Indonesian independence; and, in the 1950s, the female squads in the rebel armies of Kahar Muzakkar and Usman Balo'.

Modern oral *to-warani* stories follow in the same tradition. In these tales the quality of bravery is not just psychological or behavioural; it is also linked with the quest for special means. One of these is the possession of a magical knowledge which simultaneously confers aggression and invulnerability; the other is the possession of a magical weapon, usually a kriss, a wound from which is almost always fatal. The heroes of these stories have no other reason to fight than to prove their superiority over other champions. In stories set in the time of the struggle for Indonesian independence, or of past rebellions, the political movitations of the combatants are never mentioned: the narratives concentrate exclusively on the details of the fights, the respective roles of each warrior, how they display their bravery in challenging and attacking one another, how they show their invulnerability or how they defend their honour. In spite of its frequent cruelty, war is described as a kind of sport, the sorrows of which are compensated for to some extent by the excitement and pleasure it provides for fighters. Bravery here is seen not as a means to achieve a goal, but only as a way of asserting one's *siri'*. Another striking aspect of these stories is the presence, again, of women fighters. In one tale about the war for independence, when a group of disembarking Bugis combatants from Java are surrounded by Dutch troops, the chief's wife, seeing her husband dead and herself in danger of being captured alive, detonates a hand grenade which kills her and the Dutch soldiers around her, thus defending her honour in a way that emulates the behaviour of past South Sulawesi heroines.

The meaning of to-acca, which I translate as 'clever person', could also be given as either 'expert' or 'cunning' person. Among mythical characters of the Western tradition, Ulysses would be a good example of *to-acca*. In the Bugis narrative tradition, this 'trickster' element is not so important in the epics as in the oral stories. The prototype of the trickster and deceiver in this kind of literature is Lapong Pulando', 'Master Mousedeer' – obviously a borrowing from the Malay tradition of the Pelanduk Jinaka, but considered by the Bugis themselves as genuinely Bugis. The tricks played by the Bugis mouse-deer on the tiger, the crocodile, the buffalo and the monkeys are very similar to those related in Malay versions of the tale, but they are set in the Bugis country – where in fact there are neither mouse-deer nor tigers – and the Pulando' has been integrated into the local tradition to such an extent that its name has produced the word *ma'pulando'*, 'to act like the mouse-deer', that is, to cheat. Other *to-acca* heroes include pseudo-historical characters linked with particular kingdoms, such as La Pudaka in Wajo', La Méllong in Boné and La Sallomo' in Sidénréng, who seem to have been inspired by real historical figures. Cleverness is no more a male preserve than bravery, and there are also many stories about women *to-acca*.

The treatment of these characters, who achieve power and wealth through dishonesty, deception, lying and trickery, is often very sympathetic; by having the laughs on their side and by their very success they win forgiveness for their completely amoral behaviour. Cleverness, then, is as ambiguous a concept as bravery in Bugis stories: like bravery, it can be used both for the sake of the common good and for satisfying one's own selfish desires, and in both cases it is a means of asserting one's *siri'*.

The third of the Bugis cardinal virtues is the ability to enrich oneself. In the *La Galigo* cycle, a matchless wealth second only to that of the gods themselves characterizes all the protagonists in accordance with their own divine descent. This is manifested by the omnipresence of gold, named in these texts by an extraordinary variety of synonyms, and by a startling abundance of precious imported goods such as the silken *patola* cloths, perfumes, china wares and mirrors brought by Marangkabo traders from those mysterious western lands known collectively by the names of Jawa and Kelling. The Bugis seem never to have lost their nostalgia for this – literally – golden age: eagerness to enrich oneself still appears to be the most powerful motivation in life for many, and the main incentive for their trading enterprises. Most *ulama* even consider self-enrichment in so far as it is done honestly, as a duty, enabling oneself to contribute to the well-being of other, less fortunate, people. This is why it was long ago possible, at least in Wajo', for a wealthy man of low rank to marry a higher-ranking woman, in violation of the rule normally forbidding such unions, on the condition that 'the blood's price' was paid. It is thus not surprising that the quest for fortune prompts people to travel overseas. However, the traveller will be shamed if, after leaving the native land in search of wealth, he is not able to come back, sometimes after an absence of years, to show his family evidence of his success. Here, too, *siri'* is at stake.

In contrast to the first three cardinal virtues, there is no ambiguity about the fourth, which is represented by the *to-panrita*, a person of great religious learning, wisdom, piety and honesty. The *to-panrita* – the term, despite its Sanskrit origin (*pandita*: priest, hermit), has since islamization generally been equated with the Arabic *'alim* – never acts wrongly or out of selfishness. A pre-Islamic prototype of *to-panrita* might thus be Wé Tenriabéng, Sawérigading's twin sister, who intervenes wisely to dissuade her brother from his intention to commit incest and, using her magical powers, provides him with the ship which will bear him to Cina. Married as a *bissu* to a celestial being, she later ascends to Heaven to live there with him. From there she keeps a watchful eye on her brother, sending him welcome help or wise advice when necessary. At the end of the cycle her youngest son marries Sawérigading's youngest daughter, thus uniting at last the twin elements of the *to-warani* and *to-panrita*.

It is interesting to note that in the oral stories, while most of the *to-warani* are male and just a few female, it is the other way round with the *to-panrita*. When these are men, they are usually represented as elderly (*to-matoa*), individuals who have left behind them all the wrong deeds they may have committed during their youth. For example, a passage in the Wajo' chronicle describes how La Ta'dampare', who under the name of Puang ri Ma'galatung later became the kingdom's wisest ruler, has to quit the land of Boné because of his bad conduct. Arriving at the river which marks the border between Boné and Wajo', he unbinds his loincloth and casts it into the current as a sign of renunciation of his former behaviour. In the present Islamic context, the passage from being a *tau 'lao sala* – rascal, good-for-nothing – to a *to-panrita* would more probably be marked by the decision to go on *hajj*, the holy pilgrimage to Mecca.

In modern oral stories, the *to-panrita* are always exemplary – and in most cases female – Muslims who sometimes fall victim to false accusations or random mistreatment. Accepting their fate without demur, unshaken in their trust in God and surrendering themselves to his grace, they finally find justification and triumph over their enemies. The latter, almost always men, are sometimes described as hypocrites, false *to-panrita*, of whom there are also a few comical examples. Islam has thus brought new colour to an already existing prototype by strengthening its ethical aspects and thus decisively distinguishing the *to-panrita* from the more ambiguous images of the *to-warani*, *to-acca* and *to-sugi'*.

Resolving the Contradictions

If one acknowledges that, as seems to be the case in many Bugis stories, the end justifies the means, how is it possible to distinguish the good from the evil characters in these tales, and in real life to prevent society from crumbling into anarchy? Zainal Abidin Faried also wondered ('Exercice de l'autorité': 135–7) how it was possible that the actual behaviour of many present-day Bugis – ruthlessly competitive, unjust, treacherous, offering impunity to the powerful – was so far removed from that advocated by their ancestors, founded on respect for the democratic spirit, the love of justice, protection of the powerless, and faithfulness. He attributed the difference to a decline of cultural values brought about by internal and external wars, colonization, the aftermath of independence and poverty.

In fact, such contradictions are endemic in the ideal Bugis values, as exemplified by the tension between the demands of *siri'* and *pessé*, of competition and solidarity, of hierarchy and equality; and one cannot help wondering how the contradictory aspects of the four cardinal qualities can be reconciled with one another. A saying attributed to the renowned Arung Palakka even goes so far as to question these very qualities themselves, which had been demanded of him as a ruler: 'Don't rely too much on four things: bravery, cleverness, descent, wealth. For these four things are like worm-eaten wood: on the ground, they swarm with worms; in water, they soon become soaked; in fire, they are soon burnt' (Hasan Machmud, *Silasa*).

A possible answer to the puzzle of these contradictions might be sought in the fact that Bugis society is basically constituted as a series of interlocking groups – families, territorial groups, clienteles – forming pyramids which stand to one another in the same relations of competition or solidarity as do individuals. These relations, and thus the relations between individuals, who are all members of several of these groups, are governed not so much by a universal morality as by a set of conventions or a code of conduct of the same kind as the rules of a game – or, better, as the rules which govern the relations between states. Within such a context the main purpose of an individual would be both to seek personal achievements and to contribute to the success of the groups of which he is a member, observing the rules of the game which permit fierce competition without encouraging a lapse into anarchy or endangering the functioning of society at large. In this scheme, personal qualities would not be absolute virtues but rather means of achieving the desired goals.

Puang ri Ma'galatung may well be the prototype for a number of thinkers who emerged in early historical times, when society came to be organized along contractual lines. His sayings, advice and recommendations still form the core of most of the traditional ethical teachings, together with those of other wise men such as Kajao Lali'dong of Boné, Néné Ma'lomo of Sidénréng or To Ménggu Macca-é of Luwu'. After islamization, those teachings which conformed with, or at least were not in direct contradiction of, the new religion were interwoven with those of the wise men of the Islamic period such as the Makassar Karaéng Matoaya of Tallo', and are now read from an Islamic perspective. Nevertheless, in the collective mind a number of pre-Islamic concepts and collective rules still seem to prevail. According to these implicit rules, if you resort to force you must, at peril of losing your *siri'*, choose as your opponent someone of at least equal strength, or someone who has magical powers he could use against you. If your opponent is stronger than you, it is no treachery to assault him from behind or to cheat him; the same would apply if he is richer or more powerful. In stories where pious and honest women or orphans suffer at the hands of bad people, these are considered the worse because they attack those who are weaker than themselves. In one story ('La Béu Pa'lolang', 'The Orphan Thief'), an orphan who has repeatedly fallen victim to ill-treatment and calumny takes his revenge by acquiring powerful magic and so becoming an extremely successful thief. In that story, justice is obviously not a question of ethics in either an Islamic or a Western sense, but a question of fair play.

9

Material Culture and Economic Activity

Material aspects of a culture can reveal much of a people's identity by showing how they use the means and techniques available to them in specific ways and at particular times to adapt themselves to their environment and to the prevailing historical and economic conditions. Material culture is constantly changing, sometimes so slowly as to give an impression of stability, at other times undergoing dramatic upheavals; it is a particularly significant field in ethnographic investigation.

Bugis material culture, as observed between the mid-nineteenth and mid-twentieth centuries, was the relatively stable outcome of a long history of contacts with other influences both within and outside South Sulawesi. While sharing common origins with the cultures of all South Sulawesi peoples, it had developed significant differences from that of the neighbouring Toraja but had become almost identical with that of the Makassar and Mandar, and similar in many respects to that of other western Indonesian coastal peoples, especially the Malays.

Habits of Use and Consumption

Houses and Settlements

The settlement patterns of the Bugis have undergone several changes over the centuries. The *La Galigo* texts describe set-

Plate 43   The standard Bugis house

tlements established on low hills near river mouths. In later times it seems that political insecurity led to the establishment of a number of new settlements on much higher ridges or summits. In the fourteenth century people began to occupy the lowlands; the chronicles tell us that the houses of these settlers were sometimes isolated, sometimes grouped in small clusters and sometimes loosely assembled near cultivated land. These settlements were not necessarily permanent; the texts often mention their rapid growth or sudden desertion, and the movement of people to new locations.

In the centre of most *wanua* was a defensive enclosure made of an earthern talus topped by stockades; these were not properly speaking cities, nor even fortified settlements, but fortified areas, where in times of war the people of the surrounding *wanua* could take refuge. The fortified site was not a completely built-up area, but included fields, plantations, gardens and of course a few small settlements. On his visit of 1840, James Brooke described Tosora, the heart of ancient

Wajo', as 'a large straggling city, greatly in decay; the ancient boundary of which is marked by a fortification, which embraces a space of several miles in circumference, and occupies to the eastward a slightly elevated ridge, and to the westward sinks to a swamp' (Brooke, *Narrative of Events*:). He was correct in his description, but not in his interpretation: the fact that the area was only partly settled had nothing to do with decay, for it had probably always been thus. Some settlements were quite important: in 1840 Brooke estimated Lagosi, the capital of Pammana, to contain 'at least a thousand houses', and accordingly a population of perhaps 10,000; but this, too, was less a city than an extended cluster of villages.

Factors favouring the mobility of Bugis settlements and the absence of cities as the term is understood in the West are reflected in the physical characteristics of the south-east Asian house, of which the Bugis home is a typical example. Construction of these houses is a progressive process: even today they are made of interchangeable elements and can quite easily be modified and enlarged. Thus one might begin with a very simple bamboo hut, then replace it with a still fairly straightforward wooden house which could be improved in stages a little at a time. The materials necessary for building – wood, bamboo and plant-derived coverings such as palm leaves, sugar-palm fibre, *Imperata* grass or bamboo tiles – were readily available, inexpensive and could be processed everywhere. Even large houses could be taken down and reassembled somewhere else, since the method of construction was exclusively by jointing and binding. The smaller bamboo dwellings could even be moved without being dismantled; however, the posts of the bigger wooden houses were sunk deep into the ground and had to be cut if the house was to be removed in one piece. Since probably the second half of the nineteenth century an increasing number of wooden houses have had their posts not planted but laid on stone bases – a technique possibly learnt from the Malays – which means that even the larger ones may be moved.

The wooden Bugis house, from its earliest documentary depictions in the seventeenth century to the present day, is of the Malay type of south-east Asian house, present also in Acheh and South Sumatra as well as Borneo (Dumarçay,

House, 1987: 30). In its basic form it has a roof with two planes joined by a straight ridge, in contrast to the curved ridge of the Toraja, Batak and Minangkabau houses as well as those of tenth-century Java as shown in the Borobudur reliefs. The walls are light, and the floor is raised about 2 metres – sometimes more – above the ground, the space beneath usually being completely open. The frame is made of pieces fitted into each other without the use of either pegs or nails; the development of this technique depended, of course, on the availability of the necessary carpentry tools and therefore on the development of local iron working. The posts reach from the ground to the attic and carry the weight of the roof; rectangular holes are cut in them through which floor beams and attic beams pass lengthwise, and upper and lower binding beams pass crosswise. Formerly, houses with planted posts had no lower binding beams, and the floor beams did not pass through the posts but were tied to them; this technique can still be seen in a few surviving archaic examples such as those in Ussu'. The frame of the roof, unlike that of the body of the house, is not fitted but nailed together; in former times its elements were tied with rattan bonds.

The basic structural unit of a Bugis house (Pelras, 'Maison Bugis') consists of three sets of three posts, making a rectangle with one post at each angle, one post in the middle of each side, and one post in the centre; this last is the 'house's navel' (*posi' bola*). An ordinary house would consist of four posts lengthwise and four posts crosswise; to one of its long sides would be added a penthouse or covered gallery with a slightly lowered floor, with the front entrance at one end and, if there is no separate kitchen-house, the cooking earth at the other end. Other elements may be added, making more or less complex plans, but the rectangular form underlies them all. In former times there were no inside partitions, or some-times just a single one across the middle separating the front part, where unrelated male visitors were received, from the rear, more private part. There was very little furniture, too, apart from mats and pillows: clothes and other belongings were simply stored in jars, baskets and boxes of various kinds. Cupboards, beds, tables and chairs are relatively recent introductions.

Innovations in furniture, as in other areas, were formerly the preserve of the aristocracy: for example, only they were permitted to use posts that were square or octagonal in cross-section instead of round. Certain peculiarities of house construction, too, were attached to specific upper ranks in the hierarchy, the most conspicuous of these being the number of panels constituting the gable: two for *tau décéng*, three for *ana' céra'*, five for *ana' ma'tola* and seven for the rulers of the main Bugis kingdoms – Luwu', Boné, Wajo', Soppéng and Sidénréng. Only *ana' céra'* and above had the right to a staircase ascending at right-angles to the façade of the house instead of parallel to it; and only the highest nobility could have, instead of an ordinary staircase, an inclined plane of bamboo called a *sapana* (from the Sanskrit, probably through Malay: *sopana*, 'stairs'; see Gonda, *Sanscrit in Indonesia*: 95).

Clothing

About 1785, Thomas Forrest wrote:

The Buggess [*sic*] cambay, though only one garment . . . shrowds from head to heels when the wearer sleeps . . .; being chequered, it much resembles tartan and is often wore like a sash gathered up on one shoulder over a tight waistcoat, and breeches that reach within a span of the knee. Altogether, a Buggess resembles much a Scotch highlander, when the ends of the plaid are sewed together. (Forrest, *Voyage from Calcutta*: 80)

Many early European texts, indeed, described the South Sulawesi sarong (Bugis *lipa'*) as a very large 'sash' of a man's length, wide enough for a couple to sleep together in one.

In 1840 James Brooke set down this description of a Bugis aristocrat:

His dress was magnificent, composed of puce-coloured velvet, worked with gold flowers: the trousers, rather loose, of the same material, reached half-way down the calf of the leg, and were fastened by six or eight real gold studs. The baju (or jacket), buttoned close up, was fastened with the same material at the throat, and down the breast, and each sleeve had a row of golden buttons up the fore-arm. A blue gold-embroidered sarong, or kilt, was round his waist, over a hand-

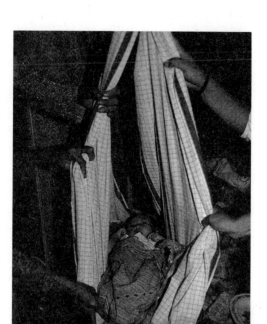

Plate 44   An alternative use of the sarong as suspended rocking cradle

some and jewelled kriss; and on his head a light skull-cap of gold, neatly and elaborately carved. The other rajahs were richly dressed in cloth of gold. (Brooke, *Narrative of Events*: 57–8)

At the court of Boné, he observed

a body of 3000 or 4000 men . . . ranged within and without the court-yard, dressed precisely alike, in skull caps and blue sarongs over the kriss . . . Eight or ten spearmen, clad in coats of bright chain armour, guarded the entrance . . . Behind the monarch were half a dozen handsome boys . . .; and two rows of young rajahs were seated cross-legged on his right hand. Like those without, they were naked to the waist, wearing only skull-caps and sarongs. (Brooke, *Narrative of Events*: 131–2)

Notwithstanding a degree of continuity in the dress of high-ranking Bugis since the times of the *La Galigo* texts, Brooke's descriptions draw attention to a number of innovations, adopted possibly between the fifteenth and the late eighteenth century. One is the introduction of breeches, which early European descriptions enable us to date from about the second half of the sixteenth century and the early seventeenth. This seems to point to a cultural influence from the areas of the archipelago that were islamized before South Sulawesi. The breeches worn by men (Bugis *sulara'*) remained part of the traditional costume until the 1930s, and were of two types, one reaching below the knee, the other much shorter, choice between the two being a matter of personal preference. The men wearing them usually wore their sarong over the shoulder; only if meeting a superior, or to perform their prayers, did they knot the sarong at the waist. On festive occasions, women could also wear tight knee-length breeches under their sarongs.

Shirts or tunics worn by men must have been introduced during the seventeenth century, since they bear in Bugis, as in Malay, a name of Portuguese origin, *waju kaméja* (from *camisa*), although they appear not to have been very common at that time: the Spanish Jesuit Navarrete describes the Makassar Sultan Hasanuddin wearing a European jacket without a shirt (Navarrete, *Travels and Controversies*). Long cassocks of Arabic cut, still worn with turbans by some Muslim scholars, were fashionable among those rulers who wished to express their orthodoxy, and were also quite commonly worn by bridegrooms as their wedding attire.

Another innovation was the kind of cap which Brooke calls a 'skull-cap'. This refers to the brimless cap, *songko' to-Boné*, worn only by the well-off, the aristocracy and their retainers. They were plaited by women of the Boné nobility from the thin fibres of a species of wild orchid collected in the forests of south-east Sulawesi; gold thread was plaited into those to be worn by aristocrats, in proportion according to the rank of the wearer. In 1840 Brooke wrote that at the court of Boné,

no one appears with a handkerchief about the head in the presence of the patamankowè. The lower class wear the skull-cap on the back of the cranium. The sovereign and his brother wear it cocked to the left side; other nobles to the right, and cocked according to the rank!

While skull-caps distinguish the young rajahs who compose the bodyguard.

Of Bugis women, Brooke wrote:

The dress of the women is plain . . . A sarong reaching to the feet, and a muslin baju worn loose, and showing all the bust and bosom, compose the dress. The hair, long and black, is generally drawn tight off the face, *à la Chinoise*, and turned up behind. Women of rank, and the females of their household, wear the thumbnail long, and enclosed in a preposterously long case. (Brooke, *Narrative of Events*: 81–2)

That Bugis women, to Brooke's eyes, 'appear[ed] less fond of ornamenting their persons than the men' can be attributed to the fact that only the Bugis chiefs, giving him an official reception, had dressed in a formal fashion; had he been invited to a Bugis wedding, he would have been impressed by the many golden anklets, bracelets, rings, necklaces and hair ornaments worn by the women on these occasions. He depicts Bugis women wearing the coloured, transparent blouse of age-old design which remains characteristic of South Sulawesi female clothing. Formerly, certain colours for blouses were restricted to certain groups of people: green was the prerogative of the nobility; white of the noble children's wet-nurses; yellow, that of the ritual practitioners (*sanro*). The traditional colour code for the various life-stages is still followed: pink for unmarried girls, light red for young married women, deep red for women who have had their first child, brown for older women with a married child, black for the elderly. The pink blouses were made of transparent gauze, and until brassières began to be worn (probably in the 1930s) the breasts were visible; as the colours grew darker, so the cloth grew thicker, and the brown blouses were barely transparent, while the black ones were quite opaque. The youngest girls went bare-breasted until puberty, when at a special ceremony they were given their first blouse to wear.

Food, Meals and Cooking

Rice is the staple food of the Bugis and is served at all three daily meals. At breakfast, the main food may be glutinous rice

Plate 45 A villager's kitchen

or cassava (roasted or boiled), often accompanied by preserved fish (salted, smoked or dried in the sun). At lunch and dinner, boiled, unsalted 'white rice' is accompanied by a number of dishes of vegetables, fish and sometimes chicken; goat meat and beef are usually served only at feasts. Glutinous rice, prepared in four colours – natural white and 'black', yellow from *Curcuma longa* and red from *Morinda citrifolia* – constitutes the basis of the offerings which are presented by traditionally minded Bugis to the 'invisible beings' who consume its 'fine part' or essence, leaving the 'coarse part' or substance to be eaten by humans. The spirits are also said to be very fond of puffed glutinous rice. Bugis pastry, which is made in many varieties and from either glutinous or normal rice flour, is usually eaten in the form of snacks and delicacies between meals, and also features in offerings.

Families usually take their meals in the kitchen, or in the rear part of the house if there is no separate kitchen. However, when male guests unrelated to the family are present, the men often eat alone in the front part of the house and the women, including female guests, in the kitchen or the rear part. When a feast is given in the house the kitchen is crowded with women of the family cooking and making pastries, and on these occasions honoured female guests may be seated in the front part; men and women remain in separate groups, although the segregation is not always very strict. For ordinary meals, people sit in a circle on a large mat, each with a dish; for feasts, long white cloths are spread over mats and people sit in rows opposite each other, arranged according to hierarchy: the best positions are those at the front of the house and at the side furthest from the entrance. The meal is brought in by the serving women on large trays, the cooked rice in a big basket or colander and the accompaniments in soup dishes. (Those of high birth used formerly to be served on individual brass trays set on pedestals, called *bôsara'*; at princely weddings or on very formal occasions, the highest-ranking guests are still welcomed by being presented with an appropriate number of sweetmeats on such *bôsara'*, up to twelve times twelve for the highest dignitaries of all.) Each guest helps himself from the tray, putting rice and a little of each accompanying dish into his own dish. Solid food is eaten with the fingers of the right hand, after rinsing them in a finger bowl. People eat fairly quickly, without much talking; they drink only after finishing their food, and only boiled water – not a recent innovation, since it was noticed with some amazement by early travellers. According to Anthony Reid (*Age of Commerce*), drinking boiled water was first known in east and south-east Asia and was introduced from there to Europe, not the other way around.

The excellence and delicacy of Bugis cooking, which can be experienced not only among aristocratic families but also in very simple and even poor households, is based on relatively unsophisticated means and techniques. Until very recently the cooking arrangements consisted only of simple hearths of hard earth where pots and pans were set on three stones over a fire of wood or coconut shells. On occasions when many guests were to be fed, these hearths were supplemented with small, makeshift terracotta furnaces, while for still bigger feasts fires were lit outside in the open. The kitchen utensils consisted of rounded pans of metal and earthenware, similar to the Chinese *wok*, and cooking pots of various dimensions, with and without lids.

Some recipes formerly used fell into disuse with the Islamic prohibition on the consumption of blood. One rather un-Islamic dish was the relish for hunters, *lawa' dara*, well described by James Brooke in 1840:

> The game being killed, chillies, salt and limes (always carried to the field) are brought; the heart taken out; and, with portions of the liver and inside of the thigh, is minced and eaten raw with these ingredients – the sauce being blood! This is the real lor dara, or feast of blood; and neither record nor tradition (that I could hear of) describes it as a practice in war. The lor dara, as I have described it, would, no doubt, shock the fastidious; but I ate of it, and found it by no means bad or revolting. (Brooke, *Narrative of Events*: 129)

What Brooke is referring to when he speaks of 'a practice in war' is a story reported by Raffles (*History of Java*, appendix F, 'Celebes': CLXXXIV) about this *lawar darah* (Malay) being made not only with game, but also with the hearts and livers of human enemies. This practice may actually have been followed in ancient times, for there are allusions to it in the *La Galigo* texts as well as in oral tales. There are in fact many kinds of *lawa'*: coconut milk, rasped and roasted coconut, pepper and salt may be used as well as chillies and limes. Raw foods prepared in this way include shrimps, cuttlefish, squids and other kinds of fish, certain kinds of seaweed and wild vegetables, and some young fruit.

A different category of Bugis cooking is that of sweets and pastries, which are produced in innumerable variety. After his reception at the court of Boné, Brooke wrote: 'I must mention the collation of sweetmeats, which was excellent, various and delicate: coffee, which would have been considered good in Stamboul or Paris, and tea fit to drink even in Canton' (*Narrative of Events*: 133). Certain recipes which are required in particular circumstances, such as feasts at rite of passage celebrations or weddings, or in ritual meals presented as offerings, seem to function as powerful tokens of Bugis identity. This is particularly conspicuous, for example, in the case of migrant Bugis in Malaya, who have adopted many aspects of

Malay cooking but retain a number of these recipes, which both they and their neighbours consider to be indicators of their ethnic identity.

Subsistence

Agriculture

Even though other staple foods are available to the Bugis, including several kinds of tubers, sago (in Luwu') and banana (in Mandar), to complement and sometimes even temporarily replace it in cases of poor harvest, rice has been central to the Bugis agricultural economy, based on paddy cultivation, since the beginning of their written history. The fact that agricultu-

Plate 46   Harvesting with a rice knife

Plate 47   Harvesting the new IRRI rice with a sickle

ral rites involve rice alone, and the importance accorded to the myth of the rice goddess Sangiang Serri, testify to its pre-eminence (Maeda, 'Agricultural Rites'; Pelras, 'Herbe divine'; Sofian Anwarmufied, 'Ritus tanah').

The adult daily requirement of rice is about half a litre, which means that a representative family of, say, a couple with three children and one widowed parent, would need about one tonne a year, or a little over, to meet its needs for everyday consumption, for any offerings that might be made, and for the feasts to celebrate the rites of passage of family members. In a successful agricultural year, a Bugis family could manage this with one hectare of traditionally cultivated paddy field, which in South Sulawesi yields on average about 1.2–1.4 tonnes a year. Until fairly recently, most such fields in South Sulawesi were exclusively rain-fed. Like irrigated paddy fields, they are surrounded by dikes in which openings are made to let water in and out. Very little is done to bring water in: at best, a short channel is connected to a small river or stream nearby, but there is no real irrigation to enable rice to grow at any time other than the rainy season – certainly nothing to compare with the irrigated terraces of Java and Bali. Rain-fed paddy fields can be found either in plains or in mountain valleys; some plots are higher than others, allowing water to run from the highest to the lowest. Regulating the depth of water in the fields is not easy, because while any peasant is free to let water out of his plot, he is not free to let it in if he has to take it from a higher field. This situation, of course, can easily give rise to disputes; hence the importance attached by the peasants both to adequate techniques and to the observance of agricultural rites as guarantees of a good harvest – as well as listening to the advice of village elders and local experts in matters agricultural, which in turn usually draw heavily on agricultural manuscripts.

Bugis agricultural manuscripts convey the entire knowledge of the ancients in agricultural matters, including most import-antly the determination of time from observation of the con-stellations and natural phenomena at different seasons, and the enumeration of the agricultural tasks to be performed at each period, following a system of reckoning the time based on the solar year (Pelras, 'Ciel et jours'). In this calen-dar, the names of the days of the week are borrowed from the Arabic, the names of the months from the Portuguese. Dates are determined, and the due times for the beginning of agricultural tasks marked, by the observation of the positions of certain stars and constellations at dusk and dawn. Nine constellations play significant roles during the year: *Tekko soro*, 'the Pushed Plough' (perhaps Triangulum); *Worong-mporong*, 'the Tuft' (the Pleiades); *Wara-wara*, 'the Burning Coal' (Aldebaran); *Tanra tellu*, 'the Triple Beacon' (Orion's belt); *Manu'*, 'the Chicken' (Canopus, Sirius and Procyo); *Watang-mpata*, 'the Job's Tears Stalk'; *Eppang*, 'the Lame' or *Bola képpang*, 'the Crooked House' (the Southern Cross); *Walu*, 'the Widow' (Alpha Centauri); and *Lambaru*, 'the Rayfish' (part of Scorpio). However, as the timing of the wet and dry seasons differs from one place to another in South Sulawesi, these manuscript calendars have local value only, since the appropriate agricultural tasks at any given date will differ from place to place.

The standard cycle of wet rice cultivation among the Bugis is regularly punctuated by rituals, and individual ploughing cannot begin before both collective and individual opening rites have been performed. As soon as the rains begin, people are busy repairing the dikes around the fields and the openings for letting water in and out; when the soil is sufficiently soaked, ploughing can start. The plough used is wooden, with a tooth-like iron ploughshare and an iron ear, and is traditionally drawn by a pair of buffalo; horses were – and still are – used only in Soppéng district. Ploughing is followed by harrowing, intended to remove tufts of grass and homogenize the mud, using a comb-like, articulated wooden harrow or rake whose angle can be adjusted. The soil is then ready for planting, first in a small field which is used as the nursery for the seedlings.

Until quite recently the seeds were taken from sheaves of the previous harvest of the numerous local varieties of rice. In one village near Singkang I was able to list twenty-six varieties with different growing times; some of them were kinds of glutinous rice, the type necessary for ritual offerings and also particularly desirable in pastry-making. After the seeds have been separated from the stalks by gentle treading with bare feet on a buffalo skin, they are put in a humid place for twenty-four hours for pre-germination to occur. They are then planted in the nursery for the first growing phase. After about thirty days the seedlings are tall enough to be transplanted. In this operation the farmer is usually helped by a group of relatives and friends, and will return the favour when requested. If previous calculations have been inaccurate, and the nursery cannot provide enough seedlings to plant all the fields, it is acceptable to ask a neighbour for additional seedlings; however, the opposite problem is more frequent, and as there is a ritual prohibition on discarding excess seedlings, they must be left to grow in the nursery.

During the period of growth, which for traditional varieties lasts from 110 to 150 'nights', the main task is to prevent the growing rice from being overwhelmed by weeds, attacked by diseases or destroyed by pests. Then comes harvest time, preceded by the ritual of 'opening the harvest'. Rice was traditionally cut not with a sickle but with a small, transverse reaping knife which enabled the harvest worker to pick out the ripe from the unripe ears and to avoid spoiling the grains. This practice is followed less and less now, but is still used on a small scale, especially with the glutinous varieties. The ears of rice are collected into bunches, six to ten bunches making one sheaf, which yields about 8 kg of paddy or grain. Like transplanting, the harvest is a collective endeavour involving family members, neighbours and friends, men, women and children alike; some will give help and receive it in their turn, while others who do not own ricefields themselves come as hired workers, receiving as payment one out of every eight or nine sheaves they reap.

Collectively organized irrigation was not introduced until after the Dutch colonization, and has only really been developed since the 1970s. New, highly productive and, in recent cases, pest-resistant varieties of rice have been introduced, most of them from the Philippines-based International Rice Research Institute (IRRI), so that in these irrigated areas it is now sometimes possible to harvest five times in two years, with average yields reaching 7 tons per hectare. These advances in turn call for new methods and practices, such as the use of fertilizers and pesticides; new planting techniques; mass harvesting, partly by hired labourers using sickles; threshing of the harvested rice in the field immediately after it is cut, and its storage in sacks; and mechanical hulling in the village's rice processing unit. More recently, the use of mini-tractors has also become increasingly common.

The techniques described above are the most commonly followed but not the only ones, even for wet rice cultivation; other agricultural techniques used in South Sulawesi have been well described by the Japanese soil scientist Furukawa ('Rice Culture'). He describes tidal irrigated ricefields in Luwu' that have recently been opened up by transmigrants from Sidénréng–Rappang and Tanah Toraja. At high tide river water enters the fields, where it is retained by dikes; three years after the fields have been opened, the remaining roots and stumps have rotted away and the fields can be worked with plough and harrow (Furukawa, 'Rice Culture': 40–1). This technique may have been borrowed recently from Bugis settlers in Sumatra, who themselves learned it from Banjar migrants. Elsewhere in Luwu' Furukawa witnessed the use of buffalo for trampling the soil in place of ploughing, and, in harder soils, transplanting with the help of a dibble ('Rice Culture': 43); these, by contrast, are probably ancient techniques. Furukawa also saw several other cases of buffalo trampling in Boné, on calcareous soils as well as in wet lowlands. In Sidénréng, on the western shore of Lake Témpé, he observed the transplanting of rice in the dark alluvial clay left by the receding lake waters in September and October. Similar conditions prevail in the swampy area around Tosora, the former heartland of Wajo', where small lakes are inundated in April and May by the Cénrana river; here too seedlings are transplanted in June and July when the water starts to recede. The rice plants here were as tall as 1.5 metres (Furukawa, 'Rice Culture': 45).

On the lower reaches of the same river, not far inland, Furukawa noticed yet other techniques:

In March, farmers prepare the first dry nurseries . . . They use the salt tolerant *sawé* variety . . . [In the fields] farmers cut down the weeds with a parang, collect them with a J-shaped branch, and pile them on ridges. Then they break up the shallow layer of soil containing grass roots with a hoe and trample the soil with their feet . . . . Thirty-or forty-day-old seedlings are transplanted . . . either by hand or with a dibble . . . The crop is often harvested from a boat. Flooding occurs when three conditions coincide: high water in lake Témpé, heavy rainfall from the southeastern monsoon and high tides (Furukawa, 'Rice Culture': 45–6).

In Jé'néponto, Furukawa observed pre-germinated seeds sown by being scattered directly on to the unirrigated ricefields in an area where the rainy period is very short ('Rice Culture': 49–50). In similar conditions I saw direct sowing by dibbling in Wajo' before the start of the rains; this was followed, after the rains had begun and the plants had grown, by what Furukawa calls 'thinning transplanting': 'Farmers, when weeding, thin the densely sown rice plants and transplant them into those paddy fields which are not planted in normal years' ('Rice Culture': 51). As Furukawa remarks, adaptation to prevailing conditions is very important in Bugis wet rice agriculture. This adaptation is seen in the tendency of Bugis who migrate to Jambi, on the eastern coast of Sumatra, from places in, for example, Wajo' or Boné where the ricefields are rain-fed or even properly irrigated, to switch to tidal cultivation, a technique which they themselves had never previously practised.

Slash and-burn agriculture probably held an important place in the South Sulawesi economy in ancient times, and was still practised by a few Bugis mountain communities in south Boné as late as the 1930s (Friedericy, 'Ponré'). The rotation period was fourteen years. When the part of the forest to be cleared had been determined by the local lord and the *sanro wanua*, individual plots were allocated to each family. Clearing was a collective task, but each plot-holder provided food for all the workers when his plot was being cleared. The seed was prepared in the same way as for wet rice cultivation and sown directly by hand in the swidden without prior germination in a nursery bed. Originally a swidden was never cultivated for more than two consecutive years, after which it was left fallow for twelve years; but the gradual growth of population meant that the fallow period had to be reduced over time. There were protected areas of forest: 'stem forests', where only trees for building the lord's house could be felled; 'hunting preserves', reserved for hunting parties ordered by the lord or his suzerain; and 'sacred forests'. Nonetheless, an ever-expanding process of clearance led progressively to extensive deforestation of the whole Bugis country.

Fishing and Fish Farming

The numbers of fishermen and fish farmers in South Sulawesi, compared to those of peasants working on the land, are relatively small even when deep sea fishing is included along with coastal fishing, freshwater fishing and fish farming. However, fishing is no less a basic activity of the Bugis than agriculture. Fish is a basic element of the Bugis diet and nearly every meal includes it in some form. On an ordinary market day near Paré-Paré I was able to count forty-five different types – and Bugis fishermen of course catch many more than these: I have myself listed about 120 names of fish in Paré-Paré.

Offshore fishing probably represents the apogee of fishing activity for the Bugis, while in mythical and ritual terms one type of fish, the flying fish, is the paragon of deep sea fishing,

Plate 48 Fishing from Lake Témpé with a casting net

occupying almost the same place as rice does in agriculture. The campaign in pursuit of the flying fish takes place mostly in the Makassar strait during the east monsoon, approximately from the beginning of April to the end of August. The beginning of the season is signalled by the rising at dawn of the constellations *Walu* and *Eppang*; in May the sky is dominated by the *Worong-mporong*; then the *Tanra tellu* takes the most prominent position, until its disappearance in August marks the season's end. As early as February the fishermen are beginning to prepare their basket traps as well as recaulking and repainting their boats. The basket traps (of which ten to twenty are carried on each boat) are in the form of a cylinder about 75 cm long and 25 cm in diameter and are made of bamboo laths: at each end long triangular laths are set in a cone pointing towards the interior, so that a fish swimming into the cone can get inside the trap but cannot get out. Each trap is provided with two floats made of bamboo tubes; when it is empty the tops of these are visible, whereas when it is full

Plate 49 A fishing canoe fitted with an outboard engine

they sink just below the surface. The traps are hung with a certain kind of seaweed called *gossé*. Once the fishing vessels have arrived on the fishing ground in the middle of the Makassar strait early in the morning the traps, tied up to a palm-fibre rope at intervals of about 21 metres – that is, about eight traps to a rope of approximately 150 metres – are set floating. The fish, which are in their laying season, come to lay their eggs on the weed and are then caught in the trap. Usually the traps are pulled up after three or four hours. The fish are then cleaned and salted; once ashore, they are usually smoked. The eggs, a valued delicacy, are now mostly exported to Japan. Five to eight voyages may be made in one season.

Another, specifically Bugis, kind of fishing takes place about 15–25 nautical miles from land in depths of 600–1,000 fathoms.[1] The craft used are *rompong*, a kind of bamboo raft

---

[1] The unit 'fathom' as used to measure depths is a translation of the Bugis *reppa*, the span of both extended arms; this, of course, is a relatively imprecise length, which cannot be precisely converted into metres.

about 10 metres long and 2 metres wide, from which ropes about 5 metres long are hung. To these ropes are attached coconut palm fronds which attract swarms of fish, among others scad and silvery batfish, which are caught by quickly surrounding the raft with a net. The nets, positioned with floats and sinkers, are similar to seine nets, with two symmetrical, rectangular, wide-mesh 'wings' and narrower mesh parts where the fish are caught by the gills. In a good season, the *rompong* fishermen may make up to ten sorties in a month.

At about the same distance from land, and with about the same frequency, expeditions are made to catch tuna fish and scad with long, rectangular drifts nets called *puka'*. These nets are also used by some to catch flying fish. Also in the same area, some Bugis fishermen follow the Mandar practice of fishing with floating long lines. Most, however, use hand lines 80 fathoms long with sinkers and scad as bait to catch deep sea fish. The use of short hand lines is common everywhere as a complement to deep sea fishing, and is much practised by sailors during long voyages. To catch garfish, which are able to cut through the line with their very sharp teeth, hooks are replaced by slipknots.

A fishing device much in use among the Bugis is the *bagang* or fishing platform, of which there are two kinds: floating and 'planted', or stationary, platforms. The first kind, which is supported by two large canoes each with mast and sails, is reminiscent of the Polynesian double-hulled canoe; the second is established on stilts driven into the bottom in relatively shallow water. Both kinds have a square opening in the middle through which a square dip-net can be lowered and hauled up by pulleys. Fishing from the platform takes place at night, using lights to attract the fish – except at full moon, when this method does not work. The catch, which includes pony fish, small scad, anchovies, sardines and cuttlefish, is sent ashore every morning by canoe.

A different kind of dip-net is the horizontal, rectangular *banrong*, used to catch milk-fish and silvery batfish, among others. Two corners are tied to two slanting poles and the other two corners to long draw-ropes which pass over a high bamboo scaffolding planted in the sand. At rest, the two poles are almost horizontal and the net is under water. A lookout is posted on the scaffolding in the early morning. When he sights a shoal of fish, he signals to other men who pull on the draw-ropes, causing the poles to stand up and the net to emerge from the water. Placed in depths of about 3 fathoms, a large *banrong* may measure 10 fathoms by 5 fathoms and need a dozen men to pull it.

Many of the implements used for onshore fishing are smaller versions of those used offshore. Shore seines called *séssé* are also used, to catch toli shad, anchovies and sardines: the two ends are pulled towards the shore, first by boats, then, when the water becomes shallower, by a dozen men. Mullet, pony fish and grunter are caught using the *palla' lariang*, a small drift net about 2 fathoms long, operated close to the shore. The fish are scared into the net by two men striking the water with canes. In depths of under 2 fathoms where the bottom is sandy or muddy a casting net of up to 3 fathoms diameter with lead sinkers is sometimes used to catch mullet, toli shad, torpedoes, sardines and crayfish. Various kinds of dragnet are used specifically for shore fishing: all bag-shaped, with the mouth kept open by bamboo laths, they include the *lanra*, which is pulled by three walking men to catch small mullet, and the *bunré*, a shrimping net which is pushed by one or two men and is not made from mesh netting but woven, with a twined warp (*dari*) made on a weaving loom of unspun vegetable fibre. Similar in shape, but smaller and operated by a single man from a canoe, is the *sodo*, a landing net made of gauze used to scoop up fish around floating logs and in fish traps.

The most common fish trap used by the Bugis is the *belle'* (Malay *belat*), which is set on shallow coral reefs and consists of two long, converging fences of wood and bamboo with a third one in the middle running at right angles to the coast through a narrow opening into a circular enclosure. The fish which swim into it at rising tide cannot find their way out at ebb tide, when they can be caught with a *sodo*. The catch from these traps is mainly mullet, rabbit fish, grunter, ladyfish, sea perch, pig-face bream, parrot fish and garfish. Large rectangular basket traps (*buwu*) are also used on reefs. Another kind of fence trap, similar to the *belle'*, is the *bulo*, which is placed across the mouth of a stream or inlet to catch the fish at ebb tide: any fish which try to leap over the fence are caught by drift nets placed just behind it. Finally, mention should be made of the *salekko*, a cone-shaped openwork basket trap with a wide opening at the bottom and a narrow opening at the top. This is carried in shallow clear water, where the fisherman puts it over a fish or crab which is then caught by hand through the upper opening.

Freshwater fishing in South Sulawesi is practised both in still water – lakes, swamps and flooded paddy fields – and in running water. The catch is less varied than in sea fishing. Some species, such as gobbies, catfish eels and some true eels, can live both in the sea and in rivers; some, such as eels, snakefish and the 'climbing perch' (*Anabas testudineus*) can even creep out of water and survive on dry land for a while. These are the most common catch, along with snakefish and brill from Lake Témpé and clarias or catfish from the rice-fields. Small rivers and ricefields yield crab, and in Lake Témpé a variety of small shrimps are caught which are much appreciated prepared as *lawar*.

As with onshore fishing, the techniques and implements used for freshwater fishing are for the most part smaller versions of those used in sea fishing. Similar to the *rompong*, for example, are the *bungka'*, floating 'islands' of aquatic weeds found in great quantity on Lake Témpé and in the swamps along the western bank of the Cénrana river in Wajo'. These are fixed with long bamboo poles planted in the muddy bottom, and in the dry season after harvest the numerous fish which swarm beneath them are caught with drag nets. Cast nets, weighted with a chain rather than lead sinkers, are also used. *Salekko* are used in flooded ricefields and a cylindrical version of the *buwu* in rivers. A technique formerly very common in river fishing, but now fallen into disuse, was the use of substances which paralysed the fish. Two-pronged fish spears were used until recently for fishing in the lakes and swamps from canoes by lamplight; in the same areas a rare technique was the use of blowpipes to fire small harpoons with floaters. Finally, there is line fishing with a rod whose oscillating head attracts the fish through the movement it causes in the line.

Fish farms (*émpang*) are an important additional source of fish in South Sulawesi. These are artificial ponds established

on formerly marshy coasts, filled with a mixture of sea water
and fresh water. They are partitioned by ditches and dikes
into divisions similar to ricefield plots, ranging from half a
hectare to several hectares in area, and communicate with the
sea through channels which can be closed off by water gates,
while other channels bring fresh water from neighbouring
rivers. The fish raised in this manner are mostly milkfish and
shrimps: small fry, about 1 cm long, and young shrimps are
caught on the sea shore with shrimping nets at the beginning
of the rainy monsoon and put into a small pond; when they
have grown to 7–8 cm they are transferred to another pond,
and later to a third until they are fully grown. They feed on
weeds growing in the ponds.

The farming techniques may have been imported from east
Java, but the making of ponds probably evolved from the
construction of the diked salt pans which have long been
common in the southern parts of South Sulawesi. Indeed, in
Pangkajé'né some of these ponds are used for fish farming
during the rainy season and as salt pans during the dry monsoon (Takaya, 'Land Use': 163).

Crafts

Two particular kinds of craft have important symbolic significance for Western Austronesian peoples: weaving and the art
of the smith. In their ancient dualist world-view, cloth represented the female principle, metal the male; and the union
of cloth and spear on a flag symbolized cosmic unity (Jager-
Gerlings, *Sprekende weefsels*). Sacred swords feature alongside sacred ploughs and sacred flags in the regalia of many
Bugis *wanua*. Aside from their symbolic meaning, weaving
and metal, both iron and gold, have played a long-standing
and very important part in the Bugis' economic life.

Textiles and Weaving

Weaving has long been a major source of income for the
Bugis. About 1785, Forrest wrote: 'The inhabitants of Celebes

are very industrious, weaving a deal of cotton cloth, generally cambays, which they export to all Malay countries; it is red checked and mixed with blue; they make beautiful silk belts, in which they fix their cresses [krisses].' Although nowadays South Sulawesi textiles are best known abroad – in some cases, only known – in the form of checked silk sarongs, a great variety of textiles are made. Besides cotton and silk, the Bugis weavers also make yarn from unspun *Corypha* or *Pandanus* fibres, and even use grass as weft for some long cotton-warped mats. The weaving and decorative techniques practised include plain gauze, plain warp or weft, striped or banded tabby weave, semi-twined warp, floating warp, tapestry weave, weft (and perhaps formerly warp) ikat, painted weft and supplementary weft, with continuous or discontinuous, gold or ordinary, floating or non-floating thread (Pelras, 'Textiles and Weaving'). The fabrics produced by these techniques are for the most part nowadays used in sarongs; up to the 1950s, card weaving was used to produce

Plate 50   A silk weaver at her back-tension loom

kriss belts. Mention should also be made of widely practised non-woven decorative textile techniques such as embroidery and appliqué, which are mostly used on bedsheets, pillows and curtains, as well as for the decorative canopies and hangings of bridal settees and rooms. Embroidered cloths of various kinds were mentioned in the *La Galigo* texts under many different names whose exact meanings are now unknown.

The earliest form of weaving loom used in South Sulawesi was probably similar to those used up to the present day among the Sa'dan, Rongkong and Kalumpang Toraja (type 1; see figure 1). These are of the common Indonesian back-tension type with continuous circulating warp. Among their features are a rear-beam around which the warp circulates and

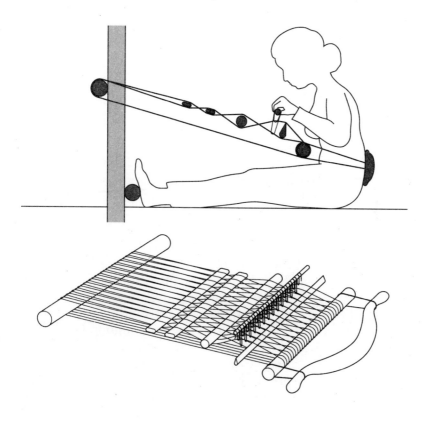

Figure 1   Type 1 loom

which, being suspended from a beam, usually of the granary, provides support for the whole loom; a shed-stick which maintains a permanently open shed between odd and even warp threads; a leash, whose loops take all the odd threads, pulled upwards by a heddle; a 'sword' used as both shed-opener and weft-beater; a front-beam around which the woven cloth circulates, and to which a back-tension yoke is attached by tension-strings.

These looms were probably used by the Bugis, as they still are by the Toraja, to weave either unspun fibres or cotton. Cotton was formerly in general use and so was cultivated and spun all over South Sulawesi. Silk, called *sabbé*, has been woven here since the end of the sixteenth century at the latest; earlier, silk cloth was a luxury imported from overseas. There are now two main types of Bugis and Makassar looms of more recent origin which are more suitable for weaving silk. Both are also of the back-tension type. One (type 2; see figure 2) has a so-called 'discontinuous rolled warp'. Its features include a warp-beam on which the warp is rolled; a warp-rod to which the warp is attached; a shed-stick; a pressing-stick which the weaver presses downwards at the same time as lifting the leashes to help separate the even warp threats, which pass over the shed-stick, from the odd threads; a leash, a heddle; a 'sword' whose blunt end rests on a sword-supporter each time it is removed from the shed; a comb acting as both warp-space and weft-rammer; a cloth-rod to which the other end of the warp is attached; a cloth-beam, either simple or composite, around which the cloth is rolled; and a back-tension yoke tied up to the cloth-beam by tension-strings.

The other type of loom (type 3; see figure 3) is again of the back-tension type. It looks like a loom with circulating warp, although in fact it is discontinuous and can thus feature a comb. This type is now found only in the south-eastern part of the peninsula along the Gulf of Boné, and among Bajo/Sama former boat-dwellers in the Pulau Sembilan archipelago; formerly, however, it was also used in other areas of Sulawesi, and is known in Flores (Sikka, Lio), the Sula Islands, Ternaté, the Sangihe Islands and Mindanao (Mandaya), which had close links with Sulawesi. It can be used for weaving any kind of yarn but seems to have been used most often for weaving

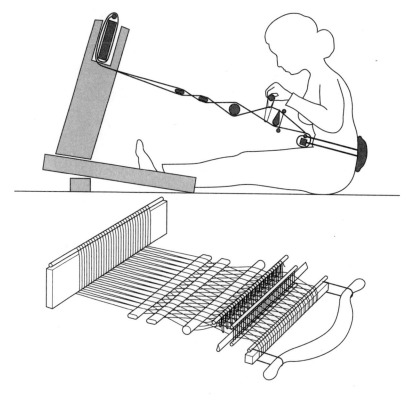

Figure 2   Type 2 loom

what in South Sulawesi was called *karoro* cloth from the unspun fibre of the *Corypha utan* palm, and in North Sulawesi *koffo* cloth from the unspun fibre of *Musa textilis*. The distinguishing feature of the discontinuous circulating warp is that its ends rejoin each other on a common warp-connecting rod, like the warp- and cloth-rods of the discontinuous flat warps; then the warp is stretched, like continuous warps, between a rear bar and a composite front bar.

As noted above, the weaving techniques used in South Sulawesi are many and various, although tabby weave predominates. The simpler decorative processes are used on material for sails made from unspun *Corypha* fibre on type 3 looms, whose comb-teeth are more widely spaced than usual. White

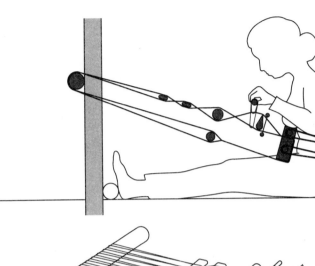

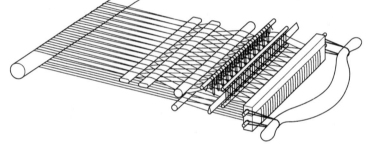

Figure 3 Type 3 loom

cotton cloth was formerly used mainly for shrouds; white cotton gauze was produced for bed curtains, mosquito nets, and for women's blouses, which were later dyed in the appropriate colours. An unusual kind of weaving still practised in the 1960s near Pangkajé'né was that of long mats with a cotton warp and a weft of blades of a particular grass, one blade for each pick. Multi-coloured fabrics produced by ground weaving include striped or banded and checked patterns. A striped pattern is said to be 'standing upright' or 'getting around', according to the appearance of the stripes on a sarong when it is worn. In simple checked cloths, a distinction is made between those with large 'empty' checks and those 'with a small motif'. A few fabrics are made using the floating warp technique, with supplementary heddles, which produces a damask effect. Cloths with discontinuous wefts of different colours, for use in sarongs, are quite popular among the Bugis; this tapestry weave is obtained by using two or more shuttles. Discontinuous wefts are interlocked where they meet so that there are no slits between adjacent areas of different colours, as is usual for instance is textiles made with a similar technique in Bali. This technique is usually known as *pucu'*, '[bamboo]-shoot', because the basic motif, on which there are many variations, is the long, triangular motif known in the literature as *tumpal*. Ikat (*ma'bebbe'*; cf. Balinese *bedbed*, Malay *bebat*) was formerly quite common.

Textiles decorated with a supplementary weft, whether of ordinary or gold thread, are produced in many patterns. Two variants of the technique of adding a decorative supplementary metallic weft are used in South Sulawesi: in one, the thread floats on the reverse of the cloth; in the other, by far the more common, the supplementary thread does not float. In this latter version, the supplementary weft has to be introduced in the even threads, i.e. those which pass over the shed-stick. Supplementary pattern-heddles or shed-sticks are seldom used to create the pattern; a mobile pointed shed-lath is all that is normally used, and the weaver thus has to keep the pattern in her head. For simple patterns the supplementary weft threads are inserted with the fingers; only for more complicated patterns does the weaver use small spools or quills. The right side may be uppermost or underneath, depending on the particular way of working followed. The 'gold thread' used in this kind of work since the distant past is imported and consists of finely beaten gold ribbon wrapped around a core fibre thread.

It has been argued in a previous chapter that weaving with the type 1 loom was probably brought to South Sulawesi by those immigrants who spoke the language from which the present languages of the peninsula derive. It remains difficult to identify the point at which the type 2 loom was introduced, although the existence of a comb strongly suggests that it came into use at the same time as silk weaving. If, as suggested by Robyn Maxwell (*Textiles*: 162), the Bugis word for silk, *sabbé*, does indeed derive from the Malay *sebai*, meaning 'scarf', this implies that silk was first known to the Bugis in the form of a type of imported cloth, not a raw material for weaving. I am inclined also to attribute the introduction of silk weaving itself to the Malays, given the similarity between the Bugis word for cloth-beam, *passa*, to the Malay term *pesa* (in contrast to the Javanese *apit*); similarly, the Bugis word for the weaver's comb, *jakka*, might correspond to a hypothetical Malay *pejanka*, 'space-gauge', whereas the common Javanese word for the same feature is *suru*. This type 2 loom may have been borrowed from those Malays who were established in trading harbours on the western coast of South Sulawesi in the fifteenth century. Familiarity with that type of loom and its main innovation, the comb, may have given birth to the transitional type 3 loom, which probably spread throughout Sulawesi and adjacent islands under Makassar influence during the seventeenth century. Later, type 2 looms progressively replaced those of type 3, but retained some of the latter's features: among these, the large front-beam resting on the weaver's lap, called *wakang*, was adapted into a new kind of cloth-beam, called not *passa* but *wakangeng*.

Metal Working

The two most important metals in Bugis culture are iron and gold. It was probably control over these two ores which gave Luwu' its original pre-eminence among Bugis kingdoms, while Bugis ironsmiths and goldsmiths appear in one way or another always to have had special connections with the holders of power. Silver, although less conspicuous than gold in Bugis jewellery, was also important for ceremonial objects, mostly related to betel consumption. Brass, introduced later, was used mainly for firearms and ceremonial tableware.

Control of the iron ore deposits, mined and smelted into ingots in the Rampi' and Séko valleys, in the upper reaches of the Kalaéna river and around Lakes Poso, Matano and Towuti, had been one of the main economic assets of the ancient kingdom of Luwu'. Nickel-bearing 'Luwu' iron' has for centuries been highly valued throughout the archipelago, especially in Java, for the manufacture of welded blades (*pamor*)

(Bronson, 'Indonesian Kris'). After the fifteenth century, however, Matano and Towuti gained in importance, and their major outlet was via Tobungku Bay in Eastern Sulawesi (the 'Tambuco' of Portuguese sources), which was mainly controlled by Ternaté; and from the seventeenth century onwards increasing amounts of scrap iron were imported from Europe. These developments contributed to the relative decline of Luwu', although its iron continued to be exported as far afield as Java and Borneo for *pamor* production. In South Sulawesi itself, while foreign iron was increasingly used for the most common tools, Luwu' iron was still strongly preferred for the fabrication of arms.

While iron smelting seems to have been limited to inland mountain areas rich in iron deposits, iron working was quite widely practised by the Bugis. In Boné, the second and partly mythical king of the local dynasty is known by the nickname of Petta Panré Bessi-é, 'His Highness the Smith', and an anvil purported to be his is still kept among the kingdom's regalia. On the western coast, in Bacukiki', a place in what is thought to be the *wanua*'s original site on Mt Aruang is called *a'manréng-é*, 'the Forge'. For a long time, however, the main iron-working centre for the whole Bugis area has been in Massépé, a large settlement in the vicinity of Tétéaji, the former capital of Sidénréng. Oral tradition tells of a sacred anvil which descended from the Heavens, and also of one Panré Baka, 'Master-Smith Baka', who, significantly, is said to have originated from Sangalla' in the Toraja country and to have moved first to Boné and then to Sidénréng, where he was invited by the ruler to stay. This tale thus encompasses three important factors specific to Bugis iron working: its sacred connotations; a presumably historical Toraja origin for iron-working techniques in the Bugis area; and a close link between mastery over iron and political rule. Certainly the rulers had an interest in controlling iron working, for two reasons: first, its production of axes, adzes, chopping-knives, sickles, dibble blades, hoes and ploughshares made it essential to the practice and development of agriculture, and therefore to the kingdom's subsistence and wealth; and secondly, its production of swords, krisses, short daggers, dart heads and lances offered superiority in war.

In the eighteenth century, indeed, a fully dressed Bugis was still a strongly armed man: 'A Buggess [*sic*] arms are sword, lance, dagger and target, sometimes a musquet and bayonet, or blenderbuss instead of the lance' (Forrest, *Voyage from Calcutta*: 80–1). Except for the addition of firearms, Bugis weaponry seems to have remained relatively unchanged from early historical times to the beginning of the twentieth century. The working of weapon blades was strongly invested with magical significance and required specific rituals. Certain smiths were considered to be endowed with supernatural powers, and some people still keep valued 'Luwu' daggers', on whose blades light hollows can be seen in places: these are said to be the fingerprints of the smiths who forged them with their bare hands. These daggers are considered to be very 'venomous'. Others are reputed to be invested with extraordinary powers, such as the ability to float on water, even to travel upriver, or to transform themselves on a Friday evening into a human being or a snake. The properties of a weapon, for example whether it is likely to bring luck or misfortune, not only in war or duel but in trade or love, can be determined by examination of the metal, noting the appearance of 'veins' or 'lines of life' and any apparent defects, and by comparison of its physical proportions with those of its owner. Guidelines for such examinations are set down in specialized *lôntara'*. In some cases a dream may be sent by the weapon's spirit guardian to the owner, bringing revelations about its past history and the identity of previous, famous owners from whom it received vital energy; possibly, too, about its desire to be returned to a previous owner. Some such weapons even have personal names, such as La Téariduni ('He who doesn't want to be put in a coffin') or La Téamusu' ('He who doesn't want war'). In fact, specific rituals seem to have been considered necessary even for ordinary iron working; in Massépé these did not fall into disuse until the twentieth century, under the influence of orthodox Islam, and a ceremony of *ma'céra'* was performed every year on the sacred *manurung* anvil until the Second World War.

The Bugis forge (Isa Sulaiman, *Dari gécong*: 20–3) is fairly typical of the specific south-east Asian model, which is found from northern Burma to eastern Indonesia, and from the southern Philippines to Madagascar (Marschall, *Metallurgie*: 187–208) and possibly originated in mainland south-east Asia in the Dongson period. Its most distinctive feature is the double bellows made of two vertical, hollowed cylinders of hard wood, such as rosewood – never of bamboo – which can be up to 1.5 metres tall and 0.4 metres in diameter. Inside each cylinder are pistons with feathers attached round the head as valves, driven by long wooden handles in an alternating motion. The air stream passes out through a hole at the base of the cylinders and down two bamboo or sometimes metal pipes joined by a clay tuyère into the hearth, bringing the burning charcoal to a high temperature. The larger the cylinders, the stronger the air blast and the higher the temperature obtained. When the work to be done is forging rather than smelting, the piston bellows needs relatively little force and is generally operated by a woman or child sitting on a high bench above the bellows.

For forging iron, the rest of the equipment consists of a small iron anvil set in a wooden base resting on the ground; a poker for the coals; tongs to manipulate the red-hot iron; a chisel to cut it into pieces; a set of hammers of different sizes and weights to hammer it into shape; a wooden pan of salt water for tempering; and a set of files with a filing stand made of two buffalo horns joined by a wooden or metal ruler. All the work is done by a master smith, crouching on the ground, with usually two helpers and a filer in charge of finishing. Many smiths specialize, producing just one or two kinds of products – agricultural instruments, nails and scissors, kitchen knives, betel cutters, or portable pestles and mortars, for example. Swords, lances and even krisses are no longer produced, but short daggers (*kawali*; Indonesian *badik*) are still occasionally made. Interestingly, although iron working has become a centralized activity – even the few smiths working outside Massépé came from there originally – the smiths adapt their production to various local demands: for example, they make different forms of hoes and choppers according to whether they are to be sold in Sidénréng, Wajo', Boné, Sinjai or the Ma'sénrémpulu'.

Copper, bronze and brass have also been worked by the Bugis. Small copper deposits exist in the mountains of Central Sulawesi, but there is no information about ancient exploitation of these resources and there seems to have been no local tradition of working pure copper sheets. On the other hand, until recently much important domestic equipment in aristocratic Bugis families was made from brass: trays, with and without pedestals (*bôsara'*), plates, glass stands, finger bowls, ewers, betel boxes, spittoons and oil lamps, with or without stands. These artefacts look quite similar to those obtainable in other coastal communities of the archipelago, for example among the Achehnese, Minangkabau or Malays, and it is unlikely that all of them were produced locally. Although Matthes (*Atlas*) gives information about brass-working techniques and equipment used in South Sulawesi itself, this activity was probably very sporadic and limited to the finishing of imported pieces. In the eighteenth and nineteenth centuries most brass objects on the peninsula, such as tableware, gongs and firearms (mostly cannons and culverins), seem to have originated in Brunei and been purchased in Singapore. Indeed, in the late eighteenth century Forrest wrote: 'They make firearms, but cannot make gun locks; they also cast small brass guns, which they call rantakkas . . . ; the larger rantakka is about 6 feet long, and carries a half pound ball . . . They get many rantakkas from Borneo proper, where they are expert in making them' (Forrest, *Voyage from Calcutta*: 81).

Gold and silver, on the other hand, were skilfully worked by Bugis smiths. Most of the gold was obtained by panning the rivers of the Toraja country, where talented goldsmiths are still at work; as with iron working, it is perhaps from the craftsmen of this area that the Bugis goldsmiths learned their trade. In any event, there is a long-standing tradition of gold working in the Bugis area, linked, of course, with the existence of a sophisticated aristocracy. Most of the precious metal was made into jewellery, with specific categories of ornaments designated as appropriate to each rank. For example, only women of *ana' ma'tola* rank could wear twenty-four bangles on each arm; those of lower rank could wear only a plated long bracelet between two ring bracelets, and commoner women could wear only a long bracelet, usually of lower quality.

Finger rings apart, very few items of jewellery were made of solid gold. Some were made out of gold sheet: bangles, ring bracelets and studs were made hollow. Bracelets, studs, diadems, bun sheaths, ear pendants, necklaces, breast or belt plates and kriss hilts and sheaths were decorated using *repoussé* or filigree techniques. The metal was valued more for

Plate 51   Bugis silverwork

its colour than for its purity: gold of a reddish tint was
preferred, and this was obtained by alloying the gold with
copper and then enriching the surface through an application
of acid followed by burnishing. The Bugis are still fond of gold
jewellery, but complete sets are now worn only at weddings;
on other occasions Bugis women prefer to wear modern jewellery made by Chinese goldsmiths.

Bugis goldsmiths worked in silver too. Where the silver originally came from is not clear. An indication that it was imported
in ancient times is the derivation of the word for silver, *salaka*,
from Sanskrit. From the seventeenth century onwards, the
silver used by the smiths of South Sulawesi was obtained from
Spanish, Dutch, Austrian or Mexican coins.[2] Objects made in
silver were of the same kinds as those made from brass,

---

[2] According to Ian Glover (personal communication), only Burma in
south-east Asia has much silver and in the seventeenth century a great deal
of this metal was imported from Mexico and Peru. Even Dutch guilders were
made from Mexican silver.

including betel sets, spittoons, ewers, and trimmings for the shafts of ceremonial spears, but not eating utensils: the silver versions were reserved for higher-ranking nobles. Silver is also used for decorating the sheaths of short daggers. Among other common silver objects were the medallions worn by children as a *cache-sexe* for so long as they went without clothes, made for girls in the shape of a heart, for boys in the shape of a penis.

At some stage – the date is unknown – a fine type of silver filigree work was developed in South Sulawesi, called 'Kendari filigree', although it is not certain that it was first made in the place in south-eastern Sulawesi which bears that name. It may already have existed at the end of the eighteenth century, as suggested by a remark made by Forrest: '[The Bugis] are curious of fillagree work, both in gold and silver' (*Voyage from Calcutta*: 81).

Sea Trade and Navigation

Bugis sea trade did not really come into its own until the fall of Makassar in 1666–7 after nearly a century of naval pre-eminence. Bugis maritime commerce was developed by the Boné people of Cénrana, Bajoé and Kajuara, and most of all by Wajo' navigators sailing from Lake Témpé – or, when they did not want to pay duties to Boné, from their own small ports of Doping and Pénéki – and above all from Makassar, where they had an important community. Their other important bases outside South Sulawesi were at Flores, Sumbawa, Lombok and Bali; Gresik in East Java; Bonératé in the Flores Sea; Kaili in north-western Sulawesi; Kutei, Pasir, Pegatan, Pulo Laut and Pontianak in eastern, south-eastern and western Borneo respectively; Batavia (Jakarta), Riau and Malaya.

Types of Ships and their Evolution

The Bugis have two basic kinds of sailing craft: the dug-out canoe (*lépa-lépa*), generally provided with outriggers; and planked boats (*lopi*), without outriggers. The former have the longer history, since the felling and hollowing of trees was

Plate 52 A lambo' *sloop under sail*

possible with only stone implements and fire. Later on, but
still with only simple tools, side planks could be added, 'sewn'
to each other with rattan by the 'lashed lugs' method. However, progress in the building of entirely planked boats was
linked to the development of iron technology, which enabled
holes to be gouged with a spoon-like implement; into these
dowels were inserted to attach the planks to one another and
the hull to the ribs. This process was observed in the eighteenth century by Forrest: 'They build their paduakans [*paduwakang*] very tight, by dowling the planks together, as
coopers do the parts that form the head of a cask, and putting
the bark of a certain tree between, which swells, and then
fit timbers to the planks, as at Bombay, but do not rabbet (as

Plate 53 An early twentieth-century innovation often wrongly considered a century-old heritage: the pînisi' *schooner*

it is called) the planks, as at Bombay' (*Voyage from Calcutta*: 80).

The boats mentioned in the *La Galigo* texts, large as they were, belonged to the 'canoe' category and, like the Borobudur ships, did have outriggers. On the other hand, we know that large ocean-going planked boats without outriggers were built and operated elsewhere in the archipelago and between there and India as early as the first few centuries of the Christian era (Manguin, 'Southeast Asian Ship'). For South Sulawesi, we know only from the earliest European writings that by the end of the sixteenth century the Bugis and Makassar probably had planked boats as well as those of the canoe type. We know, too, that at that time the main sea-trading peoples of the archipelago were the Malays and the Javanese, and that the main centres of ship-building were on the northern coast of Java and the south-eastern coast of Borneo around Pegatan, where a large number of Makassar and Bugis ships were still being built in the seventeenth century. Thus it is possible that these places may have played a role in the acquisition by the South Sulawesi peoples of this, for them, relatively new ship-building technology.

From the seventeenth century to the end of the nineteenth, the typical Sulawesi ship was the *paduwakang* or *padéwakang* (also called *padéwa'* or *paréwa*): the name is probably a borrowed one, although it is not clear from where. There were two main types, respectively called the 'long' and 'short' types according to the shape of the hull (Macknight, 'Study of Praus': 26). The 'long' type, which was also narrower, included the *binta'*, a warship with both sails and rowers, and the *palari*, or 'runner', a fast craft used for various purposes; the 'short' type included the *banawa*, for cattle transport, the *pa'palimbang*, a ferryboat, and the *pajala*, for dragnet fishing (Matthes, *Atlas*, pls 16, 17). All these variants had in common a basic characteristic which they shared with a smaller kind of vessel called *biséang* in Makassar – and indeed with all ancient Insulindian plank-built boats – namely the shape of the hull with its crescent-moon profile. This was obtained by elongating the curved keel with equally curved front and rear stems, attached by tenon and mortice, making a continuous curve. Like all south-east Asian boats of that time, they did not have the single, axial stern-post rudder of contemporary Chinese and European ships, but two oar-like quarter-rudders, like those used in Europe until the fourteenth century.

The deadworks of each variety of ship were constructed differently according to its function. The smaller planked boats were not decked, while the larger ones often had elaborate – sometimes quite inelegant – deck structures, making manoeuvring the sails and steering rather awkward. There were a few common details. One was the presence of the *sangkilang*, a king of transverse double bench fixed before the poop and jutting out over both sides, with a notch on each end where the port and starboard quarter-rudders were fixed; similar devices existed in all traditional south-east Asian craft. Alfred Wallace, who in 1856 travelled in such a boat from Makassar to the Aru Islands, gave a good description of their operation: 'The rudders were not hinged but hung with slings of rattan, the friction of which keeps them in any position in which they are placed, and thus perhaps facilitates the steering' (Wallace, *Malay Archipelago*: 310). Behind the *sangki-*

lang there might be a platform (*ambing*), sometimes jutting out over the poop to make steering easier. Towards the prow, before the mainmast, there was a transverse beam on top of a kind of riser (*salompong*); called a 'splashboard' by Horridge [*Bugis Prahus*: 4], this was made of one or two planks and rose over a short, low foredeck. Seen from the side, the bow thus seemed to be lower than the rest of the boat, presenting an appearance both strange and dubious to Western eyes: 'The paduakans have their bow lowered or cut down in a very awkward manner: a bulk head is raised a good way abast the stem, to keep off the sea, and the fore part is so low as to be often under water: they are unfit to encounter a gale of wind, not being decked' (Forrest, *Voyage from Calcutta*: 80).

Between the *salompong* and the end of the stem were wedged two crossed spars (*sarémpa*) to which a square jib was sometimes fixed. This apart, the rig consisted of one or two – very seldom three – tripod masts bearing sails (*sompe'*) of a type called *tanja'*: rectangular, each fitted to two long, parallel, tilted booms. According to Horridge, this rig

is a sophisticated fore-and-aft rig and not a square sail as is usually assumed by Western scholars. It works more like a lug sail than a square sail on a full-rigged ship, because one boom can be made into a leading edge. With the mast in the right place, a boat with a single sail of this type holds any course within a range of about 260° (not less than 50° to the wind) and little use of the rudder, because the sail can be rotated around the mast and its centre of pull can be moved forward or aft by tilting . . . Beside that, however, the [*sompe' tanja'*] can be set almost horizontally like a wing when going into the wind, so that it lifts the bows when they would otherwise be knocked back by slap. Furthermore, the sail can be reefed to any extent by rolling it around the lower boom. (Horridge, *Bugis Prahus*: 4)

The tripod masts, which had crooked heads with grooves for halyards, could also be pivoted back over the boat, as explained by Forrest:

A tripod mast . . . gave an amazing deal of room in the body of the vessel . . . which, added to that given by the galleries, made her, although only a boat of 10 to 12 tons, have the accommodation of a vessel of three times that burden. The tripod, when struck, offers itself as a boom to spread a tarpaulin upon, or cajans [*kajang*], as the Malays call palm leaves sewed together . . . The tripod mast was made of three stout bamboos . . . ; the two feet abreast were bored at the lower end across . . . and these holes received the two ends of a piece of timber which, like a main thaft, went across; on these the two ends of the two abreast parts of the tripod turned as on a hinge. The fore part of the tripod mast, like a main stay, was fixed forward to a knee amidships, with a forelock: by unlocking the forelock, the mast is struck in a moment. (Forrest, *Voyage from Calcutta*: 127–8)

This kind of mast was present as early as the ninth century in Borobudur ships, and would fit with the large outrigger boats described in the *La Galigo* texts.

The evolution of the *padéwakang*, as far as rigging is concerned, has been well explained by Horridge (*Bugis Prahus*: 26–32). From about 1830–40 triangular, Western-style jibs appeared, fixed to a light bowsprit which was itself supported by the *sarémpa*, the two oblique bars intersecting at the stem of the boat. In the second half of the nineteenth century, gaff sails were added to the *tanja'* sails and the steering bench was covered by a structure with openings on each side, which obliged the steersmen to sit in the open, a few feet above the sea. It was on a ship built in this way that Alfred Wallace made his journey from Makassar to the Aru Islands in 1856. Towards the end of the century, an uninterrupted deck appeared, and the *tanja'* sails were increasingly replaced by gaff sails. The tripod masts lost their crooked tops, rendered obsolete by the introduction of tackle, and many were elongated by the addition of a topmast to enable topsails to be used. The bowsprit also became stronger, to accommodate up to three jibs. Still later, the mizzenmast ceased to be a tripod, leaving only the foremast built in this way. By this stage, the large trading ships of the Bugis and Makassar had acquired a ketch rig called in Bugis *sompe' pînisi'* (Malay *pinas*, probably borrowed from the English 'pinnace').

There is often some confusion in the nomenclature of South Sulawesi boats, as a result of the coexistence of several terminological systems. One system is related to the boat's function (*pajala*: fishing boat using a dragnet; *pakaja*: fishing boat using basket traps; *patorani*: fishing boat to catch flying fish) or main feature (*palari*: running ship). Another system is based on the style of rigging (*pînisi*': a ketch or sometimes sloop, with standing gaffs, topsails and jibs without booms; *lambo*', a sloop, sometimes ketch, with sliding gaff, no topsail, and boomed jib or jibs; *nadé*': a gunter sail; *lété*': a two-boomed lateen, also called *sompe' Mandura* ('Madura Sail')). Yet another system has to do with the shape of the hull: *padéwakang* or *biséang*, *beggo*', *lété*', *sékoci*. A particular boat can of course be named within any of the three systems, but as not all variants exist everywhere, the same name can refer to different boats in different places and at different times. For example, in Bira the name *palari*, which used often to be applied to a *padéwakang* and then to a *pînisi*', usually refers to a *lambo*' – a name which in Boné is usually given to a boat with a *sékoci* hull and in Paré-Paré to one with a *beggo*' hull.

The *sékoci* hulls, from the Dutch *schuitje* ('small boat') but possibly inspired by the English South Seas pearling luggers (Horridge, *Sailing Craft*: 32), came into use at the beginning of the twentieth century; popular in the Moluccas at first, they were quickly adopted, together with the counter-stern, by the Buton navigators, and became increasingly popular in South Sulawesi in the 1920s. The rigging was usually of the single-masted *lambo*' type, although there were larger, two-masted *lambo*' among the Bugis ships which visited Singapore in 1949 (Gibson-Hill, 'Trading Boats': 134). According to Gibson-Hill, these ships were not very seaworthy in rough conditions; but sailing with the wind, they did 10 knots and could make the trip from Makassar to Singapore in seven or eight days. Bugis sailors say that the *lambo*' is more manoeuvrable than the *pînisi*'; for a similar size of boat, the latter would need twenty hands to the eight required for the former. *Lambo*' with *beggo*' hulls must have emerged in imitation of those with *sékoci* hulls; an example of such a boat appears under the name *palari* in a drawing done by Nieuwenkamp in the 1920s. According to Bugis sailors, *beggo*' hulls are preferable to the *sékoci* type where port facilities are poor or absent, as is the case on many of the isolated islands or out-of-the-way shores they visit. With their shallow draught, the *beggo*' can easily lay in shallow waters and enter shallow estuaries, and at low tide they can lay on their bottom with the quarter-rudders simply raised, whereas axial stern-post rudders would have to be removed. The sailors say that, even in rough seas, a *lambo' beggo'*, with its two quarter-rudders, is easier to steer than a *lambo' uri'* with a single, axial rudder.

While plank-built boats have for centuries been the Bugis' main sea-trading vessels, outrigger canoes, although mainly fishing craft, were also used for transport. Most of these types of boat are particular to a specific locality, and their names often differ from place to place; nevertheless, the many variants are often very similar in their basic features, both to each other and to other canoes in the archipelago. In many cases the difference are merely formal, and concern mainly the shape of the stem. In respect of the rigging, by contrast, the names for the sails used are of general application and correspond to sail types witnessed throughout the archipelago (Horridge, *Sailing Craft*: 49, 56–8). According to Horridge, the original Austronesian rig was the two-boomed triangular sail. He thinks that the tilted rectangular sail could have been borrowed about 2,000 years ago from the Indian Ocean, but one might wonder whether the acquisition occurred the other way round: an island people like the Austronesians are, after all, more likely to have made nautical innovations than to have borrowed them from the people of India, who are basically landsmen.

Ship Building

South Sulawesi is remarkable for the assocation of specialized craftsmen with particular localities. Just as nearly all Bugis smiths live in or come from Massépé, so nearly all the ship builders of the peninsula live in or come from Ara' and neighbouring Lémo and Tana Béru. These people are ethnic Makassar and speak a variety of the *konjo* dialect of Makassar, which is closer to Bugis than standard Makassar. They also work on contract at other Bugis boatyards, for example in Bajoé, Palanro or Paré-Paré; and now that timber has become scarce around Ara', they go in groups of ten or twenty to ply their trade wherever there is a Bugis community: to South Sumatra, central south-eastern Kalimantan, the northern coast of Java (Semarang and Gresik), Sumbawa, Sumba,

Flores and even to western New Guinea. There are, however, a few examples of Bugis navigators in places still rich in timber, like Jambi, who have built their own ships.

Although in the seventeenth and eighteenth centuries the Bugis had most of their boats built in south-east Borneo, the specialization of the Ara' people in ship's carpentry must be of very long standing, reaching back to the specific role formerly played by their ancestors (the Waniaga of the *La Galigo* texts) and their neighbours from Selayar, the two groups who are said in these texts to have provided Sawérigading's rowers. Ara', it should also be remembered, controls a junction on one of the routes between east Java and the Moluccas, at the entry into the Gulf of Boné.

Building a ship of 200 tons burden by purely traditional methods with a team of ten under a master carpenter can take three to four months. The size of Bugis ships seems to have varied widely at any given time, according to the nature of the cargoes to be transported and the types of boat most appropriate for each specific task. According to Captain Woodard, who at the end of the eighteenth century was detained for two years in Palu, the Bugis boats there had a burden of no more than 5–30 tons (Woodard, *Narrative*); but a Bugis text on boat building which may date from about the same period (Macknight and Mukhlis, 'Manuscript about Praus': 276) gives a hull length of about 18 metres from prow to stem for a *padéwakang*, which today would correspond to a capacity of about 60 tons. In the seventeenth century, the oared warships of the kingdom of Goa measured between 26 metres and 40 metres in length, with a beam of 6 metres, and could transport about 100 men each (Side', 'Expansion de Goa': 160, 169). It is possible that the Bugis might have sailed even larger ships, since a boat-building technology similar to theirs produced the Javanese ships of 500 tons (or perhaps more) that were to attack Malaka in the sixteenth century (Crawfurd, *Descriptive Dictionary*: 294, s.v. 'Navigation'). Recent research (Manguin, 'Southeast Asian Ship'; 'Vanishing Jong') has shown that a ship of this size was by no means exceptional, and that there existed an old-established tradition of south-east Asian, mainly Insulindian, ocean-going ships whose dimensions and techniques of construction filled the earliest European visitors with awe: some of them, indeed, were larger than the Europeans' own craft. According to Manguin, while the large ships of the Javanese fleet which attacked Malaka in 1512 ranged from 350 to 500 tons, some very large Insulindian ships reached 500 to 1,000 tons, as did some contemporary Chinese and Gujarati vessels.

Techniques of Navigation

Until the nineteenth century, the Bugis captain of a trading *padéwakang* was called *nakoda* or *anakoda*; his second-in-command, *juragang*. Each such vessel usually also had two *jurumudi*, 'steersmen', in charge of directing the ship's course; two *jurubatu*, 'sounders', in charge of checking the depth at the approach to the coast, reefs or shoals; and one *jurutûlisi'*, 'secretary', the agent of the ship's owner. All these names are clear borrowings from Malay, which had itself taken *nakhoda* from Persian. In the twentieth century this system has been simplified: the *juragang* is now the captain, the *jurumudi* the mate, and the two men work together to direct the ship, check the depth and look after the interests of the ship's and the cargo's owners. These two alone are empowered to operate the main, leeward, quarter-rudder. During particularly difficult manoeuvres, such as leaving port or negotiating reefs or shoals, an experienced sailor takes the second rudder; at other time it is left unmanned, acting simply as a stabilizer.

The geographical knowledge of Bugis sailors, with their well-attested enthusiasm for sea charts, has for centuries extended not only over the whole area now known as Indonesia and Malaysia, but beyond to neighbouring countries, as is obvious from names written in Bugis on a number of eighteenth-century charts which have come down to us. These include Cambodia ('Kambuja'), Cochinchina ('Kuci'), Sulu, New Guinea ('Papua') and north Australia ('Marégé'). To determine their position and therefore their course, however, Bugis sailors at sea rely hardly at all on either charts or navigational instruments. Of the latter, all they generally have on board are compasses (*padoma*) – these are mentioned in a few *La Galigo* episodes, and even if one suspects an element of anachronism here, they must at least have been known in the fourteenth century – but their use is limited. Recent fieldwork by the astronomer and anthropologist Gene Amarell ('Bugis Navigation': 220–63) has shown that once out of sight of land, Bugis navigators use a range of convergent methods, referring to the sun and stars, the maritime environment and winds.

The rising and setting points of the sun are of course used as indicators of direction. Navigation by the stars, too, involves observing their rising or setting point on the horizon, which from a particular location is known to indicate the direction of a destination. Among those mentioned by Raffles (*History of Java*, appendix F, 'Celebes': CLXXXCIII) as used by the Bugis and Makassar in this way were *Worong-mporong*, the Pleiades; a constellation known in Bugis as *Manu'*, 'the Chicken', and in Makassar as *Jangang-jangang*, which includes Sirius; and Orion's belt, *Tanra Tellu* ('the Triple Beacon'), sometimes called *Rakkala* or *Pajéko* ('the Plough'). Amarell has also noted the name *Kâppala'*, 'the Ship', for the Big Dipper in Ursa Major, which Raffles mentions under the name of Jonga-jonga. Other constellations used by Bugis navigators, as noted by Amarell, include *Walu*, Alpha and Beta Centauri; *Wari-wari* ('the Small Fly') or *Bintoing élé* ('the Morning Star'), Venus; *Mangiweng* ('the Shark'), Scorpio's tail; *Bintoing L* ('the "L" Letter', obviously a recent appellation for a constellation which must have had another, ancient, name), Altair and part of Cygnus; *Tanra Bajo* ('the Bajo Beacon') the Magellan Clouds; and *Bémbé* ('the Goat'), the 'Coal Sack' in the Milky Way near the Southern Cross. Of the nine constellations used by Bugis farmers, six are thus used by navigators; the remaining three are *Warawara* (Aldebaran), *Watang Mpata* and *Tekko soro*.

Experienced Bugis navigators also draw a great deal of information from their observation of the sea and the maritime environment: the movement of the swells, the shape of waves, the salinity, colour and temperature of the water, the presence or absence of currents, the existence and nature of flotsam, the behaviour of fish and the flight patterns of birds. Expert sailors, too, know the precise direction of the wind in each particular sector of the archipelago at every time of year.

When land is in sight, of course, specific landmarks provide the best guidance of direction. For example, to a craft approaching the southern tip of South Sulawesi, Mt Bawaka-raéng/Lompobattang is visible in the early morning or later afternoon from quite a distance: 'The Bonthain [Bantaéng] mountain, called by the natives Lampo Batan (big belly), is the highest on the south part of the island, and being seen at the distance of one hundred and twenty miles, must be about eight thousand five hundred feet above the level of the sea' (Raffles, *History of Java*, appendix F, 'Celebes': CLXXVIII).

Cargoes, Routes and Organization

In the seventeenth century the kingdom of Goa based its maritime trade mainly on the export of Moluccan spices and the import of Indian cloth, thereby posing a very serious threat to the monopolistic ambitions of the Dutch. Other imports included silver coins from Europe and Mexico (the latter coming through Manila), firearms from Europe and Japan, steel from India, gold from the Philippines, lead from Siam, copper from Japan and porcelain from China. Imports from other Insulindian areas bound for re-export included pepper from Banjarmasin and Jambi, sappanwood from Sumbawa and sandalwood from Sumba. Sulawesi itself exported tortoiseshell, rattan, wax and trepang or sea-cucumbers (Villiers, 'Makassar': 150–1). The Treaty of Bungaya, concluded between the Dutch, the South Sulawesi kingdoms and Ternaté in 1666, forbade the peoples of South Sulawesi to engage in the Moluccan spice trade. This led the Makassar and their traditional Bugis allies from Wajo' to develop their trade with the western parts of the archipelago and the shores of continental south-east Asia, particularly Malaya. It did not, however, prevent some smuggling with the eastern islands, as Thomas Forrest noted a century later:

The Dutch keep what they possess on Celebes chiefly on account of its being the west frontier to the Spice Islands . . . the Buggesses often find their way there in spite of their vigilance. I have seen, 25 years ago [i.e. in about 1760], 15 prows at a time, at Bencoolen [south-western Sumatra], with a mixt cargo of spices, wax, cassia, sandle wood, dollars, and the cloths of Celebes called cambays. (Forrest, *Voyage from Calcutta*: 79)

Forrest goes on to list goods traded from Sulawesi, such as gold, wax, rice, sago and slaves, from which the Dutch derived considerable profit, and in which the Bugis themselves must also have dealt.

There still exists among the Bugis a code of maritime law attributed to Amanna Gappa, headman of the Wajo' community in Makassar from 1697 to 1723 (Noorduyn, 'Wajo' Merchants': 5). A chapter of this code concerning freight rates includes an interesting list of the points of departure and destination of Bugis ships of that period, and also gives an idea of the routes they followed. The points of embarkation mentioned include not only Makassar and the ports of the Bugis country but also Kaili (north-west Sulawesi); the ports of east Borneo including Pasir and Berau; south Borneo with Banjarmasin; West Borneo including Pontianak and Sambas; and Sumbawa in the Lesser Sunda Islands. The points of destination included in addition Sulu to the north; to the west, Aceh, Aru, Palembang, Bangka and Belitung in Sumatra, Kedah, Selangor, Malaka, Johor and Trengganu in Malaya, and Cambodia; to the south-west, south and south-east, Jakarta, Semarang, Sumenep in Madura, other ports of east Java, Bali, and Manggarai in Flores. To the east, the inclusion of Buton, Ternaté, Ambon, Banda and Kei indicates that the Moluccan route had not been altogether abandoned. The text does not give a complete list of cargoes, mentioning only those to which specific rates apply: these included slaves; bulky goods such as rice, salt, cotton, rattan, chewing tobacco and gambir nuts (both to be consumed with betel), agar-agar and wood; and valuables, such as coins, gold and precious stones (Tobing, *Amanna Gappa*: 44–6).

A specific item in the itinerary of the South Sulawesi sailing communities, including Bugis, Makassar and Bajo navigators, was their annual expeditions to north-western Australia, in which about thirty ships, each manned by about thirty men, set off to collect trepang or sea cucumbers (*Holothuria*) (Macknight, *Voyage to Marege'*), which they sold to Chinese merchants in Makassar; this trade represented a quarter of all

Chinese trepang imports. These voyages are recorded from at least 1725 but may have been undertaken earlier; they continued until the beginning of the twentieth century.

Raffles described the organization of a Bugis trading voyage at the beginning of the nineteenth century as follows:

Each person in the prahu has his own share of the cargo, and conducts business on his own account: each person likewise carries his own provisions . . . The owner of the vessel agrees to undertake the voyage with a number of people, great or small, in proportion to its size, and apportions the vessel among them in the following manner. The two juru mudis, or steersmen, receive one pétah [Malay *pétak*] or division before the sanketan [*sangkilang*] and the whole space abast of it; the owner is entitled to two pétahs in the broadest part of the boat; and the two juru batus to the whole space between the masts; the remaining pétahs are divided among the crew; from whom the owner, or nakoda, receives a freight of one tenth or one twentieth or the price of all commodities they sell, according as they are bulky or small, in proportion to their value. The juru mudis and juru batus only pay one-half of the proportion of freight paid by the rest of the crew. Sometimes the owner supplies the crew with an advance of money for the adventure, and receives at its termination not only payment of his loan, but a third of the profits of the speculation. (Raffles, *History of Java*, appendix F, 'Celebes': CLXXXIII)

For a slightly earlier period, at the end of the seventeenth and beginning of the eighteenth centuries, the chapter headings of a printed version of Amanna Gappa's maritime law code, with Indonesian translation and comments (Tobing, *Amanna Gappa*) give an indication of the detailed commercial jurisprudence in force at that time:

1 Concerning passage-money: determination of the percentage received (*sima*) on profits made from embarked goods, varying according to the route taken.
2 Concerning profit-sharing between the ship's owner and the captain, if they are not one and the same person.
3 Concerning the costs of returning unsold goods.
4 Concerning measures to be taken if the captain changes the destination of the ship, and the rights and duties of the various categories of embarked persons: permanent crew,

free crew, embarked traders, ordinary passengers; also the places allocated in the ship for their respective goods.

5 Concerning the authority of the *jurumundi* and the *jurubatu*.

6 Concerning the prerequisites for and qualities necessary in the captain of a ship.

7 Concerning the various kinds of commercial cooperation: joint venture between travelling trader and owner of goods; part-share of the travelling trader in the benefits of the owner of goods; entrusting of goods to the travelling trader for a fixed price to be paid on return; payment on return of a price fixed in advance for goods sold during the voyage, or return of unsold goods; and entrusting of goods to a dependant of the owner of the goods.

8 Concerning indebtedness during the voyage.

9 Concerning the inheritance of traders deceased during the voyage.

10 Concerning the settlement of disputes between traders.

11 Concerning the obligation to refer disputes which arise on board ship to the captain's arbitration.

12 Concerning particular rules affecting joint ventures.

13 Concerning particular rules affecting loans and borrowing.

14 Concerning payment of debts.

15 Concerning how to handle a slave to whom goods have been entrusted and who has committed a misdemeanour on board.

16 Concerning what to do with the goods of a trader who dies during a voyage.

17 Concerning the obligation to reimburse borrowed money in the form of money, and borrowed goods in the form of goods.

18 Concerning the responsibilities of *kalula* (authorized representatives or trustees).

19 Concerning indebtedness on the part of a dependent and on the part of a slave of the owner of the goods.

20 Concerning the passage-money to be asked of shipwrecked persons who have been taken on board at sea.

21 The recommendations of Amanna Gappa concerning lending and borrowing.

10

The Modern World

Whether we think the modern era has seen our societies in progress or decline, we may agree on some general features of modernity. One is the increasing interconnectedness of the world's societies: probably no human group now remains completely isolated, almost none wholly unknown or wholly ignorant of the world outside it.[1] Production activities have become exchange-oriented in a universal trend towards market economies in which trade and money are key aspects of social life. Local communities, small polities and petty states have (with some notable exceptions) tended to become integrated into larger political units, while ideas of citizenship and political opinion have become ubiquitous. Another feature of modernity is the universal diffusion of certain ideological (religious or philosophical), cultural, social and political models increasingly marked by the development of rationality and individualism, including concepts of individual opinions, rights and freedoms. Notwithstanding the leading role played in this world-wide process of modernization by Europe and models of Western origin, it would be a mistake to consider it simply as a process of westernization, or the advent of a Western-dominated world culture. The modern world

[1] Relatively recent 'discoveries' of 'unknown tribes' in the Philippines or New Guinea have been greatly exaggerated by the media. In fact, these usually very small groups were known, and were in many cases linguistically related to, known groups living at some distance from them, from which they had split away some time in the not very distant past.

appears, rather, to encompass several interconnected and overlapping subcultures, including that – or those – of Islam, in which Bugis society participates.

Although it may seem paradoxical to those who honestly assume as self-evident that peoples little known to them, who live outside the recognized spheres of high civilization, are necessarily archaically minded, ossified and backward, the Bugis have for centuries been predisposed to modernization and in some cases have even anticipated it. Many of the aspects of modernity mentioned above have been present throughout their history. In the nineteenth and twentieth centuries, of course, this movement has been accelerated, both by external political developments, from colonization to Indonesian independence, and by internal influences including the process of islamization, the development of literacy and education in Malaysia and Indonesia, and an increasing degree of integration in a world-wide economic system

From Autonomous Traditional Polities to the Modern Integrated Nation-State

Following the creation in the Netherlands of the Batavian Republic, on 31 December 1799 the Dutch East India Company was liquidated and its entire colonial empire taken into the direct possession of the Dutch state. The Committee for East Indian Affairs in the Hague stipulated that 'the doctrine of liberty and equality . . . cannot be transferred nor applied to the East Indian possessions of the State . . . as long as the introduction cannot take place without exposing these possessions to a confusion the effect of which cannot be imagined' (Vlekke, *Nusantara*: 236–42). For the Indies, this precluded the enforcement of free trade as well as the abolition of slavery and, in those places where it was in force, of compulsory cultivation of export crops or communal ownership of farm lands. Nevertheless, the beginning of the nineteenth century in the East Indian archipelago saw the foundations laid on which not only the colonial but even, much later, the independent Indonesian state would rest. The principles implemented by the Dutch Bonapartist Governor-General, H. W. Daendels, in the reorganization of the bureaucracy and administration, at first only in Java but later in other islands as well – such as his division of the country into provinces and regencies under government-appointed officials, albeit chosen from among the local aristocracy – and of the administration of justice, have been followed ever since.

In 1810, soon after the incorporation of the Netherlands into the French Empire, Britain took pre-emptive action to prevent the French army and fleet making the Indies into a stronghold threatening British interests in the East and, having already taken Malaka from the Dutch in 1795, now determined on taking possession of the rest of the Dutch East Indies. Ambon fell into British hands in February 1810, Makassar in June and Ternaté in August; finally, in September 1811, Java was captured. Thomas Stamford Raffles, appointed the new British Lieutenant-Governor in Java, took the administrative reforms initiated by Daendels still further: he deprived native princes of most of their powers in the management of their states, completed the replacement of the former feudalistic system of local government by a modern territorial bureaucracy, and radically reformed the state financial and tax system. Henceforth a land rent would be paid by all farmers, thus introducing at the village level a money economy previously known only to the princely and merchant classes. On their return in 1817, as a result of an agreement reached with the British, the Dutch decided to leave all these reforms in place (Vlekke, *Nusantara*: 261–76), and moreover began to apply them outside Java as well.

From 1830 to about 1870, Java and a few other parts of the archipelago, including some districts of Sumatra, North Sulawesi and the Moluccas, were subjected to the so-called 'Culture System', which involved the exploitation of the lands under Dutch direct rule as though they constituted one huge plantation owned by the government; it also brought further administrative reform with the appointment of *controleurs* alongside the indigenous regents. Later, in the last years of the nineteenth century, an official shift to liberalism occurred – albeit only a limited one, since the agrarian law of 1870 prohibited the sale of landed property owned by Indonesians to non-Indonesians.

Although these changes left the peoples of South Sulawesi untouched, they had consequences for their immediate environment, and for the colonial system which was later to be imposed on them.

The Traditional Powers of South Sulawesi: Resilience and Decline, 1810–1906

The political situation in South Sulawesi at this time was quite different from that in Java. Although most of the Bugis states were nominally vassals of the government in Batavia and were located at the very centre of an area recognized by international treaties between Western powers as being under Dutch overlordship, they remained in practice virtually independent throughout the nineteenth century. However, while the Dutch for the most part had little say in their internal affairs during this period, they did make repeated attempts to encroach on their autonomy and progressively gain control over the area, culminating in the military action of 1905 which effectively established Dutch administration throughout the peninsula.

When the British occupied Makassar in 1810, a number of Bugis rulers, led by the *datus* of Tanété and Suppa', refused to acknowledge their authority, arguing that the end of Dutch rule meant that they were free again. Further friction with the British arose later in Boné, whose ruler refused to hand over the main regalia of Goa, the Sudanga sword, which had fallen into Boné hands in 1785 after the Sangkilang rebellion. The British Resident in Makassar appointed in 1812, Captain Phillips, sent a military expedition against Suppa', but it was repulsed by the Bugis; Boné armies even retook the 'Northern Provinces' around Maros and part of Bulukumba, which had previously been under the direct control of the Dutch. During these conflicts Goa, Soppéng and Sidénréng sided with the British (*Peristiwa*: 93–6; St John, *Indian Archipelago*, II: 79–80).

When Dutch rule in Makassar was resumed in 1817, Boné and its allies persisted in their assertion of independence. In 1824, at a time when armed uprisings were brewing all over the archipelago, the Governor-General, van der Capellen, came to Makassar with the aim of getting all the South

Sulawesi rulers to reaffirm the 'Short Declaration' of allegiance to the Netherlands, first signed earlier that year. This the rulers of Boné, Tanété and Suppa' refused to do, leading to several punitive expeditions which met with fierce resistance. Hostilities with Boné lasted until 1838, when the Dutch succeeded in imposing on the kingdom a new ruler totally loyal to them, and broke out again in 1857 when, after his death, the new female ruler of Boné, Bessé Kajuara, once more refused to sign the declaration of allegiance. This clash resulted in 1859 in the demotion of Boné from the status of 'ally' to that of mere 'subject' and the loss of its authority over the Bugis territory around Sinjai, south of the Tangka river, which became the 'Eastern District' under direct Dutch control. In the following years the Dutch also consolidated their control over the former Goa vassals of the 'Southern Districts' (*Peristiwa*: 96–106; Sutherland, 'Power and Politics': 166). This control, however, was far from uniformly solid, and intermittent confrontations occurred with armed dissenters, usually under noble leaders (Sutherland, 'Power and Politics': 186–93).

During this period Wajo' was suffering from chronic instability caused by repeated dynastic disputes which from time to time left the office of Arung Matoa vacant. In an attempt to escape from this constant insecurity, the people of Wajo' migrated overseas in even greater numbers than formerly. This was the situation observed by James Brooke on his visit of 1840, at a time moreover when the Wajo' aristocracy was split into two factions disputing the succession in Sidénréng. This struggle was won by the side supporting La Pang'uriseng, who subsequently reigned until 1882. Under his leadership Sidénréng strengthened its authority within the Aja'tappareng confederation and grew in importance within the peninsula, resisting Dutch claims to suzerainty and progressively building up a war-fighting force supplied with English weapons and ammunition which, in contravention of the strict Dutch regulations on the matter, were imported from Singapore in a continuous stream through the port of Paré-Paré (Staden ten Brink, *Zuid-Celebes*: 53; Sutherland, 'Power and Politics': 166–9). In fact, Sidénréng's growing prosperity was directly linked to that of this thriving port, a former possession of Suppa', with its natural outlet on the west coast: In 1873 the income accruing to the ruler of Sidénréng from trade passing through Paré-Paré amounted to 20,000 guilders a year (Sutherland, 'Power and Politics': 167).

Paré-Paré had developed rapidly since the blockade of the ports of Boné during the 1859–60 war, with many merchants moving in from Boné, Wajo' and Soppéng, finding it more convenient for trading with Singapore (Sutherland, 'Power and Politics': 167). It was also the main port of pilgrimage for the then still autonomous South Sulawesi kingdoms, and closely connected to the Islamic networks of Singapore, Malaya, Sumatra, Borneo and north Java. In addition, it offered an outlet for the slave trade, now banned in Makassar, and from about 1885 for the export of coffee. This diversion of the coffee trade led to military action by Boné in 1897 in defence of Luwu', through which it had previously been routed, in an attempt to drive Sidénréng forces from the Toraja area. Although the expedition was at least partly successful, the coffee trade nevertheless remained in the hands of Sidénréng and its Duri allies until after the First World War (Bigalke, 'Slave Trade': 53, 345–51).

In 1905, on the pretext that the Boné ruler La Pawawoi was interfering unduly in the affairs of other Bugis states, the Dutch landed in Bajoé, conquered Boné within a few weeks and took La Pawawoi prisoner. He was later exiled to Bandung. The ruler of Goa, accused of hostility towards the invading Dutch, was summoned to Makassar to explain himself; he refused to come and the Dutch set out to seize him. He died while being pursued in the Aja'tappareng region. Using various pretexts for intervention, the Dutch also subdued the other independent South Sulawesi kingdoms, arresting most of their rulers and installing more compliant aristocratic appointees of their own.

Colonial Manipulation of the Traditional Political System

Having established their authority over the whole of South Sulawesi, the Dutch endeavoured to create 'a fixed, stable, streamlined and hierarchical state which would deliver taxes and maintain *rust en orde* [peace and order]. From their chiefs and allies they wanted reliability and obedience, and a simple line of succession' (Sutherland, 'Power and Politics': 192). The former system of flexible contractual relationships between more or less autonomous Bugis kingdoms, domains or chieftainships was replaced by a rigid hierarchy of principalities divided into districts and sub-districts on the model long applied in Java. In Wajo', the grouping of the constituent *wanua* in three *limpo* on the basis of the allegiance of each to one of the three *ranreng* was changed into a mere territorial partition into three continuous areas, with the result that many of the *wanua* had to be transferred from one *limpo* to another. Elsewhere, *wanua* considered to be too small were compelled to merge with each other or to be taken over by larger ones, being classified as mere *kampung*, 'villages', a lower-level entity which had not previously existed in the Bugis system. Boundaries between former political entities, which had also, like political relationships themselves, been subject to frequent modification through treaties which took into account their specific historical circumstances, now became fixed borders between administrative jurisdictions, based on purely bureaucratic criteria. The new boundaries were often drawn in disregard of local traditions: for example, a 'North Boné' division, with Pompanua as its county town, included not only the northern part of the old kingdom of Boné, but also Soppéng and Wajo'. The territorial organization imposed on these so-called 'self-ruling territories' was imported wholesale from colonial Java, with its districts or *afdelingen* ('divisions') and sub-districts or *onderafdelingen* ('under-divisions'), in which Dutch officials, respectively *residents* and *controleurs*, were established as 'advisers' to the indigenous rulers. The term 'self-rule' thus represented not so much any real autonomy as indirect rule by the Dutch through indigenous intermediaries; and to ensure the smooth working of that indirect rule, the Dutch had to have a clear idea of who had authority over whom. Thus they did away with the traditional deliberative bodies such as the council of the *arung patang pulo* in Wajo' and formalized the hitherto fluid systems of collegial government prevailing in many Bugis states into a rigid hierarchy of functional posts, each with its specific tasks. To take Wajo' as an example again, here the three *ranreng* were now seen as departmental ministers, each with a specific domain of responsibility: respectively, justice, compulsory labour and finance. Similar reforms were imposed in respect of the Arung Pitu in Boné (Sutherland, 'Political Structure': 238).

The Implementation of Colonial Order, 1907–1941

One of the first measures taken by the Dutch as rulers of South Sulawesi was the introduction at village level of compulsory labour and taxes, with the concomitant bureaucratic authority and registration of personal identities. Compulsory labour, considered as another form of tax since it could be redeemed in money, was channelled mainly into building roads to replace the existing network of paths which could be used only by packhorses and pedestrians. Roads were certainly badly needed if economic development was to take place, but this kind of collective labour was foreign to the Bugis: contrary to what the colonial administrators may have imagined, it had no similarity to the services which in certain particular circumstances a follower would render to his patron, or a subject to his suzerain, such as helping to build a house or cultivating farmland. Consequently it was much resented, and many of the migrants who left for Malaya between 1910 and 1930, especially those of the petty nobility or *tau décéng*, gave the introduction of compulsory labour as one of the main factors in their decision to emigrate.

The Dutch administrators were of course well aware of the strongly hierarchical character of Bugis and Makassar societies, but they had their own ideas about its precise nature, perhaps based on what they knew about Javanese hierarchy. In particular, they made a clear-cut distinction between 'princes', who were in line to inherit the highest responsibilities in the main South Sulawesi kingdoms, and the rest of the nobility: only the former were exempted from compulsory labour and the payment of taxes. For the rest of the nobility, to be subject to a demand for compulsory labour, even though they could commute it into a financial payment, was a severe humiliation. In order to be able to discriminate between the various ranks in the aristocratic hierarchy, the Dutch established official genealogies in all the main kingdoms; for their part, members of the higher nobility began to distinguish themselves from those of lower rank by adding the term Andi' before their personal names.

The taxes instituted by the Dutch consisted of the land rent already mentioned and a poll tax paid by all males above the age of puberty, excepting only the higher nobility (from *ana' céra'* upwards). They were not particularly onerous in absolute terms, but villagers had very little money and often found it difficult to meet this new obligation. After paying the tax they received a *surat kampung*, which served simultaneously as receipt, identity card and certificate of residence, thus representing an attempt to pin the traditionally mobile population of South Sulawesi down to permanent locations (van Mens, *Statusscheppers*: 65–6). Anyone intending to make a visit of several days' duration to another village had to report to the village head, a position created by the Dutch. This function was often allocated to someone in possession of a traditional title such as *matoa* or *gellarang*, formerly used by lower-ranking officials, but these had indicated a role quite different from that of a village head as understood by the colonial administration. No real registry system was yet in existence, but the village head was charged with compiling a list of taxable inhabitants and an annual list of children born in the previous twelve months. At every level from native ruler to village head, officials' income was determined according to rank and function, by systematizing traditional practice in the light of research into customary law. Where necessary, the incomes traditionally derived mainly from the production of fields attached to a particular office were supplemented by the payment of salaries fixed according to the administrative hierarchy.

The preservation of public order and the implementation of a system of justice grafting some principles of Western law on to a foundation of customary law were primary aims of the colonial administration. In each *onderafdeling* courts of justice were established in which local experts in customary law sat in the presence of the Dutch *controleur*, whose role was to prevent the court's decisions from diverging too widely from Dutch law. For example, the death penalty for incest was replaced by imprisonment followed by banishment. In South

Sulawesi, as elsewhere in the Dutch Indies, the colonial administrators assiduously researched the customary law, and their
findings are published in the invaluable collection of the *Ada-
trechtbundels*.

One of the most persistent problems facing the Dutch in
their endeavour to maintain public order was the recurrence
of 'plundering parties' – sorties by cattle and horse rustlers.
Some of these expeditions were organized by high-ranking
members of the nobility as a means not so much of augment-
ing their income (any gains were, in any event, soon lost in
gambling) as of asserting their bravery and cleverness, to give
their followers an opportunity of showing their loyalty, now
that they could no longer be led to war, and of enhancing their
own prestige. Consequently, until the war with Japan the
Dutch had little success in suppressing these activities, for
even some of their most trusted collaborators were involved in
them (van Mens, *Statusscheppers*: 71–6). Other manifestations of unrest included the intermittent appearance of anti-
Dutch, messianic local leaders with small groups of followers;
these, however, were usually quelled very easily by prompt
military intervention.

Potentially more worrying for the colonial government was
the emergence of nationalist propaganda and the creation in
South Sulawesi of local branches of Java-based political and
religious movements. These developments marked the appearance in South Sulawesi of the pan-Indonesian national feeling
stirring in other parts of the Dutch Indies. One of its first
manifestations in South Sulawesi was the establishment in
Makassar in 1918, only six years later than in Java, of a
branch of the Partai Sarikat Islam (PSI: Party of the Islamic
Union), renamed in 1929 as the Partai Sarikat Islam Indonesia
(PSII: Party of the Indonesian Islamic Union). It was by far the
most active nationalist party in South Sulawesi, with five
branches, as well as a youth branch and a Boy Scout branch.
A branch of Sukarno's secular Partai Nasional Indonesia
(PNI: National Party of Indonesia) was also founded in
Makassar in 1929; when it was banned by the Dutch, its
members joined the Partai Indonesia Raja (Party of Greater
Indonesia), which was also banned. Some members then es-
tablished a politically much more moderate organization, the

Persatuan Selebes Selatan (South Sulawesi Union). The followers of these parties were in fact very few and exclusively from urban, educated circles (Sarita, *Sejarah perjuangan*: 31). More influential was the Muhammadiyah; although this was not a political party but an educational and social movement of a reformist Islamic bent, most of its leaders were active nationalists and many of its members played an important role later in the fight for independence (Sarita, *Sejarah perjuangan*: 32).

The Japanese Interlude, 1942–1945, and the Turmoils of Decolonization, 1945–1950

The period of Japanese occupation during the Second World War, a very harsh one indeed, did not bring many changes to the colonial structure established by the Dutch: offices and administrative divisions were simply given Japanese names and Japanese officials replaced Dutch ones. It did, however, mark a dramatic turning-point in the course of events, for European rule had been so easily overthrown, and by Asians, that Indonesian independence now appeared a possibility requiring only the right circumstances to become a reality. Japan's surrender to the Allies in August 1945 provided the opportunity. Troubled times were to follow (Anonym, *Sulawesi*; van Dijk, 'Rebellion': 155–67; Sarita, *Sejarah perjuangan*).

Plate 54   Hoisting the Indonesian flag on 17 August, National Day, commemorating the Indonesian declaration of independence in 1945

Plate 55   The Independence Heroes Monument in Soppéng

Immediately after the proclamation of Indonesian independence by Sukarno and Hatta, the North Sulawesi-born Dr Ratulangi was appointed by the new republican government as Governor of all Sulawesi, and took up his post in Makassar on 19 August. In September, however, Allied troops arrived on the island, and in contrast to other places in Java and Sumatra met with no resistance, for there were no trained guerrilla groups derived from Japanese-sponsored militias to oppose them. The Allies brought with them Dutch officers of the Netherlands Indies Civil Administration (NICA) who compelled Dr Ratulangi to stand down as Governor and began reconstituting the local colonial government, while troops of the Royal Netherlands Indies Army (KNIL) progressively took over the military role from the Allies. In the course of a tour around South Sulawesi in October, Dr Ratulangi obtained from most Bugis rulers a promise to support the Java-based Indonesian Republic; but soon after this many of them agreed to sign a declaration of collaboration with the NICA. Only a few refused to sign, among them the Boné ruler Andi' Ma'panyukki' and the highly respected woman *datu* of Témpé, Andi' Ninnong, one of Wajo's three regents.

Guerrilla groups then began to be formed, later to be brought together in a federal organization called the Sulawesi Revolutionary Fighters for the Indonesian Republic (LAPRIS).

By the end of October skirmishes began to break out between these groups and Allied and KNIL troops; but the guerrillas lacked weapons and were no match for the regular armies. In April 1946 Dr Ratulangi and his main collaborators were arrested and sent to Dutch-occupied Jakarta; many other nationalists were also jailed. A number of young opponents of the colonial regime fled to republican strongholds in Java, where young radicals from Sulawesi, including a small number of modern-minded noble youths who had divested themselves of their titles, had organized themselves into resistance groups which, together with youths from other islands, were fighting alongside the Javanese guerrillas against the Dutch army. One of these resistance groups was the Indonesian Republican Army for the Preparation of the Liberation of Sulawesi (TRIPS), which, under Kahar Muzakkar, a young man from Luwu', organized the infiltration into Sulawesi, using local boats, of arms, ammunition and trained fighters – among them two future generals of the National Indonesian Army, Andi' Mattalata and Yusuf. The Dutch authorities entrusted the task of countering these moves to one Captain Westerling, who proceeded to justify his sorry reputation: by calling on local people to denounce their fellows, executing hostages and resorting to mass killings to terrorize villagers, he managed in a fairly short space of time to suppress most of the armed resistance. After the LAPRIS headquarters were taken, those local guerrillas who remained lacked organization and survived only sporadically, although contact with Sulawesi fighters in Java was maintained.

In January 1947 Makassar became the capital city of the Dutch-sponsored federated State of East Indonesia, which included Sulawesi, the Moluccas, the Lesser Sunda Islands and Bali and was created at the same time as other Indonesian federated states in Sumatra, Borneo and west Java in a bid to isolate the Indonesian Republic, then based largely in central Java and part of Sumatra. This puppet state had the support of a large proportion of the conservative South Sulawesi aristocracy, while those of a more progressive cast of mind supported the incorporation of their lands into a unitary Indonesian Republic. Meanwhile, in Java, Kahar Muzakkar had been raised to the rank of lieutenant-colonel and made deputy commander of the Sixteenth Brigade of the Indonesian National Army, which drew together all overseas troops. In 1949 he was put in charge of coordinating the guerrilla units in all the 'outer islands', and as part of this endeavour a Union of South Sulawesi Guerrillas (KGSS) was created in August. That December the Dutch recognized Indonesian independence – but only within the framework of a federal constitution and a Dutch-Indonesian union.

The State of East Indonesia was the largest of the constituent states of the new United States of Indonesia outside Java. It retained a very conservative attitude; in South Sulawesi, for example, local authority was still in the hands of a High Council (Hadat Tinggi) of traditional rulers, the partisans of the Indonesian Republic having been replaced by conservative aristocrats. The nationalists and progressives were dissatisfied with this state of affairs and maintained their pressure for a unitary Indonesian Republic. The South Sulawesi guerrillas did not disband, and sporadic skirmishes continued between them and former KNIL troops, now officially charged with maintaining law and order but still very suspicious of the new Jakarta-based central government. In April 1950 some former KNIL units even resisted the disembarkation of troops of the National Indonesian Army from Java, and in the following months fighting between the two sides broke out on several occasions, causing hundreds of casualties in the Makassar city. In these clashes, the guerrillas gave significant support to the National Army.

Finally, in Sulawesi as on the other outer islands, the federalists lost the game and on 17 August 1950 Indonesia became a unitary republic. In South Sulawesi itself the High Council was forced to resign, as were most of the former rulers, often under pressure from local guerrillas. In South Sulawesi, too, the first stirrings were felt of a social revolution similar to, though far from as radical as, that which had taken place in Aceh and north Sumatra.

The South Sulawesi Rebellion, 1950–1965

Now that federalism had been defeated, the question of what to do with the former guerillas, numbering about 15,000, came to the fore. This was the starting-point of one of the most troubled periods in South Sulawesi's history (van Dijk, 'Rebellion': 171–217). Most of the guerrillas wanted to be incorporated into the Indonesian Army as members of a separate 'Hasanuddin Brigade'. Kahar Muzakkar, who even before the dissolution of the State of East Indonesia had been asked by the central army command to help settle the issue, supported this view; but the Minahasan Colonel Kawilarang, the territorial commander for East Indonesia appointed by the Jakarta government, rejected the proposal and issued a decree liquidating the KGSS. Incensed by this move, Kahar joined the guerrillas, who began obstructing South Sulawesi's main roads; the state military responded by occupying several of the guerrillas' bases. There followed several months of confused skirmishes, attempts at mediation and negotiations. In March 1951, following a provisional agreement, the former guerrillas were formed into a National Reserve Corps, made up of five battalions, pending the selection of those men who would be taken into the regular army and the 'return to society' of the remainder.

Misunderstandings, however, persisted. The army insisted on subjecting the men to rigorous tests which resulted in the elimination of about two-thirds of the candidates for army entry; it also wanted to incorporate battalions into the main army individually, as it did with Andi' Séllé's Bau Massépé battalion in Paré-Paré, rather than forming a single complete brigade of former guerrillas under Kahar's command. In spite of these and many other sources of friction, a grand incorporation ceremony was planned for 17 August 1951, to take place in Makassar's Karébosi Square. When the day arrived, however, Kahar and his troops failed to turn up: they had retreated into the jungle. The army, said Kahar, had not kept its promises to the former guerrillas. Mistrust of the military, most of whom were from North Sulawesi and Java, was in fact fairly general among the population of South Sulawesi. After an ultimatum issued by the Jakarta government, the army launched several campaigns in an attempt to suppress the dissidents, but met with little success; on the contrary, the rebellion took root in all of South and South-East Sulawesi, whose territory was divided up among the four former Reserve Corps battalions.

At the same time local rebellions were taking place in other parts of Indonesia, including in west Java the so-called Daru'l Islam (DI) rebellion. In 1952, Kahar accepted the offer made by its leader, Kartosuwirjo, to join forces against the Jakarta government, and took the title of Commander of the Fourth (Hasanuddin) Division of the Islamic Army of Indonesia (TII). In fact, he continued to act quite independently, although from now on his rebel organization, previously called the People's Liberation Army (TKR), took on an increasingly Islamic orientation: in 1953 it began collecting taxes in the name of the Islamic Republican State of Indonesia and implementing strict Islamic rules in the areas of South Sulawesi it controlled, namely the Makassar, Bugis, Ma'sénrémpulu' and Mandar countryside. The principles underlying this movement, as reflected in 1953 in the 'Makalua Charter', named after Kahar's stronghold in Ma'sénrémpulu', tended towards a kind of Islamic socialism, to be expressed in measures including a moderate degree of land reform; the suppression of social inequality and of all ostentation in dress and behaviour, such as the wearing of gold, jewels and silks or sumptuous feasting at weddings; the eradication of all traces of 'feudalism', such as traditional political offices and aristocratic titles, and of 'paganism', such as pilgrimages to sacred places and the performance of pre-Islamic rituals; and the implementation of the *shari'a* in its strictest form – stoning for adulterers and the amputation of a hand for thieves. Soldiers and their families, moreover, were forbidden to smoke foreign cigarettes or to eat 'delicacies originating from the cities'. A kind of 'anti-city' orientation similar to that of the Khmer Rouge was thus growing among the rebel force, which the population used to call the 'Forest Army' as opposed to the regular 'City Army', also labelled the 'Javanese Army'. As a token of their indomitability the rebels left their hair uncut, which would have immediately singled out any one of them who had yielded to the lure of a short visit to the city and its temptations.

Many of those who did not support the rebels, in particular most of the aristocracy – who, with the exception of a few who had discarded their titles and sided with Daru'l Islam ideals, were strongly traditional in their outlook – had taken refuge in the main cities of South Sulawesi. Most commoners and villagers were faced with an insoluble dilemma. If they wanted to stay in their villages, where their livelihoods were, they had to renounce traditions and practices to which most of them had a visceral attachment, accept being cut off from all the commodities they needed from the cities, and risk being branded as supporters of the rebels by the government forces. 'If the people didn't help the TNI [National Army] in the daytime, they were punished immediately; if they did, they suffered that night at the hands of the DI. Conversely, if they refused to help the DI at night, their homes were burned; if they did help the DI, they would be branded rebels by the TNI, and thrown into jail' (Harvey, 'Islam and Rebellion': 268). If they chose to escape this dilemma by fleeing to the cities, they became refugees, often with no source of income. Some gravitated to the houses of their former patrons, who, as refugees themselves, were unable to give them much help; others depended on urban relatives often as poor as themselves; many chose to migrate to Central Sulawesi, East Kalimantan or South Sumatra.

Not all of Kahar's former lieutenants followed his ideological path all the way, and some had their own personal strategies to pursue. The government side was well aware of rifts within the TII and made periodical offers of amnesty to those rebels who would accept the invitation to 'come back into the bosom of the Motherland'. Thus, as early as April 1952 Andi' Sosé and his Wolter Mongisidi battalion in Enrekang, Aziz Taba and his Arief Raté battalion in Bantaéng and part of the Forty Thousand battalion in Rappang had defected to the National Army. A few months later, Usman Balo' and his troops around Paré-Paré split away from Kahar's army to form an independent TKR rebel army and a three-sided conflict ensued between them, DI troops and the National Army; at times the National Army joined forces with Usman Balo's TKR against Kahar's men. Finally, in October 1957 Usman Balo's troops joined the government side. Further internal dissensions among the rebels led to the surrender in 1959, after Indonesia's return to the 1945 constitution,[2] of Bahar Ma'taliu', Kahar Muzakkar's

---

[2] The return to the 1945 constitution, decided on in July 1959, was a move by President Sockarno intended to put an end to political instability by

long-standing comrade-in-arms and deputy. By 1960 the rebellion was much weakened and significant resistance was
restricted to a few strongholds in the northern mountains
around Mt Latimojong, in Luwu' and in South-East Sulawesi
around Kolaka. Parts of the countryside and the main roads
were once more under National Army control, thanks to
vigorous and judicious handling of the situation by the new
head of the military command in Makasar, General M. Yusuf,
himself a Bugis and a former independence fighter in Java.
Increasing numbers of Javanese troops had been replaced by
local soldiers, including men who had formerly served under
Kahar. In 1961, direct negotiations between General Yusuf and
Kahar almost led to an agreement, but in the event hostilities
continued. Finally, the last remnants of the TII were forced to
retreat to South-East Sulawesi, where on 1 February 1965 Kahar
Muzakkar was discovered in his bivouac and shot dead.

South Sulawesi since 1965

The administrative 'rationalization' enforced by the colonial
government in South Sulawesi, in which the aristocracy retained some power, albeit on a different basis from that they
had enjoyed before 1905, remained in place even after the
dissolution of the State of East Indonesia. The former under-
districts, now called *swapraja* ('autonomous territories') were
until 1960 still headed by traditional aristocratic officers
(*datu, arung, karaéng,* etc.) and divided into *wanua*. In fact,
the political power wielded by the nobility had by this time
been reduced almost to nil by the rebellion, which had everywhere challenged their authority as 'feudalistic' and based on
pagan beliefs; many of the collections of regalia and aristocratic mansions had been destroyed and many of their *bissu*
stewards killed, while the aristocratic families themselves,
abandoned by many of their followers and deprived of their

replacing the parliamentary system with that of so-called 'directed democracy'. At the same time the Indonesian National Army was given full power
to crush the local rebellions which were taking place in several Indonsian
provinces, including South Sulawesi.

*Plate 56 A government advertisement for the family planning
programme*

traditional sources of income, had taken refuge in the cities. In
1960 an Indonesian government decree put an end, in Sulawesi as elsewhere in the republic, to these remnants of past
times, transforming the *swapraja* into *kabupatèn* (administrative districts) headed by *bupati* (civil district officers) appointed by the Governor; these *kabupatèn* were further
divided into *kecamatan* (under-districts) and *désa* (parishes),
whose boundaries would be fixed by the administration and
would not necessarily correspond to former traditional territorial units. Most former rulers were honourably discharged
in this process, although some were provisionally appointed
as *bupati* or heads of *kecamatan* or *désa*.

Thus the centuries-old rule of the descendants of the *to-
manurung* came to an end. Perhaps even more important than
this definitive act locating Bugis society within a homogene-
ous, modern nation-state, however, is the development among
the people themselves, although remaining strongly attached
to their Bugis identity, of an unquestionable national feeling

as Indonesians. Even the DI or TKR rebels did not question this new identification, struggling as they were for more provincial, but not ethnic, autonomy.

From an Ethnic to a Global World

The advent of universal religions – Christianity or Islam – in previously 'pagan' societies, in the etymological sense of that term (that is, practising the religion 'of the land' or an ethnic religion) has been an important step in these societies' progress towards modernity, for two reasons. First, the very universality of Christianity and Islam transcends ethnic and linguistic boundaries; secondly, although these religions do retain basic mythical elements, both accord an important place in theology, metaphysics and ethics to modes of reasoning and argument which lie at the very root of modern philosophical thought, both within and outside a religious framework. Since its acceptance by Indonesian peoples, including those in South Sulawesi, Islam has had just such an effect. Operating at first in a strongly hierarchical social context, it subsequently played an important role in the diffusion of the ideas of egalitarianism and of individual responsibility, values common to both modern Western and Islamic worlds.

Modern Islamic Trends in South Sulawesi

The influence of Wahabite reformist ideas began to be felt throughout the Muslim Malay world from about 1819. In the Minangkabau country of Sumatra they had provoked the upheaval known as the 'Padri war'; soon thereafter a rebellion led by the reformist Muslim Prince Diponegoro broke out in Java. In South Sulawesi, too, La Memmang To-A'pamadeng, ruler of Wajo' from 1821 to 1825, tried under the influence of a Muslim scholar just returned from the Holy Land to enforce a Wahabite-inspired religious programme, opposing superstitious practices, destroying ancient sacred places, and attempting to impose both strict Islamic law (with the penalties of stoning for adultery and amputation of hands for thieves)

Plate 57 Haji Abdulrahman Ambo' Dallé, founder of the Darul Dakwa wal Irsyad Institution

and Islamic customs originating in the Middle East (such as the veiling of women). These attempts were short-lived, but were evidence that some of the Bugis nobles had been won over to a more radical form of Islam.

At about the same time, other Bugis nobles were turning to a newly introduced branch of the Khalwatiyah mystic brotherhood. Popularly known as Khalwatiyah Samman, it was of a more egalitarian bent than that introduced in the seventeenth century by Shaikh Yusuf and consequently known as Khalwatiyah Yusuf. First brought from Arabia to Sumatra in the eighteenth century, the Samman branch arrived in Sulawesi around 1810 (Bruinessen, 'Khalwatiyya': 260–1). Some prominent individuals of the Bugis nobility, such as the Boné sovereign at the time of the British conquest of Makassar,

Sultan Idris, hitherto an adept of the Yusuf branch, were among its first adherents. Since the last decades of the nineteenth century Khalwatiyah Samman has recruited increasing numbers of commoners, including peasants, but the Yusuf branch has also remained very popular. According to the Bureau of Religious Affairs in Ujung Pandang, in 1976 there were about 150,000 adherents of the Khalwatiyah brotherhood in the province, over two-thirds of whom were in the Samman branch, the remainder in the Yusuf branch. These figures contrast sharply with under 10,000 in the Naksyabandiyah and fewer than 5,000 in the Kadiriyah, the strongest mystic brotherhoods elsewhere in Indonesia (Pelras, 'Dynamics of Islamization': 126–7).

The coexistence in Bugis society since earliest historical times of the apparently contradictory ideals of hierarchy and equality has been noted earlier in this book, and both found their expression in Bugis Islam. Until the second half of the nineteenth century, the main religious offices in the kingdoms had tended to be entrusted to members of the nobility. This was justified partly on the grounds that the *qadi*, *imam* and *khatib* fulfilled roles that placed them in positions of equality with the secular rulers, and this was admissible only if the posts were held by people of similar rank to them. Another reason was probably the perceived need to counterbalance the influence of the *bissu*, who in spite of islamization were still active in most polities, except where a particular ruler of a more orthodox cast of Islam displaced them. Sultan Idris of Boné had been among those who most favoured the progressive replacement of noble religious officials by commoners, preferably chosen from among those people most learned in religious matters. From the first decades of the twentieth century the egalitarian trend accelerated until it became dominant.

Modernism in Islam, another trend of an egalitarian character but quite opposed to the mysticism of the Khalwatiyah and the other brotherhoods, first appeared in Makassar in 1917 and gained momentum in South Sulawesi after the establishment there in 1926 of official branches of the Java-based Muhammadiyah movement. Doctrinally this movement is fundamentalist, as opposed to radical: that is to say, it is based on a return to the fundamental tenets of Islam and rejects such

later additions as those it alleges are found in the four traditional sunni schools, in shi'ism and in all kinds of mysticism.
It also advocates resort to reason to reconcile Islamic law to
the prevailing conditions of modern times. Muhammadiyah's
pioneering work in the development of private schools with a
mixed secular and religious curriculum, and of medical clinics
and institutions for social care, set an example which was later
followed by other, sunni, Islamic institutions. Indeed,
throughout Indonesia since the end of the 1920s there has
been a noticeable expansion of religious education, with a
growing number of Islamic schools established on the *madra-*
sah model, that is, with a sequence of grades defined more or
less by the age of pupils, as in secular schools, even though
only religious subjects and Arabic were taught. The first such
institution in South Sulawesi, the Madrasatul Arabiyatul Isla-
miyah, was founded by a Mecca-born Bugis in Singkang in
1930. Others, founded by traditional sunni masters, followed
in Luwu', Boné, Goa and Mangkoso'. Almost simultaneously,
madrasah of the Muhammadiyah movement were established,
with their combination of religious and secular curricula. This
dual role attracted Dutch subsidies to many of them, even
though most of the teaching staff, often drawn from Sumatra or
Java, were declared nationalists. Since Indonesian independence
an increasing number of both sunni and Muhammadiyah
madrasah have flourished, and some have experienced extraordinary development: for example, the Darul Dakwa
wal Irsjad, established in 1947 in Paré-Paré, claims over a
thousand *madrasah* in South Sulawesi alone, as well as hundreds in areas of Sumatra and Kalimantan with a strong Bugis
presence (Bruinessesn, 'Khalwatiyya': 266); and nearly 40 per
cent of the 200 Bugis studying theology at the Al-Azhar
University in Cairo come from that institution. The total
number of pupils in South Sulawesi religious schools in 1974
amounted to about 125,000 in nearly 1,400 educational
establishments, of which about thirty were government-run
training schools for religious teachers, since religion is also
taught in secular schools (Arief Said et al., *Geografi budaya*: 66).
Registered members of Muhammadiyah in South Sulawesi
numbered about 50,000 in 1975, only one-third of the membership of the Khalwatiyah; but its sympathizers are much

more numerous and are to be found in key positions at all levels of administration, teaching and business (Pelras, 'Dynamics of Islamization': 127–8). Many of those in South Sulawesi who fought for independence during the Indonesian revolution came from the ranks of Muhammadiyah; their struggle was not only against the Dutch and for the establishment of a unitary Indonesian republic, but also against what they called the 'feudal' aspects of traditional Bugis society and the 'pagan' aspects of its culture. Most of them later became followers of the Daru'l Islam rebellion led by Kahar Muzakkar, who was himself a former leader of the Hizbul Watan, the Muhammadiyah Boy Scout association. Much of Muhammadiyah's influence in South Sulawesi society, indeed, derives from the number of former pupils in its schools who are now leading members of the civil society, whether as primary and secondary schoolteachers, university lecturers, civil servants of all ranks or businessmen.

Secular Education and the Development of Literacy

The development of modern school education in South Sulawesi did not take place in the context of an absolutely ignorant and illiterate mass: on the contrary, traditional education had long since produced an appreciable proportion of men and women literate in both the local and Arabic scripts. According to Anthony Reid, who bases his analysis on reliable contemporary evidence, the degree of literacy in precolonial south-east Asian societies was, incredible as it may seem to us, considerably higher than that prevailing in European societies of the time (Reid, *Age of Commerce*: 215–25). It is hard to establish how far this general situation held true for the Bugis in particular, but an idea of the prevalence of literacy may be gained from the numbers of ancient manuscripts still to be found all over the Bugis country: a project to make an inventory of manuscripts, currently in progress in South Sulawesi, has so far succeeded in registering several thousands of Bugis, Makassar and Mandar writings in local script, scattered all over the province. Although most of them are relatively recent copies of older manuscripts, it seems from their contents that

Plate 58 Uniformed schoolchildren marching in the streets of Soppéng

the bulk of these texts originate from the eighteenth century, which might indicate a general development of literacy at that period. We should also take into account the large number which, according to more than one source, were intentionally destroyed during the DI rebellion as 'symbols of the feudal system' or 'remnants of the pagan past', and those which, for want of adequate care or interest, have been lost to insects, mould or accidental fires. As a majority of the great number of surviving texts dwell on local history, even down to that of the tiniest *wanua*, we may assume that literacy in Bugis, at least in the eighteenth century, was more or less evenly spread throughout the territory; the existence up to the present in most Bugis villages of texts of practical, especially agricultural, application confirms this supposition and seems also to indicate that literacy was never limited to aristocratic circles but extended to at least part of the peasantry.

Literacy in the traditional Bugis script was accompanied by literacy in Arabic among both advanced students in the religious schools and ordinary Muslims who had been taught to read Qur'anic texts. There was also some knowledge of Malay, which had long been written down in the Arabic-derived *jawi* script and was by the sixteenth century the language of trade and diplomatic relations among most of the indigenous coastal south-east Asian states (Reid, *Age of Commerce*: 233) as well as the language of Muslim preaching, proselytization and teaching by travelling *ulama*. The spread of Malay among people from various milieux, even though their number was not particularly large, made it 'the major mediator of Arabic, Persian and Indian ideas and literary styles in the region' (Reid, *Age of Commerce*). Both Arabic and Malay thus played an important role in opening Bugis society to the outside world with its new models in the fields of religion, thought, lifestyles and culture. Later, through the nineteenth century, the progressive extension of Dutch power further increased the importance of the Malay language, which was used all over the Netherlands Indies by the colonial administration instead of Dutch when it had to deal with the natives. This gave rise to a class of native clerks and employees who increasingly used Malay in its romanized form. The choice by Indonesian nationalists of Malay as the national language of Indonesia, henceforth called Indonesian (*Bahasa Indonesia*), was thus a logical move for which people in the region were not unprepared. In an area as open to the outside world as the Bugis and Makassar lands, the decision was favourably received.

Traditional Bugis literature itself, however, did not engage much with the outside world. Even those works adapted from a Malay, Indian or Persian origin, with the exception of a number of Islamic treatises, were mainly local in scope, and before the twentieth century traditional religious schools provided no teaching on secular matters. That the Bugis were interested in such matters is demonstrated by the existence of manuscripts, albeit limited in number, dealing with practical questions, some of which had been translated from Portuguese in the early seventeenth century, and also by the interest shown in external political affairs by those Bugis who questioned James Brooke in 1840 on the fate of Napoleon and on recent political developments in the Turkish Empire. For information on these points, however, the Bugis ordinarily had to rely on word of mouth, gleaning news brought back from abroad by traders, navigators and pilgrims returning from Mecca.

A new vehicle for exposure to the outside world came into being with the first Western-type school in South Sulawesi, founded in 1876 by B. F. Matthes, who served as its first director until his return to the Netherlands three years later. It was a teachers' training college coupled with a school for native civil servants, and took as pupils boys of noble or well-to-do commoner families, some of whom came from the hinterland. It taught Malay, Makassar, Bugis, Dutch, geography (Matthes himself had written a *Geography of South Sulawesi* and a *Geography of the Netherlands Indies* as his own teaching resources), history, arithmetic, natural history, elements of agriculture, drawing, composition and the rudiments of land surveying (Brink, *Matthes*: 102–12; *Encyclopaedie van Nederlandsch Indië*, s.v. Onderwijs: III, 104, 116).

It is not clear for which schools the teachers trained at Matthes' college were destined, as the first colonial law in the Netherlands Indies on 'people's schools' (*Volksscholen*) was not issued until 1903. However, after the conquest of 1905 such 'people's schools' were established by the Dutch throughout inland South Sulawesi. The first to be opened, in 1907, were in a dozen small towns; then, when public security was considered to be assured, similar institutions were established in a number of villages in the hinterland. These schools, which taught in Malay plus the local language, provided a basic education for three years only. In Bugis villages, the lack of appropriate existing buildings meant that many of the schools met in the open space under one of the pile-built houses. The system was extended in 1920 with the addition of 'native schools' (*Inlandsche Scholen* or IS) and 'complementary schools' (*Vervolg Scholen* or VVS), which provided respectively two or three further years of teaching. These were usually known as 'Malay schools' because quite a few of their teachers were Sumatrans.

Primary teaching to a higher level in Dutch for natives or other Asians had been provided in Makassar since before 1920 by the 'Dutch Ambonese School', 'Dutch Chinese School' and 'Dutch Native School' (*Hollandsch-Inlandsche*

School or HIS). In 1920 five more HIS were opened in other South Sulawesi towns. These took pupils from the indigenous nobility or other prominent native families known for their loyalty to the colonial government. Makassar also had a MULO school (*Meer Uitgebreid Lager Onderwijs*, 'extended primary teaching institution' or middle school) which provided a three-year curriculum in Dutch to former pupils of the HIS or other schools of the same level, as well as to Dutch pupils (Sarita, *Sejarah perjuangan*: 24–5). Although the total number of native pupils in these latter schools was not large, they were a breeding-ground for a new, educated and modern-minded local elite, a number of whom were later to be attracted by nationalist ideas. The same spirit also existed in a few private secular schools, such as those belonging to the Java-based Taman Siswa movement.[3]

In 1949, when the Dutch recognized Indonesia as an independent state, secular education in South and South-East Sulawesi was provided by 980 public primary schools, 11 lower secondary schools, 3 higher secondary schools and 3 primary teachers' training schools. Ten years later, in spite of the political troubles of the intervening years, these figures for South Sulawesi alone were 2,808, 78, 21 and 29. In 1969 they had risen again to 4,211, 233, 78 and 24. By then there were over 650,000 pupils in primary schools in South Sulawesi and over 90,000 in secondary schools; this represented about 60 per cent of children of school age (Sarita, *Sejarah perjuangan*: 29–30; Mattulada, 'Kebudayaan Bugis Makassar': 280), just at the time when primary education was about to be made compulsory throughout Indonesia and literacy campaigns were being launched aimed at illiterate adults in both rural and urban areas.

---

[3] Taman Siswa ('The Garden of the Disciples') is a cultural and educational movement founded in the 1920s by Ki Hadjar Dewantoro, a Javanese aristocrat and militant supporter of Indonesian independence. Inspired by Javanese philosophy, but also by the works of Rabindranath Tagore and Maria Montessori, it aims at the total development of individuals, peoples and the world by bringing together human welfare and happiness and the world's harmony and patterns, through a system of global education leading to the development of the conscience, free reflexion and free social participation.

Nowadays the vast majority of Bugis children are sent to school and probably about two-thirds of Bugis adults have some proficiency in Indonesian, which many can both read and write. Bilingualism in the local and national languages, formerly confined to particular groups of men, is now widespread among all levels of society, although still found among more men than women. Precise data on this point are lacking, but research carried out in 1979 in one coastal village near Pangkajene with a mixed Bugis and Makassar population (Basran Noor, *Pemakaian Bahasa Indonesia*) showed that, of a sample of adult men of whom 50 per cent had participated in primary schooling and 25 per cent in the government-sponsored programme for the elimination of illiteracy, 72 per cent had some proficiency in Indonesian (75 per cent of those under forty, 69 per cent of those over forty). In all professional groups, however, Indonesian was used only in certain particular circumstances, such as listening to the radio or writing letters (including those to family members), or by schoolteachers, not only in teaching but in public and official communications. At home or among fellow villagers, use of the vernacular dominated among all professional groups and was common even among schoolteachers, who tended however to use a mixture of the vernacular and Indonesian – as did civil servants, even in their official capacity.

Higher education in South Sulawesi was launched in 1954 with the creation of Hasanuddin University in Makassar, the fourth university in Indonesia and the first outside Java. It was followed by an Academic Institute for Teachers' Training and Pedagogy and an Academic Institute of Islamic Studies. In addition to these high-level, state-owned and managed institutions, which maintain a strict *numerus clausus*, scores of private institutes and universities have blossomed all over the province, sponsored by secular and religious (Muslim and Christian) foundations alike. The province has produced a number of academics of international stature: one of the most prominent is the nuclear physicist Professor Amiruddin, a Bugis from Soppéng who from 1981 to 1993 was South Sulawesi's first civilian Governor after a long series of military field officers.

Information and Knowledge of the Surrounding World

School education is of course a crucial grounding for economic and technological development, equipping the population at large with the basic knowledge necessary to understand and absorb further information imparted by administrators, agricultural advisers or health workers. However, school books apart, few books are to be seen in village or working-class urban houses, and the readership of the national and provincial press is limited to the urban middle and upper classes and the local modern elites of inland administrative centres. Radio and television, on the other hand, have a large audience everywhere. Radio enjoyed a rapid expansion from the end of the 1960s, after the period of the rebellion, thanks to the availability of relatively cheap Japanese transistor receivers brought in from Malaysia or Singapore by Bugis sailors. A resurgence in prosperity soon made them available in the

Plate 59 A local radio station in Singkang, Wajo'

shops of Ujung Pandang or Paré-Paré, and they became wide-spread, not needing electricity, which at this period was still confined to the cities. Listeners could receive not only the national, government-run radio station but also programmes in Indonesian and Malay broadcast from Australia, Germany, Britain, Malaysia and Singapore. Later, local, private stations, most of them commercially financed, sprang up all over the province, broadcasting mainly light music and also a few religious programmes, often in the vernacular. Even these private stations, however, as well as the Ujung Pandang official station, are obliged to relay the official news, broadcast from the national central station in Jakarta.

An official television station was created in Ujung Pandang in 1974 and, thanks to the existence of 'Palapa', the Indonesian geostationary satellite, it can now broadcast local as well as national programmes. A significant number of South Sulawesi families have been able to buy cheap television sets, while the more affluent have acquired parabolic aerials, which enable them to pick up programmes from neighbouring southeast Asian countries.

Cinemas, most of them in Ujung Pandang and Paré-Paré with a few others in several smaller cities inland, show Indonesian, Indian, Singapore and Taiwan Chinese as well as Western (mostly American; a few Italian and French) films. All foreign films, the import of which into Indonesia is subject to fixed quotas, are in English and dubbed with Indonesian subtitles. It must be admitted that the standard of films shown in South Sulawesi is generally not very high, and their representation of Indonesian as well as foreign ways of life is often quite unrealistic, but they do provide the audience with some insight into places, cultures and societies quite different from those familiar to them, and thus offer at least some opportunity to see their own milieux with a degree of detachment.

All these media and sources of communication have contributed in their various ways to the formation of a modern Indonesian popular culture common to the Bugis, Makassar, Toraja, Ambonese, Javanese, Sumatrans and others, giving rise to a kind of supra-culture which does not annihilate or supersede particular constituent cultures but rather incorporates them into a global supra-identity clearly distinct from, although completely interdependent with, the surrounding world.

New Commodities for New Needs

From ancient times on, the Bugis economy has never been an exclusive, self-sufficient peasant economy, but on the contrary has always been based in part on external exchanges controlled by a leading social group. This group derived most of its income – often, even, wealth – from the export of the specific mineral, natural or agricultural products which it controlled, as well as, at times, from trade. Bugis peasants and fishermen sustained that group through their own surplus production, and in exchange benefited from the added wealth which its trading activities brought to the society as a whole. The goods imported in return from China, mainland south-east Asia, India, the Middle East and, later, Europe, such as metal and china wares, glass, cloth or arms, were mostly luxury items, but even ordinary people could afford some of them; meanwhile, the produce from their own agricultural activity was sufficient to meet their basic needs.

From the end of the eighteenth century, the European industrial revolution brought major change to the economies of south-east Asia, as the region increasingly became a crucial source of the raw commodities needed by European manufacturers, and a vital market for their products. The impact of this new situation began to make itself felt even in the daily lifes of the south-east Asian peoples, the Bugis among them.

Consumption Products and Domestic Equipment

Before the advent of the industrial revolution in Europe, consumption products and domestic equipment used by the Bugis had for the most part been locally produced or home-made. From the eighteenth century, imported goods began to play a more prominent role. The Bugis had hitherto either been totally self-sufficient in food and beverages, or had supplemented their own produce with that of neighbouring places: coffee, for example, which began to be cultivated in Java at the beginning of the eighteenth century, could be obtained in the nineteenth from Sinjai or the Toraja lands. Up to the end of the nineteenth century, South Sulawesi's imports of other consumption products were mainly limited to tobacco, although there was some domestic supply of this from planting carried out as early as the seventeenth century, opium, which continued to be used sporadically in aristocratic circles up to the 1930s, and tea, introduced in Java around 1830.

As for domestic equipment, although local earthenware and wooden or bamboo vessels were readily available, the Bugis had long imported goods such as crockery and kitchen utensils of Chinese origin; to these were added, probably from the beginning of the nineteenth century, European metal tools such as knives and scissors. Although these traded wares were luxuries of a sort, it seems reasonable to assume that ordinary Bugis villagers would be no less able to buy them than the Aru islanders observed in 1856 by Alfred Russell Wallace at the Bugis and Chinese trading post of Dobo in the south-east Moluccas: 'We were here two thousand miles beyond Singapore and Batavia . . ., in a place unvisited by, and almost unknown to, European traders; everything reached us through at least two or three hands, often many more; yet . . . the natives of this out-of-the-way country can, in fact, buy all these things at about the same money price as our workmen at home' (Wallace, *Malay Archipelago*: 363). Since the mid-twentieth century yet more domestic equipment has become available, including drinking glasses, aluminium forks and spoons, cake tins, tin-plate or enamelled basins and trays, and kerosene stoves. Many manufactured products, such as margarine, soy sauce, wheat flour, yeast, noodles, canned food, condensed or powdered milk, caster sugar, biscuits, chocolate, syrup and soft drinks, kerosene, washing powder, toilet soap and shampoo, have also become staples of domestic life. Many of these, it could be argued, are not actually necessities; but once people have become used to having them, they are reluctant to do without them, as they had to, for example, during the period of Japanese occupation; during the Kahar Muzakkar rebellion, people from rebel zones even risked their lives to obtain supplies of some of these items from cities occupied by the National Army.

Clothing and Cloth

Discussions of Bugis clothing earlier in this book have made it clear that its form was far from fixed in past centuries, that it always had much in common with that of other peoples of the archipelago and yet was also subject to influences from outside the archipelago. All around the Indian Ocean, for example, people wear garments very similar to the Indonesian sarong. Fashions, too, circulated from one country to another: the long-sleeved, knee-length blouse sometimes worn by Bugis women between the later nineteenth century and the 1930s, called *waju labbu*, was obviously inspired by the Malay *baju labuh* worn in Malaya and Sumatra at the same period. At any given time, however, the Bugis style of dress, like that of any of their neighbours, had specific features which reflected their individual identity.

This is no longer the case. Everyday clothing has now lost much of its local or ethnic character. Out of doors, in the daytime, men usually wear Western-style shirts and trousers or shorts for working in the fields; after work, however, especially at home, they still like to wear the sarong, usually of a checked pattern, and this is also the normal attire to be worn for Muslim prayers or traditional rituals. On festive occasions, especially at weddings, a few elderly men still wear old silken or shiny cotton checked sarongs in dark colours, together with a closed jacket with a mandarin collar in the Dutch fashion of the late nineteenth century, and a plaited cap or, more rearely, a headcloth of local make or Javanese batik. Many others wear silk sarongs in soft colours with a Western-style jacket; but the Western-style suit, complete with collar and tie, is gaining ground.

For everyday wear young girls now usually dress in Western-style dresses or skirts and blouses. Many women wear Javanese-style long-sleeved blouses (*kebaya*) in the daytime, but most of them still prefer, in all circumstances, the sarong – that is, the real sarong, sewn in a tube, not the *kain panjang*, the unsewn cloth usually worn by Javanese women. On festive occasions they wear the traditional Bugis transparent blouse, these days over an ordinary or long-line brassiere. Today the colour code signifying the wearer's age or stage or life is applied much more flexibly; the tendency is for all women to wear colours formerly reserved for the younger ages, and new colours, such as blue, mauve or orange, have become more common. In fact, items in the Leiden Museum dating back to 1864 show that blue and mauve blouses were worn even then, probably only by women of the nobility, who always had the privilege of indulging in novelty; they were followed by the commoners later. Green is now also acceptable for commoner brides. The style of dress seen at civil celebrations nowadays reflects a trend towards a national rather than an ethnic mode of dress, with many wives of civil servants or military officers clad in the Javanese fashion, with tightly wound *kain panjang* of Central Javanese batik and bright lace *kebayas*.

South Sulawesi has long been famous for its weaving, especially of checked, very fine silk sarongs, usually in dark, somewhat austere, colours. The innovation in the 1930s of the 'painted weft' technique producing soft, bright colours made them even more popular. Silk yarn was always imported up to the early 1960s, when silk production was begun, mostly in Soppéng and South Wajo'. The enterprise had a promising start, but after a few years of successes the silkworms fell victim to epidemic diseases and became unable to reproduce themselves; since then, local silk has had to be produced from cocoons imported directly from Japan. The increasing use of silk, and the availability for general use of *palekat* sarongs of Indian make, as well as the importation of machine-spun cotton, made cotton cultivation less and less important in the 1930s. During the Second World War, import of thread was temporarily halted, and the Japanese made cotton planting compulsory everywhere it could be grown. These plantations were maintained after the war in the areas controlled by the rebels under Kahar Muzakkar, where men were forbidden to wear silk sarongs as contrary to Islamic prohibitions on luxury. By the 1960s, however, cotton cultivation and spinning had almost disappeared from the Bugis area, apart from a few isolated places. After independence, a shaft loom created in

1929 at the Bandung Textiel Instituut was promoted in South
Sulawesi, as elsewhere in Indonesia, by the government authorities in order to foster the development of local small indus-
tries. A number of firms have since used it to produce cotton
or synthetic cloth, either checked or with painted weft, in
larger quantities but of a lower quality than that produced by
home weaving. In 1965 a well-known woman of the Wajo'
aristocracy undertook to introduce a new kind of shaft loom
from Thailand, in the hope of developing the production of fine
silks on a large scale on the model of the renowned Thai Silks,
and invited an expert Thai weaver to instruct local weavers.
That particular initiative did not succeed; it was taken up later
by others, but still without the anticipated level of success.

Housing and Furniture

The evolution of Bugis architecture in the second half of the
nineteenth century, in so far as it can be reconstructed, was
marked by the progressive replacement of the large, heavy old
houses with their planted posts made of entire logs by smaller,
lighter houses based on a frame of squared beams simply standing on stone foundations. This transition involved a move towards finer carpentry and was related to the increased scarcity
of timber in South Sulawesi and the need to import new and
more expensive types of wood from Borneo. The technical evolution which has continued throughout the present century has
led to the general use of corrugated iron roofs and skilled joinery
in the floors, outer walls and windows, the latter now increasingly fitted with panes of glass. The division of the formerly open
inner space into a number of rooms, advocated by the provincial
administration, has become increasingly common. Since the
1960s an increasing number of South Sulawesi houses have been
built in brick or concrete, not only in the larger cities but also in
the smaller district or sub-district towns. The first of these were
constructed on quite simple models, directly on the ground, i.e.
without either raised piles or sunk foundations; they were followed by more elaborate designs, with Javanese-inspired steep
sloping roofs. In more recent years the wealthier residents of
Ujung Pandang have built huge two-or three-storeyed villas in

Hollywood fashion, with colonnades in the mock-antique style, and pale imitations of these buildings are beginning to appear in provincial towns as well.

Items of furniture, such as tables, chairs, armchairs of metal or synthetic material, cupboards with glass doors where the family's finest crockery can be displayed, spring beds with embroidered sheets and pillows, wardrobes with mirrors, are relatively recent innovations in village homes. Most of them are not only of practical use but also serve as marks of prestige to be admired by visitors.

From the Slave Trade to the Cocoa Boom

In their export activities, Bugis traders were always eclectic, constantly adapting supply to the most rewarding demands. By the end of the eighteenth century, the markets they seem to have considered the most promising – though their commerce was by no means limited to these – were for Malayan tin, east Indonesian and north Australian trepang, and slaves. According to Raffles, the other main articles traded at this time were 'cotton, which is imported from the surrounding islands and re-exported after being manufactured into cloths . . ., bird's-nests . . ., shark's fins, tortoise-shell, agar agar . . . The Bugis, indeed, is the great maritime and commercial state of the Archipelago. The cargoes of their vessels, particularly in opium, gold and cloths, often amount to fifty or sixty thousand dollars each' (Raffles, *History of Java*, CLXXXIII).

Early Nineteenth-Century Bugis Traders and the Foundation of Singapore

The tight commercial network built up by the Bugis across the archipelago was linked to international trade routes by various harbours. The most important of these was the entrepôt they had established in the early eighteenth century in the strategic Riau islands. There, beyond the reach of any foreign interference, they could conduct their business quite freely and easily compete with Dutch Malaka. As Curtin explains, they 'won easily in price competition with the Dutch, whose long-term policy was based on high unit profit but low turnover. The Bugis opened Riau to all comers. It attracted not only Bugis and Makassar but also Chinese, English, Thai and Javanese commerce to become for a time the most important port linking the trade of the South China Sea and the Java Sea with that of the Indian Ocean' (Curtin, *Cross-Cultural Trade*: 164–6). When in 1784 the Dutch decided to occupy Riau, their main aim was to stop the Bugis established there exchanging spices from the Moluccas for cloth imported by the British from Bengal, which competed with Dutch imported cloth (Nahuijs, *Brieven*: 71). As Brooke later observed: 'The Bugis . . . are checked and hampered by the Dutch restrictions, and this remark, applying most forcibly to them, is true of all the trading interests, and renders all alike inveterately hostile to the Dutch' (Brooke, *Private Letters*: 8–9).

The British interregnum offered the Bugis the opportunity to resume their commercial activities in Riau. After the Dutch came back in 1819, they used the pretext of an incident with the returning colonial power to decamp in force to the then almost deserted Singapore island, a flight almost certainly motivated by their desire to escape the prohibitively heavy duties levied by the Dutch on foreign, especially British, goods, and to regain room for manoeuvre in their maritime enterprises (Brooke, *Private Letters*).

Raffles, who was made Lieutenant-Governor of the British settlement in Bengkulu on the western coast of Sumatra in 1818, deeply regretted the British decision to give the Netherlands Indies back to the Dutch, and advocated the creation of a new settlement at the outlet of the Malaka strait. This, in contravention of the trade monopoly claimed by the Dutch, would be open to free trade as 'a continuation of the policy the Bugis had followed in Riau' (Curtin, *Cross-Cultural Trade*: 166). The flight of the Riau Bugis traders to Singapore may have been among the main reasons why Raffles chose that island for his new settlement rather than the previously targeted Karimun Island. It was probably no accident, too, that the Johor sultan who sold him Singapore Island was of Bugis descent. Although they were rapidly outnumbered by new immigrants from many other places, in 1824 the Bugis, who had been allotted a residential base in Kampong Glam, still numbered 1,851 out of the town's total population of 10,683.

While the creation of this new tariff-free entrepôt was to the benefit of Western trading companies as well as the existing local network which the presence of their Bugis partners had attracted from Riau, it opened up new possibilities for the latter and very rapidly boosted their commercial activities. 'The occupation of the island of Singapore by the British,' one of its residents wrote in 1831,

and the policy pursued by them ever since, have caused a revolution of opinion throughout these islands; the state of trade has changed . . . The Bugis . . . declare that they would go to Java if they could, but the advantages held out at Singapore are so great and obvious, that they could not shut their eyes to them . . . The whole of the wants of all the people inhabiting these islands can be supplied from Madras, Bengal and Europe via Singapore; therefore Singapore is doubtless in every point of view, the general emporium or grand mart of eastern commerce so far as affects these islands . . . Merchants can afford to sell at Singapore goods . . . from 35 to 50 percent cheaper than those living at Batavia. This of course falls upon the consumers or the people of the prows [*prahu* or native ships] and makes the difference very great, added to which are the import duties on their own produce, port charges and fiscal regulations, the latter of which are intolerably troublesome to the native character. All this is avoided at Singapore. (Dalton, 'Makassar': 73–4)

According to one contemporary report, 90 Wajo' ships came to Singapore in 1824, and 120 in 1825, in spite of the war the Bugis were waging with the Dutch that year ('Commerce des Boughis': 200). Crawfurd himself viewed the Wajo' Bugis as

the most considerable and enterprising of the navigators of the Indian islands. The voyage from the shore of the lake [Lake Témpé] is commenced in the beginning of the easterly monsoon. The adventurers carry on a trading voyage as they proceed westward, until at Rhio, Malacca, Penang, and Achin, they reach the limit of the Archipelago, and are prepared to return with the change of season. The commodities which they export from their native country, or collect, in the course of their outward voyage, for the supply of the most distant islands, are the excellent and durable cotton cloths of their native country, gold-dust, nutmegs, Spanish dollars, birds'-

nests, camphor, Benjamin, or frankinsense, and tortoise-shell. They bring back from the extremities of the Archipelago, either for the supply of the intermediate tribes, or that of their own countrymen, opium, European broad-cloth, European and Indian cotton-goods, unwrought iron, and tobacco. This voyage is necessarily the most considerable and important of the adventures of the Waju merchants, but many subordinate ones are undertaken, in which the chief object is to collect materials for the markets of China, as birds'-nests, ornamental feathers and tripang, or sea slug. (Crawfurd, *History*: 149–51)

The Slave Trade

Although Crawfurd does not mention them, slaves were among the 'commodities' traded by the Bugis since the sixteenth century at least. In the seventeenth and eighteenth centuries they sold captives taken in raids on the Lesser Sunda Islands, Buton, Mindanao, Sulu and north-east Borneo for labour on the pepper plantations of Malaya and Sumatra, and in Batavia (Sutherland, 'Slavery in South Sulawesi': 267). South Sulawesi traders had become the major suppliers of slaves to the Dutch East India Company (Reid, 'Slave Systems': 172–3), which 'relied on slave labour to work in the docks and shipyards, in the artisan quarter and in officials' houses, and even to fill the gaps in the lower army ranks' (Sutherland, 'Slavery in South Sulawesi': 266). In the course of the eighteenth century this trade, for the most part sponsored by local rulers, developed into a very lucrative activity: about 3,000 slaves were exported every year from Makassar, as many as were exported at the same period by the Dutch from West Africa, at a profit of about 100 guilders per head (Sutherland, 'Slavery in South Sulawesi': 270).

To enhance their profits, South Sulawesi slave traders began to sell their own people as well: nearly 26 per cent of the slaves in Batavia in 1816 were ethnic Bugis, which made them the largest single ethnic group, ahead of the Balinese (Abeyasekere, 'Slaves in Batavia': 291). According to Raffles:

Of the thousands exported annually from Makasar, the greatest portion consisted of persons who had been kidnapped by people acting under the authority of the European residents, or of the princes of the country. The sale of their subjects constituted one chief source of revenue of the Rajahs, and the factors at the different Dutch residencies traded in slaves. It is reported of one factor that he exported nine hundred in a year. (*History of Java*, CLXXXIX)

These kidnapped persons were kept in secret private gaols in the city of Makassar itself until their embarkation, with the tacit tolerance of the Dutch authority (Raffles, *History of Java*: CLXXXIX–CXCVII). After a brief hiatus during the period of British rule in Makassar, this activity resumed when the Dutch returned, as testified by the famous description by Abdullah Munshi of the arrival in Singapore of a Bugis ship full of captives from Mandar and Manggarai for public sale (Abdullah Munshi, *Hikayat Abdullah*: 232–5) – despite the fact that the slave trade had already been banned in 1807 by an Act of Parliament in Britain. In the Dutch-controlled areas, the slave trade, though not slavery itself, was theoretically abolished in 1818, and it was decreed that all slaves should be registered; but this did not apply to native-owned slaves in Sulawesi, and the Bugis slave trade shifted from Dutch Makassar to independent Boné, Palopo and Paré-Paré. Even after slavery was eventually made illegal in the Netherlands Indies in 1860, Bugis traders continued to bring slaves, most of them Bugis, clandestinely to Arabia, Borneo and even Singapore, with the occasional help of English smugglers. After around 1880 most of the slaves were Toraja people, some purchased by Luwu' and Sidénréng traders with the help of Toraja dealers (Bigalke, 'Slave Trade': 343–50). This trade finally came to an end only when the Dutch definitively conquered the Bugis and Toraja lands in 1906.

The Elusive Bugis Pirates

There seems to be a natural link between slave trading and piracy, and so it is perhaps not surprising that the Bugis have long enjoyed a reputation as fearsome pirates – a reputation, moreover, of which many contemporary Bugis are still quite proud, and which has been fostered by serious historians as

well as by novelists and travelogue writers. In fact, the case is
very far from proven. Very few nineteenth-century sources
directly incriminate South Sulawesi Bugis for specific acts of
piracy, and in the most detailed Dutch report on the subject,
written in 1846 (Cornets de Groot, 'Pirateries'; Lombard,
'Pirates malais': 234) they are hardly mentioned among the
perpetrators of such deeds. In 1837, G. W. Earl wrote that he
'had never heard of a single instance of piratical attack by a
Bugis trader; and on the contrary, several circumstances,' of
which he gives two examples, 'have come to my knowledge
which would to go prove that their inclinations tend the
contrary way' (Earl, *Eastern Seas*: 391).

There is in fact considerable evidence of Bugis trading stations and ships being the targets of piratical attacks at this
time. The Singapore-based merchant Dalton, whose jottings
usually display a very poor opinion of the Bugis, writes, for
instance, about his voyage in 1827 from Singapore to Samarinda with a fleet of Kutei Malay and Bugis prows: 'The
principal danger arises from the numerous pirates that infest
the numerous islands in this part of the world . . . particularly
those of the island of Lingin [Lingga] . . . Malayan and Bugis
prows are the favorite objects' (Dalton, 'Voyage': 30). Among
many other sources mentioning the people of South Sulawesi
as the victims of pirates is a report by James Brooke about a
fleet of Lanun pirates which had 'pillaged the bay of Boni and
other places in Celebes and passed through the Straits of
Makassar'; and the *Singapore Free Press* of 31 October 1851
printed news of the capture of a Mandar rajah by another
Lanun fleet. This is not to deny, of course, that a few individual Bugis may have been members or even leaders of bands of
pirates, as indeed was stated in the *Singapore Free Press* of 24
October 1851 in a report of the attack in 1850 on the Dutch-
controlled island of Bawean by 'pirates under two Bugis
chiefs' (St John, *Indian Archipelago*, II: 129, 351). It also
seems that some of the rajahs indulging in piracy in Central
Sulawesi (Kaili), East and South-East Borneo (Pegatan) or the
Singapore straits were of Bugis descent.

According to Cornets de Groot's analysis ('Pirateries': 12–
13), piracy had probably developed to the extent observed in
the first half of the nineteenth century as a result of the decline

of native trade, hampered as it was by Dutch power and monopolies; the abolition of the Dutch monopoly in the Moluccas, the declaration of Makassar as a free port, and other, similar measures giving a new impetus to native sea trade did as much as navy steamship patrols almost to eradicate piracy completely after 1850.

The Evolution of Bugis Sea Trade

During the first half of the nineteenth century, Bugis sea trade remained in the condition described by Crawfurd in 1820. Bugis ships were based not only in South Sulawesi itself, but also in many other places. The anonymous text already cited ('Commerce des Boughis': 200) estimated, presumably on the basis of information given by Wajo' traders established in Singapore, that in 1825 Wajo' trading vessels numbered about 100 in Makassar, 100 in Mandar, 100 in Kaili, 50 in Wajo', 10 in Paré-Paré, 50 in Flores, 40 in Sumbawa, 50 in Bali and Lombok, 50 in Bonératé (an island in the Flores Sea south of Sulawesi), 66 in eastern and south-eastern Borneo, 20 in western Borneo and 50 in Java, making a total of nearly 700 ships operated by the Wajo' Bugis alone.

Bugis traders used these various ports as bases for collecting local products and as starting-points for their coastal trading voyages to the main ports of the archipelago and to Singapore. To Singapore they brought, from New Guinea, birds of paradise and *masoya* bark; from the eastern islands (the Moluccas, the eastern Lesser Sunda Islands and south-eastern Sulawesi) and from northern Australia, mother-of-pearl, shells, tortoiseshell, agar-agar, trepang and birds'-nests; from North and Central Sulawesi, gold-dust, sandalwood, birds'-nests, tortoiseshell; from Borneo, gold-dust, birds'-nests, beeswax, trepang and tortoiseshell; and from their own land, cotton sarongs, rice and coffee. From Singapore they brought back British and American firearms and gunpowder, Chinese opium, Chinese and Siamese crockery, Chinese raw silk, Bengalese cotton fabrics, European woollen cloth, fine cotton linen and gauze, and old iron; from Java they brought back fine sugar, tobacco and brass goods from Gresik ('Commerce des

Boughis': 203; Dalton, 'Voyage', passim; Brooke, *Narrative of Events*: 117–18; Crawfurd, *Dictionary*: 89, s.v. 'Celebes').

At that time Bugis ships from South Sulawesi heading for Singapore left Makassar preferably in October, at the end of the strongest east winds. The direct voyage took from ten to twenty days: the southern route went to Surabaya first and then along the north Javanese coast to Sumatra; the northern route followed the Borneo coastline to Pontianak. The voyage back from Singapore to Sulawesi would be commenced preferably in December or January, when the west wind began to pick up. The trip to the Moluccas was best undertaken between December and March, sailing with the western monsoon and preferably from South Sulawesi's eastern coast: the northern route was via Kendari, the Tomini Gulf, Ternaté, North Halmahera and New Guinea; the southern route, via Buton, Ambon and the Kei and Aru islands. Between April and August, with the eastern monsoon, they either sailed back to South Sulawesi or went on to Timor, Flores and Sumbawa, whence they could sail north to Sulawesi or on to the western part of the archipelago (Horridge, 'Bugis Prahus': 36; Abu Hamid, *Pasompe*': 6).

The sizes attributed to the Bugis trading ships of that time by various reports vary from 20 to 80 tons, with an average of about 40–50 tons ('Commerce des Boughis': 3; Crawfurd, *Dictionary*: 89, s.v. 'Celebes'; 293, s.v. 'Navigation'). The ship on which Dalton sailed in October 1827 from Singapore to Kutei, a voyage of one month's duration, had a capacity of 30 tons and forty people on board; that on which Alfred Wallace went in December 1856 from Makassar to the Kei islands in fifteen days, and in two more on to the Aru Islands, had a capacity of 70 tons and a crew of thirty; the return trip directly back to Makassar in July 1857 took them less than ten days (Wallace, *Malay Archipelago*: 312–17, 369).

Around 1850 the conditions of sea trade in the archipelago began to change as a result of the marked increase of overseas and colonial European-rigged shipping of large tonnage, with an average burden of around 400 tons; even in 1830 one huge vessel, belonging to an Arab ship-owner of Semarang, was recorded at around 1,100 tons (Broeze, 'Fleet of Java'): 262–5). Until the middle of the century ships such as these had kept to a small number of the more important ports, such as Makassar, Manado, Ternaté, Ambon, Bima and Kupang in eastern Indonesia, and Banjarmasin, Sambas and Pontianak in Borneo. However, 'the Dutch declaration of Makassar as a free port in 1847 opened the eastern archipelago to competing merchants – European, Arab and Chinese – commanding more capacious, square rigged vessels that could more economically carry larger cargoes than the smaller *paduwakang* of the Bugis' (Acciaioli, 'Searching': 53). After the opening of the Suez Canal in 1869, increasing numbers of Western steamships travelled to Singapore and the main harbours of the archipelago. Steamships engaging in the Java trade displaced the Java-based Dutch, Chinese and Arab sailing ships, which were thus thrown into competition with the Bugis traders (Dick, 'Prahu Shipping': 75); and the competition was rendered even fiercer by the initiation in 1891 by the Royal Dutch Navigation Company (KPM) of regular steamship services even to secondary harbours, such as Bajoé or Palopo in South Sulawesi (Acciaioli, 'Searching': 53).

Thus, by the later nineteenth century Bugis and other local sea trade was being increasingly reduced to what has until recently been its main role as a complement to 'modern' shipping: able to enter shallow waters and to sail upriver to reach places without proper harbours, to act as a link between isolated islands or villages and the outer world, accepting lower prices to carry, besides the traditional sea and forest products, the sundry goods of petty local traders and the products of local industry, such as coconut oil, palm sugar and silk sarongs from Mandar and Wajo', and the crops of smallholder plantations, such as copra and maize. On their return voyages they carried crockery, hardware, tools, knives, matches, fishing lines and plaited ropes. As a consequence of this constriction of their role, the average size of Bugis ships gradually diminished, and while in 1881 the *padéwakang* registered on the Australian north coast during a trepang fishing campaign had an average burden of around 20 tons (Macknight, 'Voyage': 133–4), in 1935 only 9 per cent of *prahus* were larger than 17.5 tons and just 1.4 per cent over 35 tons; in 1940 the average size of *prahus* entering the port of Surabaya had dropped to about 8 tons (Dick, 'Prahu

Shipping'). However, according to information collected in Bira and in Paré-Paré, at the end of the 1930s and in the early postwar years the size of the *pînisi'*, the largest type of Bugis vessel, began to increase again, soon reaching 30–70 tons. This may have been because one of their main cargoes was now timber from Borneo and Central or south-east Sulawesi, which needed much more space than the commodities previously carried. Attempts were made to build still larger *pînisi'*, up to 175 tons burden; but they proved difficult to manoeuvre and suffered from both vulnerability to shipwreck and the difficulty of finding sufficient cargo. In 1949 the dimensions of the Bugis *pînisi'* reaching Singapore set down by Gibson-Hill put the average burden at about 50 tons (Gibson-Hill, 'Trading Boats': 112–13). However, in 1975, during Dick's fieldwork, *pînisi'* of about 100 tons had become common again, and the largest observed was about 150 tons.

The timber trade, on which the fortunes of *prahu* shipping had largely rested, experienced its real boom around 1955 as a result of strong demand on Java. Heavy logs were mostly brought from South Borneo to Surabaya and from south-east Sulawesi to Makassar. Copra, used in the manufacture of coconut oil, margarine and soap, was also quite important; until the Second World War the main market had been Singapore, but domestic demand in Indonesia grew considerably after 1945. It was brought from all over Sulawesi and the Moluccas to Surabaya where the mills were located. Among other bulky cargoes were rattan, carried from Borneo and South Sulawesi to Makassar; salt from Makassar to Borneo; glass sand from Tanjung Pandan to Jakarta and Surabaya; and live cattle from Madura and Paré-Paré to south and east Borneo (Dick, 'Prahu Shipping': 91, 97, 100, 102). Cement, furniture, kitchen implements, crockery, flour and caster sugar were taken on the return voyages.

In the 1970s commercial practice became simpler than it had been under the Amanna Gappa code with the disappearance of 'travelling traders'. Remuneration of officers and crew was now based, as in fishing, on sharing of the profits made. Once the cargo had been delivered to the trade agent in the destination port, freight costs calculated and the costs of feeding the crew deducted, the remaining sum was first divided into two, half reserved for the ship's owner and half for the officers and crew. This latter half was then further divided: 20 per cent went to the *juragang*, 5 per cent to the *jurumudi*, and the remainder was divided equally among the whole crew, including the *juragang* and *jurumudi*. This system did not prevent the *juragang* from acting as a forwarding agent for some owners of cargoes, and negotiating the sale of these goods on their behalf to prospective buyers in the ports visited; likewise, crew members could still take on board a few goods of their own and negotiate their sale at any of their ports of call.

The 1970s, in fact, witnessed the swan-song of Bugis *prahu* shipping in the face of harsh competition from an increasing number of motor vessels of all tonnages undertaking shorter voyages with more predictable schedules, and an increasing reluctance on the part of insurance companies to insure *prahu* cargoes. The obvious solution was motorization of the *prahus*: hence the appearance of the so-called PLM (*prahu layar motor* = 'motorized sailing ships'). This locally built hybrid was not technically very effective, but has at least enabled Bugis petty sea trade to continue for the time being. In 1977 20 per cent of inter-island freight in Indonesia was transported on board PLM, and by 1983 that proportion had risen to 50 per cent.

The Search for Remunerative Cash Crops

Cash crops are no novelty to Indonesia: for centuries, cloves and nutmeg in the Moluccas, pepper and gambier in Sumatra have been cultivated as a source of income, while the capacity to produce a substantial rice surplus may have been a major contributory factor in the replacement of the Sumatran by the Javanese kingdoms as the leading political powers in the archipelago. From the end of the eighteenth century, however, the increase in European demand created conditions particularly favourable to the development of new cash crops, and the Bugis were quick to grasp these opportunities.

Coffee was probably the first commodity the Bugis attempted to use in this way. Introduced in the early seventeenth century to Java, where it was mostly grown in the western highlands, coffee had generated handsome returns, first for

the Dutch East India Company and then at the turn of the
nineteenth century, in an extraordinary boom, for the Netherlands Indies government (Vlekke, *Nusantara*: 194–9, 245). It
may have been around then, possibly in the brief period of
British rule, that the Bugis began to cultivate coffee on their
own account in the low hills of north Sinjai and south Boné;
certainly in 1840 James Brooke reported the export of coffee
from South Sulawesi to Singapore (Brooke, *Narrative of
Events*: 117–18). At that time, while still on a limited scale,
production must have been competitive compared with West
Javan coffee and later with that produced under the 'Culture
System' in other Dutch-ruled areas, such as North Sulawesi,
the west coast of Sumatra or the Tapanuli highlands, for the
plantations were further developed under the monopoly of
local rulers in the mountains of north Sidénréng and the
Toraja country. Later, in 1869 and 1870, the high prices paid
for coffee on the international market led to a new boom: in
1872 coffee worth two and a half million guilders was exported from Makassar harbour alone, while unregistered
quantities were also exported from independent Palopo,
Wajo' and Paré-Paré (Staden ten Brink, *Zuid-Celebes*: 57–8).
The Bugis engaged in two kinds of trade in coffee: first, the
relatively new (to them) activity of growing coffee in their own
lands for export; secondly, the traditional trade in the inland
products of coastal states, levying export duties at Paré-Paré
and Palopo on coffee produced in the Toraja lands. This latter
activity led to fierce competition between Sidénréng and
Luwu' and, from 1885 to 1897, the so-called 'coffee war',
after which the coffee trade remained in the hands of the
Sidénréng merchants and their Duri allies until after the First
World War (Bigalke, 'Slave Trade': 53, 245–51).

Tobacco had been cultivated in some parts of South Sulawesi since the early seventeenth century, but only on a small
scale; until well after the middle of the nineteenth century
production was insufficient even to meet the increasing local
demand, and contemporary sources reveal that it was one of
the main Bugis imports from Java. Tobacco was used not only
for smoking but also for chewing, either on its own or, like
gambier, as an addition to betel. When tobacco began to be
grown in the present main area of cultivation, north Soppéng,

remains obscure. The economic pattern of the tobacco trade was different from that of coffee. Development of the plantations enabled the Bugis to achieve local self-sufficiency and offered new opportunities for business enterprise in Soppéng and for the retail trade in the rest of the peninsula. From the point of view of South Sulawesi, it also enabled a better balance of external trade to be achieved. However, the tobacco boom which occurred there in the late 1960s, just after the end of the rebellion and the restoration of order in the province, did not outlive the 1970s: general relative enrichment and the evolution of taste led many people to give up local tobacco and cigarettes, which came to be branded as boorish, for the more prestigious *krétèk* cigarettes produced in Java.

Coconut has been a providential tree for the peoples of Indonesia and the Pacific from time immemorial. Among other uses, cooking oil had for centuries been obtained from the scraped flesh of the fruit, until someone thought of using it as a component for a cheaper alternative to butter, margarine. Copra, the dried flesh of the coconut, then became a much sought-after raw product, and from around 1870 the newly established coconut plantations in the Netherlands Indies became a significant source of income. Once again, the Bugis were quick to latch on to this opportunity, and to look for appropriate locations for such plantations. These they found on the coastline, at first in a number of areas in southeast and Central Sulawesi where coconut plantations had long been established already, and then later around Pontianak, also an area of ancient Bugis settlement, which had the advantage of being much nearer to Batavia and Singapore, both highly important markets for copra in the region. Finally, by the end of the nineteenth century the Bugis had discovered the availability almost free of charge of appropriate uncultivated land in south-west Johor at the southern end of the Malay peninsula, adjacent to Singapore. Once the forest was cleared, the land drained and the trees planted, the Bugis planters in Johor limited themselves to picking the coconuts and drying the copra; in contrast to their compatriots in Sulawesi or Pontianak, their transport costs to Singapore were minimal. The coconut plantations here developed steadily until the effects of the world economic crisis of 1929 reached Malaya.

In the 1920s maize enjoyed some popularity for a while, becoming the second most important crop after rice. It was grown, mainly as a secondary crop, all round Lake Témpé, in the dry season on the alluvial soils from which the lake's waters had receded, and taken by river boats down the Cénrana river to the small harbour of Pallima where a special landing-stage had been built to allow the crop to be loaded on to Dutch motor vessels. At their 1920s peak, maize exports averaged 2,700,000 *pikul*, (about 16,000 tons) a year; but the 'maize craze' was short-lived and did not survive the Second World War. In the postwar years other secondary crops, such as peanuts and sesame, each had their period of success. These crops represented economic behaviour more typical of peasant societies: supplementing a main crop intended for domestic consumption with a secondary annual crop to be sold for cash.

During the 1970s a new kind of plantation emerged, that of the clove tree (*Eugenia aromatica*). As is well known, clove-growing had for centuries been exclusive to a limited number of islands in the Moluccas, until in 1767 it was introduced to the Isle de Bourbon (Mauritius), as well as to Penang, Sri Lanka and later to Zanzibar and Pemba. These latter islands became the principal producers of cloves in the world, while Indonesia, which uses vast quantities in the manufacture of its *krétèk* cigarettes, has since the 1950s been the principal consumer, importing 60–70 per cent of global production (Charras, 'Giroflier': 144). Obviously there was every reason to attempt to restore Indonesian self-sufficiency in cloves by planting clove trees in all appropriate locations throughout the archipelago, and the government offered various incentives to encourage such development. For the Bugis, the main incentive was the knowledge of the high returns to be gained on a modest investment in the seeds. Moreover, planting could be carried out on hitherto unproductive ground, either sterile grassland in deforested areas or newly cleared forest tracts; within a few years, hectares of hilly country in north Sinjai, south Boné, north Sidénréng and north Wajo' were covered in clove trees. However, this enthusiasm for cloves was shared by many other Indonesian regions, and the overproduction which resulted in the mid-1980s automatically checked its excesses.

The latest economic venture into which the Bugis have plunged is cocoa planting. Since the early 1980s Bugis planters have played a pre-eminent role in the Indonesian 'cocoa boom'. In 1979/80 cocoa production in Indonesia was no higher than 7,000–10,000 tonnes; in 1991 it reached about 200,000 tonnes, making the country the world's seventh largest producer, and experts predict that it will rank second before long. In contrast to the boom in clove production, the surge in cocoa took place without any involvement on the part of the government, which in fact always underestimated cocoa production in its official statistics, and it caught both national planners and international cocoa specialists by surprise. It resulted from completely spontaneous initiatives by small planters: 60 per cent of Indonesian cocoa production comes from smallholders, of which half (compared to 2 per cent in 1980/1) comes from farms in South and south-east Sulawesi, and appreciable amounts from Mamuju, Poléwali and south Luwu'. Most of these farms are owned and managed by Bugis planters who moved there from the core of the Bugis country with the specific object of growing cocoa; many came from Soppéng as the tobacco boom there ended (Ruf, 'Cocoa Boom').

The first experiments in Bugis cocoa farming seem to have been made in the late 1960s in Mamuju, then ruled by the famous warlord Andi' Séllé, who was well known for his independent economic initiatives and his direct trading relations with the Malaysian state of Sabah in north Borneo, from where both information about the possibilities of cocoa, and materials for planting, came. The industry really took off, however, in the 1970s when word got round that 'cocoa is money'. The leading role played by Bugis farmers in the cocoa boom is attributed by Ruf ('Cocoa Boom') to their information network concerning planting and trade; and, in contrast to other peoples, they can handle the intermediate stages of marketing by themselves.

Migration as a Market-Economy Strategy

In most tales told by or about migrant Bugis, the reasons given for their leaving their home country are generally connected with the resolution of a personal conflict, an affront received, political insecurity or the desire to escape either unsatisfactory social conditions or undesirable repercussions of an act of violence perpetrated at home. Such circumstantial explanations alone do not, however, seem sufficient to account for the scattering of Bugis settlements all over the archipelago which has occurred since the end of the seventeenth century, or for the fact that out-migration has been a permanent feature of Bugis life up to the present, despite changing historical circumstances. According to the Indonesian census of 1990, about 25 per cent of the people who acknowledge Bugis as their first language live outside Sulawesi, making Bugis one of the most widespread languages in Indonesia, after the national language and Javanese. In the postwar decades a regular outflow of Bugis, but not Makassar, has kept South Sulawesi's population increase well below the Indonesian average; between 1969 and 1980 there was even a fall of 8,762 (Mukhlis and Robinson, *Migrasi*: VII). This has occurred despite the fact that since the 1930s parts of the province, especially in Polé-wali and Luwu', have been the targets of Javanese 'transmigration' – which itself is sufficient proof that the outflow is not a simple consequence of overpopulation or a lack of available cultivable land.

It has already been noted that by the end of the eighteenth century there were already Bugis settlements in many places. On mainland Sumatra, an immigrant Bugis minority was living in Bengkulu, where some of them had been entrusted with important political offices. Bugis whose main occupation was trade constituted the majority population in the Riau archipelago, and also held influential positions in the Riau–Johor sultanate. Other Bugis controlled substantial parts of the exports of tin and certain forest products from the Malayan peninsula. In Borneo, Bugis settlements in areas around Pontianak and Mampawa on the west coast and in Pulau Laut, Pegatan, Pasir, Kutei (especially in Samarinda), Bulungan and Gunung Tabur, controlled the upriver trade. On the opposite side of the Makassar strait, many ancient Bugis settlements were to be found around the Palu Bay in Donggala, Banawa and Kaili; there were also pockets of settlement in Sumbawa, which had a long-standing tradition of close relations with South Sulawesi, and at Endeh in Flores. Finally, in Java important groups of Bugis traders existed in several places, including Surabaya, Gresik and Batavia. This brief list, of course, takes no account of the many other trading ports where Bugis communities were settled. Since the eighteenth century Bugis migrants have continued to gravitate to most of these places, and a few others as well, such as the area between the delta of the Indragiri river and Jambi in Sumatra; the west coast of Johor in Malaya; Sabah in Borneo; and the Lindu region and the south-eastern peninsula in Sulawesi.

Each settlement, of course, has its own story; nevertheless, there are a number of common and enduring features. We may take as an example the case of the Samarinda Bugis. In the early eighteenth century the Wajo' prince La Ma'dukelleng, Arung of Singkang and a fierce opponent of the Dutch and their Boné allies, left South Sulawesi with a group of about 3,000 followers for Pasir in east Borneo, just across the Makassar strait from South Sulawesi, where a small community of Bugis traders from Wajo' was already established. Engaging in trade, he stayed there until 1737, when he returned to South Sulawesi as the newly elected Arung Matoa of Wajo' to wage war against Boné and its Dutch allies (Noorduyn, 'Arung Singkang'). In east Borneo, La Ma'dukelleng concluded political matrimonial alliances with local rulers just as he would have done in his home country; thus he married one of his sons to one of the Sultan of Pasir's daughters and, later, their daughter to Sultan Idris of Kutei, while he himself became Sultan of Pasir. He was also active in organizing further Wajo' communities all down the east coast of Borneo, each under its elected chiefs. Having obtained from the previous Sultan of Kutei the right of settlement for Bugis in Samarinda, a strategic settlement near the mouth of the Mahakam river, somewhat downriver from the Kutei capital, he later also obtained from Sultan Idris monopoly rights over the export of products from the hinterland, including gold-dust, benzoin, camphor, damar, gaharu wood, rattan, birds'-nests, beeswax, bezoar stones and rhinoceros horn (for which, however, only Kutei Malays were permitted to trade upriver), and of sea products such as tortoiseshell, turtles' eggs, agar-agar and trepang. The Samarinda Bugis also had the monopoly on

imports of rice, salt, spices, coffee, tobacco, opium, china-
ware, textiles, iron, firearms, saltpetre and slaves. Moreover,
their right to self-government was recognized and they organized themselves under the authority of a chief entitled Pua'
Ado (the daughter of the first bearer of this title had married
another of La Ma'dukelleng's sons) and a council of a number
of *nakhoda* or rich sea traders. Some Bugis leaders were
granted titles by the Sultan which put them on a par with the
Malay nobility and qualified them for intermarriage with
the ruling dynasty. The Samarinda Bugis eventually obtained
the right to control the upriver trade, and a Bugis was appointed *shahbandar*, an officer whose main function was to
levy port taxes (K. K. D., 'Samarinda': 4–18; Peluso, 'Bugis
Strategies'). Peluso notes: 'The Bugis' ability to monopolize
and control interior territories hinged on their access to and
control of other goods. Bugis merchants supplied the sultan
with arms and ammunitions for his army, but they could stop
the supply at any time . . . In addition, the Bugis held the
monopoly on imports of salt, tobacco and opium . . . which
people had physiological needs for or psychological dependencies on' ('Bugis Strategies': 22).

A contrasting type of migration is that which was linked not
with trade but with cash crop plantations, and which had no
political implications, such as that which took place between
about 1885 and about 1920, first to Johor, Malaya, and then
to Sumatra. This was a time when many new areas in Borneo,
Sumatra and Malaya were undergoing forest clearance and
being planted in the first instance with gambir, and later with
rubber, cocoa, coconut, oil palms and other crops in response
to the increasing demands of the international markets. The
Bugis, together with many Javanese, Madurese, Boyanese,
Banjar and others, were quick to seize these new opportunities
and to open plantations in the western parts of the archipelago.

In the case of Johor, the opportunities open to exploitation
on its south-western coast were discovered and publicized by
the captains of Bugis ships which had been bringing Javanese
contract labourers to work on the big estate opened by a rich
Arab Johor family near Kukup, just across from Singapore
island. The highly progressive Sultan of Johor at that time,

who combined a European education with an acute political sense which had so far enabled him to maintain his independence from the British, had instituted an ambitious voluntary settlement and land development policy in the still largely uncultivated areas of his state. Tracts of virgin forest and mangrove swamp were allotted at negligible cost to any settler prepared to open them up and establish plantations. Alongside the Chinese, the first to take advantage of this opportunity in appreciable numbers were the Javanese who had come to Johor as contract labour on the Kukup estate; then some Javanese newcomers opened their own small plantations in the surrounding area.

When rubber cultivation started in Malaya, Javanese settlers began planting rubber trees along the coastline from Muar to Kukup, some distance inland. The Bugis who came later opted instead to open up the forest and mangrove swamps between these plantations and the sea shore, considering these areas more suitable ground for coconut plantation, which they preferred to rubber because it gave quicker results and, once the initial phase of plantation was over, required less work. Their first main settlements were around Sungai Kuali, not far from Kukup, and later ones were added around Benut and Rengit. Many of these Bugis had already had experience of coconut plantation and the copra trade in Pontianak; here they found the soil more suitable, and the geographical location more economically favourable.

Most of the Johor Bugis came from the lands around Lake Témpé; some were from Sidénréng or Batu-Batu in north Soppéng, but most came from Wajo', especially from the *wanua* north of Témpé. They sailed to Malaya usually on Bugis ships from Doping, Paré-Paré or Makassar, in groups each headed by a leader belonging to either the middle nobility or the sea trading class, and often to both. These leaders had the start-up capital necessary to buy tools, materials and the first seeds and seedlings, and to feed their followers for as long as required; they were also able to lend money on very cheap terms to those of their followers who later on wished to open up their own plantations (Lineton, 'Study of the Bugis': 191). At the outset of the enterprise, they could mobilize the manpower of their poorer relatives, of followers and even at that time of slaves, who were used to build provisional dwellings, clear the forest and plant the food crops needed for subsistence until the first returns came in from the plantations. Another task of the initial phase, that of digging drainage canals (*parit*) was entrusted to teams of hired Javanese specialists.

In the newly cultivated areas, subsistence crops were abandoned as soon as the first returns on the cash crops came in. As a consequence, increasing quantities of rice had to be imported, mainly from Sumatra. When the price of coconut fell during the First World War, around 1917, while that of rice rose, a number of Bugis from Benut crossed over to Sumatra to open up new land there for rice cultivation in the area around the Indragiri delta between Tembilahan and Kuala Enok, already targeted by Banjar and Javanese settlers (Lineton, 'Study of the Bugis': 173–80). Just as in Malaya, before this marshy land could be exploited *parit* had to be dug; here, however, they remained open to the tide, which has an influence on river levels, and a precise knowledge of water movement enabled them to be used to irrigate the ricefields. This technique, called 'tidal swamp cultivation', had also long been used extensively in south Borneo.

After 1920 Bugis colonization in Sumatra extended from Kuala Tungkal south-east along the coast of the Jambi regency. Where they settled, Bugis tended to form clusters of people from the same origin, often interrelated: Wajo' Bugis and Boné Bugis rarely mixed (Lineton, 'Study of the Bugis': 181–2).

During the Second World War, when foodstuffs were again difficult to obtain and very expensive in Malaya, trade in rice across the Malaka strait was forbidden, although Malaya and Sumatra were placed under the same Japanese command. A number of Malayan Bugis moved to Jambi to undertake rice cultivation there, while others engaged in rice smuggling and a few went back to Sulawesi. After Indonesian independence migration to British Malaya became increasingly difficult, with the country under a State of Emergency because of communist guerrilla activity. On the Indonesian side of the Malaka strait, economic conditions were generally bad, but nevertheless many Bugis chose to leave South Sulawesi between 1950 and 1965 to escape the dangers of the rebellion there, emigrating to Riau, Jambi and Indragiri. By 1956 over 10,000 members of the South Sulawesi-born population of Jambi and Riau were classified as refugees. Lineton also reports, on the basis of interviews with migration organizers, that more than 10,000 migrants from South Sulawesi passed through Tanjung Priok in 1955 on their way to Sumatra (Lineton, 'Study of the Bugis': 23–4, 181). At that time the inflation rate in Indonesia was high and copra production not profitable, and many Bugis who had previously engaged in coconut planting now shifted to tidal swamp rice cultivation. Some of those who persisted with coconut, however, took advantage of the armed Confrontation of 1962–5 between the newly born Malaysia and Indonesia by smuggling copra to Singapore. In the 1970s the price of coconut in Indonesia rose again and Bugis in east Sumatra invested considerable amounts in opening large areas further inland for coconut plantation and in increasing their involvement in copra marketing (Tanaka, 'Bugis and Javanese Peasants': 121, 127). More recently, with the establishment of pineapple canneries, other Bugis have taken to pineapple cultivation, which seemed to be more profitable in areas with a lighter soil (Abu Hamid, 'Spontaneous Transmigrants').

Obviously, Bugis migrants in Malaya and Sumatra are not traditional peasants but economy-minded entrepreneurs. In east Sumatra, in contrast to their Javanese neighbours, whose idea of success was the ability to acquire more ricefields or plantations in order to intensify and improve agriculture in the area, Bugis rice growers interviewed by Tanaka thought further ahead. Once they had made enough money, they planned either to reinvest in transportation or commerce, or to rent out their land to Javanese farmers or Bugis newcomers and then move on in search of a more advantageous place (Tanaka, 'Bugis and Javanese Peasants': 130). Lineton also illustrates this trend with a number of life stories which show frequent movement from one settlement to another in search of a better livelihood (Lineton, 'Study of the Bugis': 177).

An example of a third, and again different, type of Bugis migration is provided by those who settled in the Lindu area in west central Sulawesi. Bugis had long been established in this region, but nearer to the sea, either in coastal villages or in petty Bugis kingdoms around the Palu Bay, though some occasionally visited the hinterland to trade. Settlement in the highland Lindu plain, where the incomers lived mostly by fishing in Lake Lindu, began only in 1957, again with flight from South Sulawesi to escape the insecurity of the Kahar Muzakkar rebellion. The original pioneering family already knew the place, having formerly been kiosk owners in Dong-gala on the Palu Bay; they were followed by successive contingents who moved for similar reasons but independently of their predecessors, each with their own strategy for their new life. They recruited kinspeople to live with them in their homes and work as client fishermen. Young bachelors, without any fixed purpose or occupation, arrived later, usually living as clients with families already settled, and sometimes eventually marrying a daughter of the house. Others came in the 1970s, well after the rebellion was over, from areas where fertile land was scarce, specifically to develop wet rice agriculture. Some of these settlers, having amassed a small capital, set up kiosks in neighbouring market towns or started their own enterprises, either in the fishing business, or as land brokers or rice traders (Acciaioli, 'Searching': 58, 104–36). In response to Acciaioli's enquiries, some Bugis said that they were searching 'for good fortune'. This, says Acciaioli, 'encodes more than a pursuit of profit . . . It is a search for knowledge as well as riches, embracing a way of seizing one's fate that reveals both a complex conception of the relationships of personality and destiny and a commoner ideology contrasting with the manner in which nobility evaluates fundamental hierarchy' ('Searching').

The Social and Economic Decline of the Bugis Nobility

For centuries, the pre-eminence of the Bugis nobility had been economic as well as social. Even in the *La Galigo* texts, the rulers were described as having priority in trade with visiting merchant ships, and they probably had a monopoly on a number of South Sulawesi's rare raw materials, such as gold, iron and forest and sea products. Much later, at the beginning of the nineteenth century, Raffles noted that the sovereign princes . . . make their power subservient to their love of gain, by establishing in their own favour monopolies against their subjects. Monopolies are common in every state on the island, but most of them are only of a temporary nature. The sovereign of Luwu monopolized the trade in brass; the Raja in Soping that of *siri* [betel leaf], which yields him three hundred dollars a month; and the Raja of Sedendreng that of salt and opium. (Raffles, *History of Java*: appendix F, CLXXXII).

From about the fourteenth century, rice had become another important source of income for the rulers, in the form of either the produce from their own ricefields or taxes to which they were entitled.

In the nineteenth century the development of the sea trade, together with the establishment of Bugis settlements overseas in which, alongside a number of exiled nobles, many people of lower rank played important roles, offered the latter great opportunities for social advancement and thus gave birth to a middle class of wealthy traders and *nakhoda* of either petty nobility or commoner origin. This class, which was concentrated particularly in Wajo', Makassar and Singapore, was far from being opposed to the prevailing social order; on the contrary, many of its members sought to improve their social status further by marrying into noble families, which for their part often sought marriage with wealth to boost their own fortunes. This practice was formalized in customary law as *mang'elli dara*, blood acquisition, an arrangement permitting rich commoners or men of the petty nobility to marry women of the highest ranks upon payment of very high fees. Nevertheless a new elite was forming with a different social background, a different role, different interests and different values from those of the traditional Bugis high nobility. The latter, although it had intermarried to some extent with other, mainly Malay, aristocracies, was strongly centred on South Sulawesi and only fully recognized there. The emerging class, while having its original roots in the Bugis homelands, constituted a polycentred network extending all over the Insulindian world with connections reaching even further afield, to the Middle East, since marriages with Arab traders were not infrequent. Indeed, marriage outside the Bugis community was a strategic aim in order to extend the trading network.

To this new trading elite, founded not on birth but on enterprise, the old ideology of a nobility of *manurung* descent of course meant nothing. Their ruling ideology was Islamic, and included several different threads. A number became members and proselytizers of the Khalwatiyah brotherhood's Samman branch; others, upholders of the Wahabite ideas represented by the *kaum muda* and later by the Muhammadiyah movement, which championed an egalitarian conception of society. Similar Islamic and egalitarian trends characterized Bugis migrant colonists and cash-crop cultivators. Once out of South Sulawesi, even if they had left in the train of a noble leader, they acknowledged the authority of these men on the basis not of their mythical origins but of their status as patrons. In this new, overseas Bugis society as it was to develop later, a person earned superior status and influence by success in business, judicious management of his plantations, or else recognized wisdom or religious knowledge. In this context the declarations of egalitarianism in such sayings as 'we are all the same' or 'all are equally members of humankind' did not rule out economic competition which created new differences in wealth; what they were opposed to was inequality on grounds of birth, and the display of disparities in wealth by ostentation in behaviour or dress. Indeed, many successful emigrants liked to visit their native lands from time to time to show those who had stayed behind how successful they had been; and this, naturally, induced some others to try migration for themselves.

In South Sulawesi itself, despite the existence of this new middle class, the old hierarchical system remained in force. The possibility of migration in order to 'search for good fortune' abroad may even have contributed to the maintenance of social stability in South Sulawesi, since those ambitious individuals who lacked scope at home and might have become frustrated and disruptive could always find an outlet overseas. Later, the colonial government even entrenched the hierarchical system further, with its codification into a bureaucratic structure introduced by Dutch students of customary law and its registration and systematization of the services and taxes attached to different offices and responsibilities. In this way colonial rule may have prevented a natural evolution and

perhaps dilution of the system. Confident of the future preservation of their position in society, most of the Bugis nobility
were simply not interested in providing their children with a
good school education; as a consequence the wealthy middle
class benefited most from the progress in this domain registered between the two World Wars. By sending their children
to government schools or to privately run modern Islamic
institutions, they fostered the development of a new kind of
partly Western-educated elite which progressively challenged
the nobility for possession of political power. One of the first
signs of this impending conflict was the banishment pronounced in the early 1940s by the customary court in Palopo
against the man who was to head the South Sulawesi rebellion, the Muhammadiyah-educated Kahar Muzakkar, for having publicly expressed doubts about the sacred origin of the
Luwu' dynasty.

During the war of independence in Indonesia, many members of the Bugis nobility, along with traditionally minded
Islamic officials, chose to support the returning Netherlands
Indies Civil Administration, and later the State of East Indonesia. This support was based, of course, on their hopes for the
maintenance of the ancient social system, while the modern-
minded minority of Bugis nobles who, with the modernist
Muslims, sided with the Indonesian republicans, were prepared to sacrifice their traditional privileges and former power
for the sake of their ideals. Later, the former independence
fighters who rebelled under Kahar Muzakkar, and who to a
large extent had adopted the Daru'l Islam ideology under his
influence, applied themselves to eradicating from South Sulawesi every trace of the 'feudal' past. In these circumstances
Bugis nobility was again divided into a traditional majority,
which took refuge in areas controlled by the Indonesian National Army, and a minority who supported the rebels. One
might wonder why, in this context, such marked opposition
between the majority of the nobility and the *pemuda* did not
result in a bloody 'social revolution' such as that which took
place at the same period in north Sumatra and Acheh. It seems
that in their declared war against 'feudalism' the rebels
targeted their hostility more at the permanent symbolic bases
of the old society, such as sacred places where dynastic ances-

tors were revered or the regalia from which rulers drew mystic energy, rather than at the actual individuals who were the transitory holders of power. Some members of the nobility did indeed fall victim to the rebels' violence, but probably less as nobles than as members of warring groups. For despite the existence of clashing ideologies and of clear competition between recognizable classes of people, this conflict looked more like a huge vendetta between client groups, their members, though of varying social status, linked to one another by various ties of interdependence.

Shattered by the wars of independence and the period of rebellion, Bugis nobility completely lost its formal political role when in 1960 the Indonesian government abolished the last remnants of the autonomous governing institutions; and as a result they also lost the revenues attached to the various positions they had once held. In fact, since most of the territories which produced these revenues had for years been under rebel control, they had long been deprived of the income from these sources; and as they had attempted in the intervening period to maintain their status by keeping to the prescribed ceremonial when organizing weddings or family rites, and by supporting sometimes large numbers of followers who had followed them in their exile to the province's main cities, much of their wealth had already gone.

New Leaders and Modern Elites

During a period of transition between about 1960 and 1977 after the abolition of the traditional forms of government, because of the lack of trained administrative personnel many administrative offices, such as those of *kepala desa* (village chief), *camat* (under-district chief) and members of the district staff were still filled by their former noble occupants. This was often the case even when a vote had been held among the citizens to elect officials; people seemed to prefer being governed by people they considered to be innately superior to themselves and thus naturally endowed with the authority, talent and knowledge necessary to govern, rather than by their equals whom they supposed to lack these qualities. Later,

*Plate 60 The Bugis Governor of South Sulawesi province marching
in 1984 to a ceremony in the company of civilian and military
officers*

these offices were increasingly given to military personnel
invested with civilian functions, or to alumni of the Administration Academy – who could in either case, indeed, also be
members of the nobility. The latter, however, were by this
time in a minority, though they still often appeared to possess
greater personal authority than their commoner colleagues.
Nevertheless, power now derived from appointment by the
government, not from birth.

An additional source of status now is an academic education; whether in the arts, sciences, law, engineering, trade,
management or any other field, this became the best passport
to a leading position in government or business. As the gov-
ernment-owned Hasanuddin University and Teachers' Training Institute operate a strict *numerus clausus* policy, many
private (though still government-controlled) universities have
sprung up and are flourishing, with branches in all important
secondary towns. A bachelor's diploma, not to mention a

doctorate, is now almost as good a qualification for a good marriage as genuine noble birth.

As the political and economic role of the nobility declined, many of their followers were forced to look for other patrons, not so much among the political elite as among an economic elite made up in great part by commoners. That elite, which included rich peasant farmers, ship-owners, traders and businessmen, had existed since the seventeenth century, but began to come into its own at the beginning of the twentieth. It did, of course, include noblemen, but by virtue of their pursuit of economic rather than political ends. Today, clientship based on the ancient political role of the nobility survives only as the mere shadow of a glorious past; but new clientships founded on an economic base are to be observed everywhere in South Sulawesi. In this form of relationship the patron is now called a *punggawa*, a word of Sanskrit origin used in the nineteenth century to mean only a military chief or ship's captain, while the client is called *sawi*, whose nineteenth-century meaning was simply 'crew member'. Still used in maritime affairs, these two terms have now been appropriated for use in many other fields as well (Pelras, 'Patron–Client'). At the village level, ancient-style *a'joareng* (see the section on 'Clienteles' in chapter 7) and new-style *punggawa*, in their role as leaders of society, may also be called *to-matoa* or 'elders' (Millar, *Bugis Weddings*: 32–5, 40–2). In agriculture, a *punggawa* may not be a large landowner but just someone who indirectly controls large tracts of land which are either owned by members of his family or rented to supplement his own holdings from a number of people living elsewhere or from smallholders whose individual plots would be insufficient to provid a living. Planting and harvesting on these large areas calls for between 30 and 100 helpers, who are each paid a proportion of the harvest yield (up to 20 per cent in total) and given their food. These people, however, are not just hired seasonal labour; they come because they have been personally summoned by their patron. They are his regular clients and would be ashamed not to be called. For his part, the patron may give the needy more than their strict due, considering that by doing so he, both as a good Muslim and as a good patron, will be fulfilling his duty towards his fellow Muslims and clients. At the same time the client will be morally obliged to his patron and will voluntarily offer help in any other circumstances, such as a wedding. Such a *punggawa* usually has influence locally, is considered to be a *tomatoa* in his village, and is consulted by the authorities on matters of local importance.

A similar *punggawa–sawi* relationships is also the general rule in aquaculture, fishing, crafts and trade. In fishing, the pattern of patron – client ties is apparent on several levels. Almost all fishermen depend on a *punggawa pa'kaja* (fishermen's patron), but the specific obligations vary. In some cases the patron is simply an intermediary between the fishermen and the fish traders; others are fishermen themselves; yet others lend the fishermen the money they need to buy their fishing gear, or own the gear themselves and lease it to the fishermen in return for a share of the catch. Other kinds of *punggawa* captain the bigger boats or direct operations with dragnets or fishing platforms. The catch-sharing conventions also vary. Often one *punggawa* fulfils several different functions and thus has several sources of income, so that his annual earnings may be up to fifteen times those of a simple *sawi*. Despite this great disparity in wealth, however, the relationship is usually founded on feelings of confidence and loyalty on the part of the *sawi* and of responsibility on the part of the *punggawa*, and the links are often explicitly described by those to whom they apply as analogous to those which formerly existed between *arung* and dependant. The *punggawa pa'kaja* can give his *sawi* many kinds of help: he may lend money to his family to buy food when he is at sea; or pay his expenses when he suffers a misfortune, or when he wants to celebrate a birth or marry a child (the *punggawa* sometimes even arranges marriages between the children of his *sawi*). The debt is then repaid in instalments by deduction from the sale price of the fish. If the fisherman has a series of poor catches, the repayment is delayed, or a new loan may even be made. The *punggawa* does not act simply as a moneylender; at the same time he provides the services of an insurance company and a pension fund.

The new Bugis economic elites are not, however, limited to the traditional fields of economic activity such as agriculture, fishing, the ancient crafts or trading on sailing ships; they now also cover modern forms of industry and business, which provide new examples of Bugis entrepreneurship. In the Who's Who of Indonesian entrepreneurs, *Apa dan Siapa: se-jumlah orang Indonesia, 1985–1986*, 3 per cent of the 213 businesspeople selected for inclusion are Bugis, that is to say twice their proportion in the Indonesian population. A good example of the new Bugis entrepreneur is the Kalla 'dynasty'. Haji Kalla, from Bukaka (Boné), founded a textile factory in Boné and seven firms in Makassar. In the late 1960s he obtained an import–export licence through contacts with the Nadhatul Ulama Islamic movement and created the Haji Kalla Trading Company. In 1968 his son, then recently graduated form the Hasanuddin University, took over his father's group and, after further business studies in France, rapidly expanded into agribusiness and other industrial activities. He has set up several new companies, including PT Bukaka Teknik Utama, a factory for heavy equipment which he founded in 1978 in Bogor (west Java) in partnership with the Ternatan Fadel Muhammad, one of Indonesia's celebrated 'new entrepreneurial heroes'. The firm, which still depends on government orders for 80 per cent of its sales, won the tender for the Sukarno–Hatta airport avio-bridges, is exploring markets in Malaysia, Bangladesh, Pakistan, the Middle East and Africa, and exports components to the USA. Kalla has obtained the sole agency for Toyota in the whole of eastern Indonesia. He chairs various bodies, including the South Sulawesi Chamber of Commerce and Industry. His group of companies is dominant in the corporate life of the province (Raillon, 'Indonesian Capitalists': 89–9, 105–6).

In the Bugis society of today, power based on belief in the divine origin of a few has definitely come to an end. Leadership, however, remains in the hands of those four categories which the Bugis have honoured since ancient times: the *to-sugi'* (nowadays, the successful entrepreneurs); the *to-warani* (the military); the *to-acca* (the holders of academic diplomas); and the *to-panrita* (the Islamic masters).

11

Conclusion

Like that of a human individual, a people's personality at each period of its life derives both from inherited characteristics and from the multiple features it acquires in the course of its history, its interaction with neighbouring and other peoples, and its own reactions to its experiences. Again like an individual, a people remains fundamentally the same even though it is constantly changing, and sometimes experiences dramatic mutations. Thus it is with the Bugis.

Broadly speaking, one might divide Bugis socio-cultural history into eight periods. The first would be what we may call the proto-Bugis period, extending from the time of their appearance over most of the first millennium of the Christian era. For this period it is possible to make tentative reconstructions with the help of comparative linguistics and ethnography. These, of course, have to be collated with archaeological findings, which are still scarce, but research in progress is giving more and more shape to our representations of that remote time. For the present, my view of these proto-Bugis is that of a group, perhaps still few in number, who settled near the western coast of South Sulawesi, having come from overseas – perhaps from Borneo, with which they certainly had connections – with the aim of controlling part of the trade in natural and mineral products from the hinterland. As they expanded into the central part of what is now the Bugis country, they became increasingly distinct from other related groups, such as the Makassar, Mandar and Toraja, and at the same time merged with the relatively sparse previous Austronesian population of the region, which progressively adopted the newcomers' language. Thus a new mixed culture developed, including components from the original inhabitants and innovations brought by the newcomers such as weaving, the art of the smith, and new religious concepts and practices. Society remained hierarchically split into two sharply divided strata: the dominating noble class, whose wealth was based on the control of trade, and the 'people of the land'.

The second, early Bugis period is what I have called for convenience the *La Galigo* times. Although it is important to realize that the *La Galigo* texts do not present us with a perfect likeness of that period, nevertheless despite their epic exaggeration and anachronism they do help us to form a picture of a socio-cultural situation from approximately the eleventh to the thirteenth century that is clearly different from both the early metal age culture of the proto-Bugis period and the feudal society of the archaic historical times which were to follow. This seems to have been a time of great prosperity linked with the expansion of inter-insular and international trade, leading to the appearance of distinct polities, such as Luwu', Cina and Soppéng, whose ruling dynasties were linked with one another through intermarriage and a common ideology of divine kingship.

In my view, the changes in political and social organization, and in the broader culture, which can be detected between this second period and the third, from the late fourteenth century to the end of the sixteenth, were contemporaneous with the emergence of a new political and economic balance in the archipelago, changes in the physical landscape of South Sulawesi, considerable population growth, the development of agricultural technology in rice cultivation and progressive occupation of territory, coupled with significant land clearance activity, and the creation of many new settlements. Whether the transition to this new situation, which may have taken place in the fourteenth century, occurred smoothly or, as Bugis tradition itself maintains, was accompanied by lasting and serious disturbances, remains a question to be resolved. Whatever the nature of the process may have been, it led to the organization of a feudal, pyramidal system based on contractual relations between suzerains, vassals and subjects, similar to those between patrons and clients. This structure opened up the possibility of intermarriage between nobles and commoners, giving rise to many intermediate social strata. Another consequence was permanent competition between noble claimants for the various political offices and between leading polities for hegemony over each other; this remained an important driving force in political developments in South Sulawesi over the following five centuries.

The following, fourth, period, extends roughtly from 1600 to 1669. It was marked at its beginning by islamization and at its end by the settlement of the Dutch in Makassar, where they were to remain for the next 280 years. This period was characterized by relentless competition between two leading polities for hegemony over the whole peninsula, with a long series of victories by the Makassar people of Goa finally halted, with Dutch help, by Boné Bugis. These years also saw the beginning of the long dominance in the archipelago of South Sulawesi's Bugis, Makassar and Mandar fleets. The fifth period, covering the later seventeenth and eighteenth centuries, might be called the Bugis classical period. The Dutch presence had brought relative political stability to the peninsula, although sporadic disturbances still occurred. This period also witnessed important literary activity, the consolidation of Islam, the construction of an increasingly important sea-trading network, bold overseas ventures by ambitious migrants and the progressive emergence of a merchant middle class which was later to play a prominent role in Bugis life.

The sixth, precolonial, period of the nineteenth century was characterized mainly by increasing pressure from the Dutch colonial government, increasing interdependence with a global economy, the development of cash crops both in South Sulawesi itself and in the areas settled by Bugis migrants (mostly in the western parts of the archipelago) and the growing importance of the more modern and Islamic-minded merchant middle class. The brief seventh period is the true colonial period of 1906–49, including the Japanese interlude and the years of the Indonesian wars of independence. Although the colonial regime had apparently entrenched existing traditional institutions, surface continuity masked their transformation into entities based on quite different principles which paved the way for the present modern system of rationalized administration. At the same time, the spread of education and literacy led to the growth of the new elite of today.

In the eighth and present period, both the South Sulawesi Bugis and those who have migrated to Sumatra or Kalimantan have become full members of a national Indonesian state, while others in Malaya or Sabah are Malaysian citizens and a few more are citizens of Singapore. Although a significant proportion still live in villages and derive their income from agriculture, fishing or navigation, increasing numbers of Bugis are now urban dwellers in small and medium-sized cities as well as in the major metropolises of Ujung Pandang, Surabaya, Jakarta, Kuala Lumpur and Singapore. They seem to have very little in common with their ancestors; but they are still Bugis. What remains, above all, is the Bugis identity. In Malaya, people of Bugis descent in Linggi, although apparently

Plate 61   Bugis motto and concrete four-tiered gable on the district council building of Sidénréng. The motto reads 'Only by toiling 'away without tiring can one usually get good results.'

no different from other Malays, are keen to call themselves
Bugis; and in Singapore there are apparently Malay people
living in modern flats and working in the big offices of international firms whose identity cards bear, on their own request, the word 'Bugis' as ethnic identification. In such a
multi-ethnic state as Indonesia, Bugis identity is even stronger.

Throughout the socio-cultural history of the Bugis one can
detect the persistence of a number of remarkable traits from
the earliest times to the present. One is their extraordinary
propensity always to seek out the best economic opportunity
in any place at any time; another, closely related, is their
remarkable capacity to adapt themselves to prevailing circumstances. Conflicting tendencies which seem always to have
been at work among them – hierarchical and egalitarian
trends; impulses to competition and compromise; the sense of
individual honour and solidarity with fellow Bugis – combined with the valued qualities of bravery, cleverness, religious belief and business acumen, have been consistent driving
forces in their development. These qualities, I believe, are also
the guarantee of their endurance in the future as a dynamic
and strongly individualized people.

References

Abbreviations

ARB	*Adatrechtbundels, bezorgd door de Commissie voor het adatrecht en uitgegeven door het Koninklijk Instituut voor de Taal-, Land- en Volkenkunde van Nederlandsch Indië*
ASEMI	*Asie du Sud-Est et Monde Insulindien*, Centre de Documentation et de Recherches sur l'Asie du Sud-Est et le Monde Insulindien
BKI	*Bijdragen tot de Taal-, Land- en Volkenkunde*, Koninklijk Instituut voor de Taal-, Land- en Volkenkunde
JMBRAS	*Journal of the Malaysian Branch, Royal Asiatic Society*
JRAS	*Journal of the Royal Asiatic Society*
KITLV	Koninklijk Instituut voor de Taal-, Land- en Volkenkunde
MMBRAS	Monographs of the Malaysian Branch, Royal Asiatic Society
PLPIIS	Pusat Latihan Penelitian Ilmu-ilmu Sosial
RIMA	*Review of Indonesian and Malaysian Affairs*
TKNAG	*Tijdschrift van het Koninklijk Nederlandsch Aardrijkskundig Genootschap*

TNI   *Tijdschrift voor Taal-, Land- en Volkenkunde van Nederlandsch Indië*

VKI   *Verhandelingen van het Koninklijk Instituut voor Taal-, Land- en Volkenkunde*

Abdul Rahman Al-Ahmadi, 'Sejarah hubungan': 'Sejarah hubungan Kelantan/Patani dengan Sulawesi Selatan', unpublished dissertation, Ecole des Hautes Etudes en Sciences Sociales, Paris, 1981

Abeyasekere, S., 'Slaves in Batavia': 'Slaves in Batavia: Insights from a Slave Register', in Anthony Reid, ed., *Slavery, Bondage and Dependency in Southeast Asia*, St Lucia (Queensland), 1983

Abu Hamid, 'Spontaneous Migrants': 'The Buginese Spontaneous Transmigrants in Desa Tangkit Baru, Province of Jambi', in Toshimichi Someya and Makoto Ito, *The Formation of Life World among Transmigrants in Indonesia*, Department of Social Anthropology, Tokyo Metropolitan University, 1989

Acciaioli, Greg, 'Searching': 'Searching for Good Fortune: The Making of a Bugis Shore Community at Lake Lindu, Central Sulawesi', unpublished dissertation, Australian National University, Canberra, 1989

Adelaar, K. A., 'Asian Roots': 'Asian Roots of the Malagasy: A Linguistic Perspective', *BKI*, 151(3), 1995: 325–56

—— 'Borneo as a Cross-roads': 'Borneo as a Cross-roads for comparative Austronesian Linguistics', in Peter Bellwood et al., eds, *The Austronesians in History*, Canberra, 1995

Adriani, N., and Kruyt, A. C., *Bare'e Toradja's: De Bare'e sprekende Toradja's van Midden Celebes*, 2nd edn, Amsterdam, 1950–1; Eng. edn *The Bare'e-speaking Toradja of Central Celebes*, trans. Jenni K. Moulton, London, 1950

Ammarell, Gene, 'Bugis Navigation': 'Bugis Navigation', unpublished dissertation, Yale University, 1994

Andaya, Leonard Y., 'Aquatic Populations': 'Historical Links between the Aquatic Populations and the Coastal Peoples of the Malay World and Celebes', in Muhammad Abu Bakar et al., *Historia: Essays in Commemoration of the 25th Anniversary of the Department of History, University of Malaya*, 1984: 34–51

—— *Arung Palakka: The Heritage of Arung Palakka: A History of South Sulawesi (Celebes) in the Seventeenth Century*, VKI, 91, The Hague, 1981

Andaya, *Maluku: The World of Maluku: Eastern Indonesia in the Early Modern Period*, Honolulu, 1993

—— 'Treaty Conceptions': 'Treaty Conceptions and Misconceptions: A Case Study from South Sulawesi', *BKI*, 137, 1978: 275–95

Arief Said et al., *Geografi budaya: Geografi budaya daerah Sulawesi Selatan*, Proyek Inventarisasi dan Dokumentasi Kebudayaan, Departemen Pendidikan dan Kebudayaan, Jakarta, 1976–7

Barros, João de, *Decadas: Da Asia e . . . dos feitos, que os Portugueses fizeram o decubrimento, e conquista dos mares e terras do Oriente*, Decada IV, 2nd edn, vol. 8, Lisbon, 1977

Bartstra, G.-J., 'Note': 'Note on New Data Concerning the Fossil Vertebrates and Stone Tools in the Walanae River in South Sulawesi (Celebes)', in G.-J. Bartstra and W. A. Casparis, eds, *Modern Quaternary Research in Southeast Asia*, Rotterdam, 1978: 71–2

Basran Noor, *Pemakaian Bahasa Indonesia: Efektivitas pemakaian Bahasa Indonesia dalam masjarakat pedesaan: studi kasus di desa Bori Appaka, Kabupaten Pangkep*, PLPIIS, Hasanuddin University, Ujung Pandang, 1979

Battesti, Térésa, and Schubnel, Henri-Jean, 'Trésor des Philippines': 'Trésor des Philippines: un archipel de rites', *Revue de Gemmologie*, Muséum National d'Histoire Naturelle, special issue, Paris, June 1994

Bellwood, Peter, 'Horticultural Prehistory': 'Plants, Climate and People: The Early Horticultural Prehistory of Austronesia', in J. Fox et al, eds, *Indonesia: The Making of a Culture*, Canberra, 1980: 57–73

—— *Prehistory: Prehistory of the Indo-Malaysian Archipelago*, Sydney, 1985

Berg, E. J. van den, 'Poelau Makasar': 'Poelau Makasar', *Cultureel Indië*, 1, 1939: 366

Bosch, F. D. K., 'Buddha-beeld': 'Buddha-beeld van Celebes' Westkust', *TNI*, 73, 1933: 495–513

Boxer, C. R. *Francisco Vieira: Francisco Vieira de Figueiredo, a Portuguese Merchant-Adventurer in Southeast Asia, 1624–1667*, *VKI*, 52, The Hague, 1967

Brink, H. van den, *Matthes: Dr Benjamin Frederick Matthes. Zijn leven in dienst van het Nederlandsch Bijbelgenootschap*, Amsterdam, 1943

Broeze, F. J. A., 'Fleet of Java': 'The Merchant Fleet of Java 1820–1850: A Preliminary Survey', *Archipel*, 18, 1979: 251–69

Bronson, Bennett, 'Indonesian Kris': 'Terrestrial and Meteoritic Iron in Indonesian Kris', *Journal of Historical Metallurgy*, 21(1), 1987: 8–15

—— 'Metal Trade': 'Patterns in the Early Southeast Asian Metal Trade', in I. Glover, P. Suchitta and J. Villiers, eds, *Metallurgy*,

Trade and Urbanism in Early Thailand and Southeast Asia, Bangkok, 1992: 65–116

Brooke, James, *Narrative of Events*: *A Narrative of Events in Borneo and Celebes down to the Occupation of Labuan*, ed. R. Mundy, London, 1848

Bruinessen, Martin van, 'Khalwatiyya': 'The Tariqa Khalwatiyya in South Celebes', in H. A. Poeze and P. Schoorl, eds, *Excursus in Celebes*, *VKI*, 147, 1992: 251–69

Buccellati, Giorgio, and Buccellati, Marilyn Kelly, 'Terqa': 'Terqa: The First Eight Seasons', *Les annales archéologiques arabes syriennes: revue d'archéologie et d'histoire*, 32(2), 1983: 46–67

Bulbeck, David, 'Historical Archaeology': 'A Tale of Two Kingdoms: The Historical Archaeology of Gowa and Tallok (South Sulawesi, Indonesia)', unpublished dissertation, Australian National University, Canberra, 1992

Bulbeck, David, et al., *Survey Soppéng: Survey pusat kerajaan Soppéng*, final report to the Australian Myer Foundation, 1989

Caldwell, Ian, 'Bugis Texts': 'South Sulawesi AD 1300–1600: Ten Bugis Texts', unpublished dissertation, Australian National University, Canberra, 1988

Casparis, J. G. de, *Prasasti Indonesia: Prasasti Indonesia*, vol. 2, Bandung, 1954

Chabot, Hendrik T., *Verwantschap: Verwantschap, stand en sexe in Zuid-Celebes*, Gröningen/Jakarta, 1950

Charras, Muriel, 'Giroflier': 'Le Giroflier: évolution de l'agriculture et transformation de l'espace en pays Minahassa', *Archipel*, 34, 1987: 143–64

Chau Ju-Kua, *Chu-fan-tsi: Chau Ju-Kua. His Work on the Chinese Trade in the Twelfth and Thirteenth Centuries, Entitled Chu-fan-tsi*, trans. and ann. F. Hirth and W. W. Rockhill, St Petersburg, 1991

'Commerce des Boughis': 'Commerce des Boughis (extrait d'une lettre de Sincapour)', *Le Tour du Monde*, 2nd ser., 4, 1825: 197–210

Cornets de Groot, J. P., 'Pirateries': 'Notices historiques sur les pirateries commises dans l'Archipel indien oriental', *Le Moniteur des Indes*, 1846–7, 1847–8

Couto, Diogo de, *Decadas: Da Asia, e ... dos feitos que os Portugueses fizeram no descubrimento, e conquista dos mares e terras do Oriente*, Decada V, 2nd part, 2nd edn, Lisbon, 1779

Crawfurd, John, *Descriptive Dictionary: A Descriptive Dictionary of the Indian Islands and Adjacent Countries*, London, 1856

—— *History*: *History of the Indian Archipelago, Containing an Account of the Languages, Institutions and Commerce of its Inhabitants*, Edinburgh, 1820

Curtin, Philip D., *Cross-Cultural Trade*: *Cross-Cultural Trade in World History*, Cambridge, 1984

Dalton, John, 'Makassar': 'Makassar: The Advantages of Making it a Free Port', *Notices of the Indian Archipelago and Adjacent Countries*, Singapore, 1838: 73–8

—— 'Voyage': 'Journal of a Voyage from Singapore to Coti', ibid.: 30–5

Dars, Jacques, 'Jonques chinoises': 'Les jonques chinoises de haute mer sous les Song et les Yuan', *Archipel*, 18, 1979: 41–56

Dick, H. W., 'Prahu Shipping': 'Prahu Shipping in Eastern Indonesia', *Bulletin of Indonesian Economic Studies*, 11(2), 1975: 69–107, 81–103

Dijk, C. van, 'Rebellion': 'The Rebellion of South Sulawesi: Disaffected Guerrillas', in *Rebellion under the Banner of Islam*, VKI, 94, The Hague, 1983: 155–418

Dumarçay, Jacques, *House*: *The House in South-East Asia*, Singapore, 1987

Dunn and Dunn, 'Marine Adaptations': 'Marine Adaptations and Exploitation of Marine Resources in Sundaic Southeast Asian Prehistory', in P. van de Velde, ed., *Prehistoric Indonesia: A Reader*, VKI, 104, The Hague, 1984: 264–73

Eredia, Manuel Godinho de, 'Description of Malacca': 'Description of Malacca, Cathay and Meridinal India', trans. and ann. J. V. Mills, *JMBRAS*, 7, 1930: 1–21

—— 'Golden Khersonese', 'Report on the Golden Khersonese', trans. J. V. Mills, *JMBRAS*, 8(1), 1930: 227–37

Errington, Shelly, *Meaning and Power*: *Meaning and Power in a Southeast Asian Realm*, Princeton, 1989

Fontein, Jan, *Sculpture of Indonesia*: *The Sculpture of Indonesia*, with essays by R. Soekmono and Edi Sedyawati, New York, 1990

Forrest, Thomas, *Voyage from Calcutta: A Voyage from Calcutta to the Mergui Archipelago*, London, 1792

Fraassen, Ch. F. van, 'Plaatsnamen': 'Drie plaatsnamen uit Oost-Indonesië in de Nagara-Kertagama: Galiyao, Muar en Wwanin wn de vroegere handelsgeschiedenis van de Ambonse eilanden', *BKI*, 132, 1976: 293–305

Friberg, Timothy, and Friberg, Barbara, 'Geografi dialek': 'Geografi dialek bahasa Bugis', *Lontara, Majalah Universitas Hasanuddin*, Ujung Pandang, 28, 1985: 20–47

Friedericy, H. J., 'Ponré': 'Ponré: Bijdrage tot de kennis van adat en adatrecht van Zuid-Celebes', *BKI*, 89, 1932: 1–34

Furukawa, Hisao, 'Rice Culture': 'Rice Culture in South Sulawesi', in Narifumi Maeda and Mattulada, eds, *Villages and the Agricultural Landscape in South Sulawesi*, Centre for Southeast Asian Studies, Kyoto, 1982: 29–72

Gervaise, Nicolas, *Description historique*: *Description historique du royaume de Macaçar*, 2nd edn, Regensburg, 1700 (1st edn Paris, 1688; Eng edn *An Historical Description of the Kingdom of Macassar in the East Indies*, London, 1701)

Gibson-Hill, C. A., 'Trading Boats': 'The Indonesian Trading Boats Reaching Singapore' *JMBRAS*, 23(1), 1950: 103–38

Glover, Ian, 'Late Stone Age': 'The Late Stone Age in Eastern Indonesia', in P. van de Velde, eds., *Prehistoric Indonesia: A Reader*, *VKI*, 104, The Hague, 1984: 274–95

—— 'Léang Burung 2': 'Léang Burung 2: An Upper Palaeolithic Rock Shelter in South Sulawesi, Indonesia', ibid.: 329–72

Glover, Ian, and Syme, Belinda, 'Bronze Age': 'The Bronze Age in Southeast Asia: Its Recognition, Dating and Recent Research', *Man and Environment*, 18(2), 1993: 41–74

Goedhardt, O. M., 'Bonthain': 'De inlandsche rechtsgemeeschappen in de onderafdeeling Bonthain (1920)', *ARB*, 26, 1933.

Gonda, J. *Sanscrit in Indonesia*: *Sanscrit in Indonesia*, New Delhi, 1973

Gremmen, W. H. E., 'Palynological Investigations': 'Palynological Investigations in the Danau Tempe Depression, Southwest Sulawesi (Celebes), Indonesia', *Modern Quaternary Research in Southeast Asia*, 11, 1990: 123–34

Grimes, Charles E., and Grimes, Barbara D., *Languages*: *Languages of South Sulawesi* (Materials in Languages of Indonesia), Pacific Linguistics Series D, 78, Canberra, 1987

Haan, P. A. J. de, 'Aanteekeningen betreffende het zuidwestelijk schiereiland van Celebes', *Jaarverslag van den Topographischen Dienst in Nederlandsch-Indië*, Batavia, 15(2), 1920: 1–68

Hadimuljono and Macknight, Campbell C., 'Imported Ceramics' 'Imported Ceramics in South Sulawesi', *RIMA*, 17, 1983: 66–91

Hamid Abdullah, *Manusia Bugis-Makassar*: *Manusia Bugis-Makassar: suatu tinjauan historis terhadap pola tingkah laku dan pandangan hidup manusia Bugis-Makassar*, Jakarta, 1985

Hamonic, Gilbert, 'Cosmogonies': 'Pour une étude comparée des cosmogonies de Célèbes-sud. A propos d'un manuscrit inédit sur l'origine des dieux bugis', *Archipel*, 25, 1983: 35–62

—— 'Fausse femmes': 'Les fausses femmes du pays bugis', *Objets et Mondes*, 17(1), 1977: 39–46

Hamonic, *Langage des dieux*: *Le langage des dieux. Cultes et pouvoirs pré-islamiques en pays bugis, Célèbes-sud, Indonésie*, Paris, 1987

—— '*Mallawolo*': '*Mallawolo*. Chants bugis pour la sacralisation des anciens princes de Célèbes-sud. Textes et traductions', *Archipel*, 19, 1980: 43–79

—— 'Travestissement et bisexualité': 'Travestissement et bisexualité chez les bissu du Pays Bugis', *Archipel*, 10, 1975: 121–34

Hamzah Daéng Mangemba, 'Femmes bugis': 'Le statut des femmes bugis et makassar vu par leurs propres sociétés', *Archipel*, 10, 1975: 153–7

Harvey, Barbara S., 'Islam and Rebellion': 'Tradition, Islam and Rebellion: South Sulawesi, 1950–1965', unpublished thesis, Cornell University, New York, 1974

Hasan Machmud, Andi' Bau, *Silasa*: *Silasa: setetes embun di tanah gersang*, Ujung Pandang, 1976

Hasan Walinono, *Tanété*: *Tanété. Suatu studi sosiologis politik*, Ujung Pandang, 1979

Haudricourt, André G., and Delamarre, Mariel J.-B., *Homme et charrue*: *L'homme et la charrue à travers le monde*, 2nd edn, Paris, 1986

Heekeren, H. R. van, *Bronze-Iron Age*: *The Bronze-Iron Age of Indonesia*, The Hague, 1958

—— *Stone Age*: *The Stone Age of Indonesia*, 2nd edn, The Hague, 1972

Horridge, Adrian, *Bugis Prahus*: *The Konjo Boatbuilders and the Bugis Prahus of South Sulawesi*, Maritime Monographs and Reports no. 40, National Maritime Museum, Greenwich, London, 1979

—— *Sailing Craft*: *Sailing Craft of Indonesia*, Singapore, 1986

Isa Sulaiman, M. *Dari gécong*: *Dari gécong ke rotary*, PLPIIS, Ujung Pandang, 1979

Jacobs, Hubert, 'First Christianity': 'The First Demonstrable Christianity in Celebes, 1544', *Studia*, Rome, 17, 1966: 251–305

—— *Portuguese Presence*: *The Portuguese Presence at Makassar in the 17th Century*, Fifth European Colloquium on Indonesian and Malaysian Studies, Sintra, Portugal, 1985

Jager-Gerlings, J. H., *Sprekende weefsels*: *Sprekende weefsels*, Amsterdam, 1952

Kaptein, Nico, '*Berdiri Mawlid*': 'The *Berdiri Mawlid* Issue among Indonesian Muslims in the Period from circa 1875 to 1930', *BKI*, 149(1), 1993: 124–53

Kern, Rudolph A., *Catalogus* I: *Catalogus van de Boegineesche, tot den I La Galigo-cyclus behoorende handschriften der Leidsch*

Universiteitsbibliotheek, alsmede van die in andere europeesche bibliotheken, Leiden, 1939

—— Catalogus II: *Catalogus van de Boeginese, tot den I La Galigo-cyclus behoorende handschriften van Jajasan Kebudjaan Sulawesi Selatan dan Tenggara te Makassar*, Makassar, 1950

—— Cerita Bugis: *I La Galigo: cerita Bugis kuno*, trans. La Side' and M. D. Sagimun, Jakarta, 1989

King, Victor W., *Borneo: The Peoples of Borneo*, Oxford/Cambridge, Mass., 1993

K.K.D., 'Samarinda': 'Sejarah ringkas Samarinda seberang, dipetik dari sejarah lama', *Setia, Bulletin hiburan dan santapan rohani pemuda, Persatuan Pemuda Setia Samarinda Seberang*, 29 April 1968: 4–6, 21, 75–80

Kooreman, P. J., 'Feitelijke toestand': 'De feitelijke toestand in het gouvernementsgebied Celebes en Onderhoorigheden' *Indische Gids*, Amsterdan, 5(1), 1883: 167–200, 358–84, 482–98, 637–55; 5(2), 1883: 135–69

Kroef, Justus van der, 'Transvestism': 'Transvestism and the Religious Hermaphrodite in Indonesia', in *Indonesia in the Modern World*, vol. 2, Bandung, 1956: 182–97

Lat, J. de, and Keizer, J., *Atlas: Atlas van Oost-Indië*, 1735–47 Almelo & Deventer

Lineton, Jacqueline, 'Study of the Bugis': 'An Indonesian Society and its Universe: A Study of the Bugis of South Sulawesi (Celebes) and their Role within a Wider Social and Economic System', unpublished dissertation, University of London, 1975

Lombard, Denys, 'Pirates malais': 'Regard nouveau sur les "pirates malais" (Ière moitié du XIXème siècle)', *Archipel*, 18, 1979: 231–50

Lubeigt, Guy, 'Palmier à sucre': 'Une civilisation du palmier à sucre en Asie', *Le Courier de l'UNESCO*, Paris, March 1982

Macknight, Campbell C., *Early History: The Early History of South Sulawesi: Some Recent Advances*, Centre of Southeast Asian Studies, Working Paper no. 81, Monash University, Clayton, Australia, 1993

—— 'Emergence of Civilization': 'The Emergence of Civilization in South Celebes and Elsewhere', in A. Reid and L. Castles, eds, *Pre-colonial State Systems in Southeast Asia*, MMBRAS no. 6, Kuala Lumpur, 1975: 126–35

—— Voyage to Marege': *The Voyage to Marege': Macassan Trepangers in Northern Australia*, Carlton, Australia, 1976

—— 'Rise of Agriculture': 'The Rise of Agriculture in South Sulawesi before 1600', *RIMA*, 17, 1983: 92–116

—— 'Study of Praus': 'The Study of Praus in the Indonesian Archipelago', *The Great Circle*, 2(2), 1980: 117–28

Macknight, Campbell C., and Mukhlis, 'Manuscript about Praus': 'A Bugis Manuscript about Praus', *Archipel*, 18, 1979: 271–82

Maeda, Narifumi, 'Agricultural Rites': 'An Inventory of Agricultural Rites in Amparita', in Mattulada and Narifumi Maeda, eds, *Transformation of the Agricultural Landscape in Indonesia*, Kyoto University, 1984: 123–40

Manguin, Pierre-Yves, 'Southeast Asian Ship': 'The Southeast Asian Ship: An Historical Approach', *Journal of Southeast Asian Studies*, Singapore, 11(2), 1980: 266–76

—— 'Vanishing Jong': 'The Vanishing Jong: Insular Southeast Asian Fleets in Trade and War (Fifteenth to Seventeenth Centuries)', in A. Reid, ed., *Southeast Asia in the Early Modern Era: Trade, Power and Belief*, Ithaca/London, 1993: 197–213

Marschall, Wolfgang, *Metallurgie: Metallurgie und frühe besiedlungsgeschichte Indonesiens*, Ethnologica 4, Cologne, n.d.

Matthes, Benjamin Frederick, *Atlas: Ethnographisch Atlas, tot ophelslering bijgevoed aan de Boegineesch-Hollandsch woordenboek*, The Hague, 1874

—— *Boegineesche spraakkunst: Boegineesche spraakkunst*, Amsterdam, 1875

Mattulada, 'Bugis Makassar': 'Bugis Makassar: manusia dan kebudanaannya', *Berita Antropologi*, Jakarta, 16, 1974, special issue

—— 'Kebudayaan Bugis Makassar': 'Kebudayaan Bugis Makassar', in Koentjaraningrat, ed., *Manusia dan Kebudayaan di Indonesia*, Jakarta, 1971: 264–83

—— *La Toa: La Toa: satu lukisan analitis terhadap antropologi politik orang Bugis*, Yogyakarta, 1985

Mattulada et al., eds, *Sawérigading: Sawérigading, Folktale Sulawesi*, Palu, 1987

Maxwell, Robyn, *Textiles: Textiles of Southeast Asia: Tradition, Trade and Transformation*, Canberra/Oxford, 1990

Mens, Lucie van, 'Statusscheppers': 'De Statusscheppers. Socialie mobiliteit in Wajo', 1905–1950, mimeographed dissertation, Leiden University, 1987

Miksic, John N., *Javanese Gold: Old Javanese Gold*, Singapore, 1990

Millar, Susan B., *Bugis Weddings: Bugis Weddings: Rituals of Social Location in Modern Indonesia*, Monograph Series no. 29, Center for South and Southeast Studies, University of California at Berkeley, 1989

—— 'Interpreting Gender': 'On Interpreting Gender in Bugis Society', *American Ethnologist*, 10(3), 1983: 477–93

Mills, J. V., 'Chinese Navigators': 'Chinese Navigators in Insulinde about AD 1500', *Archipel*, 18, 1979: 41–56

Mills, Roger F., 'Reconstruction': 'The Reconstruction of Proto South Sulawesi', *Archipel*, 10, 1975: 205–24

—— 'Proto South Sulawesi': 'Proto South Sulawesi and Proto Austronesian Phonology', unpublished dissertation, University of Michigan, 1975

Milner, A. C., 'Malay Kingship': 'Islam and Malay Kingship', *JRAS*, 1, 1981: 46–70

Mukhlis and Robinson, Kathryn, eds, *Migrasi: Migrasi*, Yayasan Ilmu-ilmu Sosial, Hasanuddin University, Ujung Padang, 1985

Nahuijs van Burgst, Baron Huibert G., *Brieven: Brieven over Bencoolen, Padang, het rijk van Menangkabau, Rhiouw, Sincaporra en Poelo-Pinang*, Breda, 1827

Navarrete, Domingo, *Travels and Controversies: The Travels and Controversies of Friar Domingo Navarrete, 1618–1686*, trans. J. S. Cummins, 2 vols, Cambridge, 1962

Ngo Sy-Hong, 'Sa-Huynh': 'Sa-Huynh: An Indigenous Cultural Tradition in Southern Vietnam', conference on 'The High Bronze Age of South China and Southeast Asia', Hua Hin (Thailand), 1991

Noorduyn, Jacob, 'Arung Singkang': 'Arung Singkang (1700–1765): How the Victory of Wajo' Began', *Indonesia*, 1972: 61–8

—— 'Historical Writing': 'Origins of South Celebes Historical Writing', in Soedjatmoko, ed., *An Introduction to Indonesian Historiography*, Ithaca, 1965: 137–55

—— 'Islamisering van Makassar': 'De islamisering van Makasar', *BKI*, 112, 1956: 247–66

—— *Kroniek van Wadjo: Een achttiende eeuwse kroniek van Wadjo. Buginese historiografie*, La Haye, 1955

—— 'Wajo' Merchants': 'The Wajo' Merchants' Community in Makasar', Second International KITLV Workshop on Indonesian Studies, 'Trade, Society and Belief in South Sulawesi and its Maritime World', Leiden, 1987

Nur, S. R. 'Sawérigading di Gorontalo': 'Sawérigading dan Rawé dalam cerita rakyat di Gorontalo', in Mattulada et al., eds, *Sawérigading, Folktale Sulawesi*, Palu, 1987: 439–54

Pallesen, A. Kemp, *Culture Contact: Culture Contact and Language Convergence*, Manila, 1985

Pelras, Christian, 'Ciel et jours': 'Le ciel et les jours. Constellations et calendriers agraires chez les Bugis,' in B. Koechlin et al., eds, *De la voûte céleste au terroir, du jardin au foyer*, Paris, 1987: 19–39

—— 'Dynamics of Islamization': 'Religion, Tradition and the Dynamics of Islamization in South Sulawesi', *Archipel*, 29, 1985: 107–35

—— 'Herbe divine': 'Herbe divine. Le riz chez les Bugis', in *Agriculture et sociétés en Asie du Sud-Est, Etudes Rurales*, 53–6, 1974: 357–74

—— 'Hiérarchie et pouvoir': 'Hiérarchie et pouvoir traditionnels en pays Wadjo', *Archipel*, 1, 1971: 169–91; 2, 1971: 197–224

Mills, 'Maison Bugis': 'La maison Bugis: formes, structures et fonctions', *ASEMI*, 6(2), 1975: 61–100

—— 'Mer et forêt': 'La mer et la forêt, lieux de quête, d'exil et d'errances. Quelques aspects de l'univers légendaire bugis, Célèbes, Indonésie', *Le Monde Alpin et Rhodanien*, 1982 (1–4): 313–21

Pelras, Christian 'Mitos': 'Mitos, kebatinan dan perobahan dalam bidabg agama dan kepercayaan di Tanah Bugis', Second International KITLV Workshop on Indonesian Studies, 'Trade, Society and Belief in South Sulawesi and its Maritime World', Leiden, 1987

—— 'Oral et écrit': 'L'oral et l'écrit dans la tradition Bugis', *ASEMI*, 10(2–4), 1979: 271–97

—— 'Panthéon': 'Le panthéon des anciens Bugis vu à travers les textes de La Galigo', *Archipel*, 25, 1983: 63–96

—— 'Patron–Client': 'Patron–Client Ties among South Sulawesi Peoples', in G. Acciaioli and C. van Dijk, eds, *Power and Authority in South Sulawesi*, KITLV, Leiden, forthcoming

—— 'Premières données': 'Les premières données occidentales concernant Célèbes-sud', *BKI*, 133(2–3), 1977: 227–60

—— 'Regards nouveaux': 'Regards nouveaux sur l'histoire et la géographie de Célèbes-sud avant le XVIIè siècle', forthcoming

—— 'Rituel populaire': 'Les éléments du rituel populaire bugis', in W. Marschall, ed., 'Der grosse Archipel', *Ethnologica Helvetica*, 10, 1985: 183–201

—— 'Témoignages étrangers': 'Célèbes-sud avant l'islam, selon les premiers témoignages étrangers', *Archipel*, 21, 1981: 153–60

—— 'Textiles and Weaving': 'Textiles and Weaving of the South Sulawesi Muslim Peoples: A Preliminary Report', in M. L. Nabholz-Kartaschoff et al., eds, *Weaving Patterns of Life: Indonesia Textile Symposium 1991*, Museum of Ethnography, Basle, 1993: 397–418

Peluso, Nancy L. 'Bugis Strategies': 'Merchants, Manipulation and Minor Forest Products on the Mahakam: Bugis Political-Economic Strategies in Pre-colonial Kutai', Second International KITLV Workshop on Indonesian Studies, 'Trade, Society and Belief in South Sulawesi and its Maritime World', Leiden, 1987

Pigeaud, Theodore G. T., *Nagarakertagama: Java in the XIVth Century: A Study in Cultural History: The Nagarakertagama by*

Rakawi Prapanca of Majapahit, 1365 AD, 5 vols, The Hague, 1960–3

Pires, Tomé, *Suma Oriental*: *The Suma Oriental: An Account of the East, from the Red Sea to Japan*, trans. Armando Cortesão, London, 1944

Postma, Antoon, 'Laguna Copperplate': 'The Laguna Copperplate Inscription: A Valuable Philippine Document', *Bulletin of the Indo-Pacific Prehistory Association*, 11, 1991: 160–71

Ptak, Roderick, 'Northern Route': 'The Northern Route to the Spice Islands: South China Sea–Sulu Zone–North Moluccas (14th to early 16th Century)', *Archipel*, 43, 1992: 27–56

Raffles, Thomas Stamford, *History of Java*: *History of Java*, 2 vols, London, 1817

Raillon, François, 'Indonesian Capitalists': 'How to Become a National Entrepreneur: The Rise of Indonesian Capitalists', *Archipel*, 41, 1991: 89–116

Reid, Anthony, *Age of Commerce*: *Southeast Asia in the Age of Commerce, 1450–1680*, vol. 1: *The Lands Below the Winds*, New Haven/London, 1988

—— 'Rise of Makassar': 'The Rise of Makassar', *RIMA*, 17, 1983: 117–59

—— 'Slave Systems': ' "Closed" and "Open" Slave Systems in Precolonial Southeast Asia', in Anthony Reid, ed., *Slavery, Bondage and Dependency in Southeast Asia*, St Lucia (Queensland), 1983

Rössler, Martin, 'Striving': 'Striving for Modesty: Fundamentals of the Religious and Social Organization of the Makassarese Patuntung', *BKI*, 146(2–3), 1900: 285–324

Ruf, François, 'Cocoa Boom': 'Smallholder Cocoa in Indonesia: Why a Cocoa Boom in Sulawesi?', International Cocoa Conference, 'Challenges in the Nineties', Kuala Lumpur, 25–8 September 1991

Sà, Arturo Basilio de, *Insulindia*: *Insulindia: Documentação para a historia das Misões do Padroado Português do Oriente*, Lisbon, 1954–7

St John, Horace, *Indian Archipelago*: *The Indian Archipelago: Its History and Present State*, 2 vols, London, 1853

Sarasin, Fritz, and Sarasin, Paul, *Reisen*: *Reisen in Celebes, ausgeführt in den Jahren 1893–1896 und 1902–1903*, 2 vols, Wiesbaden, 1905

Sarita Pawiloy, *Sejarah perjuangan*: *Sejarah perjuangan angkatan 45 di Sulawesi Selatan*, Ujung Pandang, 1987

Sarkar, H. B., 'Sailendra Dynasty': 'The Kings of Sri Sailam and the Foundation of the Sailendra Dynasty of Indonesia', *BKI*, 141(2–3), 1985: 323–38

Scheurleer, Pauline Lunsingh, and Klokke, Marijke J., *Divine Bronzes: Divine Bronzes. Ancient Indonesian Bronzes: A Catalogue of the Exhibition in the Rijksmuseum Amsterdam with a General Introduction*, Leiden, 1988

Side' Daéng Tapala, La, 'Expansion de Goa': 'L'expansion du royaume de Goa et sa politique maritime aux XVIè et XVIIè siècles', *Archipel*, 10, 1975: 159–72

Sirk, Ülo, 'Basa Bissu': 'On Old Buginese and Basa Bissu', *Archipel*, 10, 1975: 225–38

—— 'Wotu Language': 'Research Needs: The Wotu Language', *Baruga, Sulawesi Research Bulletin*, 2, 1988: 10–12

Soejono, R., 'Prehistoric Indonesia': 'Prehistoric Indonesia', in P. van de Velde, ed., *Prehistoric Indonesia: A Reader*, VKI, 104, The Hague, 1984: 51–77

Sofyan Anwarmufied, 'Ritus tanah': 'Ritus tanah: studi analisa deskriptif tentang upacara tanah yang berkaitan dengan adat pertanian padi di desa Mangempang kabupaten Barru', *Masyarakat Indonesia*, 9(1), 1982: 1–56

Sollewijn Gelpke, J. H. F., 'Udama Katraya': 'The Majapahit Dependency Udama Katraya', *BKI*, 148(2), 1992: 240–5

Sopher, David E., *Sea Nomads: The Sea Nomads: A Study Based on the Literature of the Maritime Boat People of Southeast Asia*, Memoirs of the National Museum, 5, 2nd edn, Singapore, 1977

Staden ten Brink, P. B. van, *Zuid-Celebes: Zuid-Celebes. Bijdragen tot de krijgsgeschiedenis en militaire geographie van de zuijdelijke landtong van het eiland Celebes*, Utrecht, 1884

Sutherland, Heather A., 'Political Structure': 'Political Structure and Colonial Control in South Sulawesi', in R. Schefold, J. W. Schoorl and J. Tennakes, eds, *Man, Meaning and History: Essays in Honour of H. G. Schulte Nordholt*, VKI, 89, The Hague, 1980: 230–44

—— 'Power and Politics': 'Power and Politics in South Sulawesi: 1860–1880' *RIMA*, 17, 1983: 161–207

—— 'Slavery in South Sulawesi': 'Slavery and the Slave Trade in South Sulawesi, 1660s–1800s', Anthony Reid, ed., *Slavery, Bondage and Dependency in Southeast Asia*, St Lucia (Queensland), 1983: 263–85

Takaya, Yoshikazu, 'Land Use': 'Montane and Coastal Land Use in South Sulawesi', in Narifumi Maeda and Mattulada, eds, *Villages and the Agricultural Landscape in South Sulawesi*, Centre for Southeast Asian Studies, Kyoto, 1982: 147–76

Tanaka, Koji, 'Bugis and Javanese Peasants': 'Bugis and Javanese Peasants in the Coastal Lowland of the Province of Riau', in

Tsuyoshi Kato, Mukhtar Lutfi and Narifumi Maeda, eds, *Environment, Agriculture and Society in the Malay World*, Centre for Southeast Asian Studies, Kyoto University, 1986: 102–31

Tobing, Ph. O. L. *Amanna Gappa*: *Hukum pelayaran dan perdagangan Amanna Gappa*, Makassar, 1961

Valentijn, François, *Beschryvinge*: *Beschryvinge van Macassar, in Oud en niew Ooost Indië*, 3rd part, vol.2, 1726

Villegas, Ramon N., 'Tradition de l'or': 'La tradition philippine de l'or', in Térésa Battesti and Henri-Jean Schubnel, 'Trésor des Philippines: un archipel de rites', *Revue de Gemmologie*, Muséum National d'Histoire Naturelle, Paris, special issue, June 1994: 29–33

Villiers, John, 'Makassar': 'Makassar: The Rise and Fall of an East Indonesian Maritime Trading State', in J. Kathirithamby-Wells and J. Villiers, eds, *The Southeast Asian Port and Polity: Rise and Demise*, Singapore, 1990: 143–59

Vlekke, Bernard H. M., *Nusantara*: *Nusantara A History of Indonesia*, 5th edn, Brussels, 1961

Vuuren, L. van, *Celebes*: *Het gouvernement Celebes. Proeve eener monographie*, vol. 1, Weltevreden, 1920

Wallace, Alfred R., *Malay Archipelago*: *The Malay Archipelago*, London, 1869; repr. New York, 1962

Whitten, A. J., Muslimin Mustafa, and Henderson, S. H., *Ecology of Sulawesi: The Ecology of Sulawesi*, Yogyakarta, 1987

Wicki, Joseph, *Documenta Indica*, II: *Documenta Indica: Monumenta Societatis Jesu a patribus eusdem Societatis edita*, vol. II: *1550–1553*, Rome, 1955

Wolters, O. W., *Early Indonesian Commerce*: *Early Indonesian Commerce: A Study of the Origins of Srivijaya*, Ithaca, 1967

—— *Fall of Srivijaya*: *The Fall of Srivijaya in Malay History*, Ithaca, 1970

—— 'Jottings': 'A Few and Miscellaneous Pi-chi Jottings on Early Indonesia', *Indonesia*, 36, 1983: 49–64

Woodard, David, *Narrative*: *Narrative of Capt. David Woodard and Four Seamen . . . in the Island of Celebes*, 2nd edn, London, 1805; repr. 1969

Zainal Abidin Farid, Andi', 'Exercice de l'autorité': 'Exercice de l'autorité et éthique gouvernementale. Maximes de sagesse d'hommes d'Etat bugis et makassar du XVè au XVIIIè siècles', *Archipel*, 10, 1975: 135–54

—— 'La Galigo': 'The I La Galigo Epic Cycle of South Celebes and its Diffusion', *Indonesia*, 17, 1974: 161–9

Index

agriculture: early, 44; expansion of, 107; socio-economic relationships in, 332–3; annual cycle, 232; agricultural manuscripts, 231; harvesting, 102, 332; new techniques, 233; planting, 232, 332; *rakkala* (plough) 92, 100–1; tidal swamp cultivation, 102, 233, 324–5; trampling of ricefields, 102, 233–4; wet rice cultivation, 101 (introduction of 23, 39); ploughing, 101; rice farming, 10; slash-and-burn technique (swidden, shifting cultivation), 10, 101, 235; *see also* crops (cash)

Aja'tappareng confederation: constitution under Sidénréng leadership, 112; population in 1544, 1827 and 1884, 128; growing authority of Sidénréng under La Pang'uriseng onwards, 273–4; *see also* Sidénréng, 'Suppa'; *and under* places and domains: Alitta, Bacukiki', Paré-Paré, Rappang, Sawitto

archaeology of Insulindia and continental Asia: age of metal, 24–7; Bali, 54; Borneo, 22, 54; bronze (early), 24; bronze drums, 24; China, 23, 24; Dongson, 24; east Borneo Sanskrit inscriptions, 25; eye- covers and masks, 26–7, 54, 60; iron (early), 24; flake and blade technocomplex, 23; Java, 54; Kalanay, 23; Kedukan Bukit inscription, 72; Manila copper plate, 71; Niah cave, 22; Sa Huynh, 23; Santubong, 26; south Philippines, 22, 54; Tabon cave, 22; Telaga Batu inscription, 74; Wajak man, 22, 36; *see also* archaeology of Sulawesi

archaeology of Sulawesi: proto-historical, 53–6; antique trade, 55; Australian–Indonesian team, 54; Bantaéng, 54, 72; bronze (early), 24–5; bronze

concomitant with founding of new settlements and forest clearing, 98–9; also with development of agriculture, 103; 1433–83, period of expansion under king Kerrampélua', 113; 1509, unsuccessful attack on by Luwu', 114; 1535, and Goa join forces to defeat Luwu', 116; Cénrana falls into B. hands, 118; Luwu' compelled to join B., Goa and Soppéng to punish Wajo', for its neutrality, 116; 1562, beginning of confrontation between B. and Goa, 132; 1564, treaty of Caleppa between B. and Goa, 132, 133; 1611, is defeated by Goa and accepts Islamization, 137; 1635, Goa defeats B. and deposes its ruler, 142–3; 1666, under Arung Palakka, takes revenge by helping Dutch defeat Goa 143; end 17th to mid-19th century, virtual independence of, from Dutch, 143; after 1812, war against B. of British helped by Goa, Soppéng and Sidénréng, 272; B. recaptures Maros and part of Bulukumba from British, 272; after 1824, refuses to reaffirm declaration of allegiance to Dutch, 273; 1838, defeated by Dutch, 273; 1840, James Brooke in, 179, 223; 1857, new female ruler of, refuses allegiance to Dutch, 273; 1859, demotion

by Dutch to status of subject, 273; 1897, 'coffee war' opposing Sidénréng to B. and Luwu', 274; 1905, conquest of by Dutch, 274; after 1905, creation by Dutch of a 'North Boné' division, also including Soppéng and Wajo', 275; *see also under* historical figures: Andi' Ma'panukki', Arung Palakka, Bessé Kajuara, Kajao Lali'dong, Kerrampélua', La Ma'deremmeng; *under* rivers: Cénrana, Walennaé
Borneo: claims of overlordship by Majapahit over parts of, 108; early links with Sulawesi, 40–4, 47; links with Madagascar, 43; Banjarmasin, 125, 133, 140, 189, 265, 266; Banjar migrants in Malaya, 322, 324; Banjar people, 187, 233; Berau, 266; Brunei, 189, 252; Bugis control of up-river trade in east Borneo, 322; Bugis migrants in east and south-east Borneo, 320, 321; in west Borneo, 320; Bulungan, 320; Dayak shamans, 167; east and south-east Borneo, 174, 254, 310, 311, 314, 321; Gunung Tabur, 320; Kutei, 42, 134, 254, 310, 320; links with proto-South Sulawesi peoples, 174 (*see also hereunder*: Tamanic language group); Maanyan, 84; Mampawa, 320; Ngaju, 84; Pasir, 254, 266, 320,

molluscs, 23; harpoons, 46; hooks, 46; *jala* (casting nets), 46, 236; *puka'* (drift nets), 238; *rompong* (fishing rafts), 237–8; shore nets, 229; techniques and implements, 235–240; traps, 46, 236, 239–40; vegetable drugs, 46; *see also* boat construction and equipment, sea products *and under* economic activities: organization of fishing

food, cooking, beverages and stimulants: banana, 227; betel, *see under* rituals; coconut milk, 11, 44; coffee, 228, 301; cooking, 227–9; drinking water, 227; fish, 77, 226; manufactured food, 301; meals, 225–7; oil, 11, 44; opium, 123, 301; palm beer, 11, 44, 77, 134; pork (Islamic prohibition on), 134, 137; *lawa'* (preparation of raw food), 134; recipes, 228; rice, 77, 225–7, 229–30; sago, 77, 222; sugar, 11, 44; sweets, 228; tea, 228; tobacco, 123, 301, 316; tubers, 77; vinegar, 11, 44

forest and mangrove: clearing 99, 235, 323; in oral literature, 99; situation, 9; deforestation, 9, 99, 235; mangrove, 6; mangrove clearing and draining, 323, 324; palmyra palm tree (*Borassus flabelliformis*), 73; protected areas of forest, 235; sacred woods, 99

forest and mangrove products: Bajo people engaged in quest

for mangrove products, 16; dyes, 7, 17; beeswax, 17, 265, 266, 311, 321; camphor, 307, 321; damar, 321; eaglewood (aguilawood, gaharu wood), 17, 118, 321; honey, 44; mangrove bark, 17; mangrove wood, 17; rattan, 7, 265, 266, 314, 321; resins, 7, 17, 48, 71, 118; sandalwood, 7, 48, 70, 71; sappanwood, 6, 118, 125, 265, 266; wood (timber), 266, 313; vegetable poisons, 7

French trading post in Makassar, 5, 141; *see also under* travellers and writers: Gervaise

fruit and vegetables: aubergines, 11, 44; bananas, 11, 44, 118; betel nut, 44; breadfruit, 11, 44; *Canarium* almonds, 23; cucumbers, 11, 44; gourds, 11; mangoes, 118; pumpkins, 11; tomatoes, 123

funeral rites: cremation, 26, 28, 29, 54, 84, 106; death names, 96–7; disposal of corpses in caves, 106; double funerals, 47; erection of megaliths, 27; exposure, 106; funeral eye-covers and masks, 26–7, 54; funeral rites formerly similar to those practised by Toraja, 16; *gosali* (tombs in *La Galigo* texts), 84–5; house burial, 85; immersion, 46; inhumation, 26, 106; Islamic funerals, 137; jar burial, 27, 29, 106; return

together with Soppéng and Sidénréng, helps the British in their war against Boné, 272; 1824, Dutch Governor-General van der Capellen visits Makassar to have South Sulawesi rulers renew their allegiance, 272; 1847, Makassar made a free port, 311; 1905, Goa ruler dies in trying to escape Dutch, 274; 1926, creation in Makassar of Muhammadiyah branch and its role in Indonesian nationalism, 279, 292; 1929, creation in Makassar of branches of Partai Sarikat Islam and Partai Nasional Indonesia, 279; *see also under* historical figures: Daéng Mamméta, Daéng Matanré, Dato' ri Bandang, Karaéng Matoaya (Sultan Abdullah), Karaéng Pa'tingalloang, Manrio Gau', Sangkilang, Shaykh Yusuf, Sultan Ala'uddin, Tunatangka'lopi, Tunipalangga

hierarchy and stratification: in *La Galigo* texts, 81–2, 105; actual working of, 171–2, 209; origins of, 172–5; achieved status, 209, 328; anti-'feudalism', 284, 292, 293, 329; egalitarian ideology, 209, 328; genealogies, 82, 96; hierarchical ideology, 110, 328; *mang'elli dara* ('blood acquisition'), 327; marriage

across rank boundaries, 105, 155, 327; marriage across ethnic boundaries, 140, 327; marriage strategies, 184, 321, 322, 327; modern elites, 330–6; new economic elite, 332–4; principles of hierarchy by birth, 168–9; rank, 81–2, 169–71; signs of rank, 172–3; in house decoration, 222; in clothing and use of ornaments 225, 252; *see also* clienteles, commoners, nobility, slaves

Hinduism: in eastern Borneo, 25; Hindu influence in general, 94; Sivaite influence, 93

historical figures (Insulindian): Adityavarman (king of Malayu), 73; Amanna Gappa (author of Bugis code of maritime law from Wajo'), 266; Amiruddin, Professor (Bugis academic, Governor of South Sulawesi province), 331; Andi' Ma'panukki' (Boné ruler), 280; Andi' Mattalata, General (National Indonesian Army Bugis officer), 281; Andi'Ninnong (princess of Wajo'), 280; Andi'Séllé' (guerrilla leader, then National Indonesian Army Bugis officer), 283, 319; Andi' Sosé (guerrilla leader, then National Indonesian Army Bugis officer), 285; Arung Palakka (La Tenritatta, Boné ruler), 140, 142–3; Aziz Taba (guerrilla leader, then National Indonesian Army

Sulawesi), 135; To Ménggu
(Luwu' wise man), 215;
Trunajaya (Madurese
opponent to Dutch), 145;
Tunatangka'lopi (Goa ruler),
114; Tunipalangga (Goa
ruler), 111; Usman Balo'
(guerrilla leader), 212, 285;
Wé Kambo (lady ruler of
Luwu'), 211–12; Yusuf,
General (National
Indonesian Army Bugis
officer) 280, 286
historical sources: Chinese
sources, 35, 49; chronicles,
31–32, 51; Dutch sources, 35;
French sources, 35;
genealogies, 51, 96, 97; *La
Galigo* cycle as source for
history, 50–3; local sources,
50–3, 97; Malay sources, 35;
Javanese sources, 34; oral
tradition, 58–62; Portuguese
sources, 7, 17, 35, 63, 99
history (South Sulawesi): early,
49–61 (chronology, 31, 32;
emergence of early polities
94); 12th century, 55; 13th
century, 55; 14th century,
55–8, 66–7, 107–9
(presumed upheavals in, 175;
origin of dynasties 85–6,
94–7; emergence of
historical polities 53, 104);
15th century, 96, 111–12,
124 (first competition
between polities, 104); 16th
century, 63, 113–16, 117–35
(struggle for hegemony
between Goa and Boné,
129–33); 17th century, 118,
124, 254, 262, 265;
1607–11, Islamic wars,

136–7; 18th century, 252,
254, 255–6, 262, 263,
265–8, 272, 306; 19th
century, 63, 258–9, 264,
271, 272–4, 306–13;
1810–15, opposition to
British, 272; after 1812, war
against Boné of British
helped by Goa, Soppéng and
Sidénréng, 272; 1817,
resumption of Dutch rule,
272; 1824–56, opposition to
Dutch, 272–3; 1897, 'coffee
war' opposing Sidénréng to
Boné and Luwu', 274, 316;
20th century, 272, 279, 281;
1905, Dutch military action,
272; 1905–45 *see* colonial
period; 1945–present *see*
post-1945 chronology; *see
also* Boné (chronology),
contemporary South
Sulawesi, Goa (chronology),
historical figures
(Insulindian), historical
sources, Luwu' (chronology),
Sidénréng (chronology),
Soppéng (chronology), Wajo'
(chronology)

Indian subcontinent and Sri
Lanka, 54, 71, 72, 73: Chola
dynasty, 72; Coromandel
coast, 72; Indic influence on
religious ideas, 91–2, 93;
Indic influence on
agricultural techniques, 92,
100; Kalinga, 72; Kling, 72;
Muslim states, 189; Pallava
derived Indonesian scripts,
72; Sanskrit loanwords in
Bugis, 53, 71, 74, 94;
Sanskrit names, 110; Sri

involved with traders from east Java, 111; part of Islamic network, 189; 1525, introduces Islam in Gorontalo, 134; 1533, Portuguese in Ternaté hear about gold in the 'Macaçares', 125; 1540, introduces Islam in Buton, 134; 1580, under Sultan Babullah, defines with Goa limits of each other's spheres of influence, 111, 133; 1666, helps Dutch, together with Boné Bugis, in besieging and storming of Makassar, 143; cosignatory of Bungaya treaty, 265; *see also under* historical figures: Babullah; *and under La Galigo* geography: Taranati; *and under* Moluccas

Toraja: as slaves, 16, 119, 309; lifestyle, 44; basic data on, 12; differences from and similarities with Bugis, 15–16, 218; process of differentiation from the common proto-South Sulawesi stock, 41, 175; similarity of funeral rituals with those of ancient Bugis, 106; wars between Bugis and, 16, 274; type of weaving loom used by Sa'dan, Rongkong and Kalumpang, 243, 244; country, 112, 274; productive of gold, 119; productive of coffee, 316

trade (socio-economic aspects): as factor motivating migration of proto-South

Sulawesi peoples, 43, 94–5; monopolies, 70–1, 321, 327; Bugis control of tin trade in Malayan peninsula, 48, 305, 320; Bugis control of upriver trade in east Borneo, 322; competitiveness of Bugis in, 305–6; free trade concept, 306–7; cowrie shells, 119; freight rates, 266; money, 118, 119; non-money trade exchanges, 119; prices in 16th century, 118–19; smuggling, 325; *see also* pirates, sea routes, sea trade, slave trade, trade wares

trade wares: *balubu kelling* (Indian jars), 72; benzoin (frankincense), 307, 321; *bessi kelling* (Indian steel), 72, 265; betel leaf, 327; bezoar stones, 321; bird's nests, 17, 305, 307, 311, 321; brass ware, 248, 251–2, 311, 327; cattle, 314; cement, 314; ceramics, porcelain, crockery, 49, 265, 301, 311, 313, 321; cloth, 59, 118–19, 140, 266, 305, 321 (*see also hereunder* silk); copra, 314, 317, 323, 325; firearms, 265, 311, 321; flour, 314; furniture, 314; glass beads, 16; glass sand, 314; gold and gold dust, 7, 48, 71, 119–20, 125, 265, 266, 307, 311, 321; gunpowder, 311; iron, 59, 66, 71, 321; iron tools, 301; iron weapons, 59, 66, 125; scrap iron, 249, 311; kitchen implements, 314; lead, 25, 265; mirrors, 103; opium,